SECURED TRANSACTIONS UNDER THE UNIFORM COMMERCIAL CODE AND INTERNATIONAL COMMERCE

SECURED TRANSACTIONS UNDER THE UNIFORM COMMERCIAL CODE AND INTERNATIONAL COMMERCE

Second Edition

LOUIS F. DEL DUCA
Edward N. Polisher Distinguished Faculty Scholar
The Dickinson School of Law
The Pennsylvania State University

MARIE T. REILLY
Professor of Law
The Dickinson School of Law
The Pennsylvania State University

EDWIN E. SMITH
Lecturer in Law
Boston University School of Law
Morin Center for Banking and Financial Law
Partner, Bingham McCutchen LLP

PETER WINSHIP
James Cleo Thompson Sr. Trustee Professor of Law
Southern Methodist University
Dedman School of Law

ISBN: 978-1-4224-9081-5

Library of Congress Cataloging-in-Publication Data

Secured transactions under the Uniform Commercial Code and international commerce / Louis F. Del Duca . . . [et al.] -- 2nd ed.
    p. cm.
Includes index.
ISBN 978-1-4224-9081-5
1. Security (law)--United States. I. Del Duca, Louis F.
    KF1050.S44 2011
    346.7307'4--dc23

2011040352

NOTE TO USERS
To ensure that you are using the latest materials available in this area, please be sure to periodically check the LexisNexis Law School web site for downloadable updates and supplements at www.lexisnexis.com/lawschool.

Editorial Offices
121 Chanlon Rd., New Providence, NJ 07974 (908) 464-6800
201 Mission St., San Francisco, CA 94105-1831 (415) 908-3200
www.lexisnexis.com

MATTHEW◆BENDER

SECOND EDITION PREFACE

A significant body of case law from around the country, unavailable when we published our first edition in 2002, is now available.[1] We draw extensively on this new body of case law and eliminate pre-revision cases in this new edition.

Our new edition is more user friendly than our earlier edition. Inclusion at the outset of the H. Fleisig *Secured Transactions: The Power of Collateral* article puts secured transactions in a context which sensitizes students as to why a modern secured transactions law is important to creditors and debtors. Notes on "The Role of Codes, Statutes and Case Law" and "Simplifying Complicated Statutory Language" introduce students to statutory interpretation and develop skills which will help them to better understand the sometimes complicated text of Article 9, as well as other statutes. Students have found Appendix A, *Actual Text and Simplified Version of Actual Text of Selected Provisions of the UCC Pertaining to Secured Transactions*, interesting and useful in developing these skills.

Use on a continuing basis throughout the course of *Samuel Clemens Hypothetical Problems* to navigate through secured transactions from creation (Chapter 2), to enforcement (Chapter 3), to perfection and priority of the security interest (Chapter 4), continues to be unique to this secured transactions text. With this model, students work with more interesting and more easily understood problems rather than a series of unrelated hypotheticals.

Exposure of students early in the course to *In Re QDS* forces them to work with difficult and complicated statutory language to distinguish the so-called "true lease" from the "dirty lease." This early exposure not only sensitizes them to the broad scope and applicability of Article 9, but also assists them throughout the course in working with complicated UCC statutory language, and enhances their ability to work with complicated statutory language in other areas of the law.

New materials illustrating breach of the peace, notification, and commercially reasonable foreclosure requirements are included in the book. Difficult problems created by errors in financing statements in particular with reference to names of individual debtors are also addressed with new cases interpreting Revised Article 9.

Louis F. Del Duca
Marie T. Reilly
Edwin E. Smith
Peter Winship

January 2011

---

[1] Revised Article 9 was adopted and effective in all 50 states as of July 1, 2001 except for Connecticut, Alabama, Florida, and Mississippi. It was adopted in these four states to become effective January 1, 2002.

FIRST EDITION PREFACE

Student understanding and mastery of complex transactional settings, highly specialized terminology, and intricate legal secured transactions issues through the vehicle of simplified, user-friendly problems, cases, and commentary continue to be facilitated by our new edition of *Secured Transactions Under the Uniform Commercial Code and in International Commerce*. This course book develops students' skills in: (a) analyzing, applying, and interpreting relevant statutory text and related case law; (b) preparing and interpreting security agreements, financing statements, and other documents; and (c) identifying and evaluating policy alternatives involved in creating an equitable and efficient secured transaction system designed to enhance the availability of credit and working capital for developing and enriching the economy.

These materials also sensitize students to the historical evolution of basic legal principles and development of sophisticated secured financing statutes, such as the UCC and related state and federal statutes. For example, the venerable case of *Clow v. Woods*, 5 Serg. & Rawle 275 (Pa. 1819), with its classic treatment of "ostensible ownership," is included for this purpose. Illustrative documents are also generously interspersed throughout the text.

This book can be adapted to two or three credit courses. The authors have actually used the book in both types of courses. Chapter 5, "The Effects of Bankruptcy" and Chapter 6, "Introduction to International Secured Transactions," can be comfortably included in a three credit course. In order to sensitize students to these important areas within the parameters of a two credit course, these subjects are also addressed with less specificity in other chapters of the book.

Opportunities for enrichment of Secured Transactions course materials result from Revised Article 9's expanded coverage, inclusion of new techniques for creating and perfecting security interests, new priority and conflict of laws provisions, and its enactment by all 50 states. Additionally, the increase in international secured lending has generated efforts to create secured transactions regimes effective on a worldwide basis. Evaluation of these regimes provides excellent international and comparative source material.

The new edition uses a system of parallel section number citations which correlates Revised Article 9 and former Article 9 sections. Citations to Revised Article 9 sections are in bold, followed by the analogous section from former Article 9 in brackets. The same approach is utilized for the newly revised Article 1. This parallel citation system enables students to efficiently and meaningfully analyze case law under the former Article 9 and Article 1 numbering systems.

To introduce students to the subject of International Secured Transactions, Chapter 6, "Introduction to International Secured Transactions," utilizes the recently completed *Convention on International Interests in Mobile Equipment*, developed under the auspices of the International Institute for Unification of Private Law (UNIDROIT) in cooperation with the Council of the International Civil Aviation Organization. An overview of other major efforts to create international secured transactions regimes is included in Chapter 6 by introducing students to the work of the United Nations Commission on International Trade Law (UNCITRAL), with its outstanding work on the

FIRST EDITION PREFACE

Convention on Assignment of Receivables in International Trade, and the work of the European Bank for Reconstruction and Development with its *Model Law on Secured Transactions*.

Louis F. Del Duca
Egon Guttman
William H. Henning
Frederick H. Miller
Peter Winship

TABLE OF CONTENTS

TABLE OF CONTENTS

TABLE OF CONTENTS

TABLE OF CONTENTS

TABLE OF CONTENTS

TABLE OF CONTENTS

TABLE OF CONTENTS

Chapter 1

WHY CREDITORS PREFER A SECURED TRANSACTION—GENERATING WORKING CAPITAL USING "PERSONAL PROPERTY" ASSET BASED FINANCING

A. THE COMMON LAW WORLD WITHOUT A SYSTEM FOR RECORDING PERSONAL PROPERTY ENCUMBRANCES—LIMITATIONS ON CAPITAL FORMATION

1. Why Creditors Prefer a Secured Transaction

Heywood Fleisig,[1] *Secured Transactions: The Power of Collateral*
33 Fin. & Dev. 44 (1996)[2]

In many developing countries, businesses are unable to get low-cost, long-term loans from private lenders to finance investment projects. Reforms that make it easier for borrowers to use movable property as collateral would give comfort to lenders, stimulate investment, and boost productivity and growth.

The first question any private lender asks is, "How do I get my money back?" Given the risks involved in lending—borrowers may be unlucky, unwise, or dishonest—what conditions give comfort to lenders?

Two basic loan transactions have evolved in private markets: *unsecured and secured.* When a borrower offers an unsecured promise to pay, the lender must rely on the borrower's reputation, or trust that the borrower will pay back the loan in order to have access to future loans. In secured transactions, promises to repay are backed by collateral that lenders can seize and sell in the event loan payments are not made as agreed. Collateral may be real estate or personal property—tangible personal property such as inventory, equipment, livestock, and tractors; or intangible personal property such as unsecured accounts owed to merchants (accounts receivable) and secured agreements (chattel paper). Secured transactions have advantages for borrowers and lenders alike—transaction costs

---

[1] Heywood Fleisig, a U.S. national, recently retired as Economic Advisor in the World Bank's Private Sector Development Department. He is now Director of Research at the Center for the Economic Analysis of Law, located in Washington, D.C.

[2] Reprinted with permission of the author.

are lower and lenders do not need to gather as much information about borrowers.

The issue of collateral is one of great economic importance. When borrowers cannot use their assets as collateral for loans and cannot purchase goods on credit using the goods themselves as collateral, interest rates on loans tend to be higher to reflect the risk to lenders. In many developing countries, where legal and regulatory constraints make it difficult to use movable property as loan collateral, the cost of loans makes capital equipment more expensive for entrepreneurs relative to their counterparts in industrial countries; businesses either postpone buying new equipment or finance it more slowly out of their own limited savings. Small businesses, in particular, are hit hard by the scarcity of low-cost financing, but the whole economy suffers because the lack of new investment dampens productivity and keeps incomes down. Estimates put welfare losses caused by barriers to secured transactions at 5–10 percent of GNP in Argentina and Bolivia.

Legal barriers

Movable property is widely used as collateral in the industrial countries. About half the credit offered in the United States is secured by some kind of movable property: about two-thirds of bank loans are secured by either movable property or real estate, and nonbank institutions that lend against movable property—such as leasing and finance companies—do almost as much lending as banks.

In contrast, private lenders in developing countries rarely make loans secured by movable property unless at least one of two conditions is satisfied: borrowers must own real estate that can be attached if they do not pay, or borrowers must place the movable property under the physical control of the lenders, as in a pawnshop or warehouse financing. If neither of these restrictive conditions can be met, private lenders rarely make loans secured by movable property. They may still make unsecured loans, but these are likely to be smaller loans with higher interest rates and shorter maturities. This phenomenon has been studied in a broad range of countries with different traditions, income levels, macroeconomic outlooks, religions, and levels of urbanization and industrial activity. The difficulties in securing loans with movable property have been observed in Africa, Asia, Eastern Europe, and Latin America—in countries with legal and regulatory systems modeled after the Civil Codes of Continental European countries, as well as in African and Asian countries whose systems are modeled after British common law.

What prevents the use of movable property as collateral in developing and transition countries? Three obstacles stand out:

- The *creation* of security interests is difficult, expensive, and uncertain.

- The *perfection* of security interests—the public demonstration of their existence and the establishment of their priority—is not effectively possible.

- The *enforcement* of security interests is slow and expensive.

These abstract notions can be understood more easily with an example. Compare the financing available to farmers raising cattle in Uruguay with that available to their counterparts in Kansas, in the United States. Uruguay and Kansas have similar topographies and well-educated populations interested in advanced technologies and able to apply them, and both are world-class exporters of beef cattle. In Kansas, private banks view cattle as one of the best forms of loan collateral; this is also the view of the bank examiners at the Federal Reserve Bank of Kansas City. Banks with "cattle paper" are seen as solid, whereas banks with "exposure to farm real estate" are seen as risky. By contrast, in Uruguay, because of flaws in the legal framework governing secured transactions, private banks and bank examiners prefer real estate as collateral for loans: they consider a pledge on cattle worthless as collateral. The unacceptability of cattle as collateral applies to all types of transactions, including sales of cattle on credit, sales of cattle financed by third-party lenders like banks or finance companies, or working capital loans for other purposes that might be secured by cattle.

Creating security interests. First, it is difficult to create a security interest in Uruguay. Suppose a private bank in Uruguay were to lend against 100 cattle worth $200,000. Uruguayan law calls for a specific description of the property that is pledged. A pledge against cattle might identify the individual cows pledged by name (Bessie, Elmer, etc.) or by the numbers tattooed on them. The need to identify the collateral so specifically undermines the secured transaction because the bank must ensure that the cattle designated in the pledge are available to be seized in the event of nonpayment—the lender is not allowed to repossess a different group of cows.

As a result, the supervision of such loans is costly. It would not be enough, as it is in Canada and the United States, for example, to verify simply that there are enough cattle in the farmer's field: in Uruguay, the loan officer would have to verify that the cattle in the field are the ones specifically identified in the pledge. The Uruguayan bank might try to get around this problem by using a more general description of the collateral in the pledge contract—say, "100 calves." But, with a loan of one year's maturity, the calves would become cows, bulls, or steers, and the enforceability of the contract would be clouded. In Canada and the United States, however, a binding agreement can be written with a floating security interest in $200,000 worth of "cattle." Moreover, in Uruguay the bank would have to worry that the farmer might sell the cattle without notifying the bank, whereas a Canadian or US bank would have a continuing security interest in the proceeds of the sale and could automatically attach the proceeds—whether they were placed in another bank or used to buy a tractor.

Perfecting security interests. Second, Uruguayan lenders cannot easily find out whether prior and superior claims exist on their security interest. In Canada, Norway and the United States, for example, all security interests against property are registered; the registries are public and indexed by borrower, by description of security interest, and by other relevant information. Lenders can easily conduct a thorough search to ensure that they have identified any outstanding security interests: security interests that are not registered have no legal standing. By contrast, the registry in Uruguay files security interests in chronological order and does not index them. The only way lenders can find out whether a security interest exists is if borrowers inform them.

Enforcing security interests. Finally, repossession and sale of collateral takes longer in Uruguay than in Kansas. In Kansas, repossession and sale of cattle takes one to five days and can be contracted between private parties. Typically, judicial intervention or the action of government officials is unnecessary. In Uruguay, the process requires six months to two years. In the case of cattle, there is a risk that the collateral will die, disappear, or get sick. Not surprisingly, under these conditions, lenders demand collateral that is sure to outlast a lengthy adjudication process—in other words, real estate.

Economic impact

In Kansas, the ease of creating a security interest, the inexpensiveness and high degree of confidence that can be attached to the perfection of a security interest, and the speed and low cost of enforcement explain why farmers can get private loans for a large fraction of the value of their cattle at interest rates close to the prime rate. The difficulty of using cattle as collateral in Uruguay explains why Uruguayan farmers cannot get any financing for cattle. However, although both rich and poor farmers are affected, rich farmers own land and have access to some credit by virtue of their real estate holdings; poor farmers, who are often tenants, have to use their own savings to finance the additional investment required to raise their incomes. But neither rich nor poor farmers have the easy access to credit enjoyed by their Canadian and US counterparts (and competitors in the world beef markets).

With minor adjustments, the same story can be told for Argentina, Bangladesh, Bolivia, Bulgaria, Mexico, and other developing and transition economies, both urban and rural, regardless of whether their legal systems are based on civil or common law. And the same story can be told, with slight variations, for lending against all movable property in developing countries, except for loans and leases secured by automobiles or loans secured by goods stored—under the control of lenders—in warehouses and pawnshops. Barriers to using movable property as collateral block access to credit and make it difficult to obtain term financing for investment. They also make it difficult to reform banking systems burdened by risky, unsecured loans. Lacking usable collateral, developing countries do not enjoy the major benefit of financial markets—the transfer of funds from savers with limited investment opportunities to investors with insufficient savings to finance profitable projects.

Access to credit. Even in the best of circumstances, poor people do not often go to banks for loans to finance small equipment purchases. But, in industrial countries, small-scale farmers and entrepreneurs can usually purchase equipment, livestock, or inventory on credit from merchants. In developing countries, however, merchants willing to sell on credit to poor customers whose reputation is good have their own problems gaining access to credit: legal constraints as to collateral prevent merchants from getting financing secured by their inventories or accounts receivable. If merchants want to extend credit to microenterprises and small and medium-sized businesses, they typically must do so out of their own capital.

Term finance. Although operators of small industrial operations may find it possible to finance "plant"—real estate—with a mortgage, it may be impossible for them to get medium-term loans for working capital or equipment. The reason is not the loan maturities—the same lenders happily make longer-term loans secured by real estate—but the underlying collateral (equipment and inventory) is unacceptable to lenders. In the United States, movable property accounts for half of the nonresidential capital stock and two-thirds of corresponding gross investment. The difficulty of financing this investment in developing countries greatly hampers industrial and agricultural development.

Bank reform. In developing countries, well-regulated banks typically only make loans secured by real estate or make unsecured loans to those who give evidence of owning real estate. Because the costs of mortgaging property are usually quite high, most bank loans are actually unsecured but made to borrowers who own real estate on the theory that, in the event of default, banks can file a lien against the real estate.

Most bank loans in industrial countries are secured—70 percent in the United States, for example. The difference between industrial and developing countries is striking—nearly 90 percent of bank loans in Argentina are unsecured, and the figure is similar for Bulgaria. Unsecured banking systems are necessarily more risky and prone to failure. And, because mortgages are unregistered, a lender has no idea how many times a borrower has used the same property to indirectly back up a loan. If the borrower defaults, only the bank that files a lien the fastest will be able to back up the loan. Inability to use anything else as collateral means that about half of the nonresidential private capital stock is inaccessible to banks as security for loans.

Capital markets. The World Bank has supported capital market reforms that encourage the securitization of equipment loans, real estate mortgages, and credit card accounts receivable. Such mechanisms can change the conduits through which financing takes place, improve the allocation of capital, and promote competition in the financial sector. However, their effectiveness is limited by the difficulty of creating, perfecting, and enforcing the underlying secured transactions. At the most rudimentary level, the easiest securitization is one where an enforceable security interest is given in the underlying paper. Successful securitizations in Canada and the United States are based on predictable collection rates for underlying mortgages, chattel paper, leases, and accounts receivable. In countries where the underlying loans cannot be collected or leases enforced, securitization offers only limited actuarial benefits. And, if a government guarantees such securitizations, it risks accumulating large uncollectible debts.

Leasing, a type of secured transaction, may facilitate repossession by not requiring proof of ownership. Even so, repossession can be a lengthy process. Leasing is also subject to problems of creation and perfection. When these problems are not addressed, leasing primarily benefits those who can already borrow.

Seeking solutions

Some analysts have concluded that, if the private sector is unwilling to provide credit, market imperfections justify the creation of state agencies that make loans.

However, this strategy has severe limitations. First, state lenders are no more able to collect these loans than are private lenders. The main difference is that state lenders are willing to make loans despite the risk of losing money. Not surprisingly, they have lost a great deal. Second, because borrowers know that these loans are hard to collect, such lenders tend to attract a different type of client—one who specializes in getting loans from the government, not one who specializes in investments with high returns. What typically takes place with state agency lending programs is a great deal of lending, little repayment, and not much positive impact on economic growth.

To get around the difficulties of repossession and sale of collateral, some lenders simply seize and sell the collateral without the sanction of law. Some leasing operations disguise their underlying financial nature and pretend that their seizures are not repossessions, hoping that the judicial system will not uncover the equivalence of the transactions.[3] For large and valuable pieces of equipment, dealers in every developing country tell tales of dispatching armed men and bribing police to recover machinery at gunpoint.

In some countries, lenders use a postdated check to convert the civil offense of nonpayment into a criminal act. They may demand a postdated check in the amount of both the loan and the interest. On the date the loan is due, the lender requests payment. If the borrower cannot pay, the lender deposits the check in a bank. If the check is returned unpaid, the lender can take the check, stamped "check without funds," to the police station. In Bolivia, for example, writing a check without funds is prima facie evidence of a criminal act of fraud. The borrower may be arrested. If he or she fails to raise the funds, conviction is certain. (The sentence in Bolivia for writing bad checks is about four years.)

Lenders in the formal sector, obviously, cannot use such collection techniques; the risk of civil and criminal damages is too great. Therefore, the resources of the formal sector are not tapped for credit, and movable property remains the province of lending techniques in the informal sector. This is costly for developing economies—faced with the prospect of jail if they are unable to repay, business people tend to borrow less and borrow only for operations with very high returns—and costly for society, because incarcerating risk-taking entrepreneurs stifles development.

Governments can implement a number of legal reforms to address the fundamental problems in credit markets that make it so difficult to secure loans with movable property:

- Changing the law to permit a greater variety of security interests in a wider range of transactions by a broader group of people.

- Making registry records public, reforming state-operated registries, restructuring public registries to permit competition, and privatizing registry services or allowing private registry services to compete with public ones.

- Speeding up enforcement and making it cheaper, changing the law to

---

[3] [This subject is addressed in detail in Chapter 2, Section B, *infra*.]

permit private parties to contract for nonjudicial repossession and sale, and, when possible, allowing private parties to contract for repossession and sale without government intervention.[4]

2.   Cash, Unsecured and Secured Credit

Credit enables buyers and borrowers to obtain goods and services which might not be obtainable if they had to pay cash. The availability of credit to commercial, agricultural, manufacturing and industrial enterprises and consumers facilitates economic growth and achievement of higher standards of living.

Sellers of property or services must decide whether to require cash payment or to extend credit. Credit can be extended without requiring collateral (i.e., unsecured credit) or by requiring collateral (i.e., secured credit). In a cash transaction, payment is transferred from the buyer to the seller at the outset of the transaction. This strengthens the seller's procedural position because the buyer loses the advantage of being able to withhold payment because of defective performance by the seller and is generally relegated to initiating a lawsuit to obtain relief.

If unsecured credit is extended, it is the seller who may be required to initiate a lawsuit to obtain satisfaction for non-payment. On the other hand, where secured credit has been extended, a creditor who complies with procedural requirements may unilaterally declare a default and repossess and dispose of the collateral to obtain satisfaction of the indebtedness. Article 9 of the Uniform Commercial Code provides rules for creation, public notice requirements, enforcement and priority claims of a secured creditor's interest in collateral.

Moreover, under Article 9, a secured party can establish its priority at the time it perfects its security interest and give public notice of its claim in perfected collateral (i.e., usually reference to a claim of "perfection" of its interest).[5] The priority of an unsecured creditor is, however, generally established by legal process such as levy of execution, and normally occurs only after a lawsuit and judgment. In addition, in the event of a debtor's bankruptcy, a creditor who has met the UCC and bankruptcy requirements for giving public notice of the "security interest" (i.e., perfected the security interest) generally will be permitted to proceed to satisfy the claim for the unpaid indebtedness against the property duly claimed as collateral in lieu of being relegated to the status of a general unsecured creditor likely to recover only 7 or 8% rather than 100% of the unpaid indebtedness.

Article 9 sets forth secured credit contract formation rules, public notice and priority rules and procedures applicable where the creditor requires collateral as a condition for extending credit. The secured credit contract is called a *security agreement* under Article 9 terminology. The public notice requirement is generally

---

[4] This article draws on the work of several lawyers and economists who have advised the World Bank on a variety of issues related to the Bank's lending activity and economic and sector work in the area of secured transactions.

[5] The concept of "perfection" of a secured creditor's interest in collateral (i.e., a security interest) is considered in detail in Chapter 4 along with issues pertaining to priority of competing claims to collateral among various classes of creditors, buyers and other transferees.

met by filing a *financing statement* which identifies the creditor, debtor and collateral.

As suggested above, an unsecured creditor's remedy against a debtor who defaults is to initiate a lawsuit, obtain a judgment and attempt to enforce it against the debtor. This involves considerable time and expense. A properly secured creditor does not need to follow this time consuming and costly route to satisfy its claim. Under UCC Article 9, a creditor who has obtained a security interest in collateral has several options available if the debtor defaults.[6] By following prescribed procedures, such a creditor may:

(1) take possession of the collateral, if this can be accomplished peaceably;

(2) render equipment unusable without removal or dispose of the collateral.

Given the advantages which the secured creditor has over the unsecured creditor, the cost and time involved in obtaining a security interest and giving the required public notice of the security interest is usually inexpensive insurance against the potentially severe consequences of a default.

3. Limitations of Possessory Personal Property Security Interests (i.e., Pledge)—Reduced Potential for Capital Formation

The problem of "ostensible ownership" or "apparent ownership" arises when a debtor retains possession of collateral after conveying to a creditor an unrecorded property interest or "secret" lien. If secret liens were recognized, then prospective creditors dealing with a debtor would be reluctant to rely on the appearance of ownership in the debtor given the possibility that a security interest could be challenged by a secret prior lien. Prospective buyers would also be deterred from buying because of the possibility that a secret lien might exist against the item they seek to buy.

A system for recording encumbrances (or use of some other procedure for giving public notice of encumbrances) introduces a degree of certainty to secured transactions and the buying and selling of personal property by providing a mechanism for giving public notice of security interests in a routine and reliable fashion. The absence of filing or some other public notice system for encumbered personal property during the first half of the nineteenth century made courts reluctant to enforce liens unless the creditor maintained possession of the collateral. This resulted from the fact that the apparent ownership of the debtor in possession of the collateral placed an enormous burden on creditors to determine whether an asset was encumbered or unencumbered. The leading case of *Clow v. Woods* illustrates this problem of apparent ownership. Development of a public notice filing system was a prerequisite for secured transactions law to evolve beyond the common law pledge into the era of non-possessory liens.

---

[6] *See* §§ 9-609, 9-610, 9-611, 9-615, 9-617 & 9-624. We will address each of these UCC Sections subsequently in these materials as they become relevant.

CLOW v. WOODS
Pennsylvania Supreme Court
5 Serg. & Rawle 275, 9 Am. Dec. 346 (1819)

[Action in trespass by Creditor-Guarantor for wrongful seizure of property by Sheriff. Debtor operated a tanning business in partnership with Partner. Creditor-Guarantor agreed to pay debts which Debtor failed to pay. To assure repayment by Debtor if Creditor-Guarantor had to pay such debts, Creditor-Guarantor obtained a mortgage from Debtor in Debtor's unfinished skins, leather, bark (i.e., "inventory" under § 9-102(a)(48)) and tools (i.e., "equipment" under § 9-102(a)(33)). Since no recording system was in existence, the mortgage could not and was not recorded. In addition, Debtor retained possession of the mortgaged property and continued to work with the leather, bark, and tools in his tanning business. No symbolic delivery took place, nor was any schedule, inventory or appraisement of the mortgaged property provided.

[After the creation of the mortgage, Debtor and his Partner decided to voluntarily dissolve their partnership by having Partner sell his interest to Debtor. When Debtor failed to make payment to Partner, Partner obtained a judgment against Debtor and the court directed Sheriff to levy against the unfinished skins, leather, bark and tools in Debtor's tan-yard to satisfy the judgment. Neither Partner nor Sheriff knew or had notice of the mortgage before Sheriff levied.

[Creditor-Guarantor in the meantime had paid Debtor's other obligations. To recover these payments, Creditor-Guarantor instituted an action in trespass against Sheriff for wrongfully seizing and selling the skins, leather, bark, and tools. Creditor-Guarantor claimed ownership of these assets on grounds that the mortgage transferred title to the property to Creditor, subject to the Debtor regaining title if he paid the obligation secured. Conversely, Sheriff argued that the mortgage was a fraudulent transfer and therefore null and void under the statute of Elizabeth. If the mortgage was ruled void, Debtor would still have title to the property and the Creditor-Guarantor's action in trespass would not be proper.

[Agreeing on appeal with the trial court ruling that the mortgage was invalid and that the Creditor-Guarantor's action in trespass was therefore not proper, the court relied in part on the Statute of Elizabeth which *inter alia* provided that:

> All and every feoffment, gift, grant, alienation, bargain, and conveyance of lands, tenements, hereditaments, goods and chattels . . . and every bond, suit, judgment, and execution . . . made [i.e., transferred] . . . to or for any intent or purpose [to delay, hinder, or defraud creditors and others], shall be . . . deemed and taken . . . to be clearly and utterly void, frustrate and of no effect.

[The opinion of Justice Gibson on appeal to the Pennsylvania Supreme Court follows:]

GIBSON, J.—

The Statute 13 Eliz. does not, in words [i.e., expressly], declare a conveyance of goods fraudulent, where the vendor retains possession; but, in general terms, renders void all conveyances made to the end, purpose, and intent of defrauding creditors. Hence it becomes incumbent on the courts to determine, from all the circumstances of the case, whether the conveyance be or be not made with a fraudulent intention; and in judging of that, it is held that any neglect in leaving the vendor in possession is fraudulent, within the statute. *The general rule is, that the possession must be transferred to the purchaser*; and to this I propose to examine such exceptions as have been urged. It has been said the rule does not apply to conditional sales; but that is altogether without foundation, for neither this statute nor the 27 Eliz., c. 4, which provides for the securing of purchasers, makes any difference between absolute and conditional sales. The only question in any case is, whether the sale is fraudulent; and if it be, it is within the statute. *Delivery of the subject-matter of the contract is as requisite in the case of a mortgage of goods, as it is in the case of an absolute sale.* [Emphasis added.]

* * *

The law will not and ought not to permit the owner of personal property to create an interest in another, either by mortgage or absolute sale, and still to continue to be the *ostensible owner*; and where the creating of such an interest is the sole object, the conveyance will be fraudulent, whether it contains a stipulation for the retention of possession or not; for to indulge the motive that led to the arrangement would be against true policy. [Emphasis Supplied.]

* * *

Where possession has been retained without any stipulation in the conveyance, the cases have uniformly declared that to be, not only evidence of fraud, but *fraud per se*. Such a case is, not inconsistent with the most perfect honesty; yet a court will not stop to inquire, *whether there be actual fraud or not; the law will impute it*, at all events, because it would be dangerous to the public to countenance such a transaction under any circumstances. [Emphasis Supplied.]

* * *

To come however to the case before us: I do not object to the transaction, altogether on the ground of the possession not having been immediately delivered. *The hides being in the process of tanning, could not be removed without great deterioration; and until finished, were unfit for market.* The bark and tools were necessary to complete the process; and I think the fair construction of the contract is, that all was to be delivered as soon as the leather should be in a fit state to be sold. Possession of the hides in the vats, to enable the mortgagor to complete the tanning, would have been unavailing without possession of the tan-yard at the same time, which was not intended to be included in the mortgage. If the case stood clear of objection on another ground, I think a good reason might be assigned for the mortgagor continuing in possession as the agent of the mortgagee. I can see no objection to an absolute sale of an article undergoing a process of manufacture to be delivered when finished; and if such a sale would be good, a mortgage under the same circumstances would also be good. If, however, the intention were to conceal the lien thus created, and the transaction were industriously kept secret, it would amount to actual fraud. *But where, from the nature of the transaction, possession cannot be given, the parties ought in lieu, to do everything in their power to secure the public from that deception which the possession of property, without the ownership, always enables a person to practice.* [Emphasis added.]

When a ship at sea is sold, the grand bill of sale is delivered, and that divests the owner of his last badge of ownership; and when goods are too bulky to admit of manual possession, the key of the room is handed over. In every case where possession is not given, the parties must leave nothing unperformed, within the compass of their power, to secure third persons from the consequences of the apparent ownership of the vendor. Here the defect is that the articles conveyed are not described or particularized, either in a schedule or in the body of the instrument. This is fatal. In a case of this kind, the slightest neglect in any circumstance the nature of the case may admit of as an equivalent for actual possession, is unpardonable. Where there is to be delivery at the time of the sale, a schedule or description may be unnecessary, for it could not afterwards be alleged that an interest passed in anything not then delivered; but where the goods are to remain with the vendor, and nothing in particular is specified as the subject of the grant, there is imminent danger of fraud. The vendor continuing to treat the property as his own, it would be almost impossible for a third person to show, by evidence *dehors* the deed, what did or what did not pass. What was to prevent the plaintiffs here from covering any quantity of property of the kind expressed in the mortgage? The transaction being secret, [Debtor] might have continued to carry on business, and purchase hides, bark and tools as usual; and whether he should be able to shelter such property under the mortgage, would depend on the secrecy and adroitness with which the matter was managed. I do not suppose the parties had, in fact, a fraudulent view; but as such a transaction might be turned to a dishonest use, it was their duty, as far as in their power, to secure the public against it.

In *Wilt v. Franklin*, 1 Binn. 502 [2 Am. Dec. 474], a schedule was not thought necessary, as there was an assignment of the whole property; but there was an intimation that where only a part is conveyed, it may be necessary, and the want of it, even in case of a general assignment, was held to be a circumstance, though not conclusive evidence of fraud. Here the assignment was but of a part. Perhaps a more satisfactory reason for dispensing with the schedule, in *Wilt v. Franklin*, than that expressed by the court, is, that the conveyance was made with a view to immediate delivery, which was prevented by accidental circumstances. Where possession is to follow the sale, there can be no danger from the want of a specification, because from the nature of the transaction, the parties cannot pretend with success that anything passed that was not actually delivered. But there would be great danger of imposition if a contract so vague as the present should be held available when its existence was a secret to the public, and there was no act of notoriety to be performed by the parties to mark the extent of its operation. In such a case, a single circumstance of fraud should be considered conclusive evidence. I am of opinion, therefore, that judgment should be affirmed.

NOTES AND QUESTIONS

1. Creditors claimed title to the unfinished skins, leather, bark and tanning tools, but they did not have possession. Debtor had possession of these goods but, if the mortgage was effective, he no longer owned them. Third parties seeing that Debtor had possession might assume that Debtor owned the property. Debtor has, in the words of the court, "apparent ownership" (sometimes also called "ostensible ownership"). Because third parties might be misled by this apparent ownership, the court insists that the parties must make every effort "to secure third persons from the consequences of the apparent ownership." There was no public filing system in which the mortgage documents or notice of the mortgage could be filed. What steps to publicize the mortgage did the court require? Would these steps address the danger the court foresaw?

2. Assume Debtor tried to borrow money from Banker. What would Banker do to satisfy herself that Debtor was creditworthy? Would she stop her investigation by merely looking at the tan-yard? What if she examined the mortgage deed?

3. Was Partner actually misled by Debtor's apparent ownership of the property at the tan-yard? If not, why does the court decide that the mortgage is null and void?

4. What is the economic effect of the court's ruling in *Clow v. Woods*? Does it hinder or facilitate capital formation? How did the state legislatures respond to the problem created by *Clow v. Woods*? (See the discussion of the Evolution of Security Devices in Walter D. Malcolm, *The Uniform Commercial Code as Enacted in Massachusetts*, 13 Bus. Law. 490 (1958), Section A.4., *infra*; and *Why Creditors Prefer a Secured Transaction in* Heywood Fleisig, *Secured Transactions: The Power of Collateral*, 33 Fin. & Dev. 44 (1996), Section A.1., *supra*). On what basis do creditors extend secured credit?

5. Justice Gibson used the Statute of Elizabeth as the basis for this decision that the retention of possession by the Debtor created apparent ownership and was therefore void. Does the Statute of Elizabeth quoted in *Clow v. Woods*, Section A.3., *supra*, explicitly provide that the retention of possession of collateral by a debtor while the debt is outstanding is per se fraudulent? If not, what interpretive techniques does the court use to read the Statute as making the mortgage null and void? Did the court use a "plain meaning" or "purpose" rule of construction in interpreting the Statute of Elizabeth in *Clow v. Woods*?

6. The Statute of Elizabeth (13 Eliz. c. 1-29) was passed by the English parliament in 1570. How did this Statute become the law of Pennsylvania? After independence, Pennsylvania adopted a statute on the "Applicability of Colonial Law" (1 Pa. C.S.A. § 1503), which provides:

> The common law and such of the statutes of England as were in force in the Province of Pennsylvania on May 14, 1776 and which were properly adapted to the circumstances of the inhabitants of this Commonwealth shall be deemed to have been in force in this Commonwealth from and after February 10, 1777.

Most of the thirteen original states also adopted English common law and statutes, although some did so not by legislation but by judicial decision. Comparative lawyers refer to wholesale adoption or transfer of a body of law from one legal system to another as a *legal transplant*. This is distinguished from gradual assimilation of rules of law or legal procedures from one system to another system. Comparative lawyers refer to this later phenomena as *convergence* of legal systems.

7.   What types of collateral other than the inventory (i.e., hides, etc.) and equipment (i.e., machinery, vats) of the Tannery Owner in the *Clow v. Woods* case would be available to the Tannery Owner under UCC Article 9?

8.   When does the special secured transaction Law of Article 9 apply? (*See* § 9-109(a)).

4.   Evolution of Non-Possessory Personal Property Security Devices and Recording Systems—"Chattel Mortgage," "Conditional Sale," "Trust Receipt," "Factors' Lien Acts"—Use of Accounts "i.e., Intangible Personal Property" as Collateral; Need For A Unified Secured Transaction System

Walter D. Malcolm, *The Uniform Commercial Code as Enacted in Massachusetts*
13 Bus. Law. 490 (1958)[7]

[POSSESSORY SECURITY INTERESTS]

[Pledge]

The oldest security device, dating at least back to Roman law, is that of the pledge. As you well know, the essential element in a pledge is possession. A lender or secured party acquires and holds possession of the property involved (the collateral) to secure payment or performance of the secured obligation.

[Development of the Pledge Concept]

Three other security devices, currently in use today, represent a development of the pledge concept. First, it is common practice to obtain a security interest in goods in the possession of a carrier or a warehouseman, by possession of or control of the bill of lading or warehouse receipt representing them. This procedure dates back at least to about 1600.

Similarly, it is common practice to obtain security interests in shares of stock or a corporation or a government by a pledge of the certificates of stock representing

---

the obligations. This practice has existed at least since the middle of the nineteenth century.

Still later, probably since 1900, the possessory principle of the pledge was developed further by the so-called "field warehouse" device whereby a warehouse is established on the premises of the debtor by an independent warehouseman for the purpose of obtaining and retaining possession of goods that cannot be conveniently moved from the debtor's premises, e.g., raw materials and supplies going into manufacturing process.

[DEVELOPMENT OF NON-POSSESSORY SECURITY INTERESTS]

[Chattel Mortgage]

Of course in many situations it was not possible or convenient to transfer possession of the collateral to the secured party so as to create a valid pledge. To meet this situation, the chattel mortgage was developed. However, where possession of the property remained with the debtor, some procedure was required to give notice to competing creditors or the world at large and this need was met by the device of recording. In Massachusetts, statutes providing for the recording of chattel mortgages date back at least to 1832.

Due largely to the considerable age of the chattel mortgage and the fact that this device was an adaptation of the much older real estate mortgage, the chattel mortgage is traditionally a quite formal instrument; in most states, the law requires witnessing, acknowledgments, affidavits or like formalities and similarly requires quite specific identification of the mortgaged property. Consequently, it is appropriate for use in cases where the property can be specifically identified, e.g., an automobile, by make, model, engine number and maker's number, but not where identification is difficult or impossible, e.g., hides being tanned into leather.

[Conditional Sales Contract]

Conditional sales contracts, developed during the last one hundred years to secure to the seller or his assignee the unpaid purchase price of goods, have a substantially different form and appearance from the older chattel mortgage. In many states (Massachusetts included), they must comply with rigid statutory requirements as to form. In some states, they must be recorded; in others (Massachusetts included), no recording is necessary.

[Trust Receipt]

[Development of the Floating Lien]

Beginning about 1880, at common law, and in the early 1930s by statute, the trust receipt was developed. Here was a security device that was designed to give a security interest of relatively short duration while goods were actively moving through channels of trade. Because of its transitory nature and the difficulties of identification of many kinds of goods to be covered by it, a new type of filing was provided by the Uniform Trusts Receipts Act, namely, the filing with the Secretary of State of a simple financing statement specifying merely the name of the secured party, the name of the debtor and the type of property covered, e.g., wool, hides, automobiles.

[Factors' Lien Acts]

In New York in 1911 and in other states since 1940, so-called "factors' lien acts" have been enacted designed primarily to confer a security interest in raw materials, goods in process, and finished goods going through the manufacturing process. In this type of device, it is recognized that it is impossible to describe or identify specifically the goods subject to the security interest and the emphasis is upon goods going through a process rather than upon specifically identified goods. Here again public filing is required of the same general type as that for trust receipts. In Massachusetts, however, in the case of factors' liens, the filing must be both in the Secretary of State's office and in the town clerk's office in the place of business of the debtor.

[Accounts Receivable]

Finally, during the last thirty or forty years, another type of financing has developed, namely, loans on the security of assignments of accounts receivable. Since an account receivable is a purely abstract indebtedness between two parties, which indebtedness is not embodied in any written instrument, there could be no possibility of a transfer of possession as is required for a pledge and similarly no problem of possession being retained by the debtor. In 1945, Massachusetts (as did some fifteen or sixteen other states) enacted a statute validating assignments of accounts receivable, if in writing and for value, and without any requirement of public filing or recording.

[Need For Unified System]

Thus, we have a security system today that is traceable primarily to historical accident. As financing by one person for another has gradually increased and the practice of securing this financing has similarly increased, a new and different security device has developed almost for each additional need. Each device was developed in a different period of history, by different people; to meet a different need; involves different rules; appears in a different type of instrument; requires different formalities; and has different recording or filing requirements from substantially every other device.

Consequently, today, within a single state, the means of obtaining security is simply a patchwork of odd devices that are replete with variations with little logical sense; gaps that are hard to fill; unnecessary duplications; and traps for the unwary. When there is added to this confusion within a single state a very great variation in rules in almost every one of the fifty states, you have confusion worse confounded. The result simply means great inefficiency in the giving and taking of security, which inefficiency is paid for by the business community and the public as a whole.

NOTE

For an enlightening history of pre-Code security devices, see GRANT GILMORE, SECURITY INTERESTS IN PERSONAL PROPERTY chs. 1–8 (1965).

Problem 1-1: Pledge—Possessory Security Interests. John Smith needs cash to finance a vacation. He takes his $5,000 diamond ring to a pawn shop and receives a $3,000 loan. The pawnbroker retains possession of the ring until the loan is repaid. Is it feasible for John Smith to give up possession of the ring during the period of time in which the loan is outstanding and being repaid? By retaining possession of the ring until the loan is repaid, the pawnbroker has retained a "possessory security interest."

Problem 1-2: Chattel Mortgage—Non-Possessory Security Interest. Would the same type of security device (i.e., a pledge) be helpful to an enterprise engaged in a leather tanning operation seeking to obtain a loan by encumbering machinery which it already owns? Is a non-possessory secured transaction in the form of a chattel mortgage helpful to enable a business to continue to operate while the loan is being repaid?

Problem 1-3: Conditional Sale; Purchase Money Non-Possessory Security Interest. John Smith wants to start a leather tanning business and needs to purchase $50,000 worth of machinery. He has only $10,000 in cash. He plans to use the machinery to generate funds to repay the loan needed to acquire the machinery. If the lender requires collateral, will a pledge or chattel mortgage be useful? Is a conditional sale more useful? In a conditional sales contract, the seller transfers possession of the machinery to the buyer on credit with the stipulation that the seller has the right to take back the machinery (i.e., repossess it) if the buyer defaults on any of the payments due.

5. More on Distinguishing Chattel Mortgages and Conditional Sales

As illustrated by Problems 1-2 and 1-3 above, a chattel mortgage is generally distinguished from a conditional sale by the fact that the chattel mortgage uses as collateral tangible personal property which the debtor *already owns*. On the other hand, a conditional sale type of secured transaction uses as collateral tangible personal property which the debtor *is acquiring*. In general, this is the basic distinction between these two types of secured transactions. The *Pacific Metal Company v. Joslin* case that follows examines other distinctions and considers whether a transaction that fails as a conditional sale may nevertheless be enforceable as a chattel mortgage.

PACIFIC METAL COMPANY v. JOSLIN
United States Court of Appeals, Ninth Circuit
359 F.2d 396 (1966)

DUNIWAY, CIRCUIT JUDGE:

Pacific Metal Company, an Oregon corporation, a creditor of Edsco Manufacturing Co., bankrupt, appeals from a decision of the District Court for the Western Division of Washington. We affirm.

The facts are stipulated. Pacific sold certain machinery to Edsco under a conditional sale contract. The machinery was delivered to and used by Edsco at Vancouver, Clark County, Washington. The contract was duly and regularly filed, as a conditional sale contract, in the office of the County Auditor of Clark County. It is valid under the laws of Oregon. Before using the form of contract for sales in Washington, Pacific obtained the opinion of Washington counsel that the form would be valid as a conditional sale contract in that state. It used the form in reliance upon that opinion. Both Pacific and Edsco believed that the contract in question was valid and enforceable, and intended that it should be. If the contract is not valid, it is because of a mistake of law on the part of Pacific and Edsco.

[Effect of Deficiency Judgment Clause]

Edsco's trustee asserted, and the court held, that the conditional sale contract was void as against the trustee. The contract is not valid as a conditional sale in Washington, but is valid as a chattel mortgage. The reason is that the contract permits both repossession and a deficiency judgment, under the following language:

a. The portion appearing in Sec. 5(a), dealing with repossession, and reading as follows: "* * * in which event Purchaser shall remain bound for and shall and does agree to pay to Seller the balance remaining unpaid, with interest thereon in accordance with the provisions hereof, * * *."

b. The portion appearing in Sec. 5 reading as follows: "All rights and remedies of Seller shall be and are cumulative and not alternative."

The Washington Supreme Court has held that such provisions render the contract invalid as one of conditional sale, and its recording as a conditional sale ineffectual. It may still be valid against creditors, as a chattel mortgage, if recorded as such. [Citations omitted.] That court has said that the rule is one of law, not a mere rule of construction. [Citation omitted.] Pacific concedes that this is the Washington law. It sought to have the contract reformed, based upon a mutual mistake of law, by striking the language that we have quoted. This the referee and the trial court refused to do.

[Effect of Separate Conditional Sales and Chattel Mortgage Statutes]

The court rested its decision on Pacific's failure to comply with the appropriate recording statute. Washington has separate statutes for recording conditional sale contracts (R.C. Wash. § 63.12.010) and chattel mortgages (R.C. Wash. § 61.04.020). Admittedly, the latter statute was not complied with; no affidavit of good faith accompanied the contract, as that statute requires. Thus, considered as a chattel mortgage, the contract is void against the trustee, who stands in the shoes of creditors.

The section dealing with conditional sale contracts reads, in part (§ 63.12.010):

> Sale absolute unless contract filed—Exceptions. All conditional sales of personal property * * * containing a conditional right to purchase, where the property is placed in the possession of the vendee, shall be absolute as to all bona fide purchasers * * * and subsequent creditors, whether or not such creditors have or claim a lien upon such property, unless within ten days after the taking of possession by the vendee, a memorandum of such sale, * * * shall be filed in the auditor's office of the county, wherein, at the date of the vendee's taking possession of the property, the vendee resides.

The filing was within the time and with the officer specified, but, as filed, the contract was invalid on its face, as a contract of conditional sale.

[Reformation of Contract Denied]

Pacific asserts that the contract was subject to an equity of reformation, which would make it valid, that creditors (and the trustee in bankruptcy, who represents them) are not bona fide purchasers, and that therefore the contract can be reformed as against the trustee. The argument is appealing, but the law of Washington appears to be to the contrary, and the trial judge, himself an experienced Washington lawyer, so held.

The statute makes the sale absolute as to creditors as well as bona fide purchasers. And the Washington court has refused to permit reformation in order to validate a filing under it as against creditors, *Malott v. General Machinery Co.*, 19 Wash. 2d 62, 141 P.2d 146 (1943), "because an instrument cannot be reformed so as to affect the rights of innocent third parties" [19 Wash. 2d at 65, 141 P.2d at 148]. There, the mistake was an erroneous statement, in the contract, of the date of delivery of possession, so that it appeared on the face of the contract that the recording was late. Actual delivery was within the prescribed ten days, and reformation was sought to show the correct date. Pacific would distinguish the case on the ground that it involved a failure to comply with filing requirements, while here those requirements were complied with, but the contract itself was defective. We cannot follow the distinction. In either case, a creditor examining the filed contract could conclude that, as to him, the sale was absolute. And, in *Malott*, it was to avoid defeating creditors' rights that the court declined to decree reformation. We find no Washington case to the contrary.

Affirmed.

NOTES AND QUESTIONS

1. Why was the accumulation of the right to repossess and the right to recover a deficiency considered inconsistent with the conditional sale? In a conditional sale, the seller transfers title on the condition subsequent that the buyer make the payments for which he contracted for. If the buyer fails to make these payments and therefore does not satisfy the condition, who then is the owner of the goods sold? If the conditional seller is the owner and he is merely taking back "his" goods, why can't the parties agree that the buyer must also pay installments not yet due at the time of default? (*See* UCC § 9-103(a) definition of Purchase Money Obligation; § 9-103(b) Purchase Money Security Interest in Goods.)

2. How can a chattel mortgage be used when the debtor is securing a loan used *to acquire* the collateral? The court in *Pacific Metal Company v. Joslin* concluded that the transaction could be a chattel mortgage if the parties had satisfied the requirements of the Washington chattel mortgage law. What requirements of that law did the parties fail to satisfy? Were the documents filed in the proper office? Had the parties executed all the proper documents? Why are the requirements for the chattel mortgage different from those for the conditional sale?

3. As you gripe about how difficult it is to work with Article 9, you should consider whether you would have found it more difficult (and riskier) to work with pre-Code security law. In this connection, consider what responsibilities the attorneys from Oregon and Washington undertook in this multistate secured transaction. Should any of them be liable for the losses of the losing party in this case?

6. Floating Lien

Problem 1-4: Floating Lien in Inventory. John Smith wishes to buy $50,000 worth of tanning hides to process them into finished goods in his leather factory. His only asset is $10,000 in cash. If his lender requires collateral to secure repayment of the loan, will a pledge, chattel mortgage or a conditional sale be useful? Will a transaction granting a continuing right of the creditor to foreclose on the hides in John Smith's possession at the time he signs the loan agreement and also thereafter as the raw hides are used and replaced (i.e., a "floating lien") be helpful? *See* UCC § 9-204(a).

Problem 1-5: Floating Lien in Accounts. Will a transaction granting a continuing right of the creditor to foreclose on accounts receivable owed to John Smith—both at the time the security agreement is signed and also thereafter as old accounts are paid and new accounts are generated—be helpful? *See* UCC § 9-204(a).

B. INTRODUCTION TO UNIFIED ARTICLE 9 SECURED TRANSACTION SYSTEM OF THE UNIFORM COMMERCIAL CODE

Today, the principal source of U.S. law governing security interests in movable property is found in Article 9 of the Uniform Commercial Code. All jurisdictions in the United States—including Louisiana—had adopted the 1995 official text of

Article 9. That text was replaced by the 1998 official text which is now in effect in all states and the District of Columbia. The new text, supplemented by amendments promulgated in 2010, has expanded Article 9's scope of application and has adjusted the text to reflect modern financing practices and technological innovations. It has not, however, changed the basic conceptual foundation of Article 9.

A patchwork of federal and state legislation regulates consumer credit. This legislation relies on the required disclosure to consumers of specified information and the prohibition of specific practices and contract terms. Thus, a creditor must disclose it is taking a security interest in property the creditor is financing,[8] while it is an unfair credit practice for a creditor to take a security interest in household goods unless the creditor is financing the debtor's purchase of the goods.[9] Article 9 itself contains several consumer protection rules but the number of these rules is limited.[10] Creditor interests have unsuccessfully argued that it is not appropriate to include regulatory rules in a *commercial* code.[11] Moreover, they have argued, any distinction between consumer and commercial transactions would require separate forms, separate training for personnel, and difficult borderline judgments to be made. The resulting transaction costs would increase the cost of credit to all users of credit, including consumers.

Special legislation other than consumer legislation may also complement Article 9. Many states, for example, have enacted certificate-of-title laws which set out special rules for security interests in motor vehicles, pleasure boats, and similar goods.[12] For those few categories of property not within the scope of Article 9 (even fewer with the adoption of the 2000 official text), state common law will usually apply. For some specific types of property, special federal legislation may also govern. Thus, for example, there is special federal legislation with respect to intellectual property,[13] agricultural finance,[14] and mortgages of ships[15] and aircraft.[16] However, these laws are not comprehensive, and Article 9 will fill the gaps.

Federal law, in other words, plays a relatively minor role in the area of secured transactions law—with the notable exception of federal bankruptcy law. In addition to the special legislation already mentioned, federal common law governs the rights, obligations and remedies of general government lending agencies. However, the

---

[8] 12 C.F.R. §§ 226.6(c), 226.18(m) (2000).

[9] 16 C.F.R. § 444.2(a)(4) (2000).

[10] *See generally Symposium: Consumer Protection and the Uniform Commercial Code*, 75 WASH. U. L.Q. 1-672 (1997).

[11] UCC § 9-101, Comment 4j.

[12] *See, e.g.*, Uniform Motor Vehicle Certificate of Title and Anti-Theft Act, 11A UNIF. LAWS ANN. 175 (adopted 1955); Uniform Certificate of Title Act (2006).

[13] *See* Copyright Act, 17 U.S.C. §§ 101, 201–205 (1994); Patent Act, 35 U.S.C. § 261 (1994). There is uncertainty as to what law governs security interests in trademarks. The relevant federal act, the Lanham Act, is silent on the need to register a security interest. *See* Lanham Act, 15 U.S.C. § 1060 (1994). *See generally* William A. Dornbos, *Structuring, Financing, and Preserving Security Interests in Intellectual Property*, 113 BANKING L.J. 656 (1996).

[14] *See, e.g.*, Food Security Act of 1985, 7 U.S.C. § 1631 (1994).

[15] Ship Mortgage Act, 46 U.S.C. §§ 31301–31343 (1994).

[16] 49 U.S.C. §§ 44107–44110 (1994).

U.S. Supreme Court has held that, in the absence of a need to protect federal interests by a uniform rule, this federal law adopts the substance of state law (i.e., Article 9).[17]

As we shall see, the federal Bankruptcy Code has particular relevance to secured transactions. In theory, a properly-publicized security interest (i.e., a "perfected" security interest) or the value of this interest will survive a bankruptcy proceeding. A secured creditor of a debtor who files for bankruptcy, however, faces at least two general problems. First, commencement of a bankruptcy proceeding automatically triggers a stay on the right of the secured party to create, perfect or enforce its security interest until it requests the court to grant relief from the stay.[18] Second, the trustee in bankruptcy may reduce the secured claim to an unsecured claim if the trustee avoids the security interest. The trustee may avoid a security interest in movable property and fixtures if it is not "perfected" by appropriate publicity under state law.[19] In most cases, the secured party will provide this publicity by filing a notice of the security interest in a public file. The Bankruptcy Code itself also authorizes the trustee to set aside a security interest if it is a fraudulent conveyance[20] or a preferential transfer to a favored creditor shortly before bankruptcy proceedings commence.[21]

NOTE ON OTHER FORMS OF "CREDIT ENHANCEMENT"

A secured transaction reassures the secured creditor that it may look to the value of the collateral if the debtor fails to perform as promised. There are, however, other legal devices that provide similar reassurance. For example, a surety or guarantor provides an additional promise to that made by the principal debtor, as does a financial institution which issues a standby letter of credit. Other examples include creating an escrow arrangement, transferring property to a trust for the benefit of a creditor, or insuring against credit risks. Some authors use the term "credit enhancement" to describe all these different devices. These course materials, however, focus on secured transactions in personal property and fixtures.

The Uniform Commercial Code covers some, but not all, of these devices. For example, Article 5 governs letters of credit, and Article 3 covers suretyship obligations undertaken by signing negotiable instrument. Much of the relevant law, however, is governed by the common law. The American Law Institute adopted the RESTATEMENT (THIRD) OF SURETYSHIP AND GUARANTY in 1995 to provide some guidance in that field.

---

[17] *United States v. Kimbell Foods, Inc.*, 440 U.S. 715 (1979). *See, e.g., Matter of Gary Aircraft Corp.*, 681 F.2d 365 (5th Cir. 1982) (federal law requires parties to register notice of a security interest in airplane in the central Federal Aviation Authority register but leaves to state law the issue of which creditor has a prior claim to the airplane).

[18] 11 U.S.C. § 362 (1994).

[19] 11 U.S.C. § 544(a)(1) (1994).

[20] 11 U.S.C. § 548 (1994).

[21] 11 U.S.C. § 547 (1994).

C. GENERATING WORKING CAPITAL BY CREATION OF AN ATTACHED AND ENFORCEABLE SECURITY INTEREST—INTRODUCING SAMUEL CLEMENS

Samuel Clemens owns and operates a printing business in Dallas, Texas. The business is a sole proprietorship which Mr. Clemens operates under the trade name, Apex Printing. The business' principal asset is a printing machine, but its assets also include numerous smaller machines and other printing equipment, an inventory of paper products, and outstanding accounts receivable. The business is conducted in leased premises.

After consulting his accountant, Mr. Clemens decides that he needs to raise working capital. On the advice of his accountant, Mr. Clemens approaches Steady State Bank of University Park to apply for a loan. The Bank officer reviewing the loan application concludes that the Bank might be willing to make the loan if Mr. Clemens provides adequate security for his promise to repay the loan. Mr. Clemens again consults his accountant, who advises him to offer to use the sole proprietorship as collateral.

1. Alternative Sources of Financing

Problem 1-6: Options When Raising Working Capital. What options other than robbing a bank does Samuel Clemens have when he seeks to raise working capital in order to expand his printing business? Consider the table set out below, which lists possible sources of capital, and the following text, which describes the different lending institutions that might lend to him. Are any of the listed sources realistically available to Mr. Clemens?

P. Hunt, C. Williams & G. Donaldson, Basic Business Finance: A Text
112 (1974)[22]

The proliferation of financial institutions is a twentieth-century phenomenon. At the end of the nineteenth century, commercial banks and the securities markets were the primary external sources of business funds. Banks, however, were conservative in their lending policies, and the securities markets were a source of funds primarily for larger enterprises. Rapid industrial expansion and growing consumer demand for durable goods, especially the automobile, created a need for new credit institutions. Sales finance companies financed the installment sales of equipment and consumer durables by taking assignments of the contracts from the seller of the goods. Commercial finance companies financed riskier smaller ventures and looked to accounts receivable and inventory as collateral. Credit unions and personal finance companies supplied funds directly to consumers. The Depression, the war effort, and reconstruction after World War II also saw the introduction of government lending institutions that continue to be important in the financing of agriculture, transportation, and small business ventures.

---

[22] Copyright 1974. Reprinted by permission.

The markets served by these financial institutions have changed significantly, especially in the last two decades. For many years, banks were content to lend money to finance companies either directly or indirectly by the purchase of short-term commercial paper issued by the finance companies. In recent years, however, commercial banks have competed vigorously in markets formerly left to the finance companies, such as accounts-receivable financing and consumer lending. The present call for deregulation and the expansion of financial intermediaries into new markets suggests that the present trend toward greater competition in all credit markets will continue.

For the purposes of these materials, commercial banks and finance companies are the most important financial intermediaries. Among the more important restrictions in this context are the limitations on loans to any one customer (e.g., 12 U.S.C. § 84), the reserve requirements that may restrict the availability of credit (e.g., 12 U.S.C. § 461; 12 C.F.R. pt. 204), and the prohibition on banks acting as guarantors or sureties. By contrast, finance companies are usually subject to less elaborate and stringent state law regulation, except for loans to consumers. The lending of all institutions, however, is usually subject to the same state or federal usury laws that prescribe the maximum interest rates that may be charged.

While secured lending is clearly important to these institutions, one should not overestimate the importance of Article 9 security interests for either the lender or the borrower. Lenders rely primarily on the three C's (Capital, Character, Capacity) and usually look to collateral and legal proceedings as a last resort. Indeed, much short-term lending by commercial banks to business customers is unsecured. From the perspective of the businessman borrower, loans secured by collateral are only one of a variety of sources of funding, as Table 1 illustrates.

TABLE 1
Major Sources of Funds for American Business

Instrument or form in which funds are acquired	Major suppliers of funds
Normal trade credit	Vendors selling to the firm[1]
Accrued expenses	Miscellaneous creditors[1]
Accrued U.S. income taxes	U.S. government[2]
Special credits from suppliers	Major vendors[2]
Customer loans and advances	Major customers[2]
Short-term bank loans	Commercial banks[2]
Loans from specialized lending companies	Business finance companies, factors, sales finance companies[2]
Commercial paper (short-term notes payable)	Nonfinancial corporations, banks and other financial institutions[3]
Term bank loans	Commercial banks[3]
Term loans—directly placed with non-bank lenders	Insurance companies, pension funds, small-business investment companies[3]
Long-term debt instruments (bonds, notes, debentures, mortgages)	Primarily insurance companies, pension funds, savings banks and other institutional investors, (to lesser extent) individual investors[4]
Preferred stock	Individual investors, institutional investors[4]
Common stock	Individual investors, institutional investors[4]
Inflows from operations represented by retained earnings; noncash charges to earnings (depreciation, etc.)	Operations of the business[5]

Notes: The following notes indicate the broad classification of sources and the classification by length of term.

1.	Spontaneous:	Short term
2.	Negotiated:	Short term
3.	Negotiated:	Intermediate term
4.	Negotiated:	Long term
5.	Operational:	Long term

[The authors of the business finance text from which Table 1 is adapted go on to state both the importance and limitations of secured financing.]

2. Remedies of the Unsecured Creditor

Problem 1-7: Remedies of the Unsecured Creditor. If Steady State Bank decides to make the loan without requiring collateral, how will the Bank enforce its rights if Mr. Clemens defaults on his obligation to repay the loan?

The question is not whether the Bank has rights when Mr. Clemens breaches—a question you probably explored in your contracts class—but the far more practical question of how the Bank actually collects. Assuming that non-legal (and illegal) solutions are not available, you will probably answer that the Bank should sue Mr. Clemens. If Mr. Clemens has no defenses, you will no doubt expect that the judge will render judgment in favor of the Bank. When the judgment is rendered, the Bank becomes a *judgment creditor*, Mr. Clemens becomes a *judgment debtor*, and the debt sued on is merged into the judgment. But what happens next if Mr. Clemens does not pay the judgment?

The following description of what happens next is a very general description of what will happen in most U.S. jurisdictions. The relevant state law is not uniform.

In most jurisdictions, after a judge renders judgment in a particular case, the judgment creditor is entitled to ask the clerk of the court to issue a *writ of execution*. This writ is, in effect, a letter from the court to the local sheriff directing the sheriff to take possession of sufficient property of the judgment debtor to satisfy the judgment, including property not used in the business. There are some limits on the property that the sheriff may take. The sheriff will only be authorized to take property found in a particular area, such as a county (i.e., only property in the sheriff's bailiwick). The sheriff may not take property that is exempt from execution by statute, such as the essential tools of Mr. Clemens' trade. Moreover, the sheriff may only seize enough property to satisfy the judgment. With all these limits in mind, sheriffs will frequently ask the judgment creditor to assist in identifying the judgment debtor's property.

Once the sheriff takes the judgment debtor's property into his or her possession, the sheriff must arrange to sell the property at a public sale (i.e., a sheriff's sale). Statutes will frequently set out detailed rules on the time and manner of this sale. Despite official public notice of the sale, few bidders may appear. Because buyers at the sale will usually receive no warranty of title to the property purchased, the bids will usually be discounted to take this risk into account. In many jurisdictions, not only will the judgment creditor be able to bid at the sheriff's sale but the creditor may be the only bidder. Successful bidders will pay the sheriff, who will first deduct his or her fee and expenses and then return the remainder to the court clerk. The clerk will apply the proceeds to the judgment debt and return any surplus to the judgment debtor.

This collection process—bringing the law suit and enforcing the judgment—is time-consuming and expensive. The process may protect the judgment debtor from abuses by the creditor, but this protection comes at a cost. Recognizing this cost, Article 9 of the Uniform Commercial Code provides a collection process that allows secured creditors to avoid the courts and sheriff by authorizing self-help repossession and sale. Whether this alternate process strikes the right balance between protecting the debtor from an overreaching creditor and maximizing the proceeds for the benefit of both creditor and debtor is a question you should keep in mind as you study these materials.

Problem 1-8: Why a Security Interest? Why would the Bank require Mr. Clemens to grant it a security interest in the personal property assets of his sole proprietorship?

3. Risk Management Policy

P. Hunt, C. Williams & G. Donaldson, Basic Business Finance: A Text
286–88, 306 (1974)[23]

Why do lenders so frequently prefer a secured position to the status of an unsecured creditor? As suggested earlier, lenders take collateral primarily as a means of reducing the risk of loss through non-repayment of their loans. The risks of loss may be reduced by a secured position in several ways:

1. Under many security arrangements, close contact with the borrower is required in order to maintain an effective secured position. As a byproduct of the security arrangement, the lender often gains a more complete and up-to-date acquaintance with the borrower's affairs than he would have obtained as an unsecured creditor.

2. Under many security arrangements, the lender obtains a close and continuing control over assets vital to the borrower's business. This control helps to prevent the sale or diversion of assets that the lender is looking to as an ultimate source of repayment of his loan. Some lenders would be willing to accept an unsecured status provided no other creditor could obtain a prior claim. By taking key assets as security, the lender assures himself that these assets cannot be pledged to another creditor who would thereby gain priority over unsecured lenders. If the lender has full confidence in the borrower, he may seek to gain this same objective through an agreement that the borrower will not pledge assets to other lenders. Such compacts, known as *negative pledge agreements*, are used with some frequency.

3. Finally, and most basically, if the borrower encounters serious financial difficulties and cannot meet his obligations, the secured lender expects to enjoy a prior claim to the security and to the net proceeds from its disposition. . . .

[Possible Disadvantages From Injudicious Encumbrance of Assets]

Earlier in this chapter, advantages that borrowers might obtain from effective use of their assets as security for loans—greater credit, lower interest rates than on unsecured borrowing, etc.—were discussed. It is appropriate at this point to

---

[23] Copyright 1974. Reprinted by permission.

consider the serious disadvantages that can result from injudicious giving of security.

First, the increased availability of credit by giving security may encourage excessively heavy use of debt. Any borrowing involves risk to the borrower—financial risk added to the normal risks of doing business. The increased risks of debt should be appreciated and accepted only after careful and full consideration.

Second, for many firms, there is great advantage (not to say comfort) in retaining reserves of borrowing power for use in financial extremity or to finance particularly desirable investment opportunities that may develop. Obviously, security, once committed, no longer is available as the basis for further credit, and the firm that ties up all of its attractive security is in the same exposed position as the general who has committed all his reserves to battle. When secured borrowing is undertaken, the borrower should appreciate that if he concedes more security than really is required and further credit subsequently is needed, it may be hard indeed to get the old lender to release security or to dilute his own cushion by lending more against the same security.

Third, most firms depend heavily on continued trade credit from suppliers, extended on an unsecured basis. As the firm commits more and more of its best assets as security for loans, the trade creditors increasingly depend on the shrinking and poorer assets left unpledged. While it is difficult to determine in advance the exact extent to which pledging of assets can be carried without jeopardizing the continued availability of trade credit, excessive pledging of assets can result in impairment or loss of credit from alert suppliers and other unsecured creditors.

STATEMENT ON SUB-PRIME MORTGAGE LENDING[24]

Commissioner of Financial Regulation
Conference of State Bank Supervisors
American Association of Residential Mortgage Regulators
National Association of Consumer Credit Administrators

I. Introduction and Background

On June 29, 2007, the Federal Deposit Insurance Corporation (FDIC), the Board of Governors of the Federal Reserve System (Board), the Office of the Comptroller of the Currency (OCC), the Office of Thrift Supervision (OTS), and the National Credit Union Administration (NCUA) (collectively, the Agencies) publicly released the Statement on Subprime Mortgage Lending (Subprime Statement).

The Agencies developed the Subprime Statement to address emerging risks associated with certain subprime mortgage products and lending practices. In particular, the Agencies are concerned about the growing use of adjustable rate

---

[24] www.dllr.state.md.us/finance/subprimelending.htm

mortgage (ARM) products[25] that provide low initial payments based on a fixed introductory rate that expires after a short period, and then adjusts to a variable rate plus a margin for the remaining term of the loan. These products could result in payment shock to the borrower. The Agencies are concerned that these products, typically offered to subprime borrowers, present heightened risks to lenders and borrowers. Often, these products have additional characteristics that increase risk. These include qualifying borrowers based on limited or no documentation of income or imposing substantial prepayment penalties or prepayment penalty periods that extend beyond the initial fixed interest rate period. In addition, borrowers may not be adequately informed of product features and risks, including their responsibility to pay taxes and insurance, which might be separate from their mortgage payments.

These products originally were extended to customers primarily as a temporary credit accommodation in anticipation of early sale of the property or in expectation of future earnings growth. However, these loans have more recently been offered to subprime borrowers as "credit repair" or "affordability" products. The Agencies are concerned that many subprime borrowers may not have sufficient financial capacity to service a higher debt load, especially if they were qualified based on a low introductory payment. The Agencies are also concerned that subprime borrowers may not fully understand the risks and consequences of obtaining this type of ARM loan. Borrowers who obtain these loans may face unaffordable monthly payments after the initial rate adjustment, difficulty in paying real estate taxes and insurance that were not escrowed, or expensive refinancing fees, any of which could cause borrowers to default and potentially lose their homes.

Like the interagency Guidance on Nontraditional Mortgage Product Risks that was published in the *Federal Register* on October 4, 2006 (Volume 71, Number 192, Page 58609–58618), the interagency Subprime Statement applies to all banks and their subsidiaries, bank holding companies and their nonbank subsidiaries, savings associations and their subsidiaries, savings and loan holding companies and their subsidiaries, and credit unions.

Recognizing that the interagency Subprime Statement does not apply to subprime loan originations of independent mortgage lenders and mortgage brokers, on June 29, 2007, the Conference of State Bank Supervisors (CSBS), the American Association of Residential Mortgage Regulators (AARMR), and the National Association of Consumer Credit Administrators (NACCA) announced their intent to develop a parallel statement. CSBS, AARMR and NACCA strongly support the purpose of the Subprime Statement and are committed to promoting uniform application of the Statement's origination and underwriting standards for all mortgage brokers and lenders (herein referred to as providers).

The Subprime Statement identifies many important standards for subprime lending, and CSBS, AARMR, and NACCA support additional efforts to enhance subprime lending oversight. For instance, the Subprime Statement encourages

---

[25] [For example, ARMs known as "2/28" loans feature a fixed rate for two years and then adjust to a variable rate for the remaining 28 years. The spread between the initial fixed interest rate and the fully indexed interest rate in effect at loan origination typically ranges from 300 to 600 basis points.]

depository institutions to consider a borrower's housing-related expenses in the course of determining a borrower's ability to repay the subprime mortgage loan. However, the Agencies did not explicitly encourage the consideration of total monthly debt obligations. Rather than create confusion or adopt a higher standard, CSBS, AARMR, and NACCA have determined to mirror the interagency statement. We will continue to work with the Agencies and our state members to improve industry-wide mortgage lending practices.

. . .

II. Statement on Subprime Mortgage Lending

CSBS, AARMR and NACCA developed this Statement on Subprime Mortgage Lending (Subprime Statement) to address emerging issues and questions relating to subprime mortgage lending practices. The term "subprime" refers to the credit characteristics of individual borrowers. Subprime borrowers typically have weakened credit histories that include payment delinquencies, and possibly more severe problems such as charge-offs, judgments, and bankruptcies. They may also display reduced repayment capacity as measured by credit scores, debt-to-income (DTI) ratios, or other criteria that may encompass borrowers with incomplete credit histories. "Subprime loans" are loans to borrowers displaying one or more of these characteristics at the time of origination or purchase. Such loans have a higher risk of default than loans to prime borrowers. Generally subprime borrowers will display a range of credit risk characteristics that may include one or more of the following:

- Two or more 30-day delinquencies in the last 12 months, or one or more 60-day delinquencies in the last 24 months;

- Judgment, foreclosure, repossession, or charge-off in the prior 24 months;

- Bankruptcy in the last 5 years;

- Relatively high default probability as evidenced by, for example, a credit bureau risk score (FICO) of 660 or below (depending on the product/ collateral), or other bureau or proprietary scores with an equivalent default probability likelihood; and/or

- Debt service-to-income ratio of 50% or greater, or otherwise limited ability to cover family living expenses after deducting total monthly debt-service requirements from monthly income.

This list is illustrative rather than exhaustive and is not meant to define specific parameters for all subprime borrowers. Additionally, this definition may not match all market or institution specific subprime definitions, but should be viewed as a starting point from which the Maryland Commissioner of Financial Regulation (the "Commissioner") will expand examination efforts.[26]

---

[26] [2] "Subprime" and "subprime loans" are defined by the 2001 Interagency Expanded Guidance for Subprime Lending Programs. To promote consistency and uniformity, CSBS, AARMR and NACCA support these definitions for the purposes of this statement.

CSBS, AARMR and NACCA are concerned that borrowers may not fully understand the risks and consequences of obtaining products that can cause payment shock.[27] In particular, CSBS, AARMR and NACCA are concerned with certain adjustable-rate mortgage (ARM) products typically[28] offered to subprime borrowers that have one or more of the following characteristics:

- Low initial payments based on a fixed introductory rate that expires after a short period and then adjusts to a variable index rate plus a margin for the remaining term of the loan;[29]

- Very high or no limits on how much the payment amount or the interest rate may increase ("payment or rate caps") on reset dates;

- Limited or no documentation of borrowers' income;

- Product features likely to result in frequent refinancing to maintain an affordable monthly payment; and/or

- Substantial prepayment penalties and/or prepayment penalties that extend beyond the initial fixed interest rate period.

Products with one or more of these features present substantial risks to both consumers and providers. These risks are increased if borrowers are not adequately informed of the product features and risks, including their responsibility for paying real estate taxes and insurance, which may be separate from their monthly mortgage payments. The consequences to borrowers could include: being unable to afford the monthly payments after the initial rate adjustment because of payment shock; experiencing difficulty in paying real estate taxes and insurance that were not escrowed; incurring expensive refinancing fees, frequently due to closing costs and prepayment penalties, especially if the prepayment penalty period extends beyond the rate adjustment date; and losing their homes. Consequences to providers may include unwarranted levels of credit, legal, compliance, reputation, and liquidity risks due to the elevated risks inherent in these products.

CSBS, AARMR and NACCA note that many of these concerns are addressed in existing interagency guidance.[30] CSBS, AARMR and NACCA recognize that these guidance documents may not apply to state-supervised providers. However, CSBS, AARMR and NACCA believe these guidelines provide sound principles for

---

[27] [3] Payment shock refers to a significant increase in the amount of the monthly payment that generally occurs as the interest rate adjusts to a fully indexed basis. Products with a wide spread between the initial interest rate and the fully indexed rate that do not have payment caps or periodic interest rate caps, or that contain very high caps, can produce significant payment shock.

[28] [12] As noted by Agencies in the final statement, the Subprime Statement focuses on subprime borrowers; however, the statement applies to ARM products that have one or more characteristics that can cause payment shock. Providers should look to the principles of this statement when such ARM products are offered to non-subprime borrowers.

[29] [13] For example, ARMs known as "2/28" loans feature a fixed rate for two years and then adjust to a variable rate for the remaining 28 years. The spread between the initial fixed interest rate and the fully indexed interest rate in effect at loan origination typically ranges from 300 to 600 basis points.

[30] [14] The most prominent are the 1993 *Interagency Guidelines for Real Estate Lending (Real Estate Guidelines)*, the 1999 *Interagency Guidance on Subprime Lending*, and the 2001 *Expanded Guidance for Subprime Lending Programs (Expanded Subprime Guidance)*.

mortgage lending as a reference for state-supervised providers.

While the 2006 CSBS-AARMR Guidance on Nontraditional Mortgage Product Risks (NTM Guidance) may not explicitly pertain to products with the characteristics addressed in this Statement, it outlines prudent underwriting and consumer protection principles that providers also should consider with regard to subprime mortgage lending. This Statement reiterates many of the principles addressed in existing guidance relating to prudent risk management practices and consumer protection laws.[31]

4. Note on the Role of Codes, Statutes, and Case Law

Commercial law in the United States and England developed primarily by case law until the late 19th and early 20th Centuries. Today, the Uniform Commercial Code replaces and augments the early case law, as well as statutes enacted in the late 19th and first half of the 20th Century, which dealt individually with subjects like "sales,"[32] "negotiable instruments,"[33] "conditional sales,"[34] "trust receipts,"[35] "warehouse receipts,"[36] "bills of lading,"[37] and "stock transfer."[38]

Resolution of contemporary legal problems primarily requires application of codes, statutes, or administrative regulations. If the code, statute, or administrative regulation contains a provision(s) relevant to resolving the issues presented, the case law as a secondary source is properly used only if the code, statute, or regulation is ambiguous in its treatment of the issue. The relevant code, statutory, or regulatory provision(s) are the primary source. Case law is properly used as a source only if such provisions are ambiguous, and after application of the relevant code, statutory, or regulatory provision(s).

5. Simplifying Complicated Statutory Language

The concepts of "Security Interest" (§ 1-201(b)(35)), "Security Agreement" (§ 9-102(a)(73)), and the "Scope" provisions of Article § 9-109(a)(1) are fundamental in determining whether a transaction is subject to Article 9. How is "Security Interest" defined by the UCC? (*See* § 1-201(b)(35)). How is "Security Agreement" defined? (*See* § 9-102(a)(73)). Why is "Security Interest" defined in Article 1 and "Security Agreement" defined in Article 9? (*See* § 9-102(c)). Note that 9-102(a) is

---

[31] [15] As with the *Interagency Guidance on Nontraditional Mortgage Product Risks*, 71 FR 58609 (October 4, 2006), the interagency Subprime Statement applies to all banks and their subsidiaries, bank holding companies and their nonbank subsidiaries, savings associations and their subsidiaries, savings and loan holding companies and their subsidiaries, and credit unions. This statement, developed by CSBS, AARMR and NACCA, is applicable to all state-supervised mortgage providers.

[32] Uniform Sales Act (promulgated 1906, currently addressed in UCC Art. 2).

[33] Uniform Negotiable Instruments Law (promulgated 1896, currently addressed in UCC Art. 3).

[34] Uniform Conditional Sales Act (promulgated 1918, currently addressed in UCC Art. 9).

[35] Uniform Trust Receipts Act (promulgated 1933, currently addressed in UCC Art. 9).

[36] Uniform Warehouse Receipts Act (promulgated 1906, currently addressed in UCC Art. 7).

[37] Uniform Bills of Lading Act (promulgated 1909, currently addressed in UCC Art. 7).

[38] Uniform Stock Transfer Act (promulgated 1909, currently addressed in UCC Art. 8).

captioned, Article 9 "Definitions." Section 9-102(b) is captioned "Definitions in Other Articles." Section 9-102(c) is captioned "Article 1 Definitions and Principles."

Students and practitioners first encountering Article 9 of the UCC will often experience difficulties reading and understanding its text. In particular, some of the provisions are written in a "horizontal listing format" that makes it difficult to separate the categories or factors contained within the provision. The horizontal listing format is illustrated by the Actual Text of § 1-201(b)(35), defining "Security Interest." In the horizontal listing format, a series of categories are run horizontally across the page, making it difficult to identify and separate the categories and relate modifying language to the appropriate categories.

Throughout the course, we will be considering Actual Text and Simplified versions of Actual Text of selected provisions of the UCC pertaining to secured transactions. For your ready reference, see *Appendix A: Actual Text and Simplified Version of Actual Text of Selected Provisions of the UCC Pertaining to Secured Transactions.*

The vertical listing format is illustrated by the Simplified Version of the Text of § 1-201(b)(35) in Appendix A, defining "Security Interest." Compare the Actual Text of the term "Security Interest" § 1-201(b)(35) with the Simplified Version, in which each category is vertically lettered, listed, and captioned thereby making the text much more user friendly and more easily understandable.

In order to facilitate understanding and produce a more user-friendly text, various provisions of Article 9 (as well as sections from other Articles relating to Article 9), are included as they become relevant in this book in an Actual Text format alongside a Simplified Version of the text utilizing simplification techniques such as:

1. Vertical listing of categories;

2. Shortened paragraphs;

3. Use of captions not only for sections but also of subsections, and as necessary, for paragraphs as well[39]; and

4. Stating the general rules followed by exceptions rather than exception followed by the general rule.

The simplified version of § 1-201(b)(35) illustrates the vertical listing of categories (item 1 above), and use of subsection, paragraph, as well as section captions (item 3 above), simplification techniques. The use of shortened paragraphs and statement of general rules followed by exceptions simplification technique are addressed later in these materials.

Does the § 1-201(b)(35) Article 9 definition of "Security Interest" address the issue of "ostensible—apparent" ownership? See in particular the introductory

---

[39] Article 9 includes headings for the subsections as an aid to readers. Unlike section captions, which are part of the UCC, *see* § 1-109, subsection headings are not part of the official text itself and have not been approved by the sponsors. Each jurisdiction in which this Article is introduced may consider whether to adopt the headings as a part of the statute and whether to adopt a provision clarifying the effect, if any, to be given to the headings. (§ 9-101(3)).

language of the Simplified Version of §§ 1-201(b)(35), 1-201(b)(35)(A), (D). What are the effects of § 1-201(b)(35)(B), (C), and (E)? *See* Appendix A.

For more information regarding the simplification of Article 9, *see* Del Duca, DeLiberato Jr. & Hostetter, *Applying Plain English Techniques in Revising the UCC*, 29 UCC L.J. 428, 428 (1997); Del Duca, et al., *Revisiting the Application of Plain English in Revising the UCC—Current Practice Among the Fifty States on Use of Captions in Legislation*, 30 UCC L.J. 167, 167–68 (1997); Del Duca, et al., *Simplification in Drafting—The Uniform Commercial Code Article 9 Experience*, 74 CHI.-KENT L. REV. 1309 (1999); Weise, *"Plain English" Will Set the UCC Free*, 28 LOY L.A. L. REV. 317 (1994).

Chapter 2

IDENTIFYING TRANSACTIONS SUBJECT TO ARTICLE 9—CREATING ATTACHED AND ENFORCEABLE SECURITY INTERESTS

A. SETTING UP A SECURED LOAN TRANSACTION

The principal focus of this chapter is on answering the question: When is a security interest enforceable by a secured party? We explore this question by studying what steps Samuel Clemens, the owner of a small business, and his bank must take to create an attached and enforceable security interest. We will learn new legal vocabulary and concepts.

1. Documenting a Secured Transaction

After consulting with his accountant, Samuel Clemens returns to negotiate with the loan officer of Steady State Bank. He submits a completed Business Loan Application form. Following negotiations, the officer approves a working capital loan of $100,000 if Mr. Clemens will grant the bank a security interest in the assets of the sole proprietorship and if he arranges for his brother, Mark, to act as a surety or guarantor. Mr. Clemens agrees to these terms.

On September 1, 2007, Mr. Clemens signs a loan agreement and finalizes three documents of immediate interest to us:

(1) a promissory note (Document A);

(2) a security agreement (Document B);

(3) a financing statement (Document C).

Mark Clemens cosigns the note. On the same day, the bank records a credit entry in the amount of $100,000 in Mr. Clemens' business checking account.

The three documents follow. The promissory note is analyzed immediately following these documents. The security agreement is discussed in Part D of this chapter, where we examine the legal requirements for an attached and enforceable security agreement.[1] There will also be some discussion of the financing statement in Part D, when we ask whether filing a financing statement alone satisfies the formal requirements for a security agreement, but discussion of the use of a registered financing statement to "perfect" a financing statement is postponed until Chapter 4.

---

[1] For a detailed security agreement, see Appendix B, *infra*.

DOCUMENT A
DEMAND NOTE

$100,000.00 September 1, 2007

On demand, we, Samuel Clemens and Mark T. Clemens, promise to pay to the order of Steady State Bank of University Park, Texas, one hundred thousand and xx/100 dollars ($100,000.00) together with interest on the principal outstanding at the rate of fifteen percent (15%) per annum.

This note is secured by a security interest granted by Samuel Clemens in a security agreement dated September 1, 2007.

If this note is placed in the hands of an attorney for collection after default, the undersigned agree to pay all costs of collection, including reasonable attorney's fees.

/s/ Samuel Clemens

/s/ Mark T. Clemens

DOCUMENT B[2]
LOAN SECURITY AGREEMENT

I.

GRANT OF SECURITY INTEREST

September 1, 2007

Samuel Clemens ("Apex Printing"), 3412 Milton Ave., University Park (hereinafter called "debtor") hereby grants to Steady State Bank, 6518 Hillcrest Ave., University Park (hereinafter called "Bank") a security interest in the following described property:

One ABM printer, Model # 3142, Serial #76458

Two Xerox photocopy machines, Model # 5042, with attachments

One automated Miti binder/stapler

One Dell desktop computer with HP laser printer

All other equipment, inventory, accounts, instruments, chattel paper, general intangibles, and fixtures in which debtor has rights at present or in the future and which are used or acquired in connection with the printing and stationery business he operates together with all additions, accessions

---

[2] This form is adapted from Form 9:1600 in 5 UNIF. LAWS ANNOT. 363 (R. Henson & W. Davenport eds. 1968). An annotation of this form appears in RAY D. HENSON, HANDBOOK ON SECURED TRANSACTIONS 392 (2d ed. 1979). Reprinted by permission of West Group.

and substitutions, and all similar property hereafter acquired, referred to in this agreement as "collateral." Proceeds of collateral are also covered but this does not mean that Bank consents to a sale of the collateral.

II.
OBLIGATIONS SECURED

This Security Interest is Given to Secure

a) Payment of a note dated September 1, 2007, executed and delivered by debtor to Bank in the principal sum of $100,000 payable as to principal and interest as therein provided;

b) future advances to be evidenced by like notes to be made by Bank to debtor at Bank's option;

c) expenditures by Bank for taxes, insurance, repairs to and maintenance of the collateral and all costs and expenses incurred by Bank in the collection and enforcement of the note and other indebtedness of debtor; and

d) liabilities of debtor to Bank now existing or hereafter incurred, matured or unmatured, direct or contingent, and any renewal and extension and substitution.

III.
WARRANTIES AND COVENANTS

Debtor expressly warrants and Covenants

1. **Ownership free of encumbrances.** Except for the security interest granted in this agreement, debtor now owns or will use the proceeds of the advances under this agreement to become the owner of the collateral free from any prior lien, security interest or encumbrance, and debtor will defend the collateral against claims and demands claiming the collateral or any interest in it.

2. **Financing statements.** No financing statement covering the collateral or proceeds is on file and debtor will join with Bank in executing a financing statement in form satisfactory to Bank.

3. **Insurance.** Debtor will insure the collateral with companies acceptable to Bank against such casualties and in such amounts as Bank requires. All insurance policies shall be written for the benefit of debtor and Bank as their interests may appear, and policies or certificates evidencing policies shall be furnished to Bank. All policies of insurance shall provide at least ten (10) days prior written notice of cancellation to Bank.

4. **Maintenance.** Debtor (a) will keep the collateral in good condition and free from liens and other security interests, (b) will pay promptly all taxes and assessments, (c) will not use the collateral illegally or encumber it and (d) will not permit the collateral to be affixed to real or personal property without the written consent of Bank.

5. **Inspection.** Bank may examine and inspect the collateral at any time, wherever located.

6. **Reimbursement for expenses.** At its option, Bank may discharge taxes, liens, security interests, or other encumbrances on the collateral and may pay for the repair of damage to the collateral, the maintenance and preservation of it and for insurance on it. Debtor agrees to reimburse Bank on demand for payments so made and until reimbursement, the amount of the payment with interest at ten percent (10%) a year until reimbursement shall be added to the indebtedness and shall be secured by this security agreement.

7. **Change of residence or location of collateral.** Debtor will immediately notify Bank in writing of any change in debtor's residence, and debtor will not permit the collateral to be removed from the location specified in this agreement without the written consent of Bank.

IV.
ADDITIONAL WARRANTY AND COVENANTS

DEBTOR ALSO WARRANTS AND COVENANTS

The collateral covered by this agreement is to be used by debtor primarily for business other than farming operations.

V.
EVENTS OF DEFAULT

Debtor is in default under the agreement upon the happening of one of the following events or conditions:

1. Default in the payment or performance of an obligation, covenant or liability contained or referred to in this agreement;

2. If a warranty, representation or statement made or furnished to Bank by debtor proves to have been false in any material respect when made or furnished;

3. Any event which results in the acceleration of the maturity of the indebtedness of debtor to others under an indenture, agreement or undertaking;

4. Loss, theft, substantial damage, destruction, sale or encumbrance of the collateral, or the levy, seizure or attachment of the collateral;

5. If the Bank believes that the prospect of payment of the indebtedness or the performance of this agreement is impaired;

6. Death, dissolution, termination of existence, insolvency, business failure, appointment of a receiver for any part of the collateral, assignment for the benefit of creditors or the commencement of a proceeding under a bankruptcy or insolvency law by or against debtor or a guarantor or surety for debtor.

VI.
REMEDIES AND SALE ON DEFAULT

Upon default and at any time thereafter, Bank may declare all obligations secured immediately due and payable and may proceed to enforce payment and exercise the rights and remedies provided by the Texas Uniform Commercial Code and other rights and remedies possessed by Bank. Bank may require debtor to assemble the collateral and make it available to Bank at any place to be designated by Bank which is reasonably convenient to both parties. Unless the collateral is perishable or threatens to decline speedily in value or is of a type customarily sold on a recognized market, Bank will give debtor notice of the time and place of any public sale or of the time after which a private sale or other intended disposition is to be made.

Expenses of retaking, holding, preparing for sale, selling or the like shall include Bank's reasonable attorney's fees and legal expenses.

VII.
FINAL PROVISIONS

ANTI-WAIVER CLAUSE

No waiver by Bank of a default operates as a waiver of another default and the terms of this agreement are binding upon the heirs, executors, administrators, successors, and assigns of the parties.

Signed and delivered the day and year first above written.

_____ [*Signature of debtor*]

DOCUMENT C

[The financing statement form reproduced here does not reflect changes made to the form by the 2010 amendments to Article 9.]

UCC FINANCING STATEMENT **ADDENDUM**
FOLLOW INSTRUCTIONS (front and back) CAREFULLY

9. NAME OF FIRST DEBTOR (1a or 1b) ON RELATED FINANCING STATEMENT

9a. ORGANIZATION'S NAME

OR

9b. INDIVIDUAL'S LAST NAME	FIRST NAME	MIDDLE NAME,SUFFIX

10.MISCELLANEOUS:

THE ABOVE SPACE IS FOR FILING OFFICE USE ONLY

11. ADDITIONAL DEBTOR'S EXACT FULL LEGAL NAME - insert only <u>one</u> name (11a or 11b) - do not abbreviate or combine names

11a. ORGANIZATION'S NAME

OR

11b. INDIVIDUAL'S LAST NAME	FIRST NAME	MIDDLE NAME	SUFFIX

11c. MAILING ADDRESS	CITY	STATE	POSTAL CODE	COUNTRY

11d. <u>SEE INSTRUCTIONS</u>	ADD'L INFO RE ORGANIZATION DEBTOR	11e. TYPE OF ORGANIZATION	11f. JURISDICTION OF ORGANIZATION	11g. ORGANIZATIONAL ID #, if any	□ NONE

12. □ **ADDITIONAL SECURED PARTY'S** <u>or</u> □ **ASSIGNOR S/P'S NAME** - insert only <u>one</u> name (12a or 12b)

12a. ORGANIZATION'S NAME

OR

12b. INDIVIDUAL'S LAST NAME	FIRST NAME	MIDDLE NAME	SUFFIX

12c. MAILING ADDRESS	CITY	STATE	POSTAL CODE	COUNTRY

13. This FINANCING STATEMENT covers □ timber to be cut or □ as-extracted collateral, or is filed as a □ fixture filing.

14. Description of real estate:

16. Additional collateral description:

15. Name and address of a RECORD OWNER of above-described real estate (if Debtor does not have a record interest):

17. Check <u>only</u> if applicable and check <u>only</u> one box.
Debtor is a □ Trust or □ Trustee acting with respect to property held in trust or □ Decedent's Estate

18. Check <u>only</u> if applicable and check <u>only</u> one box.
□ Debtor is a TRANSMITTING UTILITY
□ Filed in connection with a Manufactured-Home Transaction — effective 30 years
□ Filed in connection with a Public-Finance Transaction — effective 30 years

FILING OFFICE COPY — UCC FINANCING STATEMENT ADDENDUM (FORM UCC1Ad) (REV. 05/22/02)

2. Comment on Demand Promissory Notes[3]

Debtors like Mr. Clemens frequently sign promissory notes setting out their obligation to pay money to their creditors. Creditors will usually want these notes to be negotiable instruments governed by UCC Article 3. They do so for two reasons: negotiable instruments may be enforced more expeditiously and less expensively than simple promises, and negotiable instruments are more easily assigned to third parties. Law school courses on negotiable instruments or payment systems explore the details of Article 3 rules on negotiability. For present purposes, what is important is (A) to point out how to recognize an Article 3 negotiable instrument and (B) to explain what a "demand" note is.

(A) To be a negotiable instrument within the scope of Article 3, an instrument must satisfy the formal rules of § 3-104. UCC § 3-104(a). These formal attributes are thought to permit the reader to determine from the face of the instrument whether or not it is negotiable. To be a negotiable promissory note, the instrument must set out "an unconditional promise . . . to pay a fixed amount of money, with or without interest or other charges described in the promise." In addition, the instrument must satisfy the following three requirements:

(1) The promise must be payable to "bearer" or to "order" at the time it is issued or first comes into possession of a holder. UCC §§ 3-104(a)(1), 3-109(b). The maker issues the note when he or she first voluntarily hands over the signed note to the creditor. UCC § 1-201(b)(15), § 3-105(a). When it takes possession of the note, the creditor becomes the holder of the note. UCC § 1-201(b)(21).

(2) The promise must be payable on demand or at a definite time. UCC §§ 3-104(a)(2), 3-108(a).

(3) The instrument must include no other undertaking to do any act in addition to the payment of money. However, this requirement is subject to the following very important exceptions noted in § 3-104(a)(3):

(i) an undertaking or power to give, maintain, or protect collateral to secure payment,

(ii) an authorization or power to the holder to confess judgment or realize on or dispose of the collateral, [and]

(iii) a waiver of the benefit of any law intended for the advantage or protection of an obligor.

In other words, even if the instrument includes one or more of the above exceptions, then the instrument will be a negotiable instrument within Article 3 if it otherwise satisfies the formalities of § 3-104(a)(1), (2) and (3).

---

[3] The citations to the provisions of Article 1 and Article 3 in this comment are to the Official Text of the UCC even though all jurisdictions have not enacted all provisions of the Official Text Article 1 and Article 3.

(B) If the promissory note is a "demand" instrument, the original creditor (or subsequent holder of the note) may demand payment at any time. Unless otherwise agreed, the demand may be made in any commercially reasonable manner and is effective when the maker receives it. UCC § 3-501(b). If the maker does not pay upon demand, the maker *dishonors* the note. UCC § 3-502(a)(1). The original creditor or subsequent holder of the note will then have six years from the date of the demand to enforce the maker's promise. UCC § 3-118(b). If no demand is made and the maker has made no payments during a ten-year period, an action to enforce the note is barred. UCC § 3-118(b).

B. SCOPE OF APPLICABILITY OF ARTICLE 9

1. Inclusion Standard

CONCEPTUAL, FUNCTIONAL AND "DEEMED TO BE" SECURITY
INTERESTS—DEFINITION OF "SECURITY INTEREST"—TRUE
LEASE DISTINGUISHED FROM "DIRTY LEASE"
(ACTUALLY A PURCHASE MONEY SECURITY INTEREST)

The applicability/scope provision of Article 9 provides:

§ 9-109. Scope

(a)   **[General scope of article.]** . . . this article applies to:

(1)   a transaction, *regardless of its form*, that creates a security interest in personal property or fixtures by contract; . . . (emphasis supplied)

(2)   an agricultural lien;

(3)   a sale of accounts, chattel paper, payment intangibles, or promissory notes;

(4)   a consignment;

. . .

The definition of security interest in part provides:

§ 1-201(b)(35).   [General Definitions]

"Security Interest" means an interest in personal property or fixtures which secures payment or performance of an obligation.

. . .

(E)[4] Whether a transaction in the form of a lease creates a "security interest" is determined pursuant to Section 1-203.

The combined effect of the *regardless of its form* phrase of § 9-109(a)(1) and the quoted excerpt of § 1-201(b)(35) mandates use of the § 1-203 functional test to

---

[4] *See* Simplified Version of Actual Text Appendix A, *infra*, for this (E) designation.

determine whether an agreement labeled "lease" is a "true lease" or a lease which in substance is a "purchase money security interest" (*see* § 9-103) secured transaction, referred to by Code commentators as a "dirty lease."

There has been considerable litigation over when a transaction denominated as a "lease" will be recharacterized as a secured transaction. The stakes are high since: (1) the split of interest in leased property does not require public notice, but a secured transaction does; (2) a security interest for which required public notice has not been given is unperfected and has virtually no priority.[5] In addition, (3) the enforcement-remedy structure and rights of the parties are different.

At the time Article 2A was enacted, § 1-201(37) also was restructured and divided into §§ 1-201(b)(35) and 1-203 to attempt to further clarify the distinction between a so-called "true lease" governed by Article 2A, and a so-called "dirty lease," which actually constitutes a secured transaction governed by UCC Article 9 and law other than Article 2A. As the Official Comment to § 1-203 notes, this distinction is important:

(1)   in determining the rights and remedies of the parties to the "lease," and

(2)   to determine the rights of third parties.

These consequences are further illustrated in the materials which follow. The distinction is also important in other contexts including tax, usury, bankruptcy, etc.

For example, in *In re Super Feeders, Inc.,* 236 B.R. 267 (D. Neb. 1999), the court ruled that an agreement for a lease of fifteen installed and completed swine nursery buildings created a security interest rather than a lease where the agreement:

(a)   did not give Lessee the right to terminate but obligated Lessee to pay rentals for the full lease term; and

(b)   provided that the facility could be purchased at the end of the lease period for the nominal price of $46,250.00.

Under U.C.C. 1-201(37) (§§ 1-201(b)(35) and 1-203 of Revised Article 1), a lease agreement creates a security interest rather than a true lease if:

(a)   the lessee does not have the right to terminate the lease and is obligated to make payments for the full lease term; and

(b)   one of the four following enumerated requirements is present:

   1.   The original term of the lease is equal to or greater than the remaining economic life of the goods;

   2.   The lessee is bound to renew the lease for the remaining economic life of the goods or is bound to become the owner of the goods;

   3.   The lessee has an option to renew the lease for the remaining economic life of the goods for no additional consideration upon compliance with the lease agreement; or

---

[5] These priority issues are addressed later in our discussions of § 9-317(a)(2) and § 544 of the Bankruptcy Code.

4. The lessee has an option to become the owner of the goods for no additional consideration or nominal additional consideration upon compliance of the lease agreement.

The court found the option price nominal because:

(a) The $46,250 option price was only 5% of the $925,000 which was the price paid by the lessor to purchase the facility;

(b) The $46,250 option price was also only 3.6% of the $1,281,987 rental payments made under the agreement; and

(c) The option price was also nominal compared to the value of the equipment at the end of the lease term. The facility would have a value of $225,000 at the end of the lease term. The $46,250 option price was only 20% of the value of the facility at the end of the lease term.

The court accordingly held the "lessor" to be a secured creditor in Debtor's bankruptcy proceeding and overruled the Motion for an Order to Set a Time by Which Debtor Must Assume or Reject the Executory Contract.

Coleman v. DaimlerChrysler Services of North America, LLC, 623 S.E.2d 189 (Ga. App. 2005), illustrates the application of §§ 1-201(b)(35) and 1-203 and the impact which the distinction between a "true lease" and "dirty lease" may have on the *rights and remedies of the parties* to an agreement which they label "lease agreement." In *Coleman*, "Lessor" brought an action seeking a deficiency judgment against "Lessee" after the Lessee/Borrower defaulted on car lease payments and the car was sold after repossession for less than the outstanding liability on the "Lease." "Lessee" alleged that "Lessor" failed to sell the car in a commercially reasonably manner as required by UCC § 9-610(b), which provides that a creditor who sells collateral repossessed from a debtor must do so in a commercially reasonable manner. The trial court did not accept this argument but instead adopted "Lessor's" argument that UCC Article 9 was inapplicable because the transaction was a "true lease." The "Lessee" argued that Article 9 of the UCC was applicable because the transaction constituted a "dirty lease" which actually involved a sale of the motor vehicle on credit with a right in Seller (labeled "Lessor" in the contract) to repossess the car from the Buyer/Debtor (labeled "Lessee" in the contract) if the Buyer/Debtor defaulted on the required monthly installment · payments. The Appellate Court concluded that factual issues were unresolved in the application of the provisions of § 1-201(37) [R§ 1-201(b)(35)] and vacated the summary judgment which had been entered in favor of the Seller/Creditor ("Lessor") and remanded the case.

The lengthy *In re QDS* decision which follows illustrates the effect the distinction between a "true lease" and a "dirty lease" has in determining the *rights of third parties*. In *QDS*, the Buyer of all of the Debtor's assets in a bankruptcy case would have no right to equipment Debtor had "leased" from Supplier if the contract was found to be a "true lease." This is because in a "true lease" there is no transfer of title or ownership from the "Lessor" to the "Lessee." If the contract was a "true lease," Debtor "Lessee" accordingly did not have any ownership rights in the equipment to transfer to Buyer in the bankruptcy sale and the property involved reverted back to the Lessor. In *QDS*, the court concluded that Buyer had not presented evidence to establish that the "lease agreement" was a "dirty" lease.

Analysis of the *QDS* case develops skill in mastering one of the most difficult and most frequently litigated provisions of the Uniform Commercial Code. Mastering this complicated statutory language will develop statutory construction, interpretation and drafting skills for effective client counseling, litigation, and drafting user friendly, readily understandable statutory language.[6]

IN RE QDS COMPONENTS, INC.
United States Bankruptcy Court, Southern District of Ohio
292 B.R. 313 (2002)

. . .

II. Factual and Procedural Background

. . .

[Lakin purchased substantially all the assets of QDS pursuant to authorization of the Bankruptcy Court. Lakin claimed two lathes under the terms of the Bankruptcy Court Sale Order which contained the following provision:

> "Any of the Purchased Assets that are subject to a lease will be transferred and conveyed to [Lakin] without further consideration in the event that the lease is deemed to be a capital lease as compared to a true lease or operating lease" (the "Capital Lease Provision").

Invoking the Capital Lease Provision, Lakin asserted that the "Lease Agreements" under which the bankrupt Debtor acquired the two lathes were in fact disguised security agreements and that the lathes were therefore property of QDS subject to the security interest of the "lessor" and were therefore properly transferred to Lakin by way of the Sale Order.

Assignees of the "lessor" asserted that the "Lease Agreement" were "true leases" and that the two lathes should therefore be returned to them. The terms of the Lease Agreements are identical. Each of the Lease Agreements requires QDS to make payments to Intech totaling $110,425. At the end of the 60-month term of the Lease Agreements, QDS has the option to purchase each Lathe for $9,065 (the "Option Amount") plus applicable taxes. The Lease Agreements provide that, if QDS does not exercise its purchase option, it may either: (1) deliver the Lathes to Intech; or (2) continue in possession of the Lathes, in which case the Lease Agreements automatically renew for successive one-month terms at the regular monthly installment amount of $1,435.

---

[6] The actual text of R§ 1-201(b)(35) and R§ 1-203, along with simplified versions of these sections, can be found in Appendix A, *infra. See also* Fred H. Miller, The ABCs of the UCC—(Revised) Article 1 General Provisions 116–17, 120–23 (Amelia H. Boss ed., 2002).

The Lease Agreements contain an "Early Termination" provision that states, in relevant part:

> EARLY TERMINATION. If no default exists under this Lease, you have the right upon thirty (30) days written notice to purchase all the Equipment, but not less than all the Equipment, and terminate the Lease. The purchase price will be the sum of (a) + (b) + (c) as follows: (a) the net present value of all unpaid Lease payments for the remainder of the term discounted at 7.0% A.P.R.; (b) the net present value of the purchase option discounted at 7.0% A.P.R.; (c) all other amounts due or that become due under the Lease. Upon our receipt from you of the purchase price we shall transfer our interest in the Equipment to you without representation, recourse, or warranty as is, where-is and we shall deliver all documents reasonably requested to transfer our interest in the Equipment to you.

Under the Lease Agreements, Intech expressly disclaimed all warranties. QDS bore the full risk of loss and was required to insure the Lathes at its own expense. In addition, QDS had to pay directly or reimburse Intech for all applicable taxes and fees. QDS also was responsible for paying all maintenance expenses. In the event of a default by QDS, the Lease Agreements afforded Intech the following remedies:

> (a) [Intech] may cancel or terminate this Lease or any or all other agreements that we have entered into with you; (b) we may require you to immediately pay us, as compensation for loss of our bargain and not as a penalty, a sum equal to (i) the value of all unpaid Lease Payments for the remainder of the term plus the value of our anticipated residual interest in the Equipment, plus (ii) all other amounts due or that become due under this Lease; (c) we may require you to deliver the Equipment to us as set forth in Section 14; (d) we or our agent may peacefully repossess the Equipment without court order and you will not make any claims against us for damages or trespass or any other reason; and (e) we may exercise any other right or remedy available at law or in equity.

> The Lease Agreements recite that Intech is the owner of the Lathes and that you agree that this transaction is a true lease. However, if this transaction is deemed to be a lease intended for security, you grant us a purchase money security interest in the Equipment (including any replacements, substitutions, additions, attachments and proceeds) and the equipment shall secure, in addition to the lease obligations, any indebtedness at any time owed by you to us. You will deliver to us signed financing statements or other documents we request to protect our interest in the equipment.

> YOU AUTHORIZE US TO FILE A COPY OF THIS LEASE AS A FINANCING STATEMENT AND APPOINT US OR OUR DESIGNEE AS YOUR ATTORNEY-IN-FACT TO EXECUTE AND FILE, ON YOUR BEHALF, FINANCING STATEMENTS COVERING THE EQUIPMENT.

Pursuant to the foregoing provision, Intech filed financing statements covering the Lathes with the Ohio Secretary of State and the Shelby County Recorder.

The dispute was submitted upon the following stipulated facts (the "Initial Stipulation"):

(1) The fair market value of the Lathes will be $12,000 at the expiration of the Lease Agreements—i.e., in May 2005;

(2) The cost of shipping and rigging the Lathes from their present location at the QDS Facility to either Portland, Oregon or Los Angeles, California would not exceed $7,200 (including insurance);

(3) The cost of shipping and rigging the Lathes from their present location to a local storage facility would be approximately $1,500 to $2,500 and would cost approximately $100 per month to store (including insurance); and

(4) The remaining useful life of the Lathes is at least five to six years—i.e., its useful life will extend until at least 2006.

In addition to the Initial Stipulation, the Court also received briefs from the Debtor, Lakin, U.S. Bancorp, and Heller addressing the issue of whether the Lease Agreements are true leases or disguised security agreements.

III. Arguments of the Parties

Lakin asserts that the Lease Agreements constitute disguised security agreements rather than true leases.

Lakin advances several arguments in support of its contention that the Lease Agreements are, in fact, disguised security agreements. First, Lakin maintains that, under § 1-203, the Lease Agreements are conclusively presumed to have created security interests because QDS: (1) could not terminate its obligation to make payments for the entire term of the Lease Agreements; and (2) had the contractual right to become owner of the Lathes for nominal consideration. In support of its contention that the Option Amount contained in the Lease Agreements is nominal, Lakin relies on U.C.C. § 1-203. According to Lakin, the nominality of the Option Amount is also demonstrated by the application of "percentage tests"—which require a comparison of: (1) the Option Amount and cost of the Lathes; (2) the Option Amount and the total stream of rental payments made by QDS under the Lease Agreements; and (3) the total payment stream and the Lathes' original cost.

. . .

IV. Opinion

1. Overview

Sections [1-201(b)(35) and 1-203], which was adopted by the California legislature in 1988 and made effective January 1, 1990, reads:

"Security interest" **(1) [General Definition]** means an interest in personal property or fixtures which secures payment or performance of an obligation . . .[7]

[Determination is one of fact]. Whether a transaction creates a lease or security interest is determined by the facts of each case . . . .

[Bright Line Test]

[Factors which create a security interest.] A transaction creates a security interest if the consideration the lessee is to pay the lessor for the right to possession and use of the goods is an obligation for the term of the lease not subject to termination by the lessee, and

    (a)   **[Length of original term of the lease.]** The original term of the lease is equal to or greater than the remaining economic life of the goods,

    (b)   **[Lessee's obligation to renew the lease or become owner.]** The lessee is bound to renew the lease for the remaining economic life of the goods or is bound to become the owner of the goods,

    (c)   **[Renewal option for no additional or nominal consideration.]** The lessee has an option to renew the lease for the remaining economic life of the goods for no additional consideration or nominal additional consideration upon compliance with the lease agreement, or

    (d)   **[Lessee's option to become owner of the goods for no additional or nominal consideration.]** The lessee has an option to become the owner of the goods for no additional consideration or nominal additional consideration upon compliance with the lease agreement.

[Factors which by themselves are inconclusive] A transaction does not create a security interest merely because it provides that

    (a)   **[Present value of lessee's consideration to pay.]** The present value of the consideration the lessee is obligated to pay the lessor for the right to possession and use of the goods is substantially equal to or is greater than the fair market value of the goods at the time the lease is entered into,

    (b)   **[Assumption of risk of loss or agrees to pay certain costs.]** The lessee assumes risk of loss of the goods, or agrees to pay taxes, insurance, filing, recording, or registration fees, or service or maintenance costs with respect to the goods,

---

[7] [Language from the definition of "security interest" was not relevant and accordingly omitted from the court's opinion. After the "General definition" of "security interest," the omitted language lists additional transactions as follows: (2) Interest of consignor or buyer under Article 9; (3) Buyer's interest in identified goods; (4) Sellers and lessors of goods. Items 2, 3, and 4 are more properly addressed in a course in Secured Transactions. Here, we address the "lease or security interest" issue.—Eds.]

(c) [**Lessee's option to renew the lease or acquire ownership of the goods.**] The lessee has an option to renew the lease or to become the owner of the goods,

(d) [**Lessee's option to renew the lease.**] The lessee has an option to renew the lease for a fixed rent that is equal to or greater than the reasonably predictable fair market rent for the use of the goods for the term of the renewal at the time the option is to be performed, or

(e) [**Lessee's option to become the Owner of the goods.**] The lessee has an option to become the owner of the goods for a fixed price that is equal to or greater than the reasonably predictable fair market value of the goods at the time the option is to be performed.[8]

[**Definitions**] For purposes of this subsection (37) [see R§ 1-203]:

[Nominality] (x) Additional consideration is not nominal if (i) when the option to renew the lease is granted to the lessee the rent is stated to be the fair market rent for the use of the goods for the term of the renewal determined at the time the option is to be performed, or (ii) when the option to become the owner of the goods is granted to the lessee the price is stated to be the fair market value of the goods determined at the time the option is to be performed. Additional consideration is nominal if it is less than the lessee's reasonably predictable cost of performing under the lease agreement if the option is not exercised;

(y) **"Reasonably predictable"** and **"remaining economic life of the goods"** [i.e., residual value] are to be determined with reference to the *facts and circumstances at the time the transaction is entered into*; (Emphasis supplied) and

(z) **"Present value"** means the amount as of a date certain of one or more sums payable in the future, discounted to the date certain. The discount is determined by the interest rate specified by the parties if the rate is not manifestly unreasonable *at the time the transaction is entered into*; otherwise, the discount is determined by a commercially reasonable rate that takes into account the facts and circumstances of each case at the time the transaction was entered into. (Emphasis supplied).

. . .

The bankruptcy court in *In re Lerch*, 147 B.R. 455, 460 (Bankr. C.D. Ill. 1992) described the structure of new § 1-203 in the following manner:

The initial portion of the first sentence of the second unnumbered paragraph [of new § 1-203] contains the basic direction that the [true lease versus disguised security agreement] determination is made based on the

---

[8] [As previously mentioned, the editors of the textbook added their own notation for § 1-201(37) [R§ 1-201(b)(35)] in order to facilitate reference to these provisions of the Code.—Eds.]

facts of each case. The latter portion of the first sentence of the second unnumbered paragraph starting with the word "however" creates an exception to the basic direction that the determination is made on the facts of each case, as it provides that without looking at all the facts, a lease will be construed as a security interest if a debtor cannot terminate the lease, and if one of the four enumerated terms is present in the lease. Absent a mandated classification, the determination is based on the facts of the case. At this point, the third unnumbered paragraph comes into effect. Focusing on the economics of the transaction, it states that a security interest is not created merely because it contains any of the five terms enumerated in the third unnumbered paragraph.

[More on The Bright Line Test]

As the *Lerch* court noted, new § 1-203 first requires a court to apply what has been referred to as the "Bright-Line Test." Under this test, the initial focus is upon the lessee's obligation under the purported lease agreement. If the consideration the lessee must pay for the term of the lease is not subject to termination by the lessee, then the transaction meets the first prong of the test.

If a determination is made that a debtor's payment obligation under a purported lease is not subject to termination, then the second prong of the test must be satisfied in order to find a security interest as a matter of law. The second part of the Bright-Line Test looks to whether any of the so-called "Residual Value Factors" is present.

The presence of one or more of the following Residual Value Factors set forth in new § 1-203 establish that a non-terminable "lease" agreement is a disguised security agreement as a matter of law:

1. First, if the original term of the lease is equal to or greater than the remaining economic life of the goods.

2. Second, if the lessee is bound to renew the lease for the remaining economic life of the goods or to become the owner of the goods.

3. Third, if the lessee has the option to renew the lease for nominal or no additional consideration upon compliance with the lease agreement.

4. Fourth, if the lessee has an option to become the owner of the goods for nominal or no additional consideration upon compliance with the lease agreement.

[I]f the lessee is bound for the entire term of the agreement and if any one of the requirements of subparagraphs (a), (b), (c), or (d) are met, then the court's inquiry ends and the transaction is deemed to have created a security interest.

2. The Bright-Line Test

a. *Terminability of Debtor's Payment Obligation*

The Lease Agreements expressly grant the Debtor a right of termination. Lakin argues, however, that the Debtor has no meaningful right to terminate its payment obligations to the Lessors. Lakin points out that the Lease Agreements condition the Debtor's right of termination on its payment of all remaining contractual obligations, including all monthly installments due through the end of the lease term, plus the Option Amount, less a 7% discount factor.

The first prong of new § 1-203's Bright-Line Test focuses not on whether a lessee has a contractual right to terminate under the agreement in question, but rather on whether "the consideration the lessee is to pay the lessor for the right to possession and use of the goods is an obligation for the term of the lease not subject to termination by the lessee." UCC § 1-203. The Lease Agreement requires the Debtor to pay the Lessors upon termination the present value of precisely what they would receive if QDS made all required monthly installment payments for the full contract term and then exercised the purchase option. Thus, the Debtor's *payment obligation* is not subject to termination within the meaning of new § 1-203.

. . .

b. *Nominality*

The parties agree that three of the four Residual Value Factors enumerated in new § 1-203 are not applicable: the original term of the Lease Agreements is not equal to or greater than the remaining economical life of the Lathes or to become the owner of the Lathes, and QDS is not afforded the option to renew the Lease Agreements for nominal or no additional consideration. *See* UCC § 1-203. Their dispute centers on whether QDS "has the option to become the owner of the goods for nominal or no additional consideration upon compliance with the [L]ease [A]greement[s]."

Section 1-203 sets forth two tests for determining whether an option price is nominal: (1) the option price is not nominal when the option to purchase is stated in the agreement to be the fair market value of the property (the "FMV Standard"); and (2) the option price is nominal if it is less than the lessee's reasonably predictable costs of performing under the lease agreement if the option is not exercised (the "Option Price/Performance Cost Test"). UCC § 1-203. Because the Option Amount is not stated in the Lease Agreements "to be the fair market value of the goods determined at the time the option is to be performed," *id.*, the FMV Standard has no application here. Accordingly, whether the Lease Agreements should be recharacterized as disguised security agreements under the Bright-Line Test will turn on application of the Option Price/Performance Cost Test, which requires a comparison of the Option Amount with the Debtor's reasonably predictable cost of performing under the Lease Agreements if the purchase option is not exercised. Lakin, Heller, and U.S. Bancorp each apply the Option Price/ Performance Cost Test in a different manner, yielding the respective results shown below.

Lakin argues that a "cost of performing" that QDS must incur if it elects not to exercise the purchase option is the lost economic value of the Lathes (the "Lost Equipment Value"). By factoring in the Lost Equipment Value, Lakin concludes that the Debtor's cost of performing under the Lease Agreements if the purchase option is not exercised exceeds the Option Amount. Lakin's calculation is set forth below:

Option Amount	Cost of Performing	
$9,065	$12,000	Lost Equipment Value
	+$7,200[9]	Cost to Remove, Crate, and Return the Lathe to the U.S. Bancorp/Marcap
$9,065	$19,200	

Heller contends that the Lost Equipment Value should not be included as a "cost of performing" under the Lease Agreement, correctly asserting that Lakin has failed to cite any authority whatsoever for the proposition that the lost economic value of equipment returned to the lessor should be deemed a cost of performance under New § 1-203. According to Heller, including the economic value a lessee opts to forego when it returns leased equipment as a "cost of performing" under New § 1-203 "would make even the most obvious true lease a security agreement." Heller applies the Option Price/Performance Cost Test as follows:

Option Amount	Cost of Performing	
$9,065	$7,200	Cost to Remove, Crate, and Return the Lathe to U.S. Bancorp/Marcap
$9,065	$7,200	

The parties' respective nominality calculations reflect their disagreement on a fundamental question: whether, and how, the Lost Equipment Value should be factored into the Option Price/Performance Cost Test. This dispute raises an issue of statutory construction, namely whether the economic value of "leased" goods, which a lessee chooses to forego when it elects not to exercise a purchase option, constitutes a "cost of performing under the lease agreement" within the meaning of new § 1-203. As explained below, given the state of the evidentiary record, the Court need not resolve this question of statutory interpretation.

New § 1-203 expressly states that a lessee's reasonably predictable cost of performing under a lease agreement is "to be determined with reference to the facts and circumstances at the time a transaction is entered into." UCC § 1-203. Here, the parties have stipulated that the cost of returning the Lathe would not exceed $7,200, including insurance. The record does not allow the Court to determine—by referring "to the facts and circumstances at the time [the Lease Agreements were] entered into"—what the Debtor's reasonably predictable cost of performing would be if it chose not to exercise its purchase option. The parties also

---

[9] [12] The First Stipulation establishes that the cost of removal and return of each Lathe could be as low as $1,500 to $2,500 if U.S. Bancorp elected to have the Debtor ship the Lathe to a local facility for storage until resale. U.S. Bancorp suggests that this is its customary practice, rather than requiring return of leased equipment to U.S. Bancorp's facility in Portland, Oregon. Yet, because U.S. Bancorp has the contractual right to require QDS to ship the U.S. Bancorp Lathe to Portland, Oregon, the Court concludes that the full $7,200 cost of removing, crating, and shipping the Lathe back to U.S. Bancorp is the appropriate figure to be used in applying the Option Price/Performance Cost Test.

stipulated as to (1) the fair market value of the Lathes at the end of the term of the Lease Agreements, and (2) the expected remaining economic life of the Lathes upon contract termination. Yet no evidence was offered to establish what, if any, projections were made by QDS and Intech at lease inception as to the Lathes' fair market value and remaining economic life upon lease termination. In place of this critical information, Lakin, Heller, and U.S. Bancorp., have offered their estimates of the fair market value and remaining economic life of the Lathes, as well as the cost to return them to the Lessors, made nearly a year after the Lease Agreements were executed. The record therefore contains no evidence establishing what the original parties to the transaction anticipated at contract inception concerning QDS's "cost of performing under the Lease Agreement[s] if the option is not exercised." UCC § 1-203. Without this evidence, the Court is unable to make the statutory calculation required under new § 1-203's Option Price/Performance Cost Test. Because it did not present the Court with the evidence needed to apply the Option Price/Performance Cost Test, Lakin has failed to demonstrate the nominality of the Option Amount under the Bright-Line Test.

. . .

c. *Retention of a Meaningful Reversionary Interest*

Having concluded that the Lease Agreements are not terminable and that none of the conditions set forth in new § 1-203 have been met, the Court must address the outcome-determinative question: Did the Lessors retain a meaningful reversionary interest in the Lathes? *See Addison*, 41 Cal.App.4th at 1296, 49 Cal.Rptr.2d at 136. Unfortunately, while new § 1-203 sends a court on a search for the lessor's residual interest, it provides no path markers to guide the way. The statute simply states that the determination of lease versus security agreement status should be based on "the facts of each case" and then enumerates five conditions (in new § 1-203) that are not sufficient, standing alone, to establish the existence of a disguised security interest. New § 1-203 provides that a transaction does not create a security interest merely because one or more of the following five conditions exist:

[More on Factors Which By Themselves are Inconclusive]

1.　That the present value of the consideration the lessee is obligated to pay the lessor is substantially equal to or greater than the fair market value of the goods at the time the lease is entered into;

2.　That the lessee assumes the risk of loss of the goods, or undertakes the obligation to pay taxes, insurance, filing, recording or registration fees or service or maintenance costs;

3.　That the lessee has an option to renew the lease or become the owner of the leased goods;

4.　That the lessee has an option to renew the lease for a fixed rent that is equal to or greater than the reasonably predictable fair market rent for the use of the goods for the term of the renewal at the time the option is to be performed; or

5. That the lessee has an option to become the owner of the goods for a fixed price that is equal to or greater than the reasonably predictable fair market value of the goods at the time that the option is to be performed.

By failing to include an explicit test for assessing whether a lessor has retained a meaningful reversionary interest, the drafters of New § 1-203 have created the same confusion and unpredictability in the case law that existed under Old § 1-203.

The cases reflect the marked lack of uniformity in the reported decisions as to the appropriate test for determining the existence of a meaningful reversionary interest. But it is not for the Court to attempt to harmonize these discordant lines of authority or select what it deems to be the most salient decisional criteria. Since California law governs, the Court follows the sound reversionary interest analysis found in *Addison*.

Addison involved a purported lease of a Ferrari 330GTC roadster having an original value of $244,800. The court began its analysis by determining that the Bright-Line Test failed to establish a per se security agreement since none of the Residual Value Factors were present. *Addison*, 41 Cal.App.4th at 1296, 49 Cal.Rptr.2d at 137. Turning to the question of whether the lessor retained a meaningful reversionary interest in the Ferrari, the court analyzed two factors: (1) whether the purchase option price is nominal; and (2) whether the agreement contains any provision for the lessee's acquisition of equity in the vehicle. *Id.* In what one leading authority characterized as "the world's easiest determination of non-nominality," *see* White & Summers, § 30-3, at 31, the *Addison* court simply confirmed the trial court's finding that an option price of $255,809.78 was not nominal. *Id.* at 1297, 49 Cal.Rptr.2d at 137. The court then rejected the lessee's contention that the lease granted him an equity interest in the Ferrari because its termination provision required him "to bear the risk of gain or loss in value upon the termination of the lease." *Id.* Because the lease did not provide for a permanent transfer of ownership of the vehicle to the lessee upon default, but merely shifted the risk of gain or loss upon its disposition to the defendant, the *Addison* court concluded that the agreement did not grant the lessee an "an equitable ownership interest" in the Ferrari. *Id.* at 1297–98, 49 Cal.Rptr.2d at 137–38.

Application of *Addison's* decisional framework here leads to the inescapable conclusion that the Lessors retained a meaningful reversionary interest in the Lathes. The Court has determined—in the context of applying the Bright-Line Test—that Lakin failed to meet its burden of demonstrating that the Option Amount is nominal.[10] Thus, the first element of *Addison's* two-prong test has not

---

[10] [21] The *Addison* court also noted that:

> The remaining terms of this document support its construction as a true lease. Paragraph 13 expressly states that the vehicle is "the sole property of Lessor, and Lessee shall have no right, title or interest therein as to the ownership thereof . . . and this instrument is a lease and not a contract of sale."

Addison, 41 Cal.App.4th at 1299, 49 Cal.Rptr.2d at 139. Although the Lease Agreements contain similar recitations, the Court places no weight on the Debtor's acknowledgment or the form of the documents. *See Triplex Marine*, 258 B.R. at 666 ("[T]his court is not bound by any 'acknowledgment' by the Debtor nor by any other language or designation of the parties contained in the agreement."); *Owen*, 221 B.R. at 629 ("[T]he labeling of the Agreement as a 'lease' and referring to the parties as 'lessor' and 'lessee'

been established. And Lakin does not allege, nor do the Lease Agreements establish, that QDS acquired an equity interest in the Lathes. Hence, under the test adopted by the *Addison* court, Lakin has not met its burden of proving that the Lessors failed to retain a meaningful reversionary interest in the Lathes.

According to Lakin, the Lessors relinquished their reversionary interest in the Lathes because, given the economics of the transactions, they could not have reasonably expected to receive back anything of value from QDS at lease end. Lakin asserts that, in view of the $7,200 cost to return each of the Lathes to the Lessors and the Lathes' remaining one to two-year economic life at lease end, the Debtor's only sensible alternative was to pay the $9,065 Option Amount in order to retain the equipment. This argument would have more persuasive force if Lakin had produced evidence showing the projections of residual value, return shipping costs, and the Lathes' estimated remaining economic life at lease end, made by the original parties at lease inception (if such projections exist). The Court has previously explained why the information contained in the stipulation is not an acceptable substitute for this evidence. Lakin's argument therefore fails on an evidentiary level. Moreover, Lakin's argument—that the Court should essentially apply a common law nominality test, i.e., the Economic Realities Test—in the context of its reversionary interest analysis is conceptually flawed. The Option Price/Performance Cost Test contained in new § 1-203 is simply a codification (and refinement) of the Economic Realities Test. Having applied new § 1-203's statutory standard to assess the Option Amount's nominality under the Bright-Line Test, it makes no sense for the Court later to apply the common law version of the test in connection with its reversionary interest analysis. Such an approach certainly would not be consonant with the methodology followed by the *Addison* court to determine the existence of a meaningful reversionary interest.

Lakin's remaining arguments are equally unavailing. Lakin also maintains that a security agreement is indicated by the fact that the Lathes were obtained from a third-party supplier (or, stated differently, that Intech and the Lessors are financiers, rather than equipment manufacturers) and the Debtor was required to make a large up-front payment under the Lease Agreements. These factors— selectively plucked from the laundry lists developed by courts employing the Multiple-Factor Approach—do not support a finding that the Lessors did not retain a meaningful reversionary interest in the Lathes. *See, e.g., Edison Bros. Stores*, 207 B.R. at 821 ("[T]he fact that the role of the lessor is that of a financier is inconclusive to show that a disguised secured transaction was intended because this kind of three party transaction is typical in true lease[s] as well as in installment sales."); *Moore v. Emery (In re American Steel Product, Inc.)*, 203 B.R. 504, 510 (Bankr. S.D. Ga. 1996) ("The fact that [the lessor] purchased equipment designated by [the debtor] for the sole purpose of leasing [the property] back to [the lessor] does not alone convert the lease to a security agreement; nor does it establish a lease."). Lakin also makes much of the fact that U.S. Bancorp obtained Heller's agreement to subordinate its interest in the U.S. Bancorp Lathe to the security interest U.S. Bancorp was granted under the Lease Agreement. But this also fails to demon-

---

in and of themselves are not controlling."); *Zaleha*, 159 B.R. at 586 ("[L]abels used by the parties are not determinative of the situation.").

strate that U.S. Bancorp surrendered its reversionary interest in the U.S. Bancorp Lathe. Filing of a financing statement by a lessor is not determinative of true lease status. *Owen*, 221 B.R. at 62 ("The fact that [the lessor] filed financing statements . . . [does not establish a disguised security agreement]. Rather, . . . the filing of the financing statement was the result of an abundance of caution to assure that [the lessor's] rights were protected."). If the filing of a financing statement by a cautious lessor does not destroy true lease status, then it stands to reason that the ultra-cautious lessor, who takes the additional step of obtaining a subordination agreement from the lessee's senior secured lender, has not thereby admitted that it has entered into a disguised financing arrangement.

In sum, Lakin has not established that the Lessors parted with their reversionary interest in the Lathes. Lakin therefore has failed to meet its burden of proving that the Lease Agreements are in fact disguised security agreements.

MORE ON CONCEPTUAL, FUNCTIONAL AND "DEEMED TO BE" SECURITY INTERESTS

When asking whether Article 9 governs a transaction, there are two major clusters of questions to be considered: Inclusion and Exclusion.

The conceptual test to determine applicability of Article 9 is to ascertain whether the transaction involves use of "personal property" or "fixtures" to secure payment or performance of the obligation. *See* UCC § 9-109. The Code does not contain a definition of *personal property*. However, in various sections it refers to and defines types of *personal property*. At this early stage, to facilitate reference in later course materials we initially call your attention to the list in Section D.1., *infra*, of "tangible, semi-intangible and intangible personal property collateral." This classification facilitates application of perfection, priority and other Code rules which are made applicable to particular types of collateral.

We will not attempt to master at this early stage all of the various categories of personal property included in this formidable list of types of property within the Article 9 concept of "personal property." However, as we work through the case and problem materials in the remainder of the course we will have opportunity to master the individual categories of personal property and identify the special perfection, priority and other rules applicable to each type of personal property.

For example, if Samuel Clemens' wife buys a washing machine on credit and the terms of the contract specify that if Madame Clemens defaults on monthly payment, Seller has the right to repossess the washing machine and resell it in order to obtain the balance due on the purchase price, Seller has a security interest in "consumer goods" (*see* § 9-102(a)(23)). If a retailer buys fifty identical washing machines, displays them, and makes them available for sale on his retail premises, a Seller who sold the fifty washers on credit under an agreement which provided that in the event of default of monthly payments Seller had the right to repossess and dispose of the collateral to obtain payment of the balance due, Seller would have a security interest in "inventory" collateral (*see* § 9-102(a)(48)).

Suppose you buy a new home for $300,000, and Seller takes a real estate mortgage from you for a balance of $250,000 plus interest payable in installments over a twenty year period. Under § 9-109(a), this transaction would not be subject to Article 9 because the collateral is real estate rather than personal property. However, if the bank which took your real estate mortgage has fifty of these real estate mortgages and wants to use the right to receive monthly payments due over a period of twenty years on these mortgages as collateral for a multi-million dollar loan from a larger bank, the right to payment which it has from all of the account debtors it has financed to facilitate their home purchases would be an intangible type of collateral which qualifies as an "account" under Article 9. (*See* § 9-102(a)(2) and Simplified Version, Appendix A, *infra*).

The applicability of Article 9 depends on whether the transaction is *functionally* one in which personal property or a fixture is being used to secure payment or performance of an obligation. The test is function, *not* form. A businessman may wish to give the transaction a particular form. For example, the businessman might structure the acquisition of equipment as a lease in order to take advantage of tax benefits. Article 9 does not prohibit the use of this form, and the Article's provisions will apply to the transaction if functionally the lessor is financing the purchase price and at the end of the lease there is no meaningful residual value. Because scope questions of this kind require looking through form to substance, they can be quite troubling to the unwary lawyer who is unfamiliar with the true nature of the transaction. UCC § 9-109 and UCC § 1-203 are the Code landmarks, but you must also look to the growing body of case law to learn to recognize the facts that show the function of a transaction.[11] Note that Article 9 includes sales of certain property that will be discussed later. *See* UCC § 9-109(a)(3).

We also note that Article 9 only applies in the main to transactions that create a security interest by contract. *See* UCC § 9-109(a)(1). The "by contract" requirement excludes common law liens and liens created by statute, but some provisions of Article 9 do apply to certain liens, such as repair liens (*See* § 9-333, "Priority of Certain Liens Arising by Operation of Law"), and agricultural liens (*See* § 9-302, "Law Governing Perfection and Priority of Agricultural Liens").

PROBLEMS

This exercise requires us to consider the full text of the inclusion provisions (*see* § 9-109(a)(1), (2), (3), and (4)—General Scope) and the text of the exclusion provisions (*see* § 9-109(c)—Extent to which Article Does Not Apply and § 9-109(d)—Inapplicability of Article). Following these problems is an excerpt on *The Deemed Security Agreements* from Ronald Cuming, Catherine Walsh & Roderick Wood, Personal Property Security Law 90–96 (2005), which addresses treatment of the subject by the Canadian Provinces' Personal Property Security Law.

---

[11] Numerous cases address the difficult issues involved in determining whether a transaction is a true lease or actually a secured transaction disguised as a lease. *See, e.g., American General Aircraft Corp. v. Washington Co. Economic Development District*, 190 B.R. 275 (N.D. Miss. 1995); *In re Eagle Enterprises, Inc., and Liberty Recovery Systems, Inc.*, 223 B.R. 290 (E.D. Pa. 1998); *In re Howell, Venn v. Howell's Auto Repair Center, Inc.*, 161 B.R. 285 (N.D. Fla. 1993).

Problem 2-1(a):   Transactions Within the Conceptual Definition of "Security Interest." Acme Retailers sells a refrigerator to John Jones for $1,000, taking a $200 down payment and extending an $800 line of credit requiring $50 a month payments for sixteen months and reserving to Acme Retailers the right to repossess the refrigerator if John Jones defaults on his monthly payments. Does Acme Retailers have a security interest in the refrigerator? If so, what is the consequence? *See* §§ 1-201(b)(35), 9-109(a).

Problem 2-1(b):   Transactions Within the Functional Definition of "Security Interest." Acme Leasing Company enters into an agreement labeled "Leasing Agreement" with Samuel Clemens covering the "Lease" of electronic printing equipment for a three-year period for a monthly payment of $10,000. The "Lease Agreement" further provides that at the end of the three-year period, Clemens has the option to purchase the equipment for $500. At the time the "lease agreement" was signed, the electronic printing equipment was valued at $300,000 with an expectancy of being technologically useful and not obsolete for a three-year period. Does Acme Leasing Company have a security interest in the electronic printing equipment? If so, what is the consequence? *See* §§ 1-201(b)(35), 9-109(a)(1).

Problem 2-1(c):   Sale of Accounts "Deemed To Be a Security Interest." Samuel Clemens has $5 million in accounts receivable. Rather than encumbering the accounts, by creating a security interest and using them as collateral for a $3.5 million loan, Clemens sells the accounts outright to Steady State Bank. Does Steady State Bank have a security interest in the accounts? If so, what is the consequence? *See* §§ 1-201(b)(35), 9-109(a)(3).

Problem 2-1(d):   Consignment "Deemed To Be A Security Interest." Acme Television, a manufacturer of television sets, consigns 1,000 television sets to Universal Retailers. Is this transaction subject to Article 9? *See* definition of "Consignment", §§ 9-102(a)(20), 1-201(b)(35), 9-109(a)(4).

Samuel Clemens has an antique desk, a family heirloom which he uses in his private study at home for personal matters. The desk has a value of $50,000. If Clemens takes the desk to an antique dealer and tells the dealer to sell it on his behalf, is Clemens deemed to have a security interest in the desk? Will Clemens be required to comply with the public notice filing provisions of Article 9? *See* "Consignment" definition, § 9-102(a)(20)(C).

Problem 2-1(e):   Retention of Title To Goods Sold and Delivered on Credit "Deemed To Be A Security Interest." Ford Motor Company sells 500 automobiles to Global Auto Dealers on credit, retaining title to the automobiles even though they have been delivered to Global Auto Dealers warehouses and showrooms. Does this transaction create a security interest and does it become subject to Article 9? *See* §§ 2-401, 9-202, 1-201(b)(35), 9-109(a)(5).

Section 2-401(1) provides, *inter alia*, that:

> . . . Any retention or reservation by the seller of the title (property) in goods shipped or delivered to the buyer is limited in effect to a reservation of a security interest.

Section 9-202 provides that:

. . . The provisions of this article with regard to rights and obligations apply whether title to collateral is in the secured party or the debtor.

MORE ON TRANSACTIONS DEEMED TO CREATE A SECURITY INTEREST—THE CANADIAN INCLUSION OF "TRUE LEASES" WITHIN THE DEFINITION OF SECURITY INTEREST

Under the § 9-109(a)(1) "Scope" provision, Article 9 applies to any transaction *which* creates a security interest in property or fixtures by contract *"regardless of its form."* As we have already seen, the functional test created by the *"regardless of its form"* language, makes Article 9 applicable to so-called "dirty leases" i.e., transactions in the form of a lease but *which* in substance constitute a secured transaction.

This result is reinforced by the explicit use of the word "lease" in the definition of security interest (*see* § 1-201(b)(35)(E); *see also* Appendix A, *infra*), and the "lease distinguished from security interest" provision of § 1-203 (*see* Appendix A, *infra*), *which* provides detailed criteria for determining whether a document labeled "Lease Agreement" or using "Lessor-Lessee" language is a "True Lease" or an agreement merely using "Lease—Lessor—Lessee" terminology, but in substance a § 9-103 purchase money security interest (i.e., conditional sale).

"To avoid third party deception" which results from the apparent ownership of lessees in possession of leased goods, all leases including "True Leases," as well as "Dirty Leases," are deemed to create security interests under the Canadian Personal Property Security Acts which are the UCC as enacted by Canadian Provinces. The excerpt entitled "The Deemed Security Agreements" from Cuming, Walsh, and Wood, *Personal Property Security Law*, which follows, discusses policy considerations and specific provisions of the Canadian enactment of the UCC which were modified to achieve this result. Although the policy of avoiding third party deception is not applied to "True Leases" under enactments of the UCC by the states in the United States, it is applied both in the United States and Canada to transactions such as a sale of accounts, chattel paper, payment intangibles, or promissory notes (*see* § 1-201(b)(35)(A) of the Simplified Version of the Actual Text); a consignment (*see* § 1-201(b)(35)(A) of the Simplified Version of the Actual Text); and a security interest arising under § 2-401 (*see also* § 1-201(b)(35)(C) of the Simplified Version of the Actual Text).

Based on the Cuming article, why has U.S. law not adopted a similar approach to Canadian law? What purpose does the exclusion from the Canadian Act of leases for a term of less than one year serve?

RONALD CUMING, CATHERINE WALSH & RODERICK WOOD, PERSONAL PROPERTY SECURITY LAW
90–96 (2005)[12]

DEEMED SECURITY INTERESTS

1) Introduction

The creation, perfection, priority, registration and conflict provisions of all Acts other than the Ontario Act apply to four types of transactions that are not functionally or conceptually security agreements: an assignment (sale) of an account; and assignment (sale) of chattel paper; a lease for a term of more than one year; and a commercial consignment.[13] The Ontario Act applies to the first two only.[14] The Acts of Atlantic Canada provinces provide a fifth type of deemed security interest, a sale of goods without change of possession. The legislative technique used to bring these transactions within the relevant provisions of the Act is to deem that they create security interests.[15] However, the deeming effect does not extend to enforcement since these transactions do not involve the types of relationships that are characteristic of secured financing arrangements.[16]

The policy reason for including these transactions in the PPSA [Personal Property Security Act—i.e., the secured transaction Article 9 of the UCC] is clear. Endemic to each type of transaction is the potential for third party deception and the consequent commercial disruptions that this entails. In the case of a lease and a consignment, there is a separation of ownership and possession, thus placing the lessee or consignee in a position to mislead third parties as to the extent of his interest in the goods in his possession. In the case of transfers of an account, the transferor retains apparent control of the account even though she no longer owns or has an interest in it. The policy basis for including transfers of chattel paper is somewhat different. Prior to the implementation of the Acts the law applicable to the various interests involved in chattel paper was unclear. One of the innovative features of the PPSA was to establish an entirely new regime for security interests in this unique type of property. Since this regime could be applied equally well to competing claims by successive transferees of chattel paper as to competing

---

[13] [3] PPSA (A, M, NB, PEI, S) s. 3 (2); (NL, NS) s. 4 (2); (NWT, N) s. 2 (2); BC s. 3.

[14] [4] OPPSA s. 2(b).

[15] [5] PPSA (A, BC, NWT, N, O, Y) s. 1 (1); (M, NB, PEI) s. 1; (NL, NS) s. 2; S s. 2 (1).

[16] [6] The question arises as to whether OPPSA s. 61(2) applies to a non-security transfer of an account or chattel paper under an agreement that gives the transferee a right of recourse against the transferor. The Act does not specifically state that Part V does not apply to these transactions. However, by inference, the Part does not apply unless there is a debtor-creditor relationship and the credit has an interest in property that secures the debtor's obligation. There is no such relationship in a recourse assignment. Nevertheless, section 61(2) expressly applies to such an assignment. This confusion does not exist in the other Acts all of which make it clear that Part V does not apply to non-security transactions governed by other features of the Act. PPSA (A, M, NB, NWT, N, PEI) s. 55(1); (BC, S) s. 55(2); (NL, NS) s. 56(2); Y s. 53(2).

security interests in chattel paper, the decision was made to include absolute transfers within its scope.

A conceptual issue arises in the context of the extension of the Act to consignments, leases and transfers of accounts. In order to bring these transactions within the operation of the Act, it is necessary to deem that these transactions create security interests and to treat a consignor, lessor or accounts transferee as a secured party and a consignee, lessee or accounts transferor as a debtor. An attachment of a security interest requires that the debtor has rights in the collateral. A requirement of attachment of a security interest is that the debtor has rights in the collateral.[17] However, under non-PPSA law, the debtors in these transactions have no rights in the collateral other than possessory rights in the case of leases and consignments. All Acts other than that of Ontario address the matter in the context of leases and consignments by providing for the purposes of the attachment requirement, a lessee under a lease for a term of more than one year and a consignee under a commercial consignment has rights in the goods when the consignee obtains possession of them pursuant to the lease or consignment.[18] However, these Acts do not address the position of the transferor of an account or chattel paper.

It is the view of the authors that this omission in the PPSA does not warrant a different approach to transfers of accounts or chattel paper. As noted above, the legislative intention behind extending the scope of the Act to absolute transfers of accounts is to avoid third party deception. The mechanism through which this is accomplished is to deem the transfer to be a security agreement providing for a deemed security interest. It follows that the account transferor is to be deemed to have rights in the account after transfer to the extent this is necessary to support the conclusion that an attached security interest exists.[19] Similar reasoning applies to sales of chattel paper.

2) A Lease for a Term of More than One Year

All Acts, other than that of Ontario, deem true leases (i.e., non-security leases) of goods having a term of more than one year to be security agreements. Leases for less than one year fall outside the Act.

Much of the uncertainty as to what constitutes a lease for a term of more than one year has been removed by the elaborate definition of the term contained in the Act.[20] In effect, the Act will apply in any case in which the lessee remains in possession of the leased property for a period of time in excess of one year.

---

[17] [7] PPSA (A, BC, M, NB, NWT, N, PEI, S) s. 12 (1); (NL, NS) s. 13 (1); O s. 11 (2); Y s. 11 (1).

[18] [8] PPSA (A, BC, M, NWT, N, S) s. 12 (2); (NB, PEI) s. 12 (3); (NL, NS) s. 13 (3); Y s. 11 (2).

[19] [9] This approach was inferentially taken in *Agent's Equity Inc. v. Hope* (1996) 40 C.B.R. (3d) 310 (Ont. Gen. Div.); and *TCE Capital Corp. v. Kolenc* (1999), 172 D.L.R. (4th) 186 (Ont. Div. Ct.) *aff'd* (1998), 3 C.B.R. (4th) 98 (Ont. Gen Div.). In these cases, the courts concluded that there is no requirement that the transferor of an account have a property interest after the transfer in order the trustee in bankruptcy to defeat the transferee's interest under section 20(1) of the OPPSA.

[20] [10] PPSA (A, BC, NWT, N, Y) s. 1 (1); (M, NB, PEI) s. 1; (NL, NS) s. 2; S s. 2(1).

A lease for an indefinite term, although determinable at the option of one of the parties, falls within the Act.[21] A lease for a term of less than one year that is automatically renewable for one or more terms the total of which exceeds one year is deemed to be a lease for a term of more than one year. In neither case is it relevant that at the time an issue arises the lessee has been in possession of the leased property for more than one year. What is important is that this potential exists under the terms of the lease.

The definition addresses the case of an over-holding lessee. Where the lease has an initial term of one year or less and the lessee remains in possession or substantially uninterrupted possession of the leased property after the expiry of the term with the consent of the lessor, the lease is deemed to be a lease for a term of more than one year as soon as, but not before, the duration of the lessee's possession exceeds one year. Accordingly, a lease for a term of one year or less that does not fall within one of the other two categories set out in the definition remains outside the scope of the Act until the lessee has been in possession or substantially uninterrupted possession for more than one year. During the initial one year term of the lease, non-PPSA law governs all priority issues associated with conflicting claims relating to the lease property. However, once the lessee's possession extends beyond the one-year period, the Act applies. The lease is thereafter treated as creating a security interest with the result that priority issues involving interests or claims arising after but not before this point are addressed by the relevant provisions of the PPSA.

Not all leases for a term of more than one year are deemed to create security interests. A lease of household furnishings or appliances as part of a lease of land where the goods are incidental to the use and enjoyment of the land and leases of prescribed goods are outside the Act.[22] In addition, the deeming effect does not apply to a lease where the lessor is not regularly engaged in the business of leasing goods. What constitutes regular engagement in the business of leasing has been addressed by courts. Under the approach taken in these decisions, the frequency with which the lessor engaged in leasing prior to entering into the lease in question was not the determining factor. So long as leasing is part of the regular business of a person to lease goods, the volume of leasing business undertaken is not significant.[23] The word "regularly" modifies "business" rather than "engaged."

1. This Act may be cited as *The Personal Property Security Act, 1993*, R.S.S. 1978, c. P-6.1

2. (1) In this Act:

---

[21] [11] Gelowitz v. Garcon Enterprises Ltd., Dorzac Holdings (1995), 132 Sask. R. 273 (Sask. Q.B.).

[22] [12] No jurisdiction has added to the exemption through regulation.

[23] [13] *Paccar Financial Services v. Sinco Trucking Ltd.* (1987), 7 PPSAC 176 (Sask. Q.B.) reversed on other grounds (1989), 57 D.L.R. (4th) 438 (Sask. C.A.); *Planwest Consultants Ltd. v. Milltimber Holdings Ltd.* (1995), 32 Alta. L.R. (3d) 397 (Q.B.); *David Morris Fine Cars Ltd. v. North Sky Trading Inc.* (1994) 8 PPSAC (2d) 112 (Alta. Q.B.) affd. (1996) 38 Alta. L.R. (3d) 428 (C.A.); *East Central Development Corp. v. Freightliner Truck Sales (Regina) Ltd. (1997)*, 12 PPSAC (2d) 328 (Sask. Q.B.)

. . .

(y) **"lease for a term of more than one year"** includes:

(i)   a lease for an indefinite term, including a lease for an indefinite term that is determinable by one or both of the parties not later than one year after the day of its execution;

(ii)   a lease initially for a term of one year or less than one year, where the lessee, with the consent of the lessor, retains uninterrupted or substantially uninterrupted possession of the leased goods for a period of more than one year after the day on which the lessee, with the consent of the lessor, first acquired possession of them, but the lease does not become a lease for a term of more than one year until the lessee's possession extends for more than one year; and

(iii)   a lease for a term of one year or less where:

    (A)   the lease provides that it is automatically renewable or that it is renewable at the option of one of the parties or by agreement of the parties for one or more terms; and

    (B)   the total of the terms, including the original term, may exceed one year;

    but does not include:

(iv)   a lease involving a lessor who is not regularly engaged in the business of leasing goods;

(v)   a lease of household furnishings or appliances as part of a lease of land where the goods are incidental to the use and enjoyment of the land; or

(vi)   a lease of prescribed goods, regardless of the length of the lease term;

. . .

(qq) **"security interest"** means:

(i)   an interest in personal property that secures payment or performance of an obligation, but does not include the interest of a seller who has shipped goods to a buyer pursuant to a negotiable bill of lading or its equivalent to the order of the seller or to the order of an agent of the seller, unless the parties have otherwise evidenced an intention to create or provide for a security interest in the goods; and

(ii)   the interest of:

    (A)   a transferee pursuant to a transfer of an account or a transfer of chattel paper;

(B)   a consignor who delivers goods to a consignee pursuant to a commercial consignment; or

(C)   a lessor pursuant to a lease for a term of more than one year;

whether or not the interest secures payment or performance of an obligation;

3.(1) Subject to section 4, this Act applies:

(a)   to every transaction that in substance creates a security interest, without regard to its form and without regard to the person who has title to the collateral; and

(b)   without limiting the generality of clause (a), to a chattel mortgage, conditional sale, floating charge, pledge, trust indenture, trust receipt, or to an assignment, consignment, lease, trust or transfer of chattel paper that secures payment or performance of an obligation.

3.(2) Subject to section 4 and section 55, this Act applies to a transfer of an account or chattel paper, to a lease for a term of more than one year and to a commercial consignment, that does not secure payment or performance of an obligation.

2.   Exclusion Standard

A transaction may meet the functional test outlined above but be excluded from the scope of Article 9 because of some extrinsic policy reason. UCC § 9-109(c) and (d) set out these exclusions. There is no unifying theme underlying the reasons for the exclusions. Each has its own policy reason. You must check UCC § 9-109 until you are familiar with the transactions excluded. You will have to be careful because a transaction may not be omitted from Article 9 for all purposes. There are two exclusionary provisions in the text of Article 9 at UCC §§ 9-109(c) and (d).

UCC § 9-109(c) is entitled *Extent to Which Article Does Not Apply*. It partially excludes application in four types of situations. For example, UCC § 9-109(c)(1) provides that Article 9 does not apply *to the extent* that a statute, regulation, or treaty of the United States preempts Article 9. An example of this is the Federal Aviation Act of 1958 (49 U.S.C. § 1403, *et seq.*), which requires registration of title and liens upon aircraft with the Civil Aviation Administration (CAA). Such registration is recognized as equivalent to filing under Article 9. However, to the extent that the Federal Aviation Act does not regulate the rights of parties to and third parties affected by such transaction, a security interest in aircraft remains subject to Article 9. *See Sanders v. M.D. Aircraft Sales, Inc.*, 575 F.2d 1086, 23 UCC Rep. Serv. 1316, Chapter 6, Section D, *infra*, holding that since the Federal Aviation Act mandates a place of filing but does not establish a system of priorities, Article 9 governs priority.

UCC § 9-109(d), entitled *Inapplicability of Article*, provides that the Article does not apply to 13 types of transactions. UCC § 9-109(d)(1), for example, provides that Article 9 does not apply to a landlord's lien, other than an agricultural lien.

Other exclusions are considered later in appropriate parts of this book.

As a matter of logical priority, you will ask scope questions first. We suggest that your analysis should follow the steps outlined above. You should note, however, that although most secured transactions will not raise scope problems, those relatively few transactions that do are often complex. We will further discuss each of these steps in later portions of these materials.

C.   REQUIREMENTS FOR ATTACHMENT AND ENFORCEMENT OF SECURITY INTERESTS

To determine whether the security interest is *enforceable* and when the security interest *attaches*, you will consult UCC § 9-203.

Article 9 regulates *consensual* security interests in personal property and fixtures. The agreement that creates or provides for a security interest is called a *security agreement. See* UCC § 9-102(a)(73). Note that Article 9 also regulates certain aspects of non-consensual liens (statutory or common law) such as a lien given to a repair shop for the value of work done. *See* UCC § 9-333. Revised Article 9 further regulates agricultural liens. *See* UCC §§ 9-102(a)(5), 9-109(a)(2).

For a security agreement to be enforceable and for a security interest to attach, UCC § 9-203(b)(3) requires:

1.   (a) a security agreement which is authenticated and which describes the collateral; or

     (b) the secured party in possession of the collateral pursuant to agreement; or

     (c) the secured party in control of the collateral pursuant to an agreement; and

2.   Under UCC §§ 9-203(b)(1), 9-201, the secured party must give *value* (for example, by making or promising to make a loan or securing a prior unsecured loan), *see* UCC § 1-204; and Problem 2-5(a) and (b) *infra* p. 67.

3.   Under UCC § 9-203(b)(2) the debtor must have *rights in the property* used as collateral. *See* UCC § 9-203(b)(2).

The Code distinguishes *enforceability* from *attachment*. A security interest attaches when it becomes enforceable against specific collateral but the parties may agree to delay the time when the security interest will attach.[24]

---

[24] Although the draftsmen made a conscious effort to avoid using terminology associated with pre-Code security devices (*e.g.*, lien, pledge, mortgage), Article 9 continues to share terms with related areas of the law. *Attachment*, for example, is used in Article 9 to refer to when a security interest comes into existence. *See* UCC § 9-203 (combining concept of attachment with that of enforceability). The term attachment, however, is also used in non-Code law to refer to the writ of attachment, which is a non-consensual judicial writ by which a party to litigation may obtain a lien on another party's property. You may have read U.S. Supreme Court decisions exploring due process limitations on state judicial process, such as prejudgment attachment. *See, e.g., Fuentes v. Shevin*, 407 U.S. 67 (1972) (summary seizure under replevin statute unconstitutional where writ issued prejudgment on ex parte application

Problem 2-2(a): Oral Security Agreement—"Non-Possessory" Security Interest. Dealer sells a washing machine to Samuel Clemens for use in his home. Samuel Clemens makes a down payment of $100. Clemens agrees to pay the remaining $360 in equal monthly installments over the next 24 months and orally grants Dealer a security interest in the washing machine to secure payments of this obligation. The washing machine is delivered to Clemens. Does Dealer have an attached security interest in the washing machine? Clemens has not signed a security agreement and Dealer does not have possession of the washing machine. *See* UCC § 9-203(b)(3)(A) & (B). Note that the contract for sale of the washing machine is enforceable because the price is less than $500 and therefore not subject to the Article 2 statute of frauds. *See* UCC § 2-201.

Problem 2-2(b): Signed Security Agreement. Suppose that Clemens had actually signed a security agreement granting Dealer a security interest in the washing machine to secure repayment of the debt. This meets the "authentication" of a security agreement requirement of UCC § 9-203(b)(3)(A). However, in order for Dealer's security interest to be enforceable, Dealer also must establish that:

(1)   value had been given as required by UCC §§ 9-203(b)(1), 1-204;

(2)   Debtor has rights in the collateral as required by UCC § 9-203(b)(2).

Has Dealer met these requirements? Note that the UCC contains a definition of "value" at UCC § 1-204. Also note that the UCC does not contain a definition of "rights in collateral." For an illustration of how the courts are coping with the absence of a statutory definition of "rights in the collateral," *see In re Studarks Foundry Products, Inc. v. Kondik v. Ebner*, 206 B.R. 475 (N.D. Ill. 1997) (holding that Debtor, the apparent owner of equipment used as collateral to secure a loan, had "rights in the collateral" to meet the requirement of UCC § 9-203(b)(2). Son had permitted Debtor company, which was managed by Mother and Father, to have possession and use the equipment in operating the company). If there is default, what does the secured party get?

Problem 2-2(c): Rights in Collateral (Possession of Equipment). Assume that Samuel Clemens owns the printing press, and has run a successful printing business in Philadelphia for a number of years. Clemens wants to move to Miami and start a new printing business without his parents, who are reluctant to leave the comforts of their established residence. Clemens leaves the printing equipment behind and allows his parents to run the printing business and use the equipment he owns. Clemens' parents decide to use the equipment as collateral to obtain a loan. However, the business subsequently goes into bankruptcy. Creditor with a security interest in the equipment tries to assert its interest. However, Clemens claims that since his parents do not own the equipment, they do not have "rights in the collateral" as required for attachment of a security interest under the UCC. Do Clemens' parents have "rights in the collateral" and thereby giving Creditor a security interest in the collateral? *See In re Standard Foundry Products, Inc. v. Ebner*, 206 B.R. 475 (N.D. Ill. 1997) (possession was deemed sufficient for one to have "rights in the collateral"). *But see Jerke Construction, Inc. v. Home Federal*

---

to court clerk without notice to possessor of property and without opportunity for prompt judicial hearing).

Savings Bank, 693 N.W.2d 59, 63 (S.D. 2005) ("Naked possession" not enough for one to have "rights in the collateral.").

Problem 2-2(d):   Rights in Collateral (Share Agreements). Being the prudent entrepreneur that he is, Samuel Clemens decided that he wants to enter the business of cattle ranching. After seeing an advertisement in the newspaper, Clemens calls Thomas Sawyer to purchase some cattle at $650 per head. Clemens went to see Mr. Sawyer, and after selecting the cattle he wanted to purchase, the two arranged a sale. Clemens did not have the financing at the time to purchase the cattle, so the two parties entered into what is termed a "share agreement," where Clemens would possess the cattle and have the option to purchase them at any time during the year for $650 per head. Clemens would also breed the cattle, calve them out, and feed them, receiving 40% of the proceeds from the cattle crop. Clemens even went so far as to brand some of the cattle to mark that the cattle were his; Mr. Sawyer reprimanded him for the branding when he learned about it.

Clemens eventually wanted to expand the size of his herd, so he took out a loan. The cattle in his possession were part of the collateral pledged. Clemens eventually had to file for bankruptcy. Once Mr. Sawyer found out, Clemens assured him that the cattle were not collateral for any loan he had. Mr. Sawyer came to Clemens' farm to retake the cattle, but was met by the sheriff and an officer of the bank where Clemens got the loan. Mr. Sawyer was not permitted to take the cattle back with him, and eventually, a number of his cattle were sent to the slaughterhouse. Mr. Sawyer now claims that, because Clemens did not own the cattle, he did not have rights in the cattle, meaning that no security interest attached. Is he correct? *See Rohweder v. Aberdeen Production Credit Association*, 765 F.2d 109 (8th Cir. 1985).

Problem 2-3:   Oral Pledge Agreement—"Possessory" Security Interest. Clemens has 1000 shares of GM stock listed at $50 per share. Bank orally agrees to lend Clemens $30,000 to be repaid $1,000 per month to be secured by the stock. The bank retains possession of the stock. Does Bank have an enforceable security agreement? *See* UCC § 9-203(b)(1), (2), (3).

Problem 2-4:   Control over a Security Entitlement (Tripartite Agreement). Suppose Clemens had purchased the 1000 shares of stock through stockbroker who did not physically deliver 1000 shares to Clemens, but did instead establish an account for Clemens and confirmed in writing to Clemens his ownership of the 1000 shares in the account. Clemens now has a "security entitlement." *See* UCC § 8-102(a)(17); *see also* UCC § 8-503. If stockbroker agrees that it will comply with entitlement orders originated by the Bank because of default by Clemens on his repayment of the loan, will Bank have the "requisite control" required by UCC § 9-203(b)(3)(D) to create an enforceable security interest? Of course, Bank must obtain in a **tripartite** agreement the consent of Clemens as owner of the security entitlement as well as of stockbroker to the control agreement. *See* UCC § 8-106; *see also* UCC § 9-106.

Problem 2-5(a):   Value. Assume that the bank does not credit Mr. Clemens' account with the amount of the loan described in the loan agreement in Section A.1., *supra*, until September 4. When does the bank have an attached and enforceable security interest? *See* UCC §§ 1-204, 9-203(b)(1). When, if ever, did the bank make a binding commitment to extend credit? *See* UCC § 1-204. Would the bank's simple promise to extend credit be "consideration" sufficient to support a simple contract? *See* UCC § 1-204. Is "value" under § 1-204 broader in coverage than "consideration?"

Lynn M. LoPucki and Elizabeth Warren wrote in SECURED CREDIT: A SYSTEMS APPROACH 175 (1995):

> The drafters of the UCC defined *value* in UCC § 1-201(44) so broadly that the requirement is virtually always met in a commercial transaction. As a result, it is difficult to discern any policy reason for the inclusion of the "value" requirement in UCC § 9-203(1).

Do you agree? Are there policy reasons for the expansive definition of "value?"

Problem 2-5(b):   Is "value" given by the creditor in the following situations?

(i) Suppose Clemens enters into an agreement with Bank giving Bank a security interest in his plant equipment in exchange for a loan of $100,000 (*see* § 1-204(1), (4)).

(ii) Suppose Clemens entered into an agreement with Bank giving Bank a security interest in his plant equipment to secure any future loans which Bank in its discretion might extend to Clemens (*see* § 1-204(1), (4)).

(iii) Suppose Bank had extended an unsecured loan of $100,000 to Clemens. When the balance due was $70,000, Bank becomes concerned about Clemens's capacity to pay off the balance and obtains from Clemens an agreement in which Clemens gives Bank a security interest in its plant equipment giving Bank the right to foreclose on the equipment in the event that Clemens defaults in paying the $70,000 balance (*see* § 1-204(2)).

NOTE ON "RIGHTS IN THE COLLATERAL"

What constitutes sufficient "rights in the collateral" is not clear. This phrase is not defined in the Code. An outright owner of goods has rights in the goods if the owner uses them as collateral. It is also clear that a thief has no rights in stolen goods. The cases between the outright owner and the thief are more difficult. The Code has not provided a definition but instead leaves the question to the courts. The Code, at § 9-204(2) (now UCC § 9-204(c)) originally listed several criteria for determining when a debtor had rights in crops, young of livestock, fish, "oil, gas or minerals," contract rights and accounts. This subsection was eliminated from the 1972 version because "it is believed that the questions considered are best left to the courts." Review Committee for Art. 9 of the UCC, Final Report, Proposal for Changes in Article 9 of the Uniform Commercial Code, at 66 (April 25, 1991). The entire subject would now appear to be a matter essentially for judicial rule making.

Professor Clark has suggested that "rights" in the collateral might be defined by UCC § 1-201(b)(34) which provides, " 'Right' includes remedy." B. CLARK, THE LAW OF SECURED TRANSACTIONS UNDER THE UNIFORM COMMERCIAL CODE, ¶ 2.4 (1980). Thus, if a person could replevy goods against a wrongful possessor (*see* UCC § 2-716(3)), sufficient rights in the goods would be established to use them as collateral for a security interest. The problem which follows illustrates the case law developments in this area.

Problem 2-6: Rights in Collateral, Equipment Collateral. Assume that Samuel Clemens owns the printing press which is the principal asset of his sole proprietorship. Will inclusion of the term "equipment" in the description of property covered by the security agreement give the bank a security interest in Mr. Clemens' printing press? *See* UCC §§ 9-102(a)(33), 9-102(a)(23), 9-102(a)(34), 9-102(a)(48), 9-102(a)(44).

D. TYPES OF ARTICLE 9 PERSONAL PROPERTY COLLATERAL—NEW AND MODIFIED TYPES OF "PERSONAL PROPERTY" COLLATERAL

1.   Note on Types of Article 9 Personal Property Collateral

Article 9 covers security interests in "personal property." The general rules found in Article 9 govern all forms of personal property. Personal property today, however, takes many forms, and special rules are sometimes needed for particular types of personal property. Later in this course, for example, we will address special rules that require a subsequent secured party with a security interest in a debtor's "inventory" to give notice to a prior secured party with an interest in the debtor's present and "after-acquired inventory." UCC § 9-324(b). As we consider these special rules later in this course, we will discover that they have proliferated as a result of the expanded scope of Revised Article 9, which brings within its scope many new forms of intangible property.

To help you classify personal property for UCC Article 9 purposes, the following table breaks the UCC personal property down into three categories: *tangible, semi-intangible*, and *intangible property*. *Tangible property* includes movable corporeal things and fixtures, as distinguished from intangible personal property, which are non-corporeal property rights such as rights to payment, copyrights, trademarks or a liquor license. *Semi-intangible property* brings together abstract rights that the law treats as being incorporated or merged into a piece of paper. Thus, a negotiable promissory note is semi-intangible property because it embodies the promise to pay by the maker of the note. If abstract rights are not incorporated in something tangible, such as paper, they are classified as *intangible property*. For a general discussion of the types of Article 9 personal property, see Comments 4, 5 and 6 of UCC § 9-102.

We illustrate the expansion of the scope of Article 9 through addition by the draftsmen of new and modified types of collateral by inclusion of problems pertaining to "commercial tort claims" and "deposit accounts" as new types of collateral. The remaining changes pertaining to modified types of collateral are merely briefly summarized for purposes of this course. Other types of Revised Article 9 new or modified collateral include electronic chattel paper, UCC § 9-102(a)(11), investment property, UCC § 9-102(a)(14) & (15), letter of credit rights, UCC § 9-102(a)(51), health-care-insurance receivables, UCC § 9-102(a)(46), accounts UCC § 9-102(a)(2), general intangibles, UCC § 9-102(a)(42), and instruments, UCC § 9-102(a)(47) & (65). These latter types of collateral are also discussed as appropriate later in the book.

TYPES OF ARTICLE 9 PERSONAL PROPERTY

(1) Tangible collateral

1. Generic category: Goods, UCC § 9-102(a)(44)

2. Subcategories:

    Consumer goods, UCC § 9-102(a)(23)

    Equipment, UCC § 9-102(a)(33)

    Farm Products, UCC § 9-102(a)(34)

    Inventory, UCC § 9-102(a)(48)

    Fixtures, UCC § 9-102(a)(41)

3. Residual category: Equipment

(2) Semi-intangible collateral

Subcategories:

     Chattel paper, UCC § 9-102(a)(11)

     Document, UCC § 9-102(a)(30)

     Instrument, UCC § 9-102(a)(47)

     Investment property, UCC § 9-102(a)(49)

         Certificated security, UCC § 9-102(b), § 8-102(a)(4), (15), (16)

         Commodity contract, UCC § 9-102(a)(15)

(3) Intangible collateral

1. Subcategories:

    Account, UCC § 9-102(a)(2)

    Commercial tort claims, UCC § 9-102(a)(13)

    Deposit account, UCC § 9-102(a)(29)

    Electronic chattel paper, UCC § 9-102(a)(31)

    General intangibles, UCC § 9-102(a)(42)

    Health-care-insurance receivable, UCC § 9-102(a)(46)

    Investment property, UCC § 9-102(a)(49)

    Letter of credit right, UCC § 9-102(a)(51)

    Securities account, UCC § 9-102(b), § 8-501(a)

Security entitlement, UCC § 9-102(b), § 8-102(a)(17)

Uncertificated security, UCC § 9-102(b), § 8-102(a)(18)

Commodity account, UCC § 9-102(a)(14)

Payment intangible, UCC § 9-102(a)(61)

2. Residual category: General intangible

The Revised Article 9 greatly expands the scope of Article 9. The expansion is achieved primarily through the inclusion of new types of collateral and the modification of the previously existing definitions of others, which we will address after our consideration of excluded and multistate transactions.

2.   Expansion of Scope of Article 9—New Applications

a.   Commercial Tort Claims

All tort claims were excluded from the scope of the 1972 Code. UCC § 9-104(b). Under the Revised Code, "commercial tort claims," UCC § 9-102(a)(13), is established as a new category of collateral, and is expressly excluded from the definition of general intangible. UCC § 9-102(a)(42). The definition covers only claims regarding business torts. UCC § 9-102(a)(13). Consumer tort claims remain excluded from coverage of Article 9. *See* UCC § 9-109(d)(12). Note, however, that once any claim in tort has been settled and reduced to a contractual obligation, Article 9 applies as that claim becomes a payment intangible because the right to payment now is a payment intangible and ceases to be a claim arising in tort. *See* UCC § 9-109, Official Comment 15.

The inclusion of "commercial tort claims" does nothing to disrupt state law that limits or restricts the assignability of a tort claim. *See* UCC § 9-102(a)(13) Official Comment 5g. Thus, no security interest may attach if governing state law prohibits the assignability of the claim.

Problem 2-7:   Tort Claims as Collateral.

Personal Tort Claim: While en route to pick up his son at school, John runs negligently into Mary, who was driving her car to pick up her daughter at church services. Mary was injured, and her car was damaged.

May Mary use her tort claim as collateral? *See* UCC §§ 9-102(a)(13), 9-109(d)(12).

Commercial Tort Claim: Driver of a truck delivering merchandise owned by Acme Corporation runs negligently into another truck driven by Jones, who was delivering goods owned by Brock Corporation. The Brock Corporation truck and goods sustained damage and Jones was killed.

May Brock Corporation use its tort claim as collateral? For damage to the truck? May the survivors of Jones use the tort claim as collateral? For the death of Jones? *See* UCC §§ 9-109(d)(12), 9-102(a)(13).

b. Deposit Accounts

Under the 1972 Code, "deposit account" was covered only as proceeds. UCC §§ 9-104, 9-105, 9-306, 9-312. Under the Revised Code, "deposit accounts" (UCC § 9-102(a)(29)) are covered as original collateral. *See* UCC §§ 9-203(b)(3)(D), 9-104. "Deposit Account" is defined as "a demand, time, savings, passbook, or similar account maintained with a bank." UCC § 9-102(a)(29); *see also* UCC § 9-102(a)(8) (definition of "bank"). Note that "[t]he term does not include investment property or accounts evidenced by an instrument." UCC § 9-102(a)(29). Moreover, the Code excludes coverage of assignments of deposit accounts in consumer transactions. *See* UCC § 9-109(d)(13). Perfection of "deposit accounts" is achieved through control. *See* UCC § 9-104.

Problem 2-8:   Deposit Account as Collateral.

(a) Clemens has a two million dollar account with Bank. In exchange for a loan of one million dollars, Clemens gives Bank a security interest in the account. Does Bank have an enforceable security interest in the account? UCC §§ 9-203(b)(3)(D), 9-109(d)(13), and 9-104(a)(1).

(b) Suppose Manufacturer extends a loan for one million dollars to Clemens in exchange for a security agreement signed by Clemens which gives Manufacturer a security interest in this Bank Account. Does Manufacturer have an enforceable security interest? *See* UCC §§ 9-109(a)(1), 9-203(b)(3)(D), and 9-104(a)(2).

(c) Suppose that Manufacturer, Bank, and Clemens enter into an agreement that the Bank will comply with instructions originated by the secured party directing disposition of the funds in the deposit account without further consent by the debtor. Does Manufacturer now have an enforceable security interest? *See* UCC §§ 9-109(a)(1), 9-203(b)(3)(D), and 9-104(a)(2).

Analogous requirements for obtaining control over other new types of collateral are found in UCC § 9-105 pertaining to control of Electronic Chattel Paper, UCC § 9-106 pertaining to Investment Property, and UCC § 9-107 pertaining to Letter-of-Credit Rights as noted in appropriate portions of the book.

3.   More on New and Modified Types of Collateral

In addition to "Commercial Tort Claims" and "Deposit Accounts," Revised Article 9 provides for new or modified types of collateral noted below.

a.   Electronic Chattel Paper

"Chattel paper" is defined in relevant part as "a record or records that evidence both a monetary obligation and a security interest in specific goods . . . ." UCC § 9-102(a)(11). A new subcategory, electronic chattel paper, is included in the Revised Code. "Electronic chattel paper" is defined as "chattel paper evidenced by a record or records consisting of information stored in an electronic medium." UCC § 9-102(a)(31). According to the Official Comment, the term includes "electric, digital, magnetic, optical, electromagnetic, or any other current or similar emerging technology." UCC § 9-102 cmt. 5b. The Comment adds that the term is to be construed liberally.

b.   Health-Care-Insurance Receivable

This new category of collateral is brought within the scope of the Revised Code as a subcategory of "accounts." "Health-care-insurance receivable" is defined as "an interest in or claim under a policy of insurance which is a right to payment of a monetary obligation for health-care goods or services provided." UCC § 9-102(a)(46). Other types of insurance claims continue to be excluded from coverage of Article 9, unless and to the extent they constitute "proceeds." *See* UCC § 9-109(d)(8).

c.   Letter-of-Credit Right

"Letter-of-Credit Right" is defined as "a right to payment and performance under a letter of credit, whether or not the beneficiary has demanded or at the time is entitled *to demand* payment or performance." UCC § 9-102(a)(51). The beneficiary's right to demand payment or performance under a letter of credit is excluded from the definition. "Letter of credit" is defined in UCC § 5-102.

Perfection may not be accomplished through filing for this new type of collateral. Perfection is accomplished only through control, *see* UCC § 9-107, unless the letter of credit is a supporting obligation. *See* UCC § 9-102(a)(77). A "supporting obligation" supports the payment of the following other types of collateral: accounts, chattel paper, documents, general intangibles, instruments, and investment property. *See* UCC § 9-102(a)(77). Perfection of the collateral supported by a letter-of-credit automatically perfects the beneficiary's right to payment.

The Revised Code also makes significant changes discussed below to definitions of other types of collateral included in the 1972 Code.

d.   Account

The definition has been expanded to cover a wider variety of payment obligations beyond those arising from the sale or lease of goods or the providing of services. The expanded definition now includes license fee payables, credit card receivables, and the newly-added collateral health-care-insurance receivables. *See* UCC § 9-102(a)(2). The definition applies regardless of whether the obligation was earned by performance.

The expanded definition of "accounts" in the Revised Code results in the narrowing of the residual category of "general intangibles." Thus, many types of collateral once categorized as "general intangibles" in the 1972 Code are now "accounts" within the Revised Code definition.

The Revised Code continues to cover sales, including securitization, of accounts. If an account is sold, the buyer must now file a financing statement where the debtor is located in order to perfect an interest in the collateral. *See* UCC § 9-102 cmt. 5a.

e.   General Intangibles

As noted above, the scope of the definition of "general intangibles" has effectively been narrowed by the broadening of "accounts." Nonetheless, notable modifications to the definition have been made in the Revised Code.

With one exception, the sale of general intangibles remains outside the scope of Article 9, thus no filing is necessary for an outright sale. The one exception to this general rule, however, is a new subcategory of general intangibles added in the Revised Code: "payment intangibles." "Payment intangible" is defined as "a general intangible under which the account debtor's principal obligation is a monetary obligation." UCC § 9-102(a)(61). While Article 9 is applicable to the sale of a "payment intangible," perfection upon the sale is automatic.

Another separately defined subcategory of general intangibles included in the Revised Code is the term "software." "Software" is defined as "a computer program and any supporting information provided in connection with a transaction relating to the program." UCC § 9-102(a)(75). Note, however, that if the program is embedded in goods, the program is no longer "software" but part of the goods. *See* UCC §§ 9-102(a)(44), 9-102(a)(75). Centralized filing in the debtor's state of location is necessary to perfect in this collateral.

Furthermore, the new definition of "general intangibles" (*see* UCC § 9-102(a)(42)) contains important exclusions. Among those are the newly-defined terms of "commercial tort claims," "deposit accounts," and "letter-of-credit rights."

f. Instruments

"Promissory note" is included in the Revised Code as a subcategory of instruments. "Promissory note" is an "instrument that evidences a promise to pay a monetary obligation, does not evidence an order to pay, and does not contain an acknowledgment by a bank that the bank has received for deposit a sum of money or funds." UCC § 9-102(a)(65). The Revised Code explicitly makes Article 9 applicable to the sale of promissory notes. *See* UCC § 9-109(a)(3). Perfection is automatic for the buyer of a promissory note. *See* UCC § 9-309(4).

The Revised Code makes a significant change in the method by which perfection in a security interest in instruments may occur. Unlike the 1972 Code, the Revised Code allows for the perfection in a security interest in instruments through filing. *See* UCC § 9-312(a). Thus, perfection may now be accomplished by possession *or* filing.

g. Investment Property

While certificated securities, uncertificated securities, a securities entitlement, and a securities account remain defined in Article 8, Revised Article 9 includes them as investment property and defines and includes a "commodity contract" (UCC § 9-102(a)(15)) and "commodity account" (UCC § 9-102(a)(14)). UCC § 9-102(a)(49). Control remains the primary method through which perfection is achieved, although filing may be an option at least against a trustee in bankruptcy. For a broker or securities intermediary, perfection is automatic.

h. Electronic Document of Title

"Document of title" is defined in UCC § 1-201(b)(16) and includes a bill of lading or warehouse receipt. The 2003 revisions to Article 1 have created two subcategories of documents of title. If the document of title is evidenced by a writing or other record inscribed in a tangible medium, the document of title is a "tangible document of title." If it is evidenced by a record consisting of information stored in an electronic medium, it is an "electronic document of title".

4.   Security Interests in Software and Other Intellectual Property Rights

Intellectual property rights have become an increasing part of the nation's wealth during the "information age," and this material explores some of the basic issues involved in taking and perfecting security interests in such property.

Suppose Moon Microsystems has developed a new software program that will enable manufacturers to streamline their operations by constantly monitoring inventory levels. Moon registers the program with the federal Copyright Office in Washington, D.C. and then makes it available pursuant to a license agreement. Allwet Spas, Inc. is considering the acquisition of a new computer system for its plant, including hardware and various software programs, and Moon's program is among the ones that Allwet wants. Allwet contacts Stargate Computers and orders a system that meets its requirements. Moon licenses Stargate to install the program on the system subject to a requirement that Allwet agree to an end-user license. Moon's end-user license agreement pops up on the screen the first time Allwet attempts to use the program, and Allwet clicks its assent. Among the terms in the license agreement is one that precludes any third person from using the program or otherwise acquiring any interest, including a security interest, in the program. Indeed, the license agreement specifies that any attempt by the end-user to create a security interest in the program constitutes a default and invalidates the license.

The following questions explore various issues that may arise as a result of the foregoing transactions:

1. Suppose Bank One provides working capital for Moon and takes a security interest in Moon's copyright. How are copyrights classified for purposes of Article 9? UCC § 9-102(a)(42). How should Moon go about perfecting its security interest in the copyright? UCC §§ 9-109(c)(1), 9-310(b)(3), 9-311(a)(1), (b), (c). Does its security interest also extend to and is it perfected in the license fees for using the property? The courts have generally held that the federal Copyright Act (17 U.S.C. § 205 *et seq.*) regulates all transfers of a registered copyright, including transfers for security purposes, and that perfection requires recordation of the security interest with the Copyright Office. *See, e.g., In re Peregrine Entertainment, Inc.,* 116 B.R. 194 (C.D. Cal. 1990) (holding that federal law preempts state methods of perfecting security interests in copyrights and related accounts).

2. Why is the copyright of value? If Moon defaults, why would a purchaser at a foreclosure sale pay for the copyright? If a third party has infringed on the copyright, can Bank One pursue Moon's claim? UCC § 9-607(a)(3), cmt. 3.

3. Upon Moon's default, does Bank One have any rights against Allwet? UCC § 9-321(a), (b).

4. Suppose Bank Two has a security interest in all of Allwet's present and after-acquired equipment and general intangibles. Does its security interest attach to the Stargate computer? Does it attach to Moon's software program? Is it perfected?

5. Suppose Bank Two has a security interest in all of Allwet's present and after-acquired equipment and general intangibles. Does the term in the license prohibiting the creation of a security interest prevent Bank Two's security interest from attaching? UCC § 9-408(a). What would be the effect of the term in the license agreement making the attempt to create a security interest an event of default? UCC §§ 9-401, 9-408(a).

6. If Allwet defaults to Bank Two, can Bank Two convey through foreclosure the right to use Moon's program? UCC § 9-408(d), cmt. 5.

7. Suppose Stargate had sold the computer system, including Moon's program, to Allwet on credit and had retained a security interest in the system as collateral for the purchase price. To what extent could Stargate acquire priority in the system if Bank Two had already perfected a security interest in all of Allwet's present and after-acquired goods and general intangibles? UCC § 9-324(f).

8. If Allwet's obligations to Stargate as described in Question 7 are set forth in record form, how will they be classified for purposes of Article 9? UCC § 9-102(a)(42). Does that classification matter to the analysis of any of the previous questions? When would it matter?

9. Suppose one of the assets that is subject to Bank Two's security interest is a piece of industrial machinery that molds plastic into a particular shape. Some of the functions of the machine are controlled by embedded software programs. Does Bank Two have to separately describe the programs for its security interest to attach to them? UCC § 9-102(a)(75), (44). If it disposes of the machine through foreclosure, will the purchaser acquire the right to use the programs with the machine? What additional information would be helpful in answering these questions?

10. What if Bank Two, instead of taking a security interest in the software program, was licensed by Stargate and then sub-licensed Allwet? What if instead Bank Two enters into a financial accommodation contract with Allwet pursuant to which, if Allwet fails to repay Bank Two, Bank Two has a contractual right to preclude Allwet's use of the computer program? *See* Uniform Computer Information Transactions Act §§ 102(a)(29)(31), 507-11. Can this be done even if UCITA is not enacted in the jurisdiction?

The foregoing problems dealt with rights under a registered copyright. Suppose instead that the intellectual property right at issue had been a trademark registered with the federal Patent and Trademark Office (PTO) pursuant to the Lanham Act (15 USC § 1060 *et seq.*). In *In re Together Development Corp.*, 227 B.R. 439 (D. Mass. 1998), the debtor granted a security interest in a registered trademark and the secured party attempted to perfect by recording its security interest with the PTO. The secured party did not file a financing statement pursuant to Article 9. The court held that the secured party was unperfected. The court reasoned that since the Copyright Act clearly requires federal recordation of security assignments but the Lanham Act refers only to assignments, Congress must have intended that it apply only to outright assignments. *See also In re Roman Cleanser*, 43 B.R. 940 (E.D. Mich. 1984), *aff'd*, 802 F.2d 207 (6th Cir. 1986). A similar result was reached with regard to a security assignment of a patent in *In re Cybernetic Services, Inc.*, 252 F.3d 1039 (9th Cir. 2001).

E. IS A SEPARATE SECURITY AGREEMENT REQUIRED?—CONFLICTING CASE LAW

1. Separate Security Agreement Required

AMERICAN CARD COMPANY v. H.M.H. CO.
Rhode Island Supreme Court
196 A.2d 150 (1963)

CONDON, CHIEF JUSTICE.

This is a partnership creditors' claim for priority as a valid security interest under the uniform commercial code. The claim was duly filed in the above-entitled equity receivership proceeding and upon consideration the receivers recommended disallowance as a secured claim but allowed it as a general claim. After a hearing thereon in the superior court, a decree adopting the recommendation of the receivers was entered and from that decree the claimants have appealed to this court.

The sole question for our determination is whether the superior court erred in holding that UCC § 9-203[25] of the code requires in a case of this kind a written security agreement between the debtor and the secured party before a prior security interest in any collateral can attach. The claimants, Oscar A. Hillman & Sons, a co-partnership, contend that a separate agreement in writing is not necessary if the written financing statement which was filed contains the debtor's signature and a description of the collateral. In support of that position they point out that UCC § 9-402,[26] recognizes that a security agreement and a financing statement can be one and the same document. They further argue that 'under the unique circumstances that exist in this case' the minimum requirements of UCC § 9-203[27] are satisfied by the agreed statement of facts and by exhibits A, B, and C appended thereto.

Those circumstances may be summarized as follows. On February 21, 1962, the debtor corporation executed a promissory note in the sum of $12,373.33 payable to claimants. On March 14, 1962, the corporation as debtor and claimants as secured parties signed a financing statement form provided by the office of the secretary of

---

[25] [UCC § 9-203. The 2001 revision of Article 9 changed some Section numbers. Accordingly, the Revised Article 9 Section number is footnoted throughout this case.—Eds.]

[26] [UCC §§ 9-504, 9-502.]

[27] [UCC § 9-203.]

state and filed it in that office in accordance with the provisions of the uniform commercial code, § 9-402.[28]

On July 2, 1962, Melvin A. Chernick and George F. Treanor were appointed co-receivers of the debtor corporation. On October 6, 1962, claimants duly filed their proof of debt and asserted therein a security interest against certain tools and dies of the debtor which were mentioned in the financing statement as collateral. Finally, there is in addition to the agreed statement of facts testimony of claimants' agent who attempted to collect the debt. He testified that the treasurer of the debtor corporation admitted the inability of the debtor to pay the debt and agreed to the execution of the promissory note and to the designation of the tools and dies as collateral security therefor.

The claimants argue that the code requires no " 'magic words,' no precise, formalistic language which must be put in writing in order for a security interest to be enforceable." And they further argue that "the definition of a security agreement indicates, the question of whether or not a security interest is 'created or provided for' is a question of fact which must be decided upon the basis of the words and deeds of the parties." They rely on the definition of "agreement" in § 9-105(1)(h)[29] for support of this latter contention.

Upon consideration of those provisions of the code, we are of the opinion that they are not decisive of the special problem posed in the instant case. The receivers contend here, as they did successfully before the superior court, that the controlling section of the code is, in the circumstances, § 9-203[30] and that in order to establish a security interest in any collateral the secured party must show that "the debtor has signed a security agreement which contains a description of the collateral * * *." They concede that such a signed agreement may serve as a financing statement if it also contains the requirements thereof, but they deny that a financing statement, absent an agreement therein, can be treated as the equivalent of a security agreement.

The pertinent language of § 9-402[31] in this regard is, "A copy of the security agreement is sufficient as a financing statement if it contains the above information and is signed by both parties." In other words, while it is possible for a financing statement and a security agreement to be one and the same document as argued by claimants, it is not possible for a financing statement which does not contain the debtor's grant of a security interest to serve as a security agreement.

In our opinion, there is merit in the receivers' contention, and since the financing statement filed here contains no such grant, it does not qualify as a security agreement. One of the prerequisites to the perfection of a security interest is stated in BANKERS MANUAL ON THE UNIFORM COMMERCIAL CODE, § 8.6, at page 123, as follows: "Security Agreement. It is equally obvious that there must be an agreement between the parties as to the security interest." And in that manual,

---

[28] [UCC §§ 9-502, 9-503, 9-504, 9-506, 9-507, 9-512, 9-521.]

[29] [UCC § 9-102(a)(44).]

[30] [UCC § 9-203.]

[31] [UCC §§ 9-504, 9-502.]

although it is further stated that no special form of agreement is prescribed so long as it contains essential requirements, a form of security agreement is set out in the appendix and numbered Form 1. And as to the requirement of filing, it is stated in § 8.7 of the manual, at page 125, "The parties can file either a financing statement signed by both the secured party and the debtor which gives the information required by 9-402 * * * or file a copy of the security agreement itself if the latter is signed by both parties and contains the extra information required by 9-402 to be put in the separate financing statement."[32]

In an article by one of the editors of the manual in 42 B.U. L. Rev. 187, entitled *Accounts Receivable Financing: Transition from Variety to Uniform Commercial Code*, it is stated at page 189: "The financing statement does not of itself create a security interest. An agreement in writing signed by the debtor 'which contains a description of the collateral' is required." In the absence of any judicial precedent, this commentary on the code is worthy of consideration in the solution of the question here.

The financing statement which the claimants filed clearly fails to qualify also as a security agreement because nowhere in the form is there any evidence of an agreement by the debtor to grant claimants a security interest. As for the testimony of the claimants' agent upon which they also rely to prove the intention of the debtor to make such a grant, our answer is that his testimony is without probative force to supply the absence of a required security agreement in writing. Therefore, the trial justice did not err in holding as she did that the financing statement and the evidence before her did not prove the existence of a security agreement within the contemplation of the language of the statute.

The claimants' appeal is denied and dismissed, the decree appealed from is affirmed, and the cause is remanded to the superior court for further proceedings.

NOTES AND QUESTIONS

1. **Holding of *American Card*.** Grant Gilmore, one of the drafters of the original Article 9, wrote as follows about the *American Card* case:

> [T]he discrepancies between § 9-203 and § 9-402 led the Rhode Island court to an unfortunate decision. To secure a debt, H.M.H. agreed to give the card company a security interest in certain tools and dies. The card company filed a financing statement which complied in all respects with the § 9-402 requirements. In an equity receivership, the card company was denied status as a secured creditor on the ground that the debtor had not signed a "security agreement" in addition to the financing statement. The court noted that a security agreement, if executed, could have been filed as a financing statement (if it met the additional requirements of § 9-402) but concluded that the reverse was not true: "it is not possible for a financing statement which does not contain the debtor's grant of a security interest to serve as a financing statement." [Is this an accurate quote?—Eds.] Certainly, nothing in § 9-203 requires that the "security agreement"

---

[32] [UCC §§ 9-502, 9-503, 9-504, 9-506, 9-507, 9-512, 9-521.]

contain a "granting" clause. The . . . financing statement contained all that was necessary to satisfy the § 9-203 statute of frauds as well as being sufficient evidence of the parties' intention to create a security interest in the tools and dies. No doubt the court would have upheld the security interest if the debtor had signed two pieces of paper instead of one. The § 9-402 provision that a short financing statement may be filed in place of the full security agreement was designed to simplify the operation. The Rhode Island court gives it an effect reminiscent of the worst formal requisites holding under the nineteenth century chattel mortgage acts. [*See* UCC § 9-203; UCC §§ 9-502 through 9-507, 9-512, 9-521.]

GRANT GILMORE, SECURITY INTERESTS IN PERSONAL PROPERTY § 11.4 (1965). Does Professor Gilmore overlook a critical factor? *See* UCC § 9-502(d).

2. **Should Drafters Have the Last Word?** Professor Gilmore was a drafter of the first official text of Article 9. Does this fact give his opinion any additional authority? Compare the criticism by the drafters themselves of the use of the treatise of Professor Samuel Williston, draftsman of the Uniform Sales Act, as authority. At a joint meeting of the Code sponsors in 1950, Karl Llewellyn supported the adoption of "Official Comments" in the following words:

> [I]f these comments are not given effective status as permissive guides to the courts, something else is going to acquire unofficial status in a surreptitious and, to my mind, outrageous fashion. That "something else" is going to be the "Authoritative Text on the Code" written by some of the Reporters. We know what happens when that kind of text turns up. We had that kind of text on the Uniform Sales Act prepared by its draftsman [Samuel Williston], and the history of that has been that through the years, two times out of three, the court has not read or applied the statute.

Transcript of Discussion, Joint Meeting on the Uniform Commercial Code 9-10 (ALI & NCCUSL 1950); *see also* Braucher, *The Legislative History of the Uniform Commercial Code*, 58 COLUM. L. REV. 798, 809 (1958) ("delegation to private persons of essentially legislative power").

2. "Composite Document" Compliance Sufficient

IN RE AMEX-PROTEIN DEVELOPMENT CORPORATION
United States Court of Appeals, Ninth Circuit
504 F.2d 1056 (1974)

PER CURIAM:

This is an appeal filed pursuant to § 24 of the Bankruptcy Act (11 U.S.C. § 47) from a judgment of the district court holding that a valid and enforceable security interest was created under the provisions of the Uniform Commercial Code.

We adopt the following opinion of the Honorable George B. Harris, United States District Judge for the Northern District of California:

This matter is on review from an Order of the Referee which declared invalid a security interest claimed by petitioner Plant Reclamation, a creditor of the bankrupt, in certain personal property in the possession of the bankrupt.

Plant Reclamation had sold equipment to the bankrupt on open account, but on October 16, 1972, substituted a promissory note for the open account indebtedness and caused a financing statement to be signed and filed. The parties intended to create a security interest in the property sold as collateral for the note, and the Referee so found.

The promissory note included the following line: "This note is secured by a Security Interest in subject personal property as per invoices." The words "subject . . . as per invoices" were handwritten in an otherwise typewritten sentence; the testimony before the Referee established that such words were added by an officer of the bankrupt in order to tie the security interest to the personal property that had been sold to the bankrupt by Plant Reclamation. The invoices referred to in the promissory note were the only ones submitted by Plant Reclamation.

The financing statement named Plant Reclamation as the secured party and recited that it covered the following types or items of property:

1—Dorr Oliver 100 Sq. Ft. Vacuum Filter

1—Chicago Pheumatic Vacuum Compression

1—Stainless Steel Augar and Drive

1—Nichols Micro 7' dryer

1—Tolhurst Centerfuge 26 inch.

Discussion

I. Did the Promissory Note "Create or Provide for" a Security Interest?

This issue turns on whether there has been compliance with the following pertinent sections of the California Commercial Code ("Cal.Com.C.") which govern the creation and enforcement of a security interest:

Section 9-105(1)(h):[33]

"Security agreement" means an agreement which creates or provides for a security interest;

Section 1-201(37):[34]

"Security interest" means an interest in personal property or fixtures which secures payment or performance of an obligation. * * *

---

[33] [UCC § 9-102(a)(73). The 2001 revision of Article 9 changed some Section numbers. Accordingly the Revised Article 9 Section number is footnoted throughout this case.—Eds.]

[34] [UCC § 1-201(b)(35).]

Section 9-203:[35]

(1) Subject to the provisions of Section 4-208 on the security interest of a collecting bank and Section 9-113 on a security interest arising under the division on sales, a security interest is not enforceable against the debtor or third parties unless (a) The collateral is in the possession of the secured party; or (b) The debtor has signed a security agreement which contains a description of the collateral . . . .

The Referee denied the claim of Plant Reclamation on the single ground that no security interest had been "granted" pursuant to the language of the promissory note, as a result of which there had been a failure to comply with the "creates or provides for" requirement of § 9-105(1)(h).[36] The referee concluded:

Creative words do not exist in the note before me. The language relied upon is passive, descriptive and informative, much like a financing statement; it is not active or creative; it does not grant or provide for. . . .

Accordingly, I conclude that the promissory note is not a security agreement under § 9-105(1)(h)[37] and that a security agreement enforceable under § 9-203(1)(b)[38] has not been proven. * * *

The court recognizes that, pursuant to General Order 47 in Bankruptcy, it is bound to accept the Referee's findings of fact unless they are clearly erroneous. Here, however, the facts are not in dispute, and the court remains free to examine the legal conclusions of the Referee and to reject them if they are erroneous. . . .

Section 9-105(1)(h)[39] [now § 9-102(a)(73)] defines a security agreement as one which "creates or provides for" a security interest. The Referee found the above-quoted words to be synonymous with the word 'grant' and therefore to require active language. A fair reading of the statute, however, will not bear such a restrictive interpretation.

It is a matter of basic statutory construction that statutes are to be given "such effect that no clause, sentence or word is rendered superfluous, void, contradictory, or insignificant." . . . In addition, absent persuasive reasons to the contrary, statutory words are to be given their ordinary meanings.

Section 9-105(1)(h)[40] nowhere uses the word "grants" nor is that word a synonym for either "creates" or "provides for" or for all of the quoted words together.

WEBSTER'S THIRD NEW INTERNATIONAL DICTIONARY (3d ed. 1965) defines "create" as a transitive verb with the following meanings *inter alia*:[41]

---

[35] [UCC §§ 9-203, 9-201.]

[36] [UCC § 9-102(a)(73).]

[37] [UCC § 9-102(a)(73).]

[38] [UCC § 9-203(1)(a); UCC § 9-203(b)(3).]

[39] [UCC § 9-102(a)(73).]

[40] [*Id.*]

[41] [1] Webster's New International Dictionary (2d ed. 1939) lists as synonyms for "create" the words "make, build, produce, fashion; invent, originate."

1: to bring into existence * * * 2: to cause to be or to produce by fiat or by mental, moral, or legal action * * * 3: to cause or occasion * * *

"Provide" is defined as a transitive verb with the following meanings *inter alia*:

2a: to fit out or fit up * * * 3: STIPULATE * * *

and as an intransitive verb with the following meanings *inter alia*:

1a: to take precautionary measures: make provision—used with against or for * * * 2: to make a proviso or stipulation * * *

"Grant" is defined as a transitive verb with the following meanings *inter alia*:

1a: to consent to carry out for a person: ALLOW, ACCORD * * *2: GIVE, BESTOW, CONFER * * *

Thus, the requirement of § 9-105(1)(h) may be satisfied not only when a security interest is caused to be or brought into existence, but also when provision or stipulation is made therefor.

No magic words or precise form are necessary to create or provide for a security interest so long as the minimum formal requirements of the Code are met. . . . This liberal approach is mandated by an expressed purpose of the secured transaction provisions of the Code:

> The aim of this Article is to provide a simple and unified structure within which the immense variety of present-day secured financing transactions can go forward with less cost and with greater certainty. The Article's flexibility and simplified formalities should make it possible for new forms of secured financing, as they develop, to fit comfortably under its provisions . . . .

Comment to § 9-101.[42]

The court in *In re Center Auto Parts*, 6 UCC Rep. 398 (C.D. Cal. 1968), upheld the validity of a promissory note as a security agreement by reading the two together. The promissory note merely recited that, "This note is secured by a certain financing statement," and the court found that such was sufficient to "create or provide for" a security interest within the meaning of § 9-105(1)(h).[43]

A similar result was reached in a case involving the North Carolina version of the UCC, *Evans v. Everett*, 279 N.C. 352, 183 S.E.2d 109 (N.C. 1971), wherein the debtor gave a promissory note which recited: "This note is secured by Uniform Commercial Code financing statement of North Carolina" and wherein a similarly worded financing statement was thereafter filed. The court found that since a security agreement could serve as a financing statement, there was no sound reason why the converse should not be true. The court held that the financing statement before it qualified as a security agreement.

---

[42] [UCC § 9-101.]

[43] [UCC § 9-102(a)(73).]

By the same token, any written agreement signed by a debtor which recites that certain personalty is being encumbered as security for a debt ought to operate as a security agreement under § 9-105(1)(h).[44] . . .

While there are no magic words which create a security interest, there must be language in the instrument which "leads to the logical conclusion that it was the intention of the parties that a security interest be created." *In re Nottingham*, 6 UCC Rep. 1197, 1199, 183 S.E.2d 113 (D. Tenn. 1969).

* * *

The cases relied upon by the trustee and cited by the Referee are not persuasive. *Shelton v. Erwin*, 472 F.2d 1118 (8th Cir. 1973), dealt with the contention that an automobile bill of sale or a title application therefor or both together adequately set forth the intent of the parties to create or provide for a security interest and did in fact create or provide for same under pertinent Missouri statutes. In finding no security agreement, the court simply reaffirmed the principle that a single piece of paper—here the title application and later certificate of title were being treated as a financing statement—could not serve as a security agreement without containing the requirements for such. There was not, as here, two documents: a promissory note which provided for a security interest and a financing statement which gave notice of it.

Shelton, together with other cases relied upon by the trustee, stem from the ruling in *American Card Company v. H.M.H. Co.*, 196 A.2d 150 (R.I. 1963), and therefore share its infirmities. There, the court found that a financing statement which did not contain a 'grant' of a security interest could not also serve as a security agreement. There is no support in legislative history or grammatical logic for the substitution of the word 'grant' for the phrase 'creates or provides for.' This case has been subject to harsh criticism, *see* G. GILMORE, SECURITY INTERESTS IN PERSONAL PROPERTY § 11.4 at 347–348 (1965); 6D Bender's Uniform Commercial Code Service 2-1680, and it cannot be relied upon as dispositive in the instant case.

Accordingly, the promissory note herein qualifies as a security agreement which by its terms "creates or provides for" a security interest.

II. Adequacy of Description of the Collateral

The trustee urges a second ground for sustaining the Order of the Referee complained of here, namely the inadequacy of the description of the collateral in the promissory note and hence the failure to comply with § 9-203(1)(b).[45]

Section 9-110[46] provides:

> For the purposes of this division any description of personal property or real estate is sufficient whether or not it is specific if it reasonably identifies what is described. Personal Property may be referred to by general kind or

---

[44] [*Id.*]

[45] [Should be § 9-203(1)(a); UCC § 9-203(b)(3)(A).]

[46] [UCC § 9-108.]

class if the property can be reasonably identified as falling within such kind or class or if it can be so identified when acquired by the debtor. * * *

Although the promissory note does not describe the collateral within the four corners of the document such description is provided (1) through incorporation by reference of the subject invoices, as well as (2) through reference to the more specific description of the collateral contained in the financing statement.

The use of such extrinsic aids is clearly permissible to identify the collateral:

> Under the Uniform Commercial Code there is no reason why parol evidence may not be admitted in aid of the description of the collateral, even where the collateral has been reasonably and sufficiently identified in the security agreement. In many instances, a description in a security agreement may be in general terms; parol evidence should therefore be admissible to explain or supplement the general description, or to resolve ambiguities.

44 CAL. JUR. 2D REV. *Secured Transactions* § 107 at 386.

The doctrine of incorporation by reference is likewise available in this area:

> There is nothing in the Uniform Commercial Code to prevent reference in the security agreement to another writing for particular terms and conditions of the transaction. There is also nothing in the Uniform Commercial Code to prevent reference in the Security Agreement to another writing for a description of the collateral, so long as the reference in the security agreement is sufficient to identify reasonably what it described. In other words, it will at times be expedient to give a general description of the collateral in the security agreement and refer to a list or other writing for more exact description. In addition, the security agreement could itself consist of separate parts, one a general description of the obligation secured and the rights and duties of the parties, and the other a description of the collateral, both such writings being signed by the debtor and stated to comprise a single security agreement or referring to each other.

Id. § 109 at 387–388.

Thus, there is no requirement that the description of the collateral be complete within the four corners of the security agreement or other single document. The description in the security agreement is sufficient, however, if it provides such information as would lead a reasonable inquirer to the identity of the collateral. . . . As summarized by one commentator:

> A description need not be so comprehensive that it enables an interested party to determine exactly what the specific collateral is, from a reading of the security agreement or financing statement alone. It is enough if the description allows a third party, aided by information which the security agreement suggests, to identify the property.

D. Lee, *Perfection and Priorities Under the Uniform Commercial Code*, 17 WYO. L.J. 5–6 (1962). Instructive here is the decision in *In re Nickerson & Nickerson,*

Inc., 329 F. Supp. 93 (D. Neb. 1971), *aff'd*, 452 F.2d 56 (8th Cir. 1971), on the issue of adequacy of description of the collateral. A security agreement in *Nickerson* described the collateral therein as:

> All gifts, novelties, souvenirs, and other merchandise inventory held for resale including but not limited to the following: See attached schedules for a list of property covered by this Security Agreement.

The financing statement filed in connection with the security agreement described the collateral in different terms:

> . . . gifts, novelties, souvenirs, and other merchandise inventory held for resale and situated in debtor's stores located in (each particular) state.

The appellate court held that the description of the collateral in the security agreement was adequate:

> As we have noted, the evidence establishes that the parties, by attaching the financing statements to the security agreement, incorporated the clarifying language of the financing statement into the security agreement, and clearly created a lien in Lugene's (the secured party's) favor upon the inventory in all of Nickerson's (the debtor's) stores.

452 F.2d 57.

A similar conclusion was reached in *In re Center Auto Parts, supra,* at 399–400, wherein the court upheld the adequacy of the description of the collateral in a security agreement through reference to a financing statement by incorporation and the resulting suggestion of inquiry or the means of identification.

The trustee properly cites *Mitchell v. Shepherd Mall State Bank*, 324 F. Supp. 1029, 1032 (W.D. Okl. 1971), *aff'd*, 458 F.2d 700 (10th Cir. 1972), for the proposition that the description of collateral contained in a financing statement may have the effect of restricting the security interest created in a security agreement but cannot enlarge it. In the instant case, a reference to the more specific description contained in the financing statement does operate to restrict, rather than to enlarge, the security interest between the parties.

A case relied upon by the trustee, *Rusch Factors, Inc. v. Passport Fashion Ltd.*, 1 U.C.C. Rep. Serv. (CBC) 507 (N.Y. Sup. Ct. 1971), may be readily distinguished. There, the parties executed a security agreement (trust receipt) whereby the trustee acknowledged receipt of:

> the documents listed on the obverse hereof representing the goods therein specified (which, together with all improvements or additions to or accessories to or products of such goods, are all hereinafter called "collateral") and . . . the existence of . . . a security interest in favor of (Itoh) in the "collateral."

Id. at 507–08. The parties stipulated as to the nature of the subject documents, but in fact no such documents had been listed or attached to the security agreement. The court concluded that because of the absence of the documents, a reasonable inquirer, upon reviewing the security agreement with or without the financing statement, would not have discovered sufficient information to provide an adequate description of the collateral. *Id.* at 510.

Rusch is pertinent here because it approves the policy of looking beyond the security agreement to the financing statement in order to ascertain the description of the collateral, but it is distinguishable on its holding because there the court found an absence of documentation. Here, however, the invoices were available but were not claimed to be physically attached to the security agreement; only if no invoices existed or could be found would the instant case be analogous to *Rusch.*

This last conclusion is bolstered by *J. K. Gill Company v. Fireside Realty, Inc.,* 262 Or. 486, 499 P.2d 813 (1972), a case similar to *Rusch* which cited and relied upon *Rusch* as authority for a similar conclusion. A security agreement executed therein described the collateral as "furniture as per attached listing." No listing was in fact attached. The financing statement made the same description of the collateral; again no listing was attached. The court noted, however, that had the subject invoices which evidenced the furniture been attached to the security agreement, the description of the collateral would have been adequate, thus supporting the theory of description through incorporation by reference.

It is manifest that the reference to the invoices in the subject promissory note, coupled with the existence of a financing statement containing a more specific description, satisfies the requirements of §§ 9-203(1)(b) and 9-110.[47]

* * *

Conclusion

For the reasons stated above, the petition of Plant Reclamation is hereby granted, and the Order of the Referee Declaring Lien Invalid, dated April 10, 1973, is hereby reversed. It is so ordered.

The judgment is affirmed.

NOTES AND QUESTIONS

1. **Holding of *Amex-Protein*.** The court in *In re Bollinger Corp.*, 614 F.2d 924 (3d Cir. 1980), comments as follows on the *Amex-Protein* case: "The Ninth Circuit . . . echoed criticism by commentators of the *American Card* rule. . . . It concluded that as long as the financing statement contains a description of the collateral signed by the debtor, the financing statement may serve as the security agreement and the formal requirements of [UCC § 9-203(b)(3)] are met." Is that what the *Amex-Protein* court holds?

2. **Proceeds.** There are several refinements to this basic scheme. If the debtor disposes of any property to which the security interest has attached, the interest will attach automatically to the identifiable *proceeds* received on the disposition unless the security agreement otherwise provides. This new interest in proceeds may be *in addition* to the interest in the property disposed of because the original

---

[47] [UCC § 9-203(1)(a); UCC § 9-203(b)(3)(A); UCC § 9-108.]

interest continues notwithstanding disposition unless the secured party has agreed to the disposition or, with some exceptions, the disposition was in the ordinary course of business. *See* UCC § 9-203(f); UCC § 9-315. A security interest will also attach automatically to other property subsequently acquired by the debtor if the security agreement includes an *after-acquired property clause* that describes the property. *See* UCC § 9-204.

F. DRAFTING EXERCISE—SECURITY AGREEMENT

Problem 2-9: Sample Security Agreement. Mr. Clemens' accountant prepares the following draft security agreement to comply with Article 9. *See* Section A.1., *supra*, Document B. Mr. Clemens consults you. Advise Mr. Clemens on what changes, if any, you would advise to the draft text. *See* UCC §§ 9-102, 9-109, 9-108, 9-201, 9-203, 9-204.

> Samuel Clemens, hereinafter called Owner, for value of $10 in hand paid, hereby contracts with and agrees to grant and convey to Steady State Bank of University Park, hereinafter called Financier, an Article 9 property right in certain specific equipment listed in Schedule A attached hereto and incorporated herein by reference, and any and all additions, accessions, and substitutions thereto or therefor, all of which shall be called Security, to collateralize the repayment of _____, hereinafter called Debt, which is provided for in a note of even date.

Which types of Article 9 collateral need to be specifically mentioned in the description of the collateral in the security agreement? In particular, should "goods" or any of the four special types of goods (*i.e.*, consumer goods, equipment, farm products, or inventory) be included in the description? What about accounts? General intangibles?

Problem 2-10: Use of Forms. After giving your advice on the draft text prepared by Mr. Clemens' accountant, you propose that a more desirable text is the properly completed form at Document B, Section A.1., *supra*. What are your reasons?

1. Ethical Concerns

A lawyer may be called on to prepare forms for a client, negotiate the terms of a specific secured transaction, advise the client on legal alternatives when a transaction goes sour, litigate issues concerning repossession and disposition of collateral following default, or sue for a deficiency. Depending on the role, the attorney must take into account different ethical considerations. *See generally* VERNON COUNTRYMAN, PROBLEMS OF PROFESSIONAL RESPONSIBILITY UNDER THE UNIFORM COMMERCIAL CODE (1969).

Consider the problem of drafting forms. Unless a transaction involves a great deal of money, it is unlikely that a lawyer will be called on to draft a security agreement specifically tailored to a particular deal. A lawyer may, however, be asked to draft forms that will then be used by the client in a variety of transactions. When drafting a form what ethical limitations must the lawyer consider? Would the following rule be helpful?

4.3 Illegal, Fraudulent, or Unconscionable Transactions

A lawyer shall not conclude an agreement, or assist a client in concluding an agreement, that the lawyer knows or reasonably should know is illegal, contains legally prohibited terms, would work a fraud, or would be held to be unconscionable as a matter of law.

Comment: Although a lawyer is generally not responsible for the substantive fairness of the result of a negotiation, the lawyer has a duty to see that the product is not offensive to the law. There are many legal proscriptions concerning contractual arrangements. Being a party to some types of agreement is a penal offense. Some types of contractual provisions are prohibited by law, such as provisions purporting to waive certain legally conferred rights. Modern commercial law provides that grossly unfair contracts are unconscionable and may therefore be invalid. Such proscriptions are intended to secure definite legal rights. As an officer of the legal system, a lawyer is required to observe them. On the other hand, there are legal rules that simply make certain contractual provisions unenforceable, allowing one or both parties to avoid the obligation. Inclusion of such provisions in a contract may be unwise but it is not ethically improper. However, under the deceptive practices statutes of some states, such may be a violation. It is not improper to include a provision whose legality is subject to reasonable argument.

A lawyer is not obliged to make an independent investigation of the circumstances of a transaction to assure that it is legally unimpeachable . . . [A] lawyer is not absolved of responsibility for a legally offensive transaction simply because the client takes the final step in carrying it out. For example, a lawyer who prepared a form contract containing legally proscribed terms is a lawyer who is involved in a transaction in which the form is used, even though the lawyer does not participate in a specific transaction.

ABA Commission on Evaluation of Professional Standards, Discussion Draft of ABA Model Rules of Professional Conduct (January 30, 1980).[48] (This proposed rule was subsequently withdrawn by the commission without comment). *See also* MODEL CODE OF PROFESSIONAL RESPONSIBILITY, EC 7-8 and EC 7-9; Vernon Countryman, PROBLEMS OF PROFESSIONAL RESPONSIBILITY UNDER THE UNIFORM COMMERCIAL CODE 86–87 (1969).

---

[48] Copyright 1980 American Bar Association. Reprinted by permission.

2. Adapting Forms to the Client's Needs

IN RE PRODUCT DESIGN AND FABRICATION, INC.
(TERPSTRA v. MICHELOSEN)
United States Bankruptcy Court, Northern District of Iowa
182 B.R. 803 (1994)

ORDER RE: TRUSTEE'S COMPLAINT TO AVOID TRANSFERS

WILLIAM L. EDMONDS, CHIEF JUDGE.

The matter before the court is the final trial of the Trustee's complaint to avoid transfers to John P. Michelosen, Jr. pursuant to 11 U.S.C. §§ 544 and 547. . . .

Findings of Fact

Product Design and Fabrication, Inc. (PDF) was a manufacturer of agricultural equipment. Its primary product was a seed corn detassler. PDF was also in the beginning stages of the manufacture of a high clearance sprayer and a square baler. In late 1991, PDF lost its primary source of operating capital and began to look for alternate financing. Irvin Janey, president of PDF, ordered an appraisal of PDF's machinery and equipment. Craig C. Hilpipre performed the appraisal and made a written report dated May 15, 1992 (the Hilpipre appraisal). The Hilpipre appraisal did not include any of PDF's inventory. PDF used the Hilpipre appraisal, which showed a total value of $314,434.00, to solicit operating funds from investors.

PDF had discussions with Michelosen about investing in the company. On June 30, 1992, Michelosen met at PDF's facility with Janey and Richard Rank, chief financial officer of PDF. At that meeting Michelosen and Janey, as president of PDF, executed a "Short Term Financing Agreement" under which Michelosen agreed to lend PDF $100,000. The Financing Agreement further provided:

> These funds will be secured by the machinery and equipment listed in the appraisal performed by the Hilpipre Auction Company . . . dated May 15, 1992, totaling $314,434.00. PDF agrees to file a [financing statement] to secure this machinery and equipment.

[Citation omitted.] Michelosen wrote a check to PDF on June 30, 1992 in the amount of $100,000. PDF deposited the funds in its Firstar Bank account the same day. [Citation omitted.]

The Financing Agreement was delivered to Robert Downer, PDF's corporate attorney. Downer prepared a security agreement on an Iowa State Bar Association form (Security Agreement) [citation omitted]. The first paragraph of the Security Agreement states that PDF grants Michelosen a security interest "in the property described in the paragraphs checked below." A check appears in the box labeled "inventory." The words "an inventory of which is attached hereto as Exhibit "A" and by this reference made a part hereof" are typed as an insert following the checked line. Exhibit A to the Security Agreement is the Hilpipre appraisal.

The second paragraph of the Security Agreement states that the security interest secures payment of the June 30, 1992 Short Term Financing Agreement together with all other of PDF's obligations to Michelosen including future advances. Paragraph 8(b) of the Security Agreement provides that Michelosen "shall not be deemed to have waived any of [his] rights hereunder or under any other agreement, instrument or paper signed by [PDF] unless such waiver be in writing and signed by [Michelosen] . . . ."

On July 24, 1992, Downer sent PDF the original and one copy of the Security Agreement, with instructions to sign both the original and the copy. [Citation omitted.] Janey signed the documents the same day he received them from Downer. He did not change the date of the Security Agreement, which was typed in as June 30, 1992. On July 28, 1992, Rank sent Michelosen a signed Security Agreement, a copy of a form UCC-1 financing statement, and Exhibits A, B and C. Exhibit A sent to Michelosen was the Hilpipre appraisal. [Citation omitted.]

On July 23, 1992, Michelosen and Marty Sixt, chairman of PDF, executed a second Short Term Financing Agreement in the same form as the agreement executed June 30, but with handwritten changes. Michelosen agreed to lend PDF an additional $50,000. The language relating to a security interest in machinery and equipment was unchanged. . . . Michelosen and Sixt are both California residents; the second Financing Agreement was executed in California. The second Financing Agreement was sent by overnight courier to PDF with a check dated July 23, 1992 in the amount of $50,000. PDF deposited the funds in its bank account July 27, 1992. [Citation omitted.]

On August 1, 1992, Michelosen and Sixt executed a third Short Term Financing Agreement, again in the same form but with handwritten changes. The agreement stated that Michelosen "will loan PDF funds in the amount of $250,000." A handwritten paragraph at the end of the form indicates that the agreement was intended to "supersede and consolidate" the two previous loans and to provide for a new loan of $100,000. [Citation omitted] Michelosen wrote a check to PDF dated August 9, 1992 in the amount of $100,000. PDF deposited the funds in its bank account August 10, 1992. [Citation omitted.] The check was returned for insufficient funds but was honored on a later date.

On August 7, 1992, a financing statement covering PDF's equipment was filed with the Iowa Secretary of State on behalf of Michelosen. [Citation omitted.]

On August 14, 1992, PDF filed a Chapter 11 bankruptcy petition. At the time of filing, PDF had assets of approximately $800,000 and liabilities of more than $2.2 million. PDF had been "balance sheet insolvent" for at least a year before the bankruptcy filing. The case converted to Chapter 7 on September 15, 1993. The Chapter 7 trustee liquidated all the property of PDF and deposited the proceeds of sale. The property sold included machinery, equipment and inventory.

Discussion

The trustee's complaint makes two claims. First, that because the "security agreement" described inventory, not machinery or equipment, Michelosen did not obtain a security interest in PDF's equipment and, therefore, may make no claim to the proceeds of sale. [The court's discussion of the second claim—that even if Michelosen obtained security interests in debtor's machinery and equipment, two of the three interests are avoidable as preferential transfers—is omitted—Eds.] Michelosen contends that he has unavoidable perfected security interests in the proceeds of the sale of machinery and equipment.

Perfected Security Interest in Equipment Under the Security Agreement

The first issue is whether PDF gave Michelosen a security interest in its equipment. In order for a security interest to attach, the debtor must sign a security agreement "which contains a description of the collateral." UCC § 9-203(1)(a).[49] The test of sufficiency of a collateral description is that of reasonable identification. UCC § 9-110.[50] The description must do the job assigned to it; it must "make possible the identification of the thing described." [Citation omitted.]

The form Security Agreement describes the collateral as:

> All of Debtor's inventory now owned or hereafter acquired[,] an inventory of which is attached hereto as Exhibit "A" and by this reference made a part hereof.

The trustee argues that in interpreting the contract's description of collateral the court should stop reading after the word "inventory." Apparently, Exhibit A, the Hilpipre appraisal, was not attached to the Security Agreement document in PDF's files. [The completed Iowa State Bar Association form security agreement], which bears an original signature by Janey, did not have staple holes. The court believes this fact is not significant for purposes of whether Michelosen had a security interest in equipment. Downer prepared two Security Agreements for signature so there would be duplicate originals. Even if no counterpart of [the Iowa State Bar Association security agreement] had the appraisal stapled to it, the Security Agreement on its face would be incomplete without the exhibit. Incorporation of Exhibit A by reference shows that the complete expression of the agreement includes the exhibit. A security agreement serves a statute of frauds function rather than notice to third parties. [Citation omitted.] The parties to the Security Agreement knew what the collateral was. Exhibit A was an identifiable document in existence at the time the Security Agreement was executed. The information on the exhibit was part of the inducement for the loan. Both PDF and Michelosen had copies of the appraisal. PDF prepared the Security Agreement documents, and Rank sent a complete set of the documents to Michelosen.

Collateral may be described by means of incorporation by reference to other identifiable documents. *In re Nickerson & Nickerson, Inc.*, 452 F.2d 56, 9 UCC Rep. Serv. 1266 (8th Cir. 1971) (security agreement referring to "attached schedules" reasonably identified collateral); *Nolden v. Plant Reclamation (In re Amex-Protein Development Corp.)*, 504 F.2d 1056, 15 UCC Rep. Serv. 286 (9th Cir. 1974) (note referencing collateral "as per invoices" created security interest); *Mitchell v.*

---

[49] [The language of the Code as revised now states that a security agreement "provides a description of the collateral . . . ." UCC § 9-203(b)(3)(A).—Eds.]

[50] [UCC § 9-108.]

Shepherd Mall State Bank, 458 F.2d 700, 10 UCC Rep. Serv. 737 (10th Cir. 1972) (security agreement used attached exhibit to describe collateral). The case *Matter of Martin Grinding & Machine Works, Inc.*, 793 F.2d 592 (7th Cir. 1986), cited by the trustee, is not to the contrary. In *Martin Grinding*, the court found the security agreement unambiguously gave a security interest in machinery, equipment, furniture and fixtures. The court did not allow extrinsic evidence to enlarge the security interest to include inventory and accounts receivable. *Id.* at 595. The additional typewritten language on the face of the Security Agreement executed by PDF expressly incorporates Exhibit A into the description of collateral. Therefore, the court finds that the description of collateral includes all items listed on the Hilpipre appraisal.

The items on the appraisal are PDF's machinery and equipment. There is no inventory on the list. The terms "inventory" and "equipment" are mutually exclusive. UCC § 9-109(2) and (4) and Official Comment 2.[51] Thus, the collateral description is ambiguous because the term "inventory" is inconsistent with the classification of items in the appraisal. The ambiguity is whether the parties intended the term "inventory" to modify the list in some way or whether the parties intended to give a security interest in all items on the appraisal. Extrinsic evidence is admissible to discover the intent of the parties to a contract when its terms are ambiguous. [Citation omitted.] In *American State Bank v. Swearingen (In re Swearingen)*, 27 B.R. 379 (Bankr. D. Kan. 1983), cited by the trustee, the court stated that the parties' intent was "immaterial" because the court found the security agreement complete and unambiguous. *Id.* at 383. Because the Security Agreement signed by PDF is ambiguous in its description of collateral, the court will consider other evidence to determine the parties' intent.

Janey testified that PDF did not intend to create a security interest in inventory. Its intent was to give a security interest in all items listed in the appraisal. The Security Agreement's reference to the June 30, 1992 Financing Agreement is consistent with Janey's testimony. The Financing Agreement shows that the parties intended to secure the loan with PDF's machinery and equipment as listed on the Hilpipre appraisal. The court concludes that the Security Agreement creates a security interest in PDF's machinery and equipment included in the Hilpipre appraisal.

* * *

Perfected Security Interest Under the "Financing Agreements"

The court also concludes that each Financing Agreement, standing alone, is sufficient to constitute a security agreement giving Michelosen a security interest in PDF's machinery and equipment. The Financing Agreements are signed by the debtor and contain a description of the collateral. UCC § 9-203(1)(a).[52] The parties intended to make a secured loan. Specific "words of grant" are not necessary to

---

[51]   [UCC §§ 9-102(a)(33), 9-108(a)(48).]

[52]   [UCC § 9-203(b)(3)(A).]

show an intention to create a security interest. [Citation omitted.] The Financing Agreement documents show an intent to "create or provide for a security interest." UCC § 9-102(1)(a).[53]

The trustee cites *Royal Bank & Trust Co. v. Pereira* (*In re Lady Madonna Industries, Inc.*), 99 B.R. 536 (S.D.N.Y. 1989), for the proposition that the existence of the "Security Agreement" prevents the court from considering other documents as security agreements. In *Lady Madonna*, the debtors had signed two security agreements covering "accounts receivable, contract rights . . . and general intangibles relating thereto or arising therefrom." Prior to signing the security agreements, the parties had executed a commitment letter covering "all assets" of Lady Madonna Industries. The *Lady Madonna* case does not stand for the proposition that a court cannot consider multiple security agreements because the case itself involved two valid security agreements. Each security agreement contained a "non-merger clause" which preserved the creditor's rights under previous agreements. PDF's Security Agreement contains a "non-waiver clause" [citation omitted] that preserves Michelosen's rights under prior agreements. In closing argument, counsel for the trustee conceded that, standing alone, the Financing Agreements would meet the requirements of a security agreement. The court in *Lady Madonna* found that the commitment letter alone did not qualify as a security agreement and would not permit the creditor to use the letter to expand its security interest. The court stated:

> [c]ases considering the extent of a security interest where there is a conflict in the collateral descriptions in the loan documents have generally held that where there is a security agreement complete on its face, the courts will not refer to other documents to expand the scope of the security interest unless the security agreement itself refers to those other documents.

99 B.R. at 542, quoting *In re H & I Pipe and Supply Co., Inc.*, 44 B.R. 949, 950 (Bankr. M.D. Tenn. 1984). The *Lady Madonna* case is distinguishable, therefore, because the collateral description in PDF's Financing Agreement does not conflict with the Security Agreement, the Financing Agreement alone meets the requirements of a security agreement, and the Security Agreement refers on its face to the Financing Agreement. The court concludes that PDF gave Michelosen a security interest in its equipment under the Financing Agreements as well as the Security Agreement.

NOTES AND QUESTIONS

1. **Bankruptcy Aspects of this Case in a Nutshell.** We will explore some basic bankruptcy law later in these materials, but to help you understand the *Terpstra* case we set out here a brief summary of some basic points.

The judge in this case is a bankruptcy judge. Bankruptcy courts are federal courts that have jurisdiction in insolvency proceedings under the federal Bankruptcy Code. *See* 11 U.S.C. § 1 *et seq.* (1994). (In these materials citation to the Bankruptcy Code will be to "BC" followed by the section number.) Bankruptcy

---

[53] [UCC § 9-102(a)(73).]

judges are not appointed pursuant to Article III of the federal Constitution and they therefore do not have lifetime appointments.

The plaintiff in this case is the bankruptcy trustee in a liquidation proceeding under Chapter 7 of the Bankruptcy Code. The trustee acts for the benefit of unsecured creditors. The interests of the unsecured creditors conflict with those of secured creditors: the secured creditors have first claim to the property subject to the security interests. One of the trustee's duties, therefore, is to test whether each security interest claimed by the secured creditors withstands the tests set by the Bankruptcy Code. If a security interest does not survive these tests, the trustee may *avoid* the interest. As a consequence, the secured creditor becomes an unsecured creditor and the property becomes available to all unsecured creditors.

The Bankruptcy Code tests for the security interest in this case are those found in §§ 544 and 547—although the case has been edited to deal only with the former. Section 544 provides for what is known colloquially as the "strong arm" power of the trustee. Later in these materials, we will study the language of § 544(a)(1) with care. At this point, we provide only the bottom line: the trustee may avoid any security interest that is *unperfected*. An Article 9 security interest is unperfected if it has not been publicized in accordance with the provisions of the Code. The following note explains how this interest was or was not publicized in this case.

2. Financing Statement—Form UCC-1; "Perfection." *See* Form UCC-1 at Section A.1., *supra*, Document C. The opinion refers to the copy of a "form UCC-1 financing statement." A security agreement is distinct from the financing statement: the former creates the security interest, while the latter is a simple notice filed in a public record. (It is true, however, that a secured party is authorized to file the security agreement as a financing statement—as long as the security agreement satisfies the requirements of a financing statement. *See* UCC §§ 9-502, 9-504.) UCC §§ 9-502 and 9-521 set out the formal requisites of a financing statement and even suggest a model form. In all states this basic form is known as a "UCC-1" or "UCC-1 form." The actual format of the forms used in these states, however, differs from state to state. In the course of revising Article 9, there has been an attempt to provide a uniform form.

The secured party files the financing statement in the office or offices indicated in UCC § 9-501.

When a properly completed financing statement is filed in the proper office in the relevant state, the security interest is said to be *perfected*. Upon perfection, the security interest has priority over a subsequent lien acquired by judicial process, such as an *execution lien*. *See* UCC § 9-317(a)(2). In the context of this case, the importance of this priority is that the security interest will have priority over the bankruptcy trustee seeking to avoid the lien by exercise of the strong-arm power discussed in the previous note.

3. Statute of Frauds Function. The court states that "a security agreement serves a statute of frauds function rather than notice to third parties." What is the function of a statute of frauds? Note the language in Official Comment 3 to former UCC § 9-203:

One purpose of the formal requisites stated in subsection (1)(a) is evidentiary. The requirement of written record minimizes the possibility of future dispute as to the terms of a security agreement and as to what property stands as collateral for the obligation secured.

Official Comment 5 to the same section refers specifically to the statute of frauds. It appears, in other words, to distinguish this evidentiary function from that of a statute of frauds. (Comparable language is in Official Comments 3 and 5 to UCC § 9-203). Are you persuaded by this distinction? If so, does the court in this case adequately take this evidentiary function into account?

4. **Proceeds.** Michelosen, the secured party, claimed a security interest in PDF's machinery and equipment. During PDF's insolvency proceedings, the trustee sold this machinery and equipment. Michelosen contends that his security interest in the machinery and equipment carries over to the proceeds received by the trustee on the sale of the machinery and equipment. Do any of the documents grant Michelosen a security interest in these proceeds? If not, does Article 9 give Michelosen such an interest? *See* UCC § 9-203(f), UCC § 9-315. (If either the security agreement or Article 9 gives Michelosen a security interest in the proceeds, the Bankruptcy Code will recognize this interest. *See* BC § 552(b).)

G. MORE ON ATTACHED AND ENFORCEABLE SECURITY INTERESTS

1. After-Acquired Property

Problem 2-11: After-Acquired Property. Assume that the Clemens' security agreement describes the collateral as "all debtor's inventory and equipment kept at debtor's premises on 3412 Milton Ave., Dallas." Does the bank have a security interest in inventory items or equipment acquired by the sole proprietorship six months after Mr. Clemens signs the security agreement? *See* UCC § 9-204(a). How about in a new machine Clemens has purchased but which is not yet delivered? *See* UCC § 9-203(b)(2). How about the purchase of a home entertainment center under a security agreement which covers existing and after-acquired components of the center? *See* UCC § 9-204(b).

American Employers Ins. Co. v. American Security Bank, 747 F.2d 1493, 1501 (D.C. Cir. 1984): "It is reasonable to read a security agreement granting an interest in all inventory or receivables to include after-acquired inventory or receivables."

Graphic Resources, Inc. v. Thiebauth, 233 Neb. 592, 447 N.W.2d 28 (1989): The court held that after-acquired equipment is not covered by a description of collateral that included "[a]ll of Debtor's equipment, including replacement parts, additions, repairs, and accessories incorporated therein or affixed thereto."

2. Future Advances

The original security agreement granted a security interest to secure, *inter alia*, "future advances." UCC § 9-204(c) authorizes such an agreement:

A security agreement may provide that collateral secures, or that accounts, chattel paper, payment intangibles, or promissory notes are sold in connection with, future advances or other value, whether or not the advances or value are given pursuant to commitment.

After the initial financing agreement was executed on June 30, Michelosen twice agreed to make additional loans. Are these loans "future advances" or separate loans?

Problem 2-12:   Future Advances. Six months after the September 1 loan to Samuel Clemens, the bank agrees to lend him $5,000 to build trade fixtures on the premises leased by the sole proprietorship. If the bank says nothing about whether this second loan is secured by the assets of the sole proprietorship, does the bank's security interest in those assets secure this new obligation to repay the $5,000? *See* UCC § 9-204(c). Would your answer be different if the loan was made for improvements to Mr. Clemens' home?

Section 9-204(c) states that "[a] security agreement may provide that collateral secures . . . future advances or other value, whether or not the advances or value are given pursuant to commitment." Must the original security agreement include a future advance clause to ensure that the security interest secures a debtor's obligation that arises after the security agreement is concluded? In which of the following cases does the secured party have a security interest?

(a) The original security agreement includes a future advance clause. A future advance is made, at which time the debtor signs another security agreement granting a security interest in the same collateral.

(b) The original security agreement includes a future advance clause, but the debtor does not sign another security agreement when the future advance is made.

(c) There is no future advance clause in the original security agreement, but when the future advance is made the debtor signs another security agreement granting a security interest in the same collateral.

(d) There is no future advance clause in the original security agreement, and when the future advance is made, the debtor does not sign another security agreement.

Professor Gilmore states:

However "covered by the security agreement" is to be read, § 9-204(5) should certainly not be taken to overrule the so-called "dragnet" cases under pre-Code law. Legitimate future advance arrangements are validated under the Code, as indeed they generally were under pre-Code law. This useful device can, however, be abused; it is abused when a lender, relying on a broadly drafted clause, seeks to bring within the shelter of his security arrangement claims against the debtor which are unrelated to the course of financing that was contemplated by the parties. In the dragnet cases, the courts have regularly curbed such abuses: no matter how the clause is drafted, the future advances, to be covered, must "be of the same class as the primary obligation . . . and so related to it that the consent of the debtor to its inclusion may be inferred."

2 GRANT GILMORE, SECURITY INTERESTS IN PERSONAL PROPERTY 932 (1965).

An Official Comment to the Revised Code rejects these tests of "similarity" and "relatedness." *See* UCC § 9-204 cmt. 5. Why?

3. Multiple State Transactions

Michelosen and Marty Sixt, chairman of PDF, are both California residents. They executed the second Financing Agreement in California and sent it to Iowa by courier. Does Iowa law or California law govern the Financing Agreement? UCC § 9-301 provides choice-of-law rules for the law governing perfection, its effect and priority [the 1972 Code also requires classification, here "ordinary" goods]. The Article 9 concept of "perfection" is explored in later materials. At this stage, you should note that the issue before the court is, at least initially, whether PDF has granted Michelosen an enforceable security interest. Or, in other words, the issue is whether the security interest has *attached. See* UCC § 9-203(a), (b).

If UCC § 9-301 is not relevant, does the Code provide any guidance? *See* UCC § 1-301.[54] In the absence of any indication that the Security Agreement had a choice-of-law clause, UCC § 1-301(d) states that the rights and obligations of the parties are determined by the law that would be selected by application of the state's conflict of laws principles. For the bankruptcy court sitting in Iowa, "this state" is Iowa, and therefore the court is bound to apply Iowa choice-of-law rules. To what state's law does that direct you? *See* Official Comment 7 to UCC § 1-301. What does this suggest?

But does any of this make any difference if both Iowa and California have enacted Article 9? What if the jurisdictions are Iowa and Canada? *See* UCC § 1-301(a) and (c)(2). Note that international secured transactions are addressed in Chapter 6.

4. Different Requirements for Descriptions of Collateral in Security Agreements and Financing Statements

A description of collateral in a financing statement as "all income" is too broad and generic under pre-revision Article 9 to sufficiently describe the collateral. *See Cottage Grove Hospital v. Glickman*, 38 UCC Rep. Serv. 2d 683 (Bankr. D. Oregon 1999). As noted later, Revised Article 9 would validate "all assets" or "all personal property" supergeneric type descriptions of collateral such as "all income" in a financing statement, but explicitly invalidates their use in a security agreement.

---

[54] No jurisdiction except the U.S. Virgin Islands enacted § 1-301. Accordingly, the Permanent Editorial Board of the U.C.C. recommended that § 1-301 be redone to be the same as old 1-105. The NCCUSL did so in 2008.

a.   Pre-Revision Article 9

Holding the "all income" financing statement description of collateral invalid in *Cottage Grove*, the Court relied on former UCC § 9-402(1), which provided in part that "[a] financing statement is *sufficient* if it . . . contains a statement indicating the types, or describing the items, of collateral" (emphasis supplied), and former UCC § 9-110, which provided that a "description of personal property or real estate is sufficient whether or not it is specific if it *reasonably identifies what is described.*" (Emphasis supplied).

The court reasoned that the term "all income" might be understood to describe "proceeds" of collateral and noted that "proceeds" is broadly defined in former UCC § 9-306(1) as *"whatever is received* upon . . . disposition of collateral . . . ."* (emphasis supplied). Unable to find any case ruling directly on whether an "all income" description of collateral in the financing statement constitutes a sufficient description, the court also equated the concepts of "all income" and "all personal property." It then concluded that an "all income" description like an "all personal property" description is too broad and generic to sufficiently describe collateral as required by former UCC §§ 9-402(1) and 9-110 for the purpose of a UCC financing statement.

In so ruling, the court also relied on *In Re Boogie Enterprises, Inc.*, 866 F.2d 1172 (9th Cir. 1989), which held that a financing statement describing collateral as "all personal property" was not sufficient to perfect a security interest in the proceeds of the settlement of a lawsuit. The *Boogie* court stated:

> The purpose of the financing statement is to put subsequent creditors on notice that the debtor's property is encumbered. . . .

* * *

> If the language, "personal property," were sufficient to perfect a security interest, creditors would never need to use any other language to designate collateral. This is plainly at odds with § 9-402's policy of requiring disclosure to potential creditors of the nature of encumbered collateral.

The *Cottage Grove* case prompts consideration of the different two-tiered systems in pre-revision and Revised Article 9 differentiating requirements for describing collateral in a security agreement and a financing statement.

Pre-revision UCC § 9-203(1) sets forth the conditions which must be met for a security agreement to become enforceable and attach, providing in part that the security agreement must contain a "description" of the collateral. UCC § 9-402(1) [*see* Revised §§ 9-502 and 9-504], as noted above, requires the financing statement to contain "a statement indicating the types or describing the items of collateral." The "reasonably identifies what is described" standard, which is to be applied in determining what constitutes a "sufficient" description in security agreements and financing statements, was set forth in UCC § 9-110.

The case law is in general agreement that these statutory provisions (*i.e.*, UCC §§ 9-203(1), 9-402(1) [now §§ 9-502 and 9-504], and 9-110 [now § 9-108]) required greater specificity in the security agreement than in the financing statement.

Courts have noted that this greater specificity is required in the security agreement because the purpose of the security agreement is to set forth the terms of the agreement between the parties and in particular to specify the collateral on which the creditor can foreclose in the event of default by the debtor. On the other hand, the purpose of the financing statement is merely to put the general public on notice of a possible security interest and prompt further investigation of whether a security interest in the debtor's property actually exists. Accordingly, under the former UCC § 9-110 requirement that to be "sufficient" a description of collateral must "reasonably identify what is described," courts interpreting former Article 9 required greater specificity in the security agreement than in the financing statement.

b. Revised Article 9 (1998)

Revised Article 9 also contains a two-tiered system for description of collateral requiring greater specifically in security agreements than in financing statements. Revised UCC § 9-203 continues to provide that a security agreement must contain a "description" of the collateral. In defining what constitutes a *"sufficient description"* of collateral, UCC § 9-108 retains in § 9-108(a) the "reasonably identifies what is described" requirement of § 9-110 of the former Code. However, UCC § 9-108(c) also explicitly provides that:

> A description of collateral as "all of the debtor's assets" or "all of the debtor's personal property" or using words of similar import does not reasonably identify the collateral.

However, regarding the description of collateral in a financing statement, UCC § 9-502 provides *inter alia* that a financing statement is sufficient if it *"indicates the collateral covered by the financing statement."* (Emphasis supplied.) UCC § 9-504 of Revised Article 9, entitled "Indication of Collateral," then further provides:

> A financing statement sufficiently indicates the collateral that it covers if the financing statement provides:
>
> (1)   a description of the collateral pursuant to § 9-108; or
>
> (2)   an indication that the financing statement covers all assets or all personal property.

Bottom Line: Under former Article 9, "All assets"/"All personal property" supergeneric type descriptions under most decisions are invalid in security agreements and financing statements. *But see In re Legal Data Systems, Inc.*, 135 B.R. 199 (D. Mass. 1991). A security agreement described the collateral as including "all of the Debtor's properties, assets and rights of every kind and nature, wherever located, whether now owned or hereafter acquired or arising, and all proceeds and products thereof, including, without limiting the generality of the foregoing: [generic categories]." The generic categories did not include "equipment, furnishings or fixtures." Judge Hillman noted that a majority of courts would not enforce super-generic collateral descriptions, such as "all goods." He wrote:

> The court has never understood the majority view. The statutory requirement is that a security agreement contain a description of the

collateral which reasonably identifies what is described. . . . One of the basic words in English is "all." It is actually easier to understand "all" than a compilation of all of the UCC generics. Why must a security agreement state 1+1+1 when 3 is easily understood?

Under Revised Article 9, "All assets"/"All personal property" supergeneric type descriptions are invalid in security agreements but valid in financing statements, certainly a political rather than a logical position. *See also* UCC § 9-108(e).

5.   Security Agreement: Description of Collateral

Problem 2-13:   Description of Collateral. The bank officer completes the fourth line of the security agreement with the following description of the collateral:

> all debtor's personal property, including inventory, equipment, accounts receivable, chattel paper, instruments, and general intangibles

Before signing the agreement, Mr. Clemens asks you to evaluate this description. He reminds you that the principal asset of the sole proprietorship is a printing machine, but its other assets include numerous smaller machines and other printing equipment, an inventory of paper products, and outstanding accounts receivable. He also notes that the business is conducted in premises leased for a five-year term, with 40 months remaining in the lease's term. Reread UCC § 9-108, and then advise Mr. Clemens.

6.   Time of Attachment and Enforceability

Problem 2-14:   Time of Attachment and Enforceability. Samuel Clemens signs the loan documents on September 1 and the bank credits his account with the amount of the loan on the same day. After these acts, does the bank have an attached and enforceable security interest in the collateral described in the security agreement? *See* UCC § 9-203(b). Exactly when does the security interest become attached and enforceable? When, if ever, would the parties postpone the time of attachment? *See* UCC § 9-203(a).

7.   Personal Property Lease

If the security agreement uses the description of the collateral set out in Problem 2-13, does the bank have a security interest in Mr. Clemens' interest as lessee? Is Mr. Clemens' interest in the lease an interest in "personal property," "other than" one of the other types of personal property covered by Article 9? *See* UCC § 9-102(a)(42), and all the definitions for the list of types of personal property. Note the definition in UCC § 9-102(a)(42), which states:

> "General intangibles" means any personal property, including things in action other than accounts, chattel paper, commercial tort claims, deposit accounts, documents, goods, instruments, investment property, letter-of-credit rights, letters of credit, money, and oil, gas, or other minerals before extraction.

8. Fixtures

Problem 2-15:   **Fixtures.** Assume Mr. Clemens owns the printing press but that under non-Code Texas law the press is a fixture. May Mr. Clemens grant the bank a security interest in the printing press? *See* UCC §§ 9-102(a)(41), 9-109(d)(11), 9-108, 9-203(b)(3), 9-334. If the security agreement uses the formula set out in Problem 2-13, does the bank have a security interest in the press? If not, what description would you propose?

Fixtures are a sub-category of *goods* listed in UCC § 9-102(a)(44), 9-102(a)(41):

> They are goods that have "become so related to particular real estate that an interest in them arises under real estate law." *See* UCC §§ 9-102(a)(41). The Code provides little further guidance. "Ordinary building materials incorporated into an improvement" are real property interests and not fixtures. *See* UCC § 9-334(a). On the other hand, property may be a fixture even if its removal would cause material injury to the freehold. *See* UCC § 9-604. As for the non-Code definitions of *fixtures*, most commentators agree that the case law even within a single jurisdiction is often unsettled. *See* RAY ANDREWS BROWN, THE LAW OF PERSONAL PROPERTY ch. 16 (Walter B. Raushenbush 3d ed. 1975) (confusion results from failure to distinguish the different contexts in which the issue is raised).

The subject of "Fixtures" is further addressed in Chapter 4, Section G.

9. "Accounts Receivable"; Proceeds

Problem 2-16:   **Accounts Receivable; Proceeds.** Mr. Clemens' sole proprietorship renders services and sells paper products from inventory for cash and on open account. Larger payments are usually made by check, which Mr. Clemens deposits in a business checking account at Steady State Bank. He also holds a promissory note made by a customer whose open account had become more than six months in arrears. May Mr. Clemens grant the bank a security interest in the open accounts, checks, deposit account, or the promissory note? If the security agreement uses the formula set out in Problem 2-13, *supra*, does the bank have a security interest in these items? If not, what description would you propose?

Are the open accounts (UCC § 9-102(a)(2)), checks (UCC § 9-102(a)(47)), deposit account (UCC § 9-102(a)(29)), and the promissory note (UCC § 9-102(a)(47)) types of personal property collateral covered by Article 9? *See* UCC § 9-109. Would the above types of collateral also qualify as "proceeds" [§ 9-102(a)(64)] under UCC § 9-315 (proceeds basically are "whatever is received upon the sale, exchange, collection, or other disposition of collateral or proceeds . . .").

Does a secured creditor with a security interest in "equipment . . . and proceeds thereof . . ." of a debtor operating video game machines and vending machines in an arcade have a security interest in the cash revenues generated by the machines? *See* UCC § 9-315. See also *In re S & J Holding Corporation, Shazamm Enterprises, Ltd.*, 42 B.R. 249 (S.D. Fla. 1984), holding that the cash received through such equipment is "not received from sale of the collateral, but rather, through the use of it." *But see* UCC § 9-102(a)(64)(B).

A special problem has arisen regarding insurance. Prior to 1972, case law was in conflict on the question of whether insurance payments covering loss or damage to collateral constituted "proceeds." *See, e.g., PPG Industries, Inc. v. Hartford Fire Insurance Co.*, 531 F.2d 58 (2d Cir. 1976) (insurance payments constitute proceeds); *Quigley v. Caron*, 247 A.2d 94 (Me. 1968) (insurance payments do not constitute proceeds). To resolve this conflict, the 1972 amendments to Article 9 of the Code explicitly provided that "proceeds" includes "insurance payable by reason of loss or damage to the collateral . . . except to the extent that it is payable to a person other than a party to the security agreement." *See also* UCC § 9-102(a)(64).

Students should also note that proceeds are sometimes referred to as "first generation, second generation, third generation, etc." If a car is sold for cash or is exchanged for a tractor, the cash and tractor constitute "first generation proceeds." If the cash or tractor is used to purchase a wagon, the wagon is "second generation proceeds," etc.

10.   Impact of Differing "Primary Use of Collateral"

Problem 2-17:   Impact of Differing "Primary Use of Collateral." Assume that Mr. Clemens owns a small truck for picking up supplies and delivering completed orders to customers. Will the bank have a security interest in the truck if the security agreement describes the collateral as "all debtor's personal property, including inventory, equipment, accounts receivable, chattel paper, instruments, and general intangibles"?

Would your answer be different if Mr. Clemens also uses the truck to carpool his daughter to school and soccer practice, a use that constitutes approximately twenty percent (20%) of the mileage and time the truck is in use?

Would the result be different if Mr. Clemens used the truck 60% of the time for his personal use and 40% for his business use? What adjustment in the description of the collateral in the security agreement would you propose if the truck is not covered?

See UCC §§ 9-109(a)(1) [Scope], 9-102(a)(33) [Equipment], 9-102(a)(44) [Goods], 9-102(a)(48) [Inventory], 9-102(a)(34) [Farm Products], 9-102(a)(23) [Consumer Goods].

Chapter 3

DEFAULT, REPOSSESSION, AND DISPOSITION

A. DEFAULT

1. Defining Default

No creditor likes to see its debtor default. Unfortunately, debtors do default, and creditors must plan for this contingency. The default provisions in Part 6 of Article 9 seek to minimize the loss to the secured party and at the same time protect the debtor from overreaching by the secured party. A representative sampling of problems that arise on default follows.

To understand what constitutes default, you should bear in mind two points. First, default is not defined in the UCC and must be derived from the security agreement. The definitions of security interests and security agreement include a failure to make payments when due. The secured party will also usually include in the security agreement a detailed definition of "default" listing events that constitute default.

Second, regardless of whether the security interest is perfected, upon default a secured party has available against the debtor all the Code's remedies. *See* § 9-601. In particular, the secured creditor acquires the right to repossess the collateral and dispose of it in a reasonably commercial manner to satisfy payment of the indebtedness owed by the debtor. *See* § 9-609.

> **Example: Repossession and Disposition of Collateral After Default.**
> Dealer sells a washing machine to Buyer, who makes a down payment and agrees to pay the balance in 24 monthly installments. The security agreement provides that if Buyer does not pay an installment when due, the debtor will be in default and Dealer shall have the rights of a secured party under the Uniform Commercial Code. After five monthly payments, Buyer fails to make a payment. Dealer repossesses the washing machine, accelerates payment of the remaining installments (note the security agreement must allow this—the statute does not provide this right), gives notice to Buyer that secured party plans to sell it by private sale after two weeks, sells it in a commercially reasonable manner, and claims a deficiency (i.e., the difference between what is owed to Dealer, including repossession and resale expenses, and what was received by Dealer from disposition of the washing machine). Buyer is responsible for the deficiency.[1]

---

[1] Note the protections the Code provides Buyer. There are limits on permissible contract clauses limiting or waiving Dealer's responsibilities in the default proceedings. *See* UCC §§ 9-602, 9-603.

The Uniform Commercial Code does not define default. Some solace can be obtained from UCC § 1-201(b)(35), which provides in part that "Security Interest" means an interest in personal property which "secures payment or performance of an obligation." The parties to a security agreement are free to define default (i.e., the nature of the obligation to be performed) subject only to the good faith obligation of UCC § 1-304 and the limitations of UCC § 9-609. Should the drafters have made an attempt? Is it relevant that Article 9 focuses on the agreement creating the security interest and not on the obligation secured?

A secured party may foreclose on collateral when the debtor is in default under a security agreement. *See* UCC § 9-601(a)(1). UCC § 9-609 provides that a secured party has on default the right to take possession of the collateral.

Failure to make payment when due under the security agreement is the most obvious and frequently used default provision. When drafting a security agreement, the secured party should consider also including some of the following conditions to serve as grounds for default if not performed by the debtor:

(a)   Submission of certified financial statements.

(b)   Maintenance of minimal levels of inventory.

(c)   Maintenance of equipment and other properties in good condition and repair.

(d)   Maintenance of insurance, with loss payee clauses.

(e)   Payment of all taxes when due.

(f)   Keeping of accurate and complete records.

(g)   Notification of any pertinent litigation.

(h)   Access to income tax returns.

(i)   Notification of any change of address or location.

(j)   Change of name, or entry into any merger, consolidation, or reorganization.

(k)   Sale, transfer, lease or disposition of substantial part of assets.

(l)   Creation of any security interest in or lien upon any asset.

(m)   Incurring of indebtedness, whether absolute or contingent.

(n)   Disposing of assets other than in the ordinary course of business.

A security agreement may also contain an acceleration clause. This clause gives the secured party the option to demand all sums due and owing at the time of the

---

Likewise, repossession must not breach the peace. *See* UCC § 9-609. After default, Buyer has the right to redeem the washing machine by tendering the total amount owed to Dealer. *See* UCC § 9-623(a), (b). If Dealer proposes to keep the washing machine in satisfaction of the amount owed ("strict foreclosure"), Buyer may force Dealer to sell the machine in the hope of realizing a surplus to be turned over to Buyer. *See* UCC § 9-620. Disposition of the washing machine requires that prior notice be given to Buyer and that all actions be taken in a commercially reasonable manner. *See* UCC §§ 9-611(b), (c), 9-610(b). Buyer may restrain Dealer or recover damages and perhaps be relieved of a deficiency if Dealer does not comply with the Code provisions. *See* UCC § 9-625(b).

debtor's default or whenever the secured party "deems himself insecure." Enforcement of such a latter term is limited by the requirement in UCC § 1-304 of good faith.

2.   Prototype Transaction

As we shall see in the later phases of the prototype transaction, Samuel Clemens' printing business prospers. However, for the purposes of analyzing "default" and the legal consequences of default, we frame the following problems on the assumption that Mr. Clemens has taken actions that might constitute default. To answer the following questions, you should reread the security agreement set out in Chapter 2, Section A.1., *supra* (hereafter Loan Security Agreement), of these materials and read Part 6 of Article 9.

Problem 3-1:   Other Security Interests. One month after Samuel Clemens enters into the secured loan agreement, he purchases a photocopy machine from an office supplier on credit. Under the agreement with the supplier, Mr. Clemens agrees to make payments in 36 monthly installments and he grants the supplier a security interest in the machine to secure these payments. Does the Steady State Bank have a security interest in the photocopy machine? (*See* § 9-204(a)). Has Mr. Clemens defaulted under the security agreement with the bank? *See* Loan Security Agreement, *supra*, V. Events of Default, (1) and (4); and III. Warranties and Covenants, (1). UCC § 9-204.

If Mr. Clemens had purchased the same machine on the same terms one month before he concluded the secured loan agreement with the bank, would Mr. Clemens be in default under the security agreement immediately after the security agreement becomes enforceable? Would your answer be different if the bank's loan officer knew about the earlier security interest and made no comment to Mr. Clemens? *See* Loan Security Agreement, *supra*, V. Events of Default, (1) and III. Warranties and Covenants, (1).

Problem 3-2:   Insurance. At the time Samuel Clemens enters into the secured loan agreement, he shows the bank's loan officer an insurance policy insuring the tangible assets of the sole proprietorship against fire, theft, and other losses in the amount of $100,000. This policy names Mr. Clemens as the beneficiary. The loan officer makes a notation in the file indicating that the policy has been shown to her. She does not, however, ask Mr. Clemens to provide a certificate or amended policy naming the bank as a co-beneficiary. Mr. Clemens does not subsequently arrange for an amended policy but does continue to pay the premiums on the original insurance policy. At no time does the bank's loan officer ask about the insurance policy. *See* Loan Security Agreement, *supra*, V. Events of Default, (1) and III. Warranties and Covenants, (3).

Assume that the bank officer reviews the file 12 months after the security agreement was executed. She asks your advice on the following questions: Has Mr. Clemens defaulted under the security agreement with Steady State Bank? Has the bank waived its right to insist upon being given an insurance policy or certificate naming it as a co-beneficiary? *See* Loan Security Agreement, *supra*, VII. Anti-Waiver Clause. If she does not wish to declare Mr. Clemens in default, what should she do?

Problem 3-3: Change of Location of Collateral. Eighteen months after Samuel Clemens entered into the secured loan agreement, the printing press begins to show signs of wearing out. After attempting some repairs, the manufacturer of the press examines it and decides to remove it to its own premises so that it can work on it more easily. If Mr. Clemens does not tell Steady State Bank that the press has been removed from the sole proprietorship's premises, has he defaulted under the security agreement? Would your answer be different if the manufacturer merely removed key components of the press? In any event, has Mr. Clemens defaulted if he tells the bank's loan officer of the removal and the officer says nothing? *See* Loan Security Agreement, *supra*, V. Events of Default, (2) and III. Warranties and Covenants, (7).

Problem 3-4: Disposition of Collateral. Assume that the manufacturer of the printing press in the preceding problem concludes that it cannot repair the printing press. The manufacturer advises Mr. Clemens to purchase a new printing press and offers to take the old printing press as a trade-in at a valuation reflecting its value as scrap. If Mr. Clemens agrees but does not tell Steady State Bank about the exchange, has he defaulted under the security agreement? Would your answer be different if the manufacturer retains a security interest in the new printing press? *See* Loan Security Agreement, *supra*, V. Events of Default, (1) and III. Warranties and Covenants, (1). If Mr. Clemens tells the bank loan officer about the exchange and she agrees to the exchange, what steps, if any, should the officer take to protect the bank's security interest? *See* UCC § 9-339.

Problem 3-5: Change in Debtor. Assume that thirty months after he enters into the secured loan agreement with Steady State Bank, Samuel Clemens agrees to create a general partnership with his brother, Mark, to run the printing business. Samuel would transfer the assets of the sole proprietorship to the general partnership and would manage the day-to-day operations of the business. Mark would contribute $5,000 to the partnership's assets. Mark would also handle sales promotion and keep the accounts of the business. The partnership would continue to run the printing business under the trade name, Apex Printing. By agreeing to this partnership without consulting the bank, has Samuel Clemens defaulted under the security agreement with the bank? If, upon being consulted, the bank agrees to the new arrangement, what modifications, if any, should be made to the original secured loan agreement? *See* Loan Security Agreement, *supra*; UCC § 9-203(d), (e).

Problem 3-6: Options Upon Default. Assume that Steady State Bank's loan officer concludes that Samuel Clemens has defaulted in any of the previous problems. She directs the bank's attorney to enforce the note by a court proceeding. The attorney files a law suit against Mr. Clemens to enforce the note and Mr. Clemens defends by denying default. The loan officer now asks if the bank can proceed to repossess the collateral. Advise her. *See* UCC § 9-601. On the options available to a secured creditor, you may also wish to consult JAMES J. WHITE & ROBERTS S. SUMMERS, UNIFORM COMMERCIAL CODE § 25-4 (5th ed. 2000).

3. Cumulative and Simultaneous Remedies on Default

What legal alternatives do the parties have after default? The Code contemplates that the parties may go to court rather than use self-help repossession. *See* UCC § 9-627(c)(1). A judicial action might seek (a) a judgment on the underlying obligation, followed by issuance of a writ of execution, levy, and a judicial sale; (b) judicial foreclosure of the security interest; or (c) a judgment in a replevin action whereby the secured party obtains possession of the collateral. In *Spillers, infra,* what did the secured party seek? Why would a secured party ever choose to go to court rather than pursue self-help repossession under the Code?

SPILLERS v. FIRST NATIONAL BANK OF ARENZVILLE
Illinois Appellate Court
400 N.E.2d 1057 (1980)

WEBBER, JUSTICE:

* * *

The background, as revealed in the record, indicates that petitioner on March 14, 1977, borrowed $25,000 from respondent and gave a judgment note therefor. The purpose of the loan was to purchase a crane which [served] as collateral [securing repayment] and petitioner added to the crane a set of concrete forms which were about 2 years old at the time.

The note was for six months' duration and at the end of that time respondent demanded payment. None was made and the duration, by agreement, was extended for 30 days. At the end of that extension, no payment having been made, respondent placed the note in judgment on December 13, 1977. This judgment was confirmed on January 27, 1978, and thereafter respondent brought citation proceedings to enforce it.

Apparently as a result of the citation proceedings, petitioner turned the crane and the forms over to respondent who proceeded to sell them. One of the principal issues in this appeal is the nature and timeliness of the notice given to petitioner of the sales of the collateral.

On March 7, 1978, petitioner's attorney received a letter from respondent's attorney stating that respondent had received a bid of $15,000 for the crane and it would be sold "[T]en days from the receipt of this notice * * * as per our agreement of February 2, 1978." Petitioner replied to this by submitting an offer of $16,000 for the crane through a corporation owned and operated by him. Respondent replied to this offer by asserting three conditions: (1) that a cashier's check for $16,000 be tendered within four days; (2) that petitioner's concrete forms be tendered to respondent at the time the crane was picked up; and (3) that petitioner sign a waiver of any and all rights in the crane, including the right to object to the sale and to exercise any right of redemption. Plaintiff felt unable to meet these conditions and all negotiations and communications between the parties then ceased.

Respondent on April 22, 1978, sold the crane to the $15,000 bidder without making any further efforts to secure other bids. Five days later this bidder sold the crane to an equipment dealer in Aledo, Illinois, named Henderson. The price of this sale does not appear in the record. On November 3, 1978, Henderson sold the crane for $27,500 to a contractor in Iowa, named Hall. At trial on May 4, 1979, Hall testified that the crane was worth all he had paid for it and that he had it for sale at a price of $35,000.

Respondent next proceeded to sell the concrete forms. One bid was received from a contractor who had his own forms mixed in with petitioner's forms on a job site. Another bid, $500 higher, was received from another contractor but was afterwards withdrawn because that bidder was unable to determine which of the intermingled forms he was bidding on. Respondent then sold the forms for $6,120 to the other bidder. It is uncontroverted that petitioner knew of the impending sale of the forms generally, but had no specific knowledge until later.

After both sales had been consummated, the crane and the forms, a deficiency of approximately $6,500 existed on the judgment. Respondent collected this through various post-judgment proceedings. In the same cause, petitioner on October 13, 1978, filed a petition for damages against respondent in which he alleged that the sales of the crane and the forms were not commercially reasonable within the meaning of the Commercial Code. After a bench trial, the circuit court found that the sales were commercially reasonable and dismissed the petition for damages. This appeal followed. We reverse.

A preliminary question to be answered is whether this transaction is governed by the Commercial Code. Section 9-501(5),[2] [§ 9-601(e), (f) in the Revised Article 9] provides as follows:

> When a secured party has reduced his claim to judgment the lien of any levy which may be made upon his collateral by virtue of any execution based upon the judgment shall relate back to the date of the perfection of the security interest in such collateral. A judicial sale, pursuant to such execution, is a foreclosure of the security interest by judicial procedure within the meaning of this Section, and the secured party may purchase at the sale and thereafter hold the collateral free of any other requirements of this Article.

The Official Comments to this section read in part as follows:

> The second sentence of the subsection (i.e., (5)) makes clear that a judicial sale following judgment, execution and levy is one of the methods

---

[2] [UCC § 9-601(e) states in relevant part that:

If a secured party has reduced its claim to judgment, the lien of any levy that may be made upon the collateral by virtue of an execution based upon the judgment relates back to the earliest of:

    (1) the date of perfection of the security interest or agricultural lien in the collateral;

    (2) the date of filing a financing statement covering the collateral; or

    (3) any date specified in a statute under which the agricultural lien was created.

Subsection (f) adds that "[a] sale pursuant to an execution is a foreclosure of the security interest or agricultural lien by judicial procedure within the meaning of this section. A secured party may purchase at the sale and thereafter hold the collateral free of any other requirements of this article."—Eds.]

of foreclosure contemplated by subsection (1); such a sale is governed by other law and not by this Article * * *.

The Illinois Comments on section 9-501 in referring to subsection (5) have this to say:

> The last sentence of Official Comment 6 makes explicit what is implicit in this Section that a judicial sale following judgment, execution and levy is governed by other law, not by this Article. However, if a secured party repossesses collateral and also reduces his claim to judgment (whether concurrently or not) and if repossession involves taking possession of collateral in any way other than pursuant to an execution issued following a judgment, his repossession and disposition of the collateral will probably be subject to the requirements of this Part.

Ill. Ann. Stat., ch. 26, par. 9-501, at 320–21 (Smith-Hurd (1974)).

We find that the Illinois Comment quoted above accurately states the law and a plain reading of the statute leads inevitably to such a result. Judgment, execution and levy are ancient procedures in the law and are governed by their own statute which dates from the earliest days of this State. "An Act concerning judgments and executions" was approved February 17, 1823. It was later repealed by "[a]n Act concerning judgments and executions" approved January 17, 1825, which remained substantially unchanged until the general codification of the Illinois statutory law in 1872. The Act of 1872, now chapter 77, Illinois Revised Statutes 1977, pars. 1 through 68, has survived virtually unchanged for over 100 years, and is most explicit in its terms. The veriest tyro at the bar can recognize an execution sale.

On the other hand, if the procedure employed does not follow the dictates of chapter 77, it necessarily falls within the ambit of chapter 26, pars. 9-501 et seq. The secured judgment creditor has his choice: chapter 77 or chapter 26. The existence of the judgment is only the first step along either road. If the creditor elects chapter 77, he must then proceed to obtain a writ of execution, a levy and a sale. If he elects chapter 26, the latter are not involved and the existence of the judgment is immaterial. He may proceed with chapter 26 with or without a judgment.

In the instant case, respondent had already reduced his claim to judgment, but there is nothing in the record remotely resembling an execution sale under chapter 77. The petitioner turned the collateral over to the respondent who proceeded to make the sales on its own. No execution writ was ever delivered to a sheriff or other officer; no such officer ever advertised a sale; no such officer ever reported a sale. The instant case is clearly a disposition of collateral after default under section 9-503[3] notwithstanding the claim had already been reduced to judgment.

---

[3] [UCC § 9-609.]

NOTE ON PRACTICAL CONSIDERATIONS:
THE BUSINESS WORKOUT

Note the court's reference in *Spillers* to the 30-day extension. Did the secured party seek to enforce the judgment note immediately after the extension expired? Creditors are not always in a hurry to enforce legal rights; frequently they will negotiate with the debtor to adjust the underlying obligation. *See* Donald Lee Rome, The Business Workout—A Primer for Participating Creditors, 11 UCC L.J. 183 (1978). If creditors in a particular industry or locality usually seek an adjustment before commencing legal action or before repossessing collateral under Article 9, is failure to seek adjustment a violation of the Code's good faith requirements? *See* UCC §§ 1-304 and 9-102(a)(43). Does the custom become a term of the contract? *See* UCC § 1-303.

COMMENT ON JUDGMENT OR COGNOVIT NOTES

The Illinois Civil Practice Act deals specifically with the judgment note (known in some other jurisdictions as a "cognovit note"). *See* 735 Ill. Comp. Stat. § 5/2-1301(c) (1992) ("any person for a debt bona fide due may confess judgment by himself or attorney duly authorized, without process"). The Illinois statute was amended in 1979 to prohibit a judgment note in a "consumer transaction" as defined by the statute. Following a federal district court decision holding that garnishment invoked in a proceeding on a judgment note violated the due process clause of the Fourteenth Amendment, local court rules in at least some Illinois circuit courts were amended to require the judgment to be confirmed after service of process.

The Supreme Court invalidated a prejudgment wage garnishment statute as being unconstitutional in a due process attack. Anything short of providing preliminary notice and a hearing at which the creditor would have to demonstrate probable cause for the garnishment prior to seizure was said to constitute taking of property without due process of law. *See Sniadach v. Family Finance Corp.*, 395 U.S. 337 (1967).

The Fourteenth Amendment provides that "no state" shall deprive any person of "life, liberty, or property" without "due process of law." Courts have analyzed due process attacks on various forms of creditor relief. Accordingly, the Fourteenth Amendment has been found violated in circumstances in which each of the following questions was answered in the affirmative:

(a)   Was there sufficient "state action"?

(b)   Has the debtor been deprived of "life, liberty, or property"?

(c)   If the debtor has been so deprived, was the deprivation "without due process"?

For a discussion of the cases which have upheld the constitutionality of self-help repossession, *see* Louis F. Del Duca, *Prenotice, Prehearing, Prejudgment Seizure of Assets Revisited*, 7 UCC L.J. 341, 342 (1975).

The Federal Trade Commission has defined as an unfair credit practice any use of a cognovit or confession of judgment term in a consumer credit transaction. *See* 16 C.F.R. § 444.2(a)(1). State legislation may also limit the use of these terms, as the 1979 amendment to the Illinois law illustrates. Section 3-306 of the (1974) Uniform Consumer Credit Code, for example, prohibits a consumer from authorizing a party to confess judgment on a claim arising out of a consumer credit transaction.

The United States Supreme Court has upheld the constitutionality of the cognovit note. *See D.H. Overmyer Co. v. Frick Co.*, 405 U.S. 174 (1972) (a business corporation that signed a cognovit note with the advice of counsel "voluntarily, intelligently, and knowingly waived the rights it otherwise possessed to pre-judgment notice and hearing, and . . . did so with full awareness of the legal consequences"). The Court in *Overmyer* indicated, however, that it might reach a different conclusion if there was unequal bargaining power or overreaching. *See generally* Dan Hopson, Jr., Cognovit Judgments: An Ignored Problem of Due Process and Full Faith and Credit, 29 U. Chi. L. Rev. 111 (1961); Louis F. Del Duca, Prenotice, Prehearing, Prejudgment Seizure of Assets Revisited, 7 UCC L.J. 341, 342 (1975).

One commentator has summarized the business use of cognovit notes as follows:[4]

> The use of cognovit clauses by lenders and installment sellers seems to serve three classes of business purposes.
>
> First, the clauses can be so written as to facilitate debt-collection by including waivers of: procedural defects in the resulting judgment, the right of appeal from the resulting judgment, the right of inquisition, and the right to notice. Given such strictly written clauses, the process of debt-collection by judgment becomes an all but automatic process and presumably allows the economics of efficiency to lower the cost of credit.
>
> Second, it is possible—and indeed it is the practice in some states—to write the cognovit clause in such a way as to allow the entry of the confession of judgment before any default in payment. This leaves the need only for execution to be levied upon the debtor's property once the actual default in payment occurs. Thus the creditor has what amounts to a judgment lien on the property of the debtor for the life of the obligation. This device is often used in place of collateral from the debtor to secure his debt.
>
> The third purpose served by cognovit notes is that they can be used to retain personal jurisdiction over out of state debtors after they have left the state in which the note was signed or whose law governs the note.

Note, *Cognovit Judgments: Some Constitutional Considerations*, 70 Colum. L. Rev. 1118, 1130 (1970).

---

[4] The authors of the casebook have taken the liberty of paragraphing each of the three purposes listed.

B. REPOSSESSION—BREACH OF THE PEACE AND OTHER LIMITATIONS ON SELF-HELP REPOSSESSION

GILES v. FIRST VIRGINIA CREDIT SERVICES, INC.
North Carolina Court of Appeals
560 S.E.2d 557 (2002)

GEE, JUDGE.

Richard Giles and Joann Giles (plaintiffs) appeal the trial court's order granting First Virginia Credit Services, Inc.'s (First Virginia) motion for summary judgment in part.

Plaintiffs filed a complaint against defendants First Virginia and Professional Auto Recovery, Inc. (Professional Auto Recovery) for wrongful repossession of an automobile. Plaintiffs alleged in an amended complaint that: (1) First Virginia and Professional Auto Recovery wrongfully converted and/or repossessed the automobile and plaintiffs' personal property located within the automobile; (2) plaintiffs made a payment on the account which First Virginia accepted immediately prior to First Virginia's repossession of the automobile and which First Virginia subsequently cashed and applied to plaintiffs' account after the repossession; (3) removal of the automobile constituted breach of the peace in violation of N.C. Gen. Stat. § 25-9-503 [§ 9-609]; (4) N.C. Gen. Stat. § 25-9-503 [§ 9-609] is unconstitutional; and (5) First Virginia was negligent in hiring Professional Auto Recovery and committed unfair or deceptive trade practices entitling plaintiffs to treble damages.

First Virginia filed an answer stating the automobile was repossessed due to the default of Joann Giles in making the payments to First Virginia on a loan secured by the automobile. First Virginia stated that N.C. Gen. Stat. § 25-9-503 [§ 9-609] permitted a secured lender to peaceably repossess its collateral upon default by a debtor and that such repossession could not, as a matter of law, constitute conversion of the collateral or an unfair or deceptive trade practice. First Virginia moved to dismiss plaintiffs' complaint for failure to state a claim pursuant to N.C. Gen. Stat. § 1A-1, Rule 12(b)(6).

Joann Giles entered into an installment sale contract on or about 18 January 1997 for the purchase of an automobile. The contract was assigned to First Virginia, which obtained a senior perfected purchase money security interest in the automobile. The terms of the contract required Joann Giles to make sixty regular monthly payments to First Virginia. The contract stated that Joann Giles' failure to make any payment due under the contract within ten days after its due date would be a default. The contract contained an additional provision agreed to by Joann Giles that stated:

> If I am in default, you may consider all my remaining payments to be due and payable, without giving me notice. I agree that your rights of possession will be greater than mine. I will deliver the property to you at your request, or you may use lawful means to take it yourself without notice or other legal action. . . .

. . .

If you excuse one default by me, that will not excuse later defaults.

REPOSSESSION BY PROFESSIONAL AUTO RECOVERY

During the early morning hours of 27 June 1999, Professional Auto Recovery, at the request of First Virginia, repossessed the locked automobile from plaintiffs' front driveway. According to First Virginia, the account of Joann Giles was in arrears for payments due on 2 May 1999 and 2 June 1999, and pursuant to the terms of the contract, repossession was permitted.

In an affidavit filed by plaintiffs in opposition to First Virginia's motion for summary judgment, plaintiffs' neighbor, Glenn A. Mosteller (Mr. Mosteller), stated that he was awakened around 4:00am

> by the running of a loud diesel truck engine on the road outside my house. Evidentially [sic] the truck was stopped because I lay in bed for a while and did not get up. I then became concerned and went to the window to see what was going on. At this time I saw a large rollback diesel truck with a little pickup truck on the truck bed behind it. The truck only had its parking lights on. The truck . . . started going toward the Giles' yard. It still only had its parking lights on. About that time, a man jumped out of the truck and ran up the Giles' driveway. Their car was parked up at their house. Then the car came flying out back down the driveway making a loud noise and started screeching off. . . . At about the same time, the rollback also pulled off real fast making a real loud diesel noise and went down [the road]. . . . I got to the phone, called the Giles and told them someone was stealing their car. . . . My lights were on . . . and the Giles' lights were on and that portion of our neighborhood had woken up. Richard Giles came out in his yard and we hollared a few words back and forth and I jumped in my truck . . . to try to get the police. About 5 minutes later a police car came up and pulled into the Giles' yard. Then another police car came then a Sheriff's Deputy car came. Then another police car came. . . . There was a great commotion going on out in the street and in our yard all to the disturbance of the quietness and tranquility of our neighborhood. . . . It scared me and it scared the Giles.

Joann Giles stated in a deposition that she was awakened by Mr. Mosteller's telephone call in which he told her that someone was stealing her car. She stated she ran to see if the automobile was parked outside and confirmed that it was gone. Joann Giles testified she woke up her husband and gave him the telephone; he ran outside into the yard and heard Mr. Mosteller "hollering" at him from across the street. Plaintiffs testified in their depositions that neither of them saw the car being repossessed but were only awakened by their neighbor after the automobile was gone. During the actual repossession, no contact was made between Professional Auto Recovery and plaintiffs, nor between Professional Auto Recovery and Mr. Mosteller.

. . .

II.

By their first assignment of error, plaintiffs argue the trial court erred in granting in part First Virginia's motion for summary judgment dismissing plaintiffs' claim for wrongful conversion and/or repossession of their automobile. Plaintiffs specifically argue that (1) the determination of whether a breach of the peace occurred in violation of N.C. Gen. Stat. § 25-9-503 [§ 9-609] is a question for the jury and not one to be determined by summary judgment, and (2) there is a dispute as to whether plaintiffs were in default.

A.

Plaintiffs first argue the trial court erred in granting partial summary judgment to First Virginia because the issue of whether a breach of the peace occurred is a question for the jury.

["BREACH OF THE PEACE"—AN UNDEFINED TERM]

*   *   *

[REV. § 9-609]

N.C. Gen. Stat. § 25-9-503 [§ 9-609], at issue in this appeal, has been replaced by N.C. Gen. Stat. § 25-9-609 (Interim Supp. 2000) (Effective 1 July 2001), which states that a secured party, after default, may take possession of the collateral without judicial process, if the secured party proceeds without breach of the peace. In Number 3 of the Official Comment to the new statutory provision, our General Assembly continued to state that, "like former Section 9-503, this section does not define or explain the conduct that will constitute a breach of the peace, leaving that matter for continuing development by the courts." N.C.G.S. § 25-9-609. The General Assembly clearly may further define and/or limit the time, place and conditions under which a repossession is permitted, but it has not yet done so.

[JUDICIAL DEVELOPMENT OF "BREACH OF THE PEACE" STANDARDS]

In a pre-UCC case, Rea v. Credit Corp., 257 N.C. 639, 127 S.E.2d 225 (1962), a defaulting debtor left his locked automobile on his front lawn. An agent of the mortgagee went to the debtor's home to repossess the automobile, saw the automobile parked on the lawn, found no one at home, and asked a neighbor where the debtor was. The agent was told no one was at home and he thereafter opened the automobile door with a coat hanger and removed the automobile on a wrecker. Our Supreme Court found that this evidence could not warrant a finding by a jury that the mortgagee's agent wrongfully took possession of the automobile because no breach of the peace occurred. In Rea, although our Supreme Court did not define breach of the peace, it reiterated the common law rule that the right of self-help repossession "must be exercised without provoking a breach of the peace[.]" *Id.* at 641–42, 127 S.E.2d at 227. Our Supreme Court thought the law "well stated" by the South Carolina Supreme Court in the case of Willis v. Whittle, that

> "if the mortgagee finds that he cannot get possession without committing a breach of the peace, he must stay his hand, and resort to the law, for the preservation of the public peace is of more importance to society than the right of the owner of a chattel to get possession of it."

Rea, 257 N.C. at 641–42, 127 S.E.2d at 227 (quoting *Willis v. Whittle*, 82 S.C. 500, 64 S.E. 410 (1909)).

[PRIOR NOTICE AND CONFRONTATION ISSUES]

In a case addressing the issue of whether prior notice of repossession is required under N.C. Gen. Stat. § 25-9-503 [§ 9-609], our Court stated that repossession can be accomplished under the statute without prior notice so long as the repossession is peaceable. *Everett v. U.S. Life Credit Corp.*, 74 N.C. App. 142, 144, 327 S.E.2d 269, 269 (1985). Without specifically defining breach of the peace, our Court explained that "of course, if there is confrontation at the time of the attempted repossession, the secured party must cease the attempted repossession and proceed by court action in order to avoid a 'breach of the peace.' " *Id.* at 144, 327 S.E.2d at 270. This indicates, as argued by First Virginia, that confrontation is at least an element of a breach of the peace analysis.

[DEFINING "BREACH OF THE PEACE"]

In that breach of the peace has not heretofore been clarified by our appellate courts, but instead only vaguely referred to, we must construe this term as the drafters intended. "In construing statutes the court should always give effect to the legislative intent." *Electric Service v. City of Rocky Mount*, 20 N.C. App. 347, 348, 201 S.E.2d 508, 509, aff'd, 285 N.C. 135, 203 S.E.2d 838 (1974). "The intent of the Legislature may be ascertained from the phraseology of the statute as well as the nature and purpose of the act and the consequences which would follow from a construction one way or another." *Campbell v. Church*, 298 N.C. 476, 484, 259 S.E.2d 558, 564 (1979). In determining what conduct constitutes a breach of the peace we consider each of these contributing elements.

[DICTIONARY AND AM. JUR. DEFINITIONS]

The phrase "breach of the peace" is defined in Black's Law Dictionary as the "criminal offense of creating a public disturbance or engaging in disorderly conduct, particularly by an unnecessary or distracting noise." Black's Law Dictionary 183 (7th ed. 1999). The phrase is also commonly understood to mean a "violation of the public order as amounts to a disturbance of the public tranquility, by act or conduct either directly having this effect, or by inciting or tending to incite such a disturbance of the public tranquility." 12 Am. Jur. 2d Breach of Peace § 5 (1997).

[CRIMINAL LAW DEFINITION]

In a criminal case, our Supreme Court defined breach of the peace as "a disturbance of public order and tranquility by act or conduct not merely amounting to unlawfulness but tending also to create public tumult and incite others to break the peace." *State v. Mobley*, 240 N.C. 476, 482, 83 S.E.2d 100, 104 (1954). *See also Perry v. Gibson*, 247 N.C. 212, 100 S.E.2d 341 (1957) (wrongful death case stating the same definition for breach of the peace). Such " '[a] breach of the peace may be occasioned by an affray or assault, by the use of profane and abusive language by one person toward another on a public street and in the presence of others, or by a person needlessly shouting and making loud noise.' " *Mobley*, 240 N.C. at 482, 83 S.E.2d at 104 (quoting 4 Am. Jur. Arrest § 30). A breach of the peace, as used in Chapter 19 of our General Statutes, entitled "Offenses Against Public Morals," is defined as "repeated acts that disturb the public order including, but not limited to, homicide, assault, affray, communicating threats, unlawful possession of dangerous or deadly weapons, and discharging firearms." N.C. Gen. Stat. § 19-1.1(1) (1999).

[RELEVANCE OF § 1-102 LIBERAL CONSTRUCTION AND UNIFORMITY POLICIES]

We must also consider the nature and purpose of Chapter 25 of the North Carolina General Statutes, the UCC, which is to be "liberally construed and applied to promote its underlying purposes and policies." N.C. Gen. Stat. § 25-1-102 (1999). Its stated purposes are:

a) to simplify, clarify and modernize the law governing commercial transactions;

b) to permit the continued expansion of commercial practices through custom, usage and agreement of the parties;

c) to make uniform the law among the various jurisdictions.

Id.

In carrying out the policy of uniformity with other jurisdictions, we consider their treatment of the term of breach of the peace. While cases from other jurisdictions are not binding on our courts, they provide insight into how this term has been analyzed by other courts and therefore are instructive.

[INCITEMENT TO VIOLENCE STANDARD]

The courts in many states have examined whether a breach of the peace in the context of the UCC has occurred. Courts have found a breach of the peace when actions by a creditor incite violence or are likely to incite violence. *Birrell v. Indiana Auto Sales & Repair*, 698 N.E.2d 6, 8 (Ind. App. 1998) (a creditor cannot use threats, enter a residence without debtor's consent and cannot seize property over a debtor's objections); *Wade v. Ford Motor Credit Co.*, 668 P.2d 183, 189 (Kan. App. 1983) (a breach of the peace may be caused by an act likely to produce violence); *Morris v. First National Bank & Trust Co. of Ravena*, 254 N.E.2d 683, 686–87 (Ohio

1970) (a physical confrontation coupled with an oral protest constitutes a breach of the peace).

[CONFLICT IN "ORAL PROTEST" CASES]

Other courts have expanded the phrase breach of the peace beyond the criminal law context to include occurrences where a debtor or his family protest the repossession. *Fulton v. Anchor Sav. Bank*, FSB, 452 S.E.2d 208, 213 (Ga. App. 1994) (a breach of the peace can be created by an unequivocal oral protest); *Census Federal Credit Union v. Wann*, 403 N.E.2d 348, 352 (Ind. App. 1980) ("if a repossession is . . . contested at the actual time . . . of the attempted repossession by the defaulting party or other person in control of the chattel, the secured party must desist and pursue his remedy in court"); *Hollibush v. Ford Motor Credit Co.*, 508 N.W.2d 449, 453–55 (Wis. App. 1993) (in the face of an oral protest the repossessing creditor must desist). Some courts, however, have determined that a mere oral protest is not sufficient to constitute a breach of the peace. *Clarin v. Minnesota Repossessors, Inc.*, 198 F.3d 661, 664 (8th Cir. 1999) (oral protest, followed by pleading with repossessors in public parking lot does not rise to level of breach of the peace); *Chrysler Credit Corp. v. Koontz*, 661 N.E.2d 1171, 1173–74 (Ill. App. 1996) (yelling "Don't take it" is insufficient).

[UNAUTHORIZED BREAKING AND ENTERING]

If a creditor removes collateral by an unauthorized breaking and entering of a debtor's dwelling, courts generally hold this conduct to be a breach of the peace. *Davenport v. Chrysler Credit Corp.*, 818 S.W.2d 23, 29 (Tenn. App. 1991) and *General Elec. Credit Corp. v. Timbrook*, 291 S.E.2d 383, 385 (W. Va. 1982) (both cases stating that breaking and entering, despite the absence of violence or physical confrontation, is a breach of the peace). Removal of collateral from a private driveway, without more however, has been found not to constitute a breach of the peace. *Hester v. Bandy*, 627 So.2d 833, 840 (Miss. 1993). Additionally, noise alone has been determined to not rise to the level of a breach of the peace. Ragde v. Peoples Bank, 767 P.2d 949, 951 (Wash. App. 1989) (unwilling to hold that making noise is an act likely to breach the peace).

Many courts have used a balancing test to determine if a repossession was undertaken at a reasonable time and in a reasonable manner, and to balance the interests of debtors and creditors. *See e.g., Clarin v. Minnesota Repossessors, Inc.*, 198 F.3d 661, 664 (8th Cir. 1999); *Davenport v. Chrysler Credit Corp.*, 818 S.W.2d 23, 29 (Tenn. App. 1991). Five relevant factors considered in this balancing test are: "(1) where the repossession took place, (2) the debtor's express or constructive consent, (3) the reactions of third parties, (4) the type of premises entered, and (5) the creditor's use of deception." *Davenport*, 818 S.W.2d at 29 (citing 2 J. White & R. Summers, Uniform Commercial Code § 27-6, at 575–76 (3d ed. 1988)).

[THE INSTANT CASE INVOLVED NO NOTICE, NON-CONFRONTATIONAL, CLANDESTINE, AFTER MIDNIGHT REPOSSESSION]

Relying on the language of our Supreme Court in *Rea*, plaintiffs argue that the "guiding star" in determining whether a breach of the peace occurred should be whether or not the public peace was preserved during the repossession. *Rea*, 257 N.C. at 641–42, 127 S.E.2d at 228. Plaintiffs contend "the elements as to what constitutes a breach of the peace should be liberally construed" and urge our Court to adopt a subjective standard considering the totality of the circumstances as to whether a breach of the peace occurred.

Plaintiffs claim that adopting a subjective standard for N.C. Gen. Stat. § 25-9-503 [§ 9-609] cases will protect unwitting consumers from the "widespread use of no notice repossessions, clandestine and after midnight repossessions" and will protect "our State's commitment to law and order and opposition to vigilante policies, opposition to violence and acts from which violence could reasonably flow[.]" If a lender is not held to such a high subjective standard, plaintiffs contend that self-help repossessions should be disallowed altogether.

First Virginia, in contrast, argues that a breach of the peace did not occur in this case, as a matter of law, because there was no confrontation between the parties. Therefore, because the facts in this case are undisputed concerning the events during the actual repossession of the automobile, the trial court did not err in its partial grant of summary judgment.

First Virginia disputes plaintiffs' contention that a determination of whether a breach of the peace occurred should be a wholly subjective standard, because if such a standard is adopted, every determination of whether a breach of the peace occurred would hereafter be a jury question and "would run directly contrary to the fundamental purpose of the Uniform Commercial Code, which is to provide some degree of certainty to the parties engaging in various commercial transactions." Further, First Virginia argues that applying a subjective standard to a breach of the peace analysis could be detrimental to borrowers, with lenders likely increasing the price of credit to borrowers to cover the costs of having to resort to the courts in every instance to recover their collateral upon default. The standard advocated by plaintiffs would "eviscerate" the self-help rights granted to lenders by the General Assembly, leaving lenders "with no safe choice except to simply abandon their 'self help' rights altogether, since every repossession case could [result] in the time and expense of a jury trial on the issue of 'breach of the peace[.]' " Finally, First Virginia argues that a subjective standard would be detrimental to the judicial system as a whole because "with a case-by-case, wholly subjective standard . . . the number of lawsuits being filed over property repossessions could increase dramatically[.]"

[ARTICLE 9 BREACH OF THE PEACE BROADER THAN CRIMINAL LAW DEFINITION]

Based upon our review of our appellate courts' treatment of breach of the peace in pre-UCC and UCC cases, as well as in other areas of the law, the purposes and policies of the UCC, and the treatment other jurisdictions have given the phrase, we find that a breach of the peace, when used in the context of N.C. Gen. Stat. § 25-9-503 [§ 9-609], is broader than the criminal law definition. A confrontation is not always required, but we do not agree with plaintiffs that every repossession should be analyzed subjectively, thus bringing every repossession into the purview of the jury so as to eviscerate the self-help rights duly given to creditors by the General Assembly. Rather, a breach of the peace analysis should be based upon the reasonableness of the time and manner of the repossession. We therefore adopt a balancing test using the five factors discussed above to determine whether a breach of the peace occurs when there is no confrontation.

In applying these factors to the undisputed evidence in the case before us, we affirm the trial court's determination that there was no breach of the peace, as a matter of law. Professional Auto Recovery went onto plaintiffs' driveway in the early morning hours, when presumably no one would be outside, thus decreasing the possibility of confrontation. Professional Auto Recovery did not enter into plaintiffs' home or any enclosed area. Consent to repossession was expressly given in the contract with First Virginia signed by Joann Giles. Although a third party, Mr. Mosteller, was awakened by the noise of Professional Auto Recovery's truck, Mr. Mosteller did not speak with anyone from Professional Auto Recovery, nor did he go outside until Professional Auto Recovery had departed with the Giles' automobile. Further, neither of the plaintiffs were awakened by the noise of the truck, and there was no confrontation between either of them with any representative of Professional Auto Recovery. By the time Mr. Mosteller and plaintiffs went outside, the automobile was gone. Finally, there is no evidence, nor did plaintiffs allege, that First Virginia or Professional Auto Recovery employed any type of deception when repossessing the automobile.

There is no factual dispute as to what happened during the repossession in this case, and the trial court did not err in granting summary judgment to First Virginia on this issue.

[DEFAULT ISSUE]

B.

Plaintiffs next argue there was a factual dispute over whether or not a default occurred in the repayment of the note and therefore summary judgment was improper.

. . .

The trial court found, and we agree, that there is no genuine issue of material fact as to whether Joann Giles' account was in default when the automobile was repossessed. The trial court did not err in granting summary judgment to First Virginia on this issue.

Plaintiffs' first assignment of error is overruled.

III.

[CONSTITUTIONAL ISSUES]

Plaintiffs next argue that the provisions of N.C. Gen. Stat. § 25-9-503 [§ 9-609] granting a secured party the right to take possession of collateral without judicial process, without notice and/or a right to be heard, are unconstitutional as applied to the facts in this case. They further argue that the waiver of notice in the contract Joann Giles signed with First Virginia deprived her of her constitutional rights under the Fourteenth Amendment to the United States Constitution.

Plaintiffs claim that the statutory scheme providing for non-judicial repossession under N.C. Gen. Stat. § 25-9-503 [§ 9-609] constitutes state action sufficient to evoke the protection of the due process clause of the Fourteenth Amendment of the United States Constitution. As support for their position, plaintiffs rely on *Turner v. Blackburn*, 389 F. Supp. 1250 (W.D.N.C. 1975). Turner, however, is distinguishable from the case before us because in Turner, the court's determination that state action was involved, thereby requiring application of the provisions of the Fourteenth Amendment, was based upon the direct participation of the clerk of court in the statutory procedure for foreclosure and sale under deed of trust. Id. at 1254–58. In the case before us, however, plaintiffs cite no participation on the part of any state official in First Virginia's self-help repossession, nor can we find any in our review of the record.

Plaintiffs argue the state action in this case, requiring our Court to declare N.C. Gen. Stat. § 25-9-503 [§ 9-609] unconstitutional, is based on our state's statutory scheme permitting the Department of Motor Vehicles to title a motor vehicle, to create and perfect a lien on a motor vehicle, to transfer title of a motor vehicle when the motor vehicle is sold pursuant to a repossession, and to transfer title absent the owner's signature. Further, plaintiffs argue state action is present through our statutory scheme which provides for repossession without judicial process, where payment of any surplus from sale of the repossessed vehicle is paid to the clerk of superior court who is liable on a bond for safekeeping the funds. Except for the reference to N.C. Gen. Stat. § 25-9-503 [§ 9-609], the statutes as recited by plaintiff, do not apply to this case and will not be addressed.

A majority of the federal circuit courts have considered the question before us and are in agreement that self-help repossession pursuant to UCC provisions does not constitute "state action" within the purview of the due process provision of the Fourteenth Amendment. *Shirley v. State National Bank of Connecticut*, 493 F.2d 739 (2d Cir. 1974); *Gibbs v. Titelman*, 502 F.2d 1107 (3d Cir. 1974), cert. denied, *Gibbs, et al. v. Garver, Director, Bureau of Motor Vehicles, et al.*, 419 U.S. 1039, 42 L. Ed. 2d 316 (1974); *James v. Pinnix*, 495 F.2d 206 (5th Cir. 1974); *Turner v. Impala Motors*, 503 F.2d 607 (6th Cir. 1974); *Nichols v. Tower Grove Bank*, 497 F.2d 404 (8th Cir. 1974); *Nowlin v. Professional Auto Sales, Inc.*, 496 F.2d 16 (8th Cir. 1974), cert. denied, 419 U.S. 1006, 95 S. Ct. 328, 42 L. Ed. 2d 283 (1974); *Adams v. Southern California First National Bank*, 492 F.2d 324 (9th Cir. 1973), cert. denied, 419 U.S. 1006, 95 S. Ct. 325, 42 L. Ed. 2d 282 (1974). While this Court is not obliged to follow decisions from other jurisdictions, these decisions are instructive in our determination of whether there was sufficient state action in this case to sustain a challenge under the Fourteenth Amendment.

We agree with First Virginia's contention that N.C. Gen. Stat. § 25-9-503 [§ 9-609] is "wholly self-executing and takes no involvement by any state employee to fully effect its purpose." In enacting N.C. Gen. Stat. § 25-9-503 [§ 9-609], our General Assembly codified a right existing at common law; it did not delegate to private parties authority previously held by the state. Therefore, plaintiffs' argument that state action was involved in this case is without merit.

Plaintiffs also claim that the waiver of notice in the contract signed by Joann Giles is void because it deprives her of her property without notice and an opportunity to be heard, as required by the Fourteenth Amendment. Because we find that there is no state action under N.C. Gen. Stat. § 25-9-503 [§ 9-609], this argument also fails. Plaintiffs' second assignment of error is overruled.

The trial court's order granting partial summary judgment for First Virginia is affirmed.

Affirmed.

NOTES AND QUESTIONS

1. **Repossession by Court Action.** If a secured party cannot use self-help repossession, the secured party may seek to take over the collateral by a replevin or claim-and-delivery action. State rules governing these actions are subject to the due process requirements of the Fourteenth Amendment. Most of these rules have been revised to comply with constitutional requirements of due process. *See* Louis F. Del Duca, *Prenotice, Prehearing, Prejudgment Seizure of Assets Revisited*, 7 UCC L.J. 341 (1975).

2. **Breach of the Peace.** Section 5-112 of the Uniform Consumer Credit Code permits the secured party to repossess "only if possession can be taken without entry into a dwelling and without the use of force or other breach of the peace." Article 9 does not define "breach of the peace." Should Article 9 elaborate?

In *Stone Machinery Co. v. Kessler*, 463 P.2d 651 (1970) (Wash. Ct. App. 1970), the court held that a creditor breached the peace in repossessing a tractor because the local sheriff had assisted in the repossession. Kessler, the debtor, had defaulted on his payments for a tractor which he had purchased in the state of Washington. Kessler subsequently moved the tractor to a worksite in Oregon. After locating the tractor and Kessler at the worksite in Oregon, Mr. Kazanis, an agent of Stone Machinery, asked the sheriff to help him repossess the tractor. Mr. Kazanis did not have a court order for the repossession of the tractor; the sheriff was only shown a copy of the conditional sales contract which he, the sheriff, believed gave Mr. Kazanis the right to repossess the tractor. However, because there was no court order or other form of judicial process, the sheriff was not authorized to remove the tractor from Mr. Kessler's possession. Mr. Kazanis, the truck driver and a truck, which was to be used in transporting the crane back to the state of Washington, and the sheriff proceeded to the worksite. The Sheriff, acting as if he had the authority to do so, ordered Mr. Kessler to relinquish the tractor. Mr. Kessler objected verbally but did not take any physical action to resist the repossession of the tractor by the sheriff and Mr. Kazanis. Because the sheriff was acting as if he had the authority to remove the tractor from Mr. Kessler when in fact he did not, the court found that, under Oregon law, a breach of the peace had occurred during the repossession of the tractor. Therefore, Stone Machinery, through its agent Mr. Kazanis, had committed a tort against Mr. Kessler by wrongfully repossessing the tractor.

It is interesting to note that while the security agreement for the tractor was negotiated and authorized in Washington and the disputes regarding a party's rights were subject to Washington law, the law applied in the case is that of Oregon. This is because the act of repossession, if done improperly, is a tort and therefore subject to the laws of the jurisdiction in which it was committed.

In *Stone Machinery*, the court noted the sheriff said to the debtor, "[W]e come over to pick up this tractor." The court intimates that if the sheriff had merely stood by it might find no breach of the peace occurred. On this point, *see Walker v. Walthall*, 588 P.2d 863 (Ariz. Ct. App. 1978) (finding that mere presence of a deputy sheriff constitutes state action, thereby invalidating repossession without notice or hearing).

3.   Debtor's Criminal Liability. Would the debtor in *Stone Machinery* have violated the following criminal statute?

§ 32.33. Hindering Secured Creditors.

(a)   For purposes of this section:

(1)   "Remove" means transport, without the effective consent of the secured party, from the state in which the property was located when the security interest or lien attached.

(2)   "Security interest" means an interest in personal property or fixtures that secures payment or performance of an obligation.

(b)   A person who has signed a security agreement creating a security interest in property or a mortgage or deed of trust creating a lien on property commits an offense if, with intent to hinder enforcement of that interest or lien, he destroys, removes, conceals, encumbers, or otherwise harms or reduces the value of the property.

(c)   For purposes of this section, a person is presumed to have intended to hinder enforcement of the security interest or lien if, when any part of the debt secured by the security interest or lien was due, he failed:

(1)   to pay the part then due; and

(2)   if the secured party had made demand, to deliver possession of the secured property to the secured party.

4.   Constitutionality of Self-Help Repossession. In the early 1970s, the courts reviewed the constitutionality of many traditional creditors' remedies. The review was based on the due process clause of the Fourteenth Amendment of the federal

Constitution. Most of the cases involving self-help repossession under Article 9 concluded that there was no state action. If there is state action, it appears that the repossession provisions of Article 9 do not meet the due process requirements of a prompt hearing by a judicial officer. The focus would then be on whether there had been a valid waiver in the security agreement of this constitutional protection. The leading case remains *Adams v. Southern California First National Bank*, 492 F.2d 324 (9th Cir. 1973).

Problem 3-7: Repossession Procedure. Assume the loan officer of Steady State Bank concludes that Mr. Clemens has defaulted. She decides to use self-help repossession but she wishes to avoid any possible liability for wrongful repossession. Advise her on the steps the bank should take when repossessing the collateral. When considering what advice to give her, consult the security agreement in Chapter 2, *supra*, UCC § 9-609, and the following draft checklist.

- Double check to make sure there actually has been a default.

- Read carefully the security agreement and other documents to see if Mr. Clemens has contract obligations which he might be asked to perform—or which the bank is obligated to carry out when repossessing.

- Consider a direct approach, asking Mr. Clemens to turn over the assets to the bank voluntarily.

- Consider hiring a professional collection agency with experience in collecting debts and repossessing collateral.

- If bank employees are sent to repossess, give clear directions.

- Direct bank employees to go during the regular office hours of the printing business.

- Direct bank employees to withdraw if anyone protests the repossession. If the person is someone other than Mr. Clemens, ask to talk with Mr. Clemens.

- Direct bank employees not to break into a locked or barred area in order to repossess the assets.

- Make sure that bank employees are given an accurate description of the collateral as determined from the security agreement. The employees should be sure to detach any items which are not part of the collateral.

- Employees should promptly make an inventory of the repossessed collateral.

Would obtaining possession by trick be a violation? For example, suppose the bank asserts on a loan secured by his truck that Clemens missed a payment, he says he paid, and the bank invites him to the bank to discuss, intending to tow the truck from the bank's parking lot? *See Ford Motor Credit Corp. v. Byrd*, 22 UCC Rep. Serv. 1294 (Ala. 1977) (holding that Creditor would be liable for conversion of the truck, even if Buyer was in default at the time the automobile was repossessed). Consider Problem 3-9, *infra*, as well.

Problem 3-8:   Enforcing Accounts Following Default. Assume the loan officer of Steady State Bank concludes that Samuel Clemens has defaulted under any of the preceding problems. She reviews the list of collateral securing the note and sees the accounts receivable. She sends letters to the debtors on these accounts receivable directing the account debtors to pay the bank rather than Mr. Clemens. Mr. Clemens asks you if the bank is authorized to take this action. Advise him. *See* UCC § 9-607(a).

NOTE: COLLECTION RIGHTS UPON DEFAULT

When the collateral consists of rights against a third person, such as the right to payment of money from an account debtor, the secured party may after default proceed to collect on the collateral under UCC § 9-607, rather than dispose of it under UCC § 9-610. What determines which approach should be used?

Collection requires that the third party owe a duty to the secured party, and this is not determined by UCC § 9-607. *See* UCC § 9-607(e). Suppose, for example, that Bank has a perfected security interest in the inventory of Tiger Appliances. Tiger sells and leases appliances in every price range. When a customer who is buying an appliance cannot pay cash, Tiger is willing to extend credit. Depending on the customer's credit rating and the price of the appliance, Tiger may use either an unsecured or a secured retail installment contract. An unsecured contract specifies the payment terms; a secured contract specifies the payment terms and creates a security interest in the appliance. The unsecured contract rights are accounts (UCC § 9-102(a)(2)) and the buyers are account debtors (UCC § 9-102(a)(3)). Both the secured contracts and the leases are chattel paper (UCC § 9-102(a)(11)), but the buyers and lessees are nevertheless categorized as account debtors.

Each account debtor's payment obligation runs initially to Tiger. However, Bank has a security interest in the accounts and chattel paper because they are proceeds of the inventory, and upon default it may proceed to collect directly from the account debtors. Note carefully that the secured party may instead proceed to dispose of the accounts and chattel paper under UCC § 9-610, in which case the purchaser at the foreclosure sale would undertake to collect from the account debtors. The following questions explore the secured party's collection rights:

1.   Account Debtor #1 (A.D. 1) bought a washer/dryer set on unsecured credit and has been making monthly payments to Tiger for almost a year at the time of Tiger's default.

    a)   What step(s) must Bank take to collect from A.D. 1? Is A.D. 1 entitled to a credit for the payments made to Tiger? UCC §§ 9-607(a), 9-406(a).

    b)   Suppose Tiger promised to repair all defects in the appliances for a period of two years after purchase and A.D. 1's washer breaks down after notice to pay Bank is received. Is Bank obligated to make the repairs? UCC § 9-402. If A.D. 1 has the repairs done elsewhere because Tiger is no longer in business, can the cost of repair be deducted from the amount still due? UCC § 9-404(a)(1). Would your answer change if the retail installment contract contained a term waiving all claims and defenses as against assignees? UCC §§ 9-404(a), 9-403. Is it important to know why A.D.1 purchased the goods?

c) Suppose the defect in the washer caused a fire that destroyed A.D. 1's home. Could A.D. 1 recover affirmatively from Bank for the loss? UCC § 9-404(b).

d) Suppose that in a separate transaction A.D. 1 bought a television set from Tiger for cash and has a claim against Tiger for the costs of repair. Can A.D. 1 assert that claim against Bank? UCC § 9-404(a)(2).

e) Suppose A.D. 1 had insisted on a term making the payment obligation nonassignable. Would any of your answers change? UCC §§ 9-401, 9-406(d).

f) If A.D. 1 fails to make a payment that is due to Bank after receipt of notice, can Bank repossess the washer and dryer and dispose of them under UCC § 9-610?

2. A.D. 2 is in the same position as A.D. 1 except that it entered in a secured retail installment contract. Would this fact change any of the answers that you gave to Question 1? Could Tiger take a security interest in the TV to better secure the debt for the washer/dryer? UCC § 9-204; FTC Credit Practices Rule, 16 CFR pt. 444.

3. A.D. 3 leased a washer/dryer set pursuant to a written lease. How do Bank's rights against A.D. 3 differ from its rights against A.D. 1?

4. Suppose that Bank, not wanting to spend exorbitant resources in its collection efforts, simply acceded to every claim and defense asserted by an account debtor and then when its collection efforts (and disposition efforts with respect to repossessed inventory) were exhausted filed suit against Tiger (or a guarantor) for a deficiency judgment. Does Bank's conduct affect its right to a judgment?

5. Suppose that Tiger had granted Bank a security interest in its checking account, which it maintained with Bank, and its savings account at Credit Union. Credit Union entered into a control agreement with Bank and Tiger.

a) How should Bank collect the funds in the checking account? UCC § 9-607(a)(4).

b) How should Bank collect the funds in the savings account? UCC § 9-607(a)(5).

Suppose that after entering into the control agreement, Credit Union had exercised its right of set off against the funds in the savings account because Tiger had defaulted on an unsecured loan made to it by Credit Union. Would Bank be entitled to the seized funds? UCC § 9-340. How could Bank eliminate the risk of set off? If A.D.2 had given Tiger a security interest in its savings account, what law applies? UCC § 9-109(d)(13). Does it matter how this is done? UCC §§ 9-109(a)(1) and 9-102(a)(29), (47).

6. Suppose Tiger was the payee of a negotiable promissory note and had granted Bank a security interest in the note. Bank left the note in Tiger's possession and perfected its security interest by filing a financing statement. Upon default, can Bank place the maker under a duty to pay it by notification? If not, what steps must Bank take to collect from the maker? UCC §§ 9-607(a)(1), (3), 9-102(a)(3), 9-607(e), Comment 6 to UCC § 9-607, UCC § 3-301. What benefit is Bank giving up by leaving the note in Tiger's possession? UCC §§ 3-201, 3-302, 3-305.

7. Suppose that as a sideline Tiger sold from inventory certain medical prosthetic devices and took from its customers an assignment of their rights against their health-insurance companies. Suppose further that the insurance policies provided that the payment rights could not be reassigned by the health-care goods provider. Does this provision prevent Bank's security interest from attaching to the payment rights? UCC §§ 9-109(d)(8), 9-102(a)(2), (46), 9-406(i), 9-408(a). Can Bank place the insurance companies under a duty to pay it by notification? §§ 9-607(e), 9-408(d). What additional information do you need to answer fully this last question?

Problem 3-9: Good Faith. Following default of an obligation secured by an Article 9 security interest, both the debtor and the secured party are under an obligation to act in good faith. True or false? UCC § 1-304.

C. DISPOSITION FOLLOWING REPOSSESSION

1. Compulsory Disposition and Redemption of Collateral

A secured party whose debtor has defaulted not only may use self-help to repossess collateral but also may dispose of the collateral without the need for state intervention. What limits are there on the actions of the secured party? Most importantly, Article 9 assumes that the self-interest of the secured party will encourage it to maximize the proceeds received on disposition of the collateral. What creditor wants to end up with a deficiency owed by a debtor who has already defaulted? Article 9 also relies on the self-interest of the debtor, who, if informed about how the secured party proposes to act, may keep track of ("monitor") how the creditor acts and may find potential purchasers of the collateral. The Code, therefore, directs the secured party to proceed in a "commercially reasonable" manner and, in particular, to notify the debtor of its plans. *See* UCC §§ 9-610, 9-611.

Article 9 supplements this minimalist regulation with several specific rules. To avoid potential abuses when the secured party has a conflict of personal interest, Article 9 regulates when the creditor may acquire the collateral either at a sale or by retaining it in satisfaction of the obligation. *See* UCC §§ 9-610, 9-620.

Problem 3-10: Compulsory Disposition of Collateral. Clemens purchases a small truck that he uses for weekend camping trips and for transporting his children to and from school. After he has paid $15,000 of the $20,000 loan obtained to finance the purchase of the truck, Clemens defaults on 3 payments. Creditor duly repossesses and seeks advice as to whether the truck may be retained and the balance of $5,000 due treated as being satisfied. *See* UCC §§ 9-103(b), 9-102(a)(23), 9-620(e). Would the result be the same if Clemens had purchased the truck primarily for use in delivering supplies and finished products in his business, but used the truck 30% of the time for weekend camping trips and to transport his children to and from school? *See* UCC §§ 9-103(a), (b), 9-102(a)(33), 9-620.

The debtor is also given the opportunity to redeem the collateral notwithstanding default by tendering "fulfillment of all obligations secured by the collateral" as well as the secured party's reasonable expenses. *See* UCC § 9-623(a), (b).

Problem 3-11: Redemption of the Collateral. After Clemens has failed to make 3 overdue monthly payments, Creditor duly repossesses the collateral and notifies Clemens of a public sale, which is to be held in the creditor's premises on a stated date. May Clemens redeem the collateral by tendering payment of the 3 overdue payments? Is Clemens required to tender the 3 overdue payments plus the balance of the loan and incidental expenses? *See* UCC § 9-623(b).

To discourage judicial second-guessing after the secured party has acted, § 9-627(c) concludes with several rules of thumb for reviewing a disposition.

2. Timeliness of Notification and Commercial Reasonableness of Disposition

Problem 3-12: Notice of Disposition. Assume that following default by Samuel Clemens, Steady State Bank has repossessed equipment. Before repossessing this equipment, a bank loan officer had learned that another bank customer would be willing to purchase some of the equipment for the amount Mr. Clemens then owed the bank, $10,856. The repossession was conducted peacefully. The loan officer writes the following notice, which she proposes to mail to Mr. Clemens:

> We have found a buyer for the equipment we have repossessed and will sell the equipment to this buyer a week from the date of this letter.

She asks you for advice on whether the letter complies with the Uniform Commercial Code. Advise her.

Consider the following guidelines. How, if at all, would you draft a security agreement to address these issues?

- How much notice? When should one begin to count the notice period? *See* UCC §§ 9-611, 9-612.

- How should the notice be sent? *See* UCC § 9-102(a)(74).

- What should the notice say? The Code requires certain information depending on whether the proposed sale is public or private. *See* UCC § 9-611.

- To whom should notice be given? Note that notice may need to be given to parties other than the obligor who borrowed the money. *See* UCC §§ 9-102(a)(28), 9-611.

- When should waiver of notice be sought? What form should the waiver take? *See* UCC § 9-624.

Problem 3-13: Notice of Disposition. Assume the same facts as in the preceding problem except that rather than a bank customer the proposed buyer is another branch of Steady State Bank. Advise the loan officer on whether the bank may proceed with the proposed sale and, if so, what notice should be given Mr. Clemens. *See* UCC §§ 9-610(c), 9-613.

Problem 3-14: Commercially Reasonable Disposition. Assume that following default by Samuel Clemens, Steady State Bank has repossessed equipment other than the printing press. To avoid any possible liability for improper disposition, the bank loan officer consults you about what steps—other than giving notice—the bank should take. Advise her. What modifications or additions would you make to the following checklist?

- Ask Mr. Clemens to work with the bank when soliciting offers and conducting the sale.

- Have guidelines for deciding on when to use public or private sale. Mr. Clemens' advice would be useful. If the decision is to have public sale, select carefully the site and person conducting the sale. Consider whether other bank clients who are in the same line of business might be potential purchasers at a private sale.

- Consider whether appraisal is desirable. There may be "blue books" that give prices of comparable equipment.

- Consider whether repair or refurbishing is desirable and record reasons for the conclusion.

- Advertise the sale in media directed to potential purchasers at a repossession sale (e.g., trade journals, local or regional business newspapers).

COXALL v. CLOVER COMMERCIAL CORP.
New York City Civil Court
781 N.Y.S.2d 567 (2004)

JACK M. BATTAGLIA, J.

[After establishing the Coxalls' default and Creditor Clover Commercial's proper repossession of the collateral, the court addressed the "reasonable notification" and "commercially reasonable" requirements of §§ 9-610 through 9-614 for disposition of the automobile collateral repossessed by Creditor. It then discusses the consequences of the Creditor's failure to meet these procedural requirements on the Creditor's right to a deficiency judgment under the "rebuttable presumption" provisions of § 9-626 and the Debtor's general right to damages and in particular to statutory damages under § 9-625.]

. . .

After Clover Commercial took possession of the Lexus, it was obligated to deal with the vehicle in accordance with the requirements of Article 9. Under Former Article 9, those requirements were contained in a single section (*see* Former UCC § 9-504), and there was much uncertainty about the consequences of the creditor's failure to comply. Revised Article 9 expands greatly upon the statutory requirements, and clears some, but not all, of the uncertainty.

For the secured party who chooses to sell the collateral, Article 9 imposes two overriding requirements: the secured party must send "a reasonable authenticated notification of disposition" to the debtor (Revised UCC § 9-611(b); *see also* Former UCC § 9-504(3)); and the sale must be "commercially reasonably" (Revised UCC § 9-610(b); *see also* Former UCC § 9-504(3).) The Court has determined that Clover Commercial failed to comply with these requirements.

[Reasonable Notification Requirement]

"The purpose of the notice requirement is 'to give the debtor an opportunity to protect his interest in the collateral by exercising any right of redemption or by bidding at the sale, to challenge any aspect of the disposition before it is made, or to interest potential purchasers in the sale, all to the end that the merchandise not be sacrificed by a sale at less than the true value.' " (Long Island Trust Co. v. Williams, 133 Misc. 2d 746, 753, 507 N.Y.S.2d 993 [Civ. Ct., NY County 1986] [quoting First Bank and Trust Co. of Ithaca v. Mitchell, 123 Misc. 2d 386, 393, 473 N.Y.S.2d 697 [Sup. Ct., Tompkins County 1984]), aff'd 142 Misc. 2d 4, 539 N.Y.S.2d 612 [App. Term, 1st Dept. 1988].)

"The notification must be reasonable as to the manner in which it is sent, its timeliness (i.e. a reasonable time before the disposition is to take place), and its content." (Official Comment 2 to Revised UCC § 9-611.) The notification must be "authenticated", as that term is defined (*see* Revised UCC § 9-102(a)(7)), a requirement not in issue here.

"Whether a notification is sent within a reasonable time is a question of fact." (Revised UCC § 9-612(a).) "A notification that is sent so near to the disposition date that a notified person could not be expected to act on or take account of the notification would be unreasonable." (Official Comment 2 to Revised UCC § 9-612.) For secured transactions other than consumer transactions, "a notification . . . sent . . . 10 days or more before the earliest time of disposition . . . is sent within a reasonable time before the disposition." (Revised UCC § 9-612(b).) The 10-day period for non-consumer transactions "is intended to be a 'safe-harbor' and not a minimum requirement." (Official Comment 3 to Revised UCC § 9-612.) The terms "consumer goods", "consumer goods transactions" and "consumer transaction" are defined. (*See* Revised UCC § 9-102(a)(23), (24), (26).)

The contents and form of the notification are prescribed generally for all transactions (*see* Revised UCC § 9-613(a)(1)) and for consumer-goods transactions (*see* Revised UCC § 9-614(a)(1)). A notification in a non-consumer transaction that does not include all of the prescribed information may still be found sufficient as a matter of fact. (*See* Revised UCC § 9-613(a)(2).) But in a consumer transaction, "[a] notification that lacks any of the [prescribed] information . . . is insufficient as a matter of law." (Official Comment 2 to Revised UCC § 9-614.)

Here, Clover Commercial mailed two letters to Jason Coxall on February 20, 2003: one advised primarily as to the time after which the sale would be made, i.e. "12 noon on 3/03/03"; the other advised primarily as to Mr. Coxall's right to redeem the automobile. Although each of these letters shows a "copy to: Utho Coxall," there is no evidence of any mailing to him. As to Utho Coxall, therefore, it appears that he may not have been sent any notification; at the least, we do not know when any notification was sent.

The Court will assume, for purposes of these actions only that separate writings that in combination provide to the debtor all of the prescribed information may be found to comply sufficiently with the "reasonable notification" requirement. Even so, and read generously, Clover Commercial's two letters did not provide Jason Coxall with all of the information it was required to provide. Neither letter stated that Mr. Coxall was "entitled to an accounting of the unpaid indebtedness" nor stated "the charge, if any, for an accounting." (*See* Revised UCC § 9-613(1)(D); Revised UCC § 9-614(1)(A).)

As to Jason Coxall, the Post Office-stamped Certificates of Mailing are sufficient to establish that Clover Commercial sent the letters to him, even if he did not receive them. (*See* American Honda Finance Corp. v. Delorio, 260 A.D.2d 416, 417, 687 N.Y.S.2d 730 [2d Dept. 1999].) First-class mail with Certificate of Mailing, a manner of service regularly designated by judges of this court for orders to show cause, is a "commercially reasonable manner." (*See* Official Comment 3 to Revised UCC § 9-612.)

In computing the period of time, the date of mailing, i.e. February 20, should be excluded and the date of sale, i.e. March 3, should be included. (*See* Fisk Discount Corp. v. Brooklyn Taxicab Trans. Co., 270 AD 491, 499, 60 N.Y.S.2d 453 [2d Dept. 1946].) Mr. Coxall was given therefore, 11 days notice before his Lexus was sold. In a consumer transaction, and in the absence of any evidence that such a prompt sale was important to obtaining the best price, 11 days notice does not appear reasonable. Although the period of notification is measured from mailing, in other areas the law recognizes that time will elapse between mailing and receipt. (*See* CPLR 2103(b)(2) [adding five days to prescribed period of time when service is by mail].) Were notification of sale to be received, say, five days before sale, the opportunity to arrange, for example, for alternate financing to redeem a necessary item such as an automobile would be quite limited.

But the Contract between the Coxalls and Clover Commercial provides that, after repossession, Clover "can sell the vehicle after 10 days notice", and that "notice will be reasonable if . . . sent . . . to your current address . . . at least 10 days . . . before seller acts on the notice." Article 9 would permit such an agreement unless it is "manifestly unreasonable." (*See* Revised UCC §§ 9-603(a), 9-602(7).) It is not necessary to a decision in these cases to determine whether the contract notice provision is enforceable, and, in the absence of evidence on the reasonableness of notice by 10-days' prior mailing, the Court will leave the question for another day.

[Commercially Reasonable Disposition Requirement]

"Every aspect of a disposition of collateral, including the method, manner, time, place, and other terms, must be commercially reasonable." (Revised UCC § 9-610(b); *see also* Former UCC § 9-504(3).) Private dispositions, as compared to public auction, are encouraged "on the assumption that they frequently will result in higher realization on collateral for the benefit of all concerned." (Official Comment 2 to Revised UCC § 9-610.) "A disposition of collateral is made in a commercially reasonable manner if the disposition is made . . . in conformity with reasonable commercial practices among dealers in the type of property that was the subject of the disposition." (Revised UCC § 9-627(b); *see also* Former UCC § 9-507(2).)

New York courts have determined commercial reasonableness by whether the secured party "acted in good faith and to the parties' mutual best advantage." (*See* 108th Street Owners Corp. v. Overseas Commodities Ltd., 238 A.D.2d 324, 325, 656 N.Y.S.2d 942 [2d Dept. 1999]; MTI Systems Corp. v. Hatziemanuel, 151 A.D.2d 649, 650, 542 N.Y.S.2d 710 [2d Dept. 1989]; Federal Deposit Ins. Corp. v. Herald Square Fabrics Corp., 81 A.D.2d 168, 184–85, 439 N.Y.S.2d 944 [2d Dept. 1981].) When a secured party is seeking a deficiency from the debtor, the secured party bears the burden of proving the sale was commercially reasonable. (*See* Revised UCC § 9-626(a)(2); Associates Commercial Corp. v. Liberty Truck Sales & Leasing, Inc., 286 A.D.2d 311, 312, 728 N.Y.S.2d 695 [2d Dept. 2001]; BancAmerica Private Brands, Inc. v. Marine Gallery, Inc., 157 A.D.2d 813, 813, 550 N.Y.S.2d 720 [2d Dept. 1990]; Mack Financial Corp. v. Knoud, 98 A.D.2d 713, 713–14, 469 N.Y.S.2d 116 [2d Dept. 1983].) "Whether a sale was commercially reasonable is, like other questions about 'reasonableness', a fact-intensive inquiry; no magic set of procedures will immunize the sale from scrutiny." (Matter of Excello Press, Inc., 890 F.2d 896, 905 [7th Cir. 1989] [applying NY law]; *see also* Federal Deposit Ins. Corp. v. Forte, 144 A.D.2d 627, 629, 535 N.Y.S.2d 75 [2d Dept. 1988].)

Here, Clover Commercial sold Mr. Coxall's Lexus in a private sale to the dealer from whom Mr. Coxall had purchased it. Clover Commercial provided no evidence on its procedure for the sale, its identification of prospective buyers, or any other details of the sale, except for the price. (*See* Mack Financial Corp. v. Knoud, 98 A.D.2d at 714.) There was no showing that dealers sell their trade-ins in the same manner or that dealers or secured parties sell repossessed automobiles in the same manner. On the other hand, one court has noted that "the sale of [a] repossessed vehicle by private auto auction is in conformity with the reasonable commercial practices of lenders disposing of motor vehicles." (Charter One Auto Finance Corp. v. Vaglio, 2003 N.Y. Misc. LEXIS 253, 2003 NY Slip Op 50638[U], *5 [Sup. Ct. Nassau County].) This case is different, however, in that the vehicle was sold back to the dealer who sold it to the debtor. (*See* Central Budget Corp. v. Garrett, 48 A.D.2d 825, 825, 368 N.Y.S.2d 268 [2d Dept. 1975]; Jefferson Credit Corp. v. Marcano, 60 Misc. 2d 138, 143, 302 N.Y.S.2d 390 [Civ. Ct, NY County 1969]; *see also* Revised UCC § 9-615(f) and Official Comment 6 to Revised UCC § 9-615; Former UCC § 9-504(5).)

All we have, therefore, as evidence of commercial reasonableness is the price. Clover Commercial received $1,500.00 on the sale of a Lexus that had been purchased by the Coxalls approximately four months earlier for $8,100.00; that is a sales price of 18.5% of the purchase price. "The fact that a greater amount could have been obtained by a . . . disposition . . . at a different time or in a different method from that selected by the secured party is not of itself sufficient to preclude the secured party from establishing that the . . . disposition . . . was made in a commercially reasonable manner." (Revised UCC § 9-627(a); *see also* Former UCC § 9-507(2).) But "while not itself sufficient to establish a violation of [code requirements], a low price suggests that a court should scrutinize carefully all aspects of a disposition to ensure that each aspect was commercially reasonable." (Official Comment 2 to Revised UCC § 9-627.)

New York courts have, indeed, scrutinized "low price" sales. "Marked discrepancies between the disposal and sale prices signal a need for closer scrutiny, especially where, as here, the possibilities for self-dealing are substantial. . . . Under these circumstances, we require some affirmative showing that the terms of the disposition were, in fact, commercially reasonable and hold that, in the absence of such a showing, we will be compelled to deny recovery in a suit for a deficiency judgment." (Central Budget Corp. v. Garrett, 48 A.D.2d at 826 [automobile]; *see also* Orix Credit Alliance, Inc. v. East End Development Corp., 260 A.D.2d 454, 455, 688 N.Y.S.2d 191 [2d Dept. 1999]; Kohler v. Ford Motor Credit Co., Inc., 93 A.D.2d 205, 208, 462 N.Y.S.2d 297 [3d Dept. 1983] [automobile]; Federal Deposit Ins. Corp. v. Herald Square Fabrics Corp., 81 A.D.2d at 184–85; Long Island Trust Co. v. Williams, 133 Misc. 2d at 751–53 [automobile] [reviewing cases].) "[A] wide or marked discrepancy in disposal and sale prices is an independently adequate reason to question the commercial reasonableness of a disposition of collateral." (Federal Deposit Ins. Corp. v. Herald Square Fabrics Corp., 81 A.D.2d at 185 n 8.)

A low price, of course, "might simply reflect a greatly depreciated piece of collateral." (Matter of Excello Press, Inc., 890 F.2d at 905–06.) But, here, Clover Commercial acknowledged that Mr. Coxall's Lexus had not sustained any physical damage while in his possession. Clover's suggestion that the low price may have been due to the mechanical difficulties experienced by Mr. Coxall was contradicted by its own testimony that the car was running fine when repossessed, and would, in any event, be specious.

As previously indicated, Clover Commercial provided no evidence as to the commercial reasonableness of the sale; it provided no evidence that any prospective buyer was contacted, other than the original seller; and provided no evidence of the fair market value of the Lexus on the date of sale, or any other evidence that would justify a sale price of $1,500.00. In short, Clover Commercial failed to sustain its burden of showing that the sale of Mr. Coxall's Lexus was commercially reasonable.

[Deficiency Rebuttable Presumption and Absolute Bar Consequences or Failure to Meet Disposition Procedural Requirements]

When the secured party has disposed of the collateral in a commercially reasonable manner after sending reasonable notification to the debtor, the debtor will be liable for any deficiency if the proceeds of the disposition are not sufficient to satisfy the debt and allowed expenses. (*See* Revised UCC § 9-615(d); *see also* Former UCC § 9-504(2).) Former Article 9 was silent, however, on whether the secured party that had failed to send reasonable notification or had not disposed of the collateral in a commercially reasonable manner or both, as here could obtain a deficiency judgment against the debtor.

"Three general approaches emerged. Some courts have held that a noncomplying secured party may not recover a deficiency (the 'absolute bar' rule). A few courts held that the debtor can offset against a claim to a deficiency all damages recoverable under former Section 9-507 resulting from the secured party's noncompliance (the 'offset' rule). A plurality of courts considering the issue held that the noncomplying secured party is barred from recovering a deficiency unless it overcomes a rebuttable presumption that compliance with former Part 5 would have yielded an amount sufficient to satisfy the secured debt." (Official Comment 4 to Revised UCC § 9-626.)

In New York, the departments of the Appellate Division were not in agreement as to which of the approaches to follow, with the Second Department alone adopting the "absolute bar" rule. (*See* Central National Bank v. Butler, 294 A.D.2d 881, 882, 741 N.Y.S.2d 643 [4th Dept. 2002]; General Electrical Credit Corp. v. Durante Bros. & Sons, Inc., 79 A.D.2d 509, 510, 433 N.Y.S.2d 574 [1st Dept. 1980]; Security Trust Co. of Rochester v. Thomas, 59 A.D.2d 242, 245–47, 399 N.Y.S.2d 511 [4th Dept. 1977]; Stanchi v. Kemp, 48 A.D.2d 973, 974, 370 N.Y.S.2d 26 [3d Dept. 1975]; Central Budget Corp. v. Garrett, 48 A.D.2d at 826; Long Island Bank v. Knight, 122 Misc. 2d 878, 879, 473 N.Y.S.2d 901 [App. Term, 2d Dept. 1983]; Avis Rent-A-Car System, Inc. v. Franklin, 82 Misc. 2d 66, 67, 366 N.Y.S.2d 83 [App. Term, 2d Dept. 1975]; Matter of Excello Press, Inc., 890 F.2d at 903–04; Siemens Credit Corp. v. Marvik Colour, Inc., 859 F. Supp. 686, 691–93 [SDNY 1994]; Stedman v. Webb, 264 B.R. 298, 301–03 [WDNY 2001].) The "absolute bar" rule appears to have been the approach required by pre-Code law. (*See* Leasco Computer, Inc. v. Sheridan Industries, Inc., 82 Misc. 2d 897, 900, 371 N.Y.S.2d 531 [Civ. Ct., NY County 1975].)

Revised Article 9 resolves the conflict and uncertainty for transactions other than consumer transactions by adopting the "rebuttable presumption" rule. (*See* Revised UCC § 9-626(a)(3).) The limitation of the "rebuttable presumption" rule to non-consumer transactions "is intended to leave to the court the determination of the proper rules in consumer transactions", and the court "may continue to apply established approaches." (Revised UCC § 9-626(b).)

It is clear, therefore, that the "rebuttable presumption" rule is now the law in the Second Department for non-consumer transactions. The question remains, however, whether the "absolute bar" rule is to be applied in these actions, involving, as they do, a consumer transaction. A review of the legislative history provides no guidance. The Report of the New York State Law Revision Committee that accompanied Revised Article 9 through enactment states only that, "with respect to consumer defaults, Revised Article 9 makes no recommendation whatsoever, leaving the courts free to shape a remedy as is appropriate in each case." (The New York State Law Revision Commission, 2001 Report on the Proposed Revised Article 9, at 158.)

Up to now, New York courts have not distinguished between consumer and non-consumer transactions in fashioning rules where the enforcement provisions of Article 9 were silent, suggesting that the "rebuttable presumption" rule will be adopted for all transactions. But at this time, for a court sitting in the Second

Department, there is an "absolute bar" rule that has not been legislatively displaced by Revised Article 9.

Having found, therefore, that Clover Commercial failed to comply with both the reasonable notification and commercially reasonable disposition requirements of Article 9, the "absolute bar" rule precludes it from recovering a deficiency from the Coxalls. Even if, however, the "rebuttable presumption" rule were to be applied, the result would be the same. Clover introduced no evidence of "the amount of proceeds that would have been realized had [it] proceeded in accordance with the provisions of" the Code relating to disposition of the collateral. (*See* Revised UCC § 9-626(a)(3)(B).)

Specifically, Clover Commercial provided no evidence as to the fair market value of the Lexus on the date of the sale, either by reference to "blue book" value, appraisal, sales of similar vehicles or other measure. (*See* Long Island Trust Co. v. Williams, 133 Misc. 2d at 754; *see also* Central National Bank v. Butler, 294 A.D.2d at 882 ["certified appraised value"]; Kohler v. Ford Motor Credit Co., Inc., 93 A.D.2d at 208 ["book value of the vehicle"].) Moreover, Clover's witness, Adam Greenberg, acknowledged that Clover considered the Lexus to be of sufficient value to serve as collateral for the secured debt, which, at the least, was the amount financed, $4,970.00.

Although Clover Commercial cannot recover for any deficiency, it may recover "the sums owed to it prior to the repossession as well as the repossession charges." (*See Avis Rent-A-Car Sys. v. Franklin*, 82 Misc. 2d at 67.) Clover's failure to comply with the enforcement provisions of article 9 "would not discharge the [Coxalls] from all liability under the contract." (*See Stanchi v. Kemp*, 48 A.D.2d at 974; *see also Bank of China v. Chan*, 937 F.2d 780, 788 [2d Cir. 1991].) At the time of repossession, three monthly payments of $333.68 were unpaid for a total due of $1,001.04, and the contract provided for a 10% late charge for each payment not made when due, for an additional charge of $100.11. Clover is entitled, therefore, to $1,101.15 for payments in default and related late charges.

The contract also provides that the debtor must pay the "cost of repossession, storage and preparation for sale" and "an attorney's fee of up to 15% of the amount due . . . unless the court sets a smaller fee." Clover Commercial includes $325 in its computation of the deficiency, which apparently is intended as a charge for repossession, storage, and preparation charges, but, unlike the late charge, the amount is not specified in the contract, and no evidence was submitted to explain or support it. Similarly, there was no evidence to support an award of attorney's fees. (*See Orix Credit Alliance v. Grace Indus.*, 261 A.D.2d 521, 521–522 [2d Dept. 1999].)

Coxall's Claim Against Clover

Jason Coxall no longer has his Lexus. His down payment was $3,798.25, and he owes $1,101.15 for overdue payments. In effect, approximately four months' use of the vehicle has cost him approximately $5,000, not including alleged repair and towing expenses. Of course, "the debtor who precipitated the sale by defaulting on a debt is certainly not to be freed lightly from fault." (*Siemens Credit Corp. v. Marvik Colour, Inc.*, 859 F. Supp at 692.) Nonetheless, does Mr. Coxall have a remedy for Clover Commercial's failure to comply with article 9, beyond being relieved of any liability for a deficiency?

"Under the common law, prior to the enactment of the Uniform Conditional Sales Act, the seller was under no obligation upon the retaking of the goods on buyer's default to make return of partial payments or any part thereof." (*Laufer v. Burghard*, 146 Misc. 39, 42 [Sup. Ct., Erie County 1932].) "A retaking of the property by a conditional vendor is not a rescission of the contract so as to require the vendor to place the buyer in a former position and return the consideration received under the contract." (*Id.* at 45.) If, however, the repossessing seller failed to comply with obligations imposed by statute after taking possession, a return of all or part of the payments made by the buyer was mandated. (*See Rivara v. James Stewart & Co.*, 241 NY 259, 262, 267 [1925], *aff'd* 274 US 614 [1927]; *La Rocca Bldrs. v. Sanders*, 230 App. Div. 594, 597 [1st Dept. 1930].)

Under article 9, "a person is liable for damages in the amount of any loss caused by a failure to comply" with the statute. (UCC § 9-625(b); *see also* former UCC § 9-507 (1).) "Damages for violation of the requirements of [the statute] . . . are those reasonably calculated to put an eligible claimant in the position that it would have occupied had no violation occurred." (UCC § 9- 625, Comment 3.) There are, however, both supplements to and limitations on this general liability principle.

"[A] debtor . . . whose deficiency is eliminated or reduced under Section 9-626 may not otherwise recover . . . for noncompliance with the provisions . . . relating to . . . enforcement." (UCC § 9-625(d).) This provision "eliminates the possibility of double recovery or other over-compensation," but "[b]ecause Section 9-626 does not apply to consumer transactions, the statute is silent as to whether a double recovery or other over-compensation is possible in a consumer transaction." (UCC § 9-625, Comment 3.) Respected commentators "argue that 'double recoveries' should be denied in consumer cases too." (*See* White and Summers, Uniform Commercial Code § 25-13, at 919 [5th ed 2000].)

The law in New York under former article 9 allowed a debtor to recover any loss resulting from the secured party's noncompliance, even though the secured party was deprived of recovery for a deficiency because of noncompliance. (*See Liberty Bank v. Thomas*, 222 A.D.2d 1019 [4th Dept. 1995].) Here again, since revised article 9 does not displace existing law for consumer transactions, this court must apply the prerevision law. At the least, denial of a deficiency to the noncomplying secured party should not preclude the debtor's recovery of the statutorily-prescribed minimum damages. (*See Jones v. Star Bank*, 142 B.R. 194, 198–199 [SD Ohio 1992]; *Wilmington Trust Co. v. Conner*, 415 A.2d 773, 781 [Del. 1980].)

Revised article 9, like its predecessor, "provides a minimum, statutory, damage recovery for a debtor . . . in a consumer-goods transaction" that "is designed to ensure that every noncompliance . . . in a consumer-goods transaction results in liability." (*See* UCC § 9-625, Comment 4; UCC § 9-625(c); former UCC § 9-507(1).) The debtor may recover "an amount not less than the credit service charge plus 10 percent of the principal amount of the obligation or the time-price differential plus 10 percent of the cash price." (UCC § 9-625(c)(2).) The statute "does not include a definition or explanation of the terms" used in the damage formula, but "leaves their construction and application to the court, taking into account the . . . purpose of providing a minimum recovery." (UCC § 9-625, Comment 4.)

Here, according to the contract, the time-price differential is $1,036.24 and 10% of the cash price is $810, for a total statutory damage recovery of $1,846.24. Mr. Coxall is entitled to this recovery even if he sustained no actual loss from Clover Commercial's failure to comply with article 9. (*See Davenport v. Chrysler Credit Corp.*, 818 S.W.2d 23, 31–32 [Tenn. Ct. App. 1991]; *Erdmann v. Rants*, 442 N.W.2d 441, 443 [N.D. 1989]; *First City Bank-Farmers Branch, Tex. v. Guex*, 677 S.W.2d 25, 29 [Tex. 1984].) But, although Clover Commercial failed to comply with both the requirement for reasonable notification and the requirement for a commercially reasonable disposition, it is obligated for only one statutory damage remedy. (*See Dunn v. Security Pac. Hous. Servs.*, 1996 Del. Super LEXIS 428, *10–11 [Super. Ct., New Castle, Aug. 22, 1996]; *Crosby v. Basin Motor Co.*, 83 NM 77, 79, 488 P.2d 127, 129 [1971].)

Mr. Coxall would also be entitled to the value of the personal property that, he says, was contained in the vehicle when it was repossessed, but which has not been returned to him. (*See Fitzpatrick v. Bank of N.Y.*, 125 Misc. 2d 1069, 1076 [Civ. Ct., Queens County 1984].) But Mr. Coxall introduced no admissible evidence of that value.

3.   Action in Which Deficiency or Surplus is an Issue—"Absolute Bar" and "Rebuttable Presumption"

Spillers v. First National Bank of Arenzville, 400 N.E.2d 1057 (Ill. Ct. App. 1980), and *Hall v. Owen County State Bank*, 370 N.E.2d 918 (Ind. Ct. App. 1977), demonstrate that under pre-revision Article 9 the extent of a creditor's recovery of debt upon a commercially unreasonable disposition of collateral depended on the governing jurisdiction's case law. In *Spillers*, the Illinois court applied the absolute bar rule test. A creditor that failed to comply with commercially reasonable standards upon disposition of collateral was barred from obtaining a deficiency judgment against the debtor to recover the balance of the debt due where the amount produced on disposition of the collateral was less than the outstanding debt.

In *Hall*, the Indiana court applied the rebuttable presumption rule. Under this rule, if a creditor fails to comply with commercially reasonable standards upon disposition of collateral, a presumption arises that any amount received from the collateral is equal to the debt. The burden is then on the creditor to rebut this presumption as a prerequisite to obtaining a deficiency judgment against the debtor to recover the balance of the debt due.

For non-consumer transactions, Revised Article 9 eliminates the absolute bar rule in favor of the rebuttable presumption rule. *See* UCC § 9-626(a), cmt. 3. Why did the drafters of the Revised Code favor this reform? Which rule best effectuates the goals of Article 9? The Code explicitly leaves for the courts to determine which rule applies to consumer transactions. *See* UCC § 9-626(b) ("The limitation of the 'rebuttable presumption' rule to non-consumer transactions 'is intended to leave to the court the determination of the proper rules in consumer transactions,' and the court 'may continue to apply established approaches.'" *See Coxall v. Clover Commercial Corp., supra.*)

What consideration do you believe induces courts to position a remedy for secured party misbehavior beyond that provided in UCC § 9-625(c). Is there another theory that arguably would better address this problem? Compare UCC § 9-626 with *Davidson v. First State Bank & Trust Company, Yale*, 609 P.2d 1259 (Okla. 1977), overruled by *Beneficial Finance Co. v. Young*, 612 P.2d 1357 (Okla. 1980), as to denial of deficiency but not as to ruling that illegal taking or wrongful assumption of rights constitutes conversion.

Problem 3-15:   Applicable Law. Manufacturer, a Texas corporation with its sole manufacturing plant in Texas, reserves a security interest in equipment sold to Dealer, a Missouri corporation with all its outlets in Missouri, to secure Dealer's promise to pay the purchase price. Dealer accepts the equipment. Following Dealer's failure to pay for the equipment, Manufacturer proceeds to foreclose using self-help. In the absence of a relevant clause in the security agreement, what State's law governs the standards for foreclosure? *See* UCC § 1-301(d).

DISPOSITION OF PROCEEDS AND PRIORITIES FOLLOWING FORECLOSURE

UCC § 9-615(a) establishes the following four-step process to govern the distribution of the cash proceeds derived from the foreclosure process (UCC § 9-608(a) establishes a similar process for the distribution of the cash proceeds derived from the collection of collateral that consists of rights to payment):

1.   The proceeds go first to reimburse the secured party that conducts the foreclosure for the costs of repossessing the collateral, storing it pending disposition, preparing it for disposition (including commercially reasonable expenses incurred in fixing it up so that it brings a higher price), and conducting the disposition (e.g., advertising costs, auctioneer's commissions). The secured party may also recover attorney's fees and other legal expenses from the proceeds if the security agreement so provides and the recovery is not otherwise prohibited by the law of the jurisdiction. There is judicial authority for reimbursement of expenses incurred in paying off liens in order to clear title. *See, e.g., Contrail Leasing Partners, Ltd. v. Consolidated Airways, Inc.*, 742 F.2d 1095 (7th Cir. 1983).

2.   The proceeds next go to the satisfaction of the indebtedness secured by the security interest of the secured party that conducts the foreclosure. Even if that secured party is junior to another secured party or other lienor, it is entitled to have its debt satisfied from the proceeds.

3.   The proceeds next go to the satisfaction of any subordinate security interest or other subordinate lien on the collateral, but only if the secured party that conducts the foreclosure receives from the subordinate secured party or lienor an authenticated demand for the proceeds before the distribution is completed. How will a subordinate secured party or lienor know to make an authenticated demand for the proceeds? *See* UCC § 9-611(c)(3). In what circumstances will a person send an authenticated notification of an interest

in the collateral under UCC § 9-611(c)(3)(A)?

Note that if a consignor has an interest in the collateral, a subordinate secured party or lienor is not entitled to participate in the distribution unless its interest is senior to the interest of the consignor. Do you understand the rationale for this rule? If not, consider the fact that the interest of a consignor, although classified as a purchase-money security interest (UCC § 9-103(d)), does not secure an obligation. *See* UCC § 9-102(a)(20)(D).

4.   The proceeds next go to a secured party that is a consignor, but only if the secured party that conducts the foreclosure receives from the consignor an authenticated demand for the proceeds before the distribution is completed. The interest of the consignor can either be senior or junior to that of the secured party.

After completion of the distribution process described above and assuming there is no consignor that is entitled to distribution, the secured party must account to the debtor for any surplus. UCC § 9-615(d)(1).

Note that, with the exception of a consignor, only a subordinate secured party or lienor is entitled to participate in the distribution process. To understand the rationale for this limitation, consider a situation in which SP-1 and SP-2 both have security interests in Debtor's equipment perfected by filing and SP-1 has priority over SP-2. Please answer the following questions:

1.   If SP-1 repossesses the equipment and sells it at foreclosure, what is the effect on SP-2's security interest? *See* UCC § 9-617(a). Why is a junior interest destroyed by foreclosure of a senior interest? What steps can SP-2 take to protect its interest? If SP-1 receives non-cash proceeds from the foreclosure sale must it make a distribution to SP-2 upon timely receipt of an authenticated demand? *See* UCC § 9-615(c) and Official Comment 3 to UCC § 9-615.

2.   If SP-2 repossesses the equipment and sells it at foreclosure, what is the effect on SP-1's security interest? *See* UCC §§ 9-317(b), 9-617(a), Official Comment 5 to UCC § 9-610. There are potential adverse practical consequences to SP-1 from SP-2's sale. For example, the buyer might disappear with the collateral or later contest SP-1's security interest. To reduce these risks, SP-1 might consider a cross-default clause in its security agreement making either the attachment of SP-2's security interest (or, at a minimum, any enforcement action by SP-2) an event of default, thereby placing itself in position to move against other collateral. How will SP-1 learn of SP-2's sale in order to trigger its rights? *See* UCC § 9-611(c)(3). If Debtor is in default should SP-1 be permitted to repossess from SP-2 and conduct its own foreclosure sale? *See* Official Comment 5 to UCC § 9-609.

3.   Same facts as Problem 2 (SP-2 holds the foreclosure sale). What is the maximum amount that a buyer should bid at SP-2's sale? Are there any hidden risks to the foreclosure-sale buyer? *See* UCC § 9-323(d).

4. Same facts as Problem 2 (SP-2 holds the foreclosure sale). Suppose the foreclosure-sale buyer is located in a different state than Debtor and SP-1 finally tracks down the collateral more than a year after the foreclosure sale. Will SP-1's filing in the name of Debtor still be effective to give it priority over the buyer? *See* UCC §§ 9-507(a), 9-316(a)(3), 9-102(a)(28)(A), 9-316(b). If SP-1 tracks down the collateral before the expiration of the year, what steps can it take to protect itself? *See* UCC §§ 9-609, 9-509(c).

5. Are the proceeds of the foreclosure sale "proceeds" of SP-1's security interest such that SP-1 is entitled to recover them from SP-2? Put another way, is SP-2 a converter? In answering this question, consider that the distribution scheme set forth above does not provide for distribution to a senior secured party. Also, consider that SP-2's security interest attached to Debtor's rights in the equipment, and those rights were at all times subject to SP-1's security interest. *See* UCC § 9-401. Thus, SP-2's security interest was limited to Debtor's equity. For a discussion of the issues raised by this problem, *see* Delaware Truck Sales, Inc. v. Wilson, 618 A.2d 303 (N.J. 1993). *See* also UCC § 9-615(g). When, if ever, would receipt of proceeds by a junior secured party violate the rights of a senior secured party?

6. Does SP-2 warrant the quality of the title received by the foreclosure sale buyer? If so, can SP-2 disclaim that liability? *See* UCC §§ 2-312, 9-610(d), (e), and (f).

7. Suppose SP-1 conducts a public foreclosure sale. Can it participate in the bidding? *See* UCC § 9-610(c). If SP-1 is the successful bidder, the price is unusually low, and SP-2 has made an authenticated demand for the proceeds, what is the effect of UCC § 9-615(f)? What is the effect on any claim SP-1 might bring against Debtor for a deficiency? The problem UCC § 9-615(f) addresses may also be the focus of other laws outside Article 9 to which its provisions are subject under UCC § 9-201, such as an anti-deficiency statute. *See, e.g.*, 1974 Uniform Consumer Credit Code § 5.103.

Chapter 4

PERFECTION AND PRIORITY

A. PERFECTION—GIVING PUBLIC NOTICE OF A SECURITY INTEREST TO ENHANCE ITS PRIORITY

Secured parties not only evaluate the likelihood that their debtors will perform as promised, they also consider whether on default by their Debtors their security interest in collateral will be satisfied before the claims of third persons who also have an interest in the same collateral. The general rule is "first in time, is first in right." This rule is subject, however, to important limitations. For example, the secured party must usually publicize its interest in order to have priority over subsequent claims. Thus, when UCC § 9-201 states that "a security agreement is effective according to its terms between the parties, against purchasers of the collateral and against creditors," the reader should remember that the sentence begins with the words "[e]xcept as otherwise provided by this Act."

One should distinguish between those third-party claims that exist at the time the secured party's interest becomes attached and those claims that arise subsequently. As for the earlier claims, the secured party will presumably have discovered and evaluated them. Most such claims will have priority over the secured party (i.e., they are "first in time" and therefore "first in right"). A potential secured party who discovers such claims has several options. It may refuse to enter into the transaction with the potential debtor. It may absorb the additional risk of its subordinate interest or adjust the terms of its transaction with the debtor. It may also seek to negotiate with the earlier claimant to have that party agree to subordinate its interest to that of the secured party. *See* UCC § 9-339. In any event, the secured party will frequently require the debtor to warrant that there are no other claims to the collateral or at least no other claims than those that have been revealed.

The secured party will also be concerned with assuring that its claim comes before as many subsequent claims as possible. Article 9 generally will give the secured party this priority if the secured party not only has an attached interest but also has publicized its interest. Publicity is usually given by filing a financing statement in a public file where third parties may inspect it. When a financing statement is properly filed and the interest has attached, the security interest is said to be perfected. Filing is not, however, the only way to perfect a security interest. A secured party may also perfect by taking possession of the collateral, by having "control" over specified types of collateral (as discussed in Section B.4., *infra*) and in some instances, security interests are automatically perfected. Moreover, a perfected security interest may be subordinate to certain later interests. As indicated later in this chapter and analyzed in greater detail in an earlier chapter of these materials, the most important of these exceptions is for "purchase money security interests." There are also special priority rules for fixtures, accession and commingled goods, and for statutory liens.

In practice you will find many disputes turn on whether or not a security interest is perfected. Although there are several exceptions noted below, perfection of the security interest occurs when the interest has attached, as described above, and is publicized. *See* UCC § 9-308. Publicity of the secured party's interest is usually given by filing a short notice (called a "financing statement") in a public file, but publicity may also be given by having the secured party take possession of the collateral. In some cases, which we will later identify, no publicity is required or an alternative action to giving publicity is required.

The consequence of perfecting a security interest is that the secured party will have priority over many, but not all, potential conflicting claims of third parties. The law may make exceptions to the secured party's priority to promote other policies. Once the secured party perfects its interest, however, it has taken all the steps possible to maximize the legal effectiveness of the interest.

To determine whether a security interest is perfected, you must take the following steps:

a) classify the collateral within the elaborate definitions of UCC § 9-102;

b) determine whether the interest is a purchase money security interest under UCC § 9-103;

c) find out if the security interest has attached under UCC §§ 9-203, 9-201 and UCC § 9-204;

d) determine if a filing is required or permitted by UCC §§ 9-310, 9-309, 9-311, 9-312 or whether an exception to filing applies. (§ 9-310(b));

e) check UCC § 9-313 to see if that section permits or requires the secured party to take possession in order to perfect the interest;

f) if filing is required or permitted, examine relevant UCC sections[1] to determine if a validly completed notice was filed in the proper office in the proper jurisdiction and has not lapsed by the passage of time.

Filing a notice in the form of a financing statement will be the normal means of perfecting a security interest in most cases you encounter. *See* UCC §§ 9-309, 9-310, 9-311. Taking possession of collateral is in theory a substitute means of perfecting in many cases and is even required in the case of negotiable instruments, negotiable documents of title, or money. *See* UCC §§ 9-312, 9-313. In addition, you should note there are other means of perfecting an interest. Notice to a bailee if the collateral is in the bailee's possession is one method. *See* UCC § 9-312. A purchase money security interest in consumer goods among others is automatically perfected on attachment without the need to file. *See* UCC §§ 9-309, 9-310. Temporary perfection without the need to file is also provided in specialized commercial contexts where

---

[1] Relevant sections are addressed later in this chapter. *See* UCC §§ 9-301, 9-303, 9-307, 9-316, 9-337, 9-501, 9-502, 9-504, 9-506, 9-507, 9-512, 9-521, 9-515, 9-516(a), 9-519, 9-522, 9-525.

the debtor has possession of very specific types of collateral for a short period of time. *See* UCC §§ 9-312, 9-315. Finally, a security interest for certain types of collateral such as investment property may be perfected by control. *See* UCC § 9-314. This method can also be used for other types of collateral.

All this detail may bewilder you at first. Remember, though, that the basic directions on how to perfect an interest are set out in UCC §§ 9-308 through 9-315. If you read these sections and follow the steps outlined above, you should be able to determine quickly and accurately whether a security interest is perfected.

One final note on a point that generation after generation of students stumbles over; the Code distinguishes between a security agreement, which creates or provides for a security interest, and a financing statement, which is the notice filed to perfect the security interest. The requirements of a security agreement under UCC § 9-203 are only two: that the debtor authenticate the agreement, and that the agreement describe the collateral. The statutory function of this writing, as noted, is to serve as a writing for statute of frauds purposes. The business function, however, is also to serve as a statement of the agreement between the parties. Thus, in certain types of secured transactions, the security agreement may run to several pages, since it will include not merely the statutory minimum requirements but many clauses covering additional rights and duties of the parties, such as a clause requiring the debtor to maintain insurance covering the collateral.

The requirements of the financing statement are found in UCC §§ 9-502, 9-503, 9-504, 9-506, 9-512, 9-521; they are likewise minimal. As a matter of practice, virtually all states have adopted a simple form that meets these requirements, and most UCC filings are made using this standard form. The function of the financing statement is simply to provide a public record that will serve to place other creditors, potential lenders, or purchasers on notice of the possible existence of a security interest in property of the debtor. We explore this distinction further in the material following this note.

B. METHODS OF PERFECTION

Under the revised Article 9, most security interests can be perfected in one or more of four major ways: by filing, by possession, automatically, or by control.

1. Perfection by Filing

Filing a financing statement remains the most important method of perfecting a security interest. *See* §§ 9-308, 9-310(a). The revised Article 9 reforms and modernizes the UCC filing system. Subject to stated exceptions addressed later in these materials, all filings governed by the revision are to be made in the jurisdiction where the debtor is located. UCC § 9-301(1). Under the pre-revision, the secured party filing was required in the state where tangible collateral was physically located. For intangible collateral, the party was required to file where the debtor was located. Revised Article 9 enables the secured party to package all types of collateral, including both tangible and intangible, into a single filing—in the state where the debtor is located. Transaction costs and time are therefore substantially reduced.[2]

2. Perfection by Possession of the Collateral

Possession is an alternative method of perfection for tangible and semi-intangible collateral, including goods, negotiable documents of title, instruments, or tangible chattel paper and certificated securities. UCC § 9-313(a). It is the exclusive method of perfecting a security interest in money. Like the current law, the revised statute does not define "possession." However, comment 3 to UCC § 9-313 states that the principles of agency apply. If the collateral is clearly in the possession of the secured party's agent, and if the agent is not also an agent of the debtor, the secured party has possession.

Revised Article 9 changes current law by allowing a security interest in an "instrument," UCC § 9-102(a)(47), to be perfected by either possession or filing. UCC §§ 9-312(a), 9-313(a). However, a security interest in instruments perfected by possession will have greater protection over a secured creditor who has perfected a security interest in instruments by filing. UCC § 9-330(d). In most cases, possession will be the method of choice for instruments. Though filing will protect the secured creditor from the debtor's trustee in bankruptcy, UCC § 9-317(a)(2), the negotiability of instruments makes filing ineffective to protect a secured party from a holder in due course, or from a purchaser who acquires a negotiable document of title by due negotiation. UCC §§ 3-302, 7-501, 9-331.

Problem 4-1: Perfection by Possession—Priority Over Unperfected Security Interest. On January 18, Steady State Bank extends a loan for $10,000 to Samuel Clemens taking a signed security agreement and an unperfected security interest in Clemens' Rolex watch. On February 15, Clemens takes his watch to Pawn Broker, who extends Clemens a loan for $8,000 and takes possession of Clemens' Rolex. Who has priority with respect to Clemens' Rolex? *See* UCC §§ 9-313(a), 9-317, 9-322(1).

Suppose on January 18, Samuel Clemens had indicated to Steady State Bank that he would need $10,000 of financing on March 15. Steady State Bank immediately files a financing statement on January 18 listing itself as the secured creditor, Samuel Clemens as the debtor, and the Rolex watch as the collateral. After pawn broker extends its loan and takes possession of the Rolex on February 15, Steady State Bank extends the loan and obtains a security interest in the Rolex on March 15. Clemens thereafter defaults. Who prevails? *See* § 9-322(a)(1). In this fact situation, is the priority resolved by the "filing" or alternatively by "perfection"?

Problem 4-2: Perfection by Possession; Priority in Bankruptcy; Perfected vs. Unperfected Security Interest. On June 14, Acme Bank extends a $50,000 loan to Clemens and files a financing statement to perfect its security interest in a promissory note issued to the order of Clemens by Wholesale Book Vendors Inc. to secure repayment of a $70,000 loan Clemens had extended to finance Wholesaler's acquisition of new book inventory. On June 26, Clemens obtains a loan of $55,000 from Steady State Bank, duly signs a security agreement, and to secure repayment

---

[2] Barkley Clark & Barbara Clark, *Special Report: New Article* 9, 31 UCC L.J. 243, 247 (1999).

gives Steady State Bank possession of the Wholesale Book Vendors Inc. promissory note. Assume that five months after Samuel Clemens entered into the loans with Acme Bank and Steady State Bank, a petition in bankruptcy against Clemens is filed. Does the trustee in bankruptcy have priority in the promissory note? *See* UCC §§ 9-308, 9-310, 9-312, 9-313, 9-317(a)(2) (instruments), 9-102(a)(47) (promissory note), 9-102(a)(65) (lien creditor), 9-102(a)(52)(C); *see also* Bankr. Code § 544(a)(1). As between Acme Bank and Steady State Bank, which bank has priority with respect to the promissory note? *See* UCC §§ 9-102(a)(47), 9-310, 9-312(a), 9-313, 9-330(d).

3.   Automatic Perfection

A security interest may also be perfected automatically, when the security interest attaches. UCC §§ 9-203(a), 9-309. Attachment requires:

1. creation of a security agreement UCC § 9-203(b)(3),

2. extension of value by the creditor to the debtor, UCC § 9-203(b)(1), and

3. acquisition of the rights in the collateral by the debtor, UCC § 9-203(b)(2).

Example: Automatic Perfection—Purchase Money Security Interest in Consumer Goods. Dealer sells a washing machine to Buyer for use in Buyer's home. By written agreement, Dealer retains a security interest in the washer to secure payment of the purchase price. Dealer does not file a financing statement. Notwithstanding the failure to file, Dealer has a perfected security interest. Dealer is a seller who retained a security interest to secure the purchase price of goods (purchase money security interest, UCC § 9-103, and the goods were bought for use primarily in the household (consumer goods) UCC § 9-102(a)(44) and UCC § 9-102(a)(23)). Dealer's security interest, therefore, is automatically perfected. *See* UCC § 9-309(1).

Problem 4-3:   Priority by Automatic Perfection. Dealer sells Samuel Clemens a computer for use in his home. Dealer retains a security interest in the computer by written agreement to secure payment of the purchase price. Dealer does not file a financing statement. Three months later, Steady State Bank extends a loan to Clemens, taking a security interest in the computer and files a financing statement to perfect a security interest in the computer. Who has priority over the computer? *See* UCC §§ 9-309(1), 9-322(a), 9-103, 9-102(a)(44), 9-102(a)(23). Has the bank a further legal problem? See 16 C.F.R. §§ 444.2(a)(4), 444.1(i), which provide:

16 C.F.R. PART 444—CREDIT PRACTICES

§ 444.1 Definitions.

. . .

(b) *Household goods.* Clothing, furniture, appliances, one radio and one television, linens, china, crockery, kitchenware, and personal effects (including wedding rings) of the consumer and his or her dependents, provided that the following are not included within the scope of the term *household goods* . . .

§ 444.2 Unfair credit practices.

(a) In connection with the extension of credit to consumers in or affecting commerce, as commerce is defined in the Federal Trade Commission Act, it is an unfair act or practice within the meaning of Section 5 of that Act for a lender or retail installment seller directly or indirectly to take or receive from a consumer an obligation that

. . .

   (4) Constitutes or contains a non-possessory security interest in household goods other than a purchase money security interest.

4.   Perfection by "Control" of the Collateral

Perfection may also be accomplished by control over the collateral. Originally, control governed perfection of investment property. However, Revised Article 9 now uses the concept for deposit accounts, UCC § 9-104, electronic chattel paper, UCC § 9-105, investment property, UCC § 9-106, and UCC § 9-107, letter-of-credit rights. In addition, under the 2003 amendments to Article 7, perfection of a security interest in an electronic document of title may be accomplished by control. UCC §§ 7-106, 9-314(a).

Deposit accounts and letter-of-credit rights must be perfected by control. Control over letter-of-credit rights occurs when the issuer consents to an assignment of proceeds. UCC § 9-107. Control over deposit accounts occurs automatically when the relevant depository institution is the secured party. Control for third parties over deposit accounts occurs when the depository institution has agreed with the debtor and the secured party that it will follow directions from the secured party without further consent by the debtor. UCC § 9-104. A similar concept applies to control of an electronic document of title under UCC § 7-106.

Control of electronic chattel paper occurs when there is a special electronic identification of the secured party on the electronic copy of the chattel paper. UCC § 9-105 defines "control" as the functional equivalent of possession of tangible chattel paper. Thus, the requirement for establishing control is that a particular copy be an "authoritative copy."

Under the 1972 Code, "deposit accounts" were covered only as proceeds [§§ 9-102(12), 9-104]. Under the Revised Article 9, "deposit accounts" (§ 9-102(a)(29)) are covered as original collateral. *See* UCC §§ 9-203(b)(3)(D); 9-104. "Deposit Account" is defined as "a demand, time, savings, passbook, or similar account maintained with a bank." UCC § 9-102(a)(29); *see also* UCC § 9-102(a)(8) (definition of "bank"). Note that "[t]he term does not include investment property or accounts evidenced by an instrument." UCC § 9-102(a)(29). Moreover, the Code excludes coverage of assignments of deposit accounts in consumer transactions. *See* UCC § 9-109(d)(13). Perfection of "deposit accounts" is achieved through control. *See* UCC § 9-104.

Problem 4-4: Perfection by Control—Deposit Account as Collateral.

(a) Clemens has a two million dollar account with Bank. In exchange for a loan of one million dollars, Clemens and Bank enter into a security agreement using the account as collateral. Does Bank have an enforceable security interest in the account? *See* UCC §§ 9-203(b)(3)(D), 9-109(a)(1), 9-109(d)(13), 9-104(a)(1). Does Bank have a perfected security interest in the account? *See* UCC §§ 9-308, 9-310, 9-314(a), 9-104(a)(1).

(b) Suppose Manufacturer extends a loan for one million dollars to Clemens in exchange for a security agreement signed by Clemens which gives manufacturer a security interest in this Bank Account. Does manufacturer have an enforceable security interest? *See* UCC §§ 9-109(a)(1), 9-203(b)(3)(D), 9-104(a)(2). Does Manufacturer have a perfected security interest? *See* UCC §§ 9-308, 9-340, 9-314(a), 9-104(a)(2).

(c) Suppose that Manufacturer, Bank, and Clemens enter into an agreement that the Bank will comply with instructions originated by the secured party directing disposition of the funds in the deposit account without further consent by the debtor. Does Manufacturer now have an enforceable security interest? *See* UCC §§ 9-109(a)(1), 9-203(b)(3)(D), 9-104(a)(2). Does Manufacturer have a perfected security interest? *See* UCC §§ 9-308, 9-310, 9-314(a), 9-104(a)(2).

Analogous requirements for obtaining control over other new types of collateral are found in UCC § 9-105 pertaining to electronic chattel paper, UCC § 9-106 pertaining to investment property, UCC § 9-107 pertaining to letter-of-credit rights and UCC § 7-106 pertaining to an electronic document of title, as noted in appropriate portions of the book.

C. REQUIRED FILINGS AND EXCEPTIONS

"Perfection" of a security interest is to be distinguished from "attachment" of a security interest. As we have seen, attachment occurs when the steps required to give the secured party an enforceable security interest in the collateral have been completed (i.e., "security agreement," "value," and "debtor rights in the collateral" requirements).

UCC § 9-308 provides that "perfection" of a security interest occurs when the security interest has attached and the performance of an applicable step for perfection has occurred. This step generally occurs by the secured creditor giving public notice of his security interest by filing a financing statement. The Code provides exceptions to this rule in UCC §§ 9-309, 9-310, 9-311, 9-312, 9-313, 9-314.

"Perfection" normally gives the secured party priority to the collateral against the debtor's creditors and transferees from the debtor. Exceptions to this general rule are discussed later in this chapter. UCC § 9-310 states the basic requirement (subject to enumerated exceptions) that a financing statement must be filed to perfect all security interests. The content and place of filing requirements of financing statements are also considered later in this chapter.

The exceptions to the general requirement that a financing statement must be filed to perfect a security interest include:

(a)   perfection by possession of the collateral; UCC § 9-310(b)(6);

(b)   temporary perfection of a security interest in instruments or documents for a 20 day period, or in proceeds for a 20 day period; UCC § 9-310(b)(5);

(c)   automatic perfection; UCC § 9-309; included *inter alia* are a purchase money security interest in consumer goods (other than goods subject to certificate of title statutes or goods which are fixtures); an assignment of an insignificant part of accounts of the assignor; an assignment for the benefit of all the creditors of the transferor;

(d)   compliance with a federal statute or treaty providing for national or international registration or certificate of title; a state certificate of title statute; and security interest subject to certificate of title statutes of another jurisdiction. UCC § 9-310(b)(3);

(e)   deposit accounts, electronic chattel paper, investment property, letter-of-credit rights or electronic documents of title which are perfected by control. UCC § 9-310(b)(8);

(f)   the security interest of a collecting bank or security interest arising under Article 2; UCC § 9-309(7);

(g)   an assignment for the benefit of all the creditors of the transferor; UCC § 9-309(12);

(h)   compliance with a federal statute or treaty providing for national or international registration or certificate of title, UCC § 9-311(a)(11);

(i)   compliance with a state certificate of title statute, UCC § 9-311(a)(2);

(j)   security interest subject to certificate of title statutes of another jurisdiction, UCC § 9-311(a)(3); and

(k)   deposit accounts, electronic chattel paper, investment property, letter-of-credit rights or electronic documents of title which are perfected by control—§ 9-310(b)(8).

Illustrative of the exceptions are those set forth in the following chart, which are considered in the materials that follow.

General Outline of Perfection Requirements and Procedures
§ 9-308 Attachment of Security Interest

§§ 9-203, 9-204, 9-205

Attachment Requirements:

(a) creation of a security agreement[3]—**§§ 9-203(b)(3) and 9-102(a)(73)**

(b) extension of value (**UCC § 1-204** by creditor to debtor—**§ 9-203(b)(1)**

(c) acquisition of rights in the collateral by debtor—**§ 9-203(b)(2)**

Performance of Applicable Step for Perfection

§§ 9-309, 9-310, 9-311, 9-312, 9-313, 9-315, 9-334

The occurrence of any one of the following will qualify for perfection:

1. Filing financing statement for personal property and fixtures—**§ 9-310(a)**;
2. Exceptions to the filing requirement
   (a) possession—**§ 9-310(b)(6)**;
   (b) 20 day rule **§ 9-312(e)–(g)** or **§ 9-315(d)**, **§ 9-310(b)(5)**;
   (c) assignment of a beneficial interest in a trust or decedent's estate—**§ 9-309(13)**;
   (d) purchase money security interest (P.M.S.I.) in consumer goods—**§ 9-309(1)**;
   (e) assignment of an "insignificant part" of accounts receivable—**§ 9-309(2)**;
   (f) security interest of a collecting bank or arising under Article 2 or 2A—**§ 9-309(6) and (7)**;
   (g) assignment for the benefit of all the creditors of the transferor—**§ 9-309(12)**;
   (h) compliance with federal statute or treaty providing for national or international registration or certificate of title—**§ 9-311(a)(1)**;
   (i) compliance with state certificate of title statutes—**§ 9-311(a)(2)**;
   (j) certificate of title statutes of another jurisdiction—**§ 9-311(a)(3)**;
   (k) deposit accounts, electronic chattel paper, investment property, letter-of-credit rights or electronic documents of title which are perfected by control—**§ 9-310(b)(8)**.

---

[3] This requirement is usually met by execution of an authenticated (which includes *inter alia* written and electronic agreements, *see* UCC § 9-102(a)(7)) security agreement. However, the UCC also permits a security agreement to be created orally if "the collateral is . . . in the possession of the secured party . . . pursuant to the debtor's security agreement." UCC § 9-203(b)(3)(B).

D. PRIORITIES

1. Overview

The final major landmark in the law of secured transactions is the area of priorities. As we noted above, the perfection of a security interest increases the protection that a secured party enjoys against third parties but does not give absolute protection. Some third party claimants are given a special priority that enables them to take priority over even a perfected security interest. Furthermore, the priority that certain claimants will enjoy against a secured party will depend in some instances upon the mode of perfection the secured party has chosen where more than one mode is available. The three most likely competing claimants will be the lien creditor (*see* UCC § 9-317),[4] the buyer (*see* UCC §§ 9-317, 9-320) (similarly treated are lessees and licensees) and another secured party (*see* UCC §§ 9-322 through 9-324).

An illustration of how a priority rule works will show the difference between priority and perfection. Assume that a retailer obtains a line of credit from a bank secured by a security interest in all the retailer's inventory. Assume further that the bank has properly perfected this security interest by filing an appropriate financing statement with the secretary of state. If at some later time the retailer files a petition in bankruptcy, the bank will receive protection against the trustee in bankruptcy as representative of the unsecured creditors of the retailer. Under both the Bankruptcy Code and the Uniform Commercial Code, the trustee has the rights of lien creditor. The strict UCC authority for the bank's protection is UCC

---

[4] A lien is an interest in or charge against property to secure payment of a debt or performance of an obligation. The holder of a lien on property has a claim against the property that can be enforced by foreclosure and that will have priority over most of the claims of unsecured creditors and subsequent lienholders. Liens may arise by judicial process, by statute, or by agreement. An Article 9 security interest might be described as a consensual lien. The lien creditor in UCC § 9-317 is a creditor who has obtained a lien without the consent of the debtor by judicial process (*e.g.*, by attachment, levy or the like) although the assignee for the benefit of creditors and the trustee in bankruptcy, whose liens might be said to arise by statute, are also deemed lien creditors. *See* UCC § 9-102.

When you come across the word *lien*, you should be careful to read it in context. A *judgment lien* usually arises when a judgment is rendered and adopted (recorded in a special book kept by the clerk of the court rendering the judgment) but, with the exception of three states, this lien only attaches to real property. A *judicial lien* includes liens that arise through legal process and may include judgment liens. See, for example, the definition of *judicial lien* in § 101(30) of the Bankruptcy Code. Unfortunately, usage is not always consistent. The Internal Revenue Code, for example, uses the term *judgment lien creditor* in a sense that includes not only the judgment lien but also liens that may arise by levy of execution. *See* 26 U.S.C. § 6321-23 (1994); 26 C.F.R. § 301.623(h)-1(g) (1996).

For the purposes of UCC § 9-317, it is important to know the date on which a lien is deemed effective. The Code does not provide an answer and unfortunately state law is not uniform. In some states, the lien may arise only when a sheriff levies on property by taking it into his custody; in some states, the lien may arise when the writ is delivered to the sheriff and continue in effect if the sheriff levies promptly; in yet other states, the lien may arise when the sheriff levies but for priority purposes be deemed to relate back to the date on which the writ was delivered to the sheriff. If you look at UCC §§ 9-317, 9-102, 9-323 closely, you will see how these different rules might lead to different results.

§ 9-201. If the security interest is unperfected, the trustee will be able to invoke a very broad exception to UCC § 9-201, to wit, UCC § 9-317(a)(2), which subordinates the interest of the unperfected security interest holder to a broad range of other claimants, including the lien creditor. Since the bank has perfected its interest, however, the trustee loses the benefit of the rights as a lien creditor under UCC § 9-317.

You should not read the above example as saying that the bank will win against all potential claimants. Indeed, strictly speaking, the only assured result of perfecting a security interest is that the secured party will not lose to a third party who can cite only UCC § 9-201 in support of the claim to priority. For example, in the above illustration, assume that an expensive item is sold out of the retailer's inventory to a consumer. Bank then attempts to assert its security interest. Good sense tells us that banks financing inventory should not, as a general rule, be able to assert that security interest against the collateral in the hands of a buyer in ordinary course; a contrary result would be disruptive of retail trade or inventory financing or both. The Code comes to the same conclusion as our common sense, in this instance in UCC §§ 9-315(a)(1), 9-320(a); *see also* UCC § 9-321 (lessees and licensees).

Note that, as a matter of logical structure, this priority for the buyer is simply another exception to the "general" rule of UCC § 9-201. The logical structure of the Code is to provide for a "general rule" of protection against third parties in UCC § 9-201. This rule is applicable as soon as the secured party has created an enforceable security interest: it does not require that the interest be perfected. However, UCC § 9-201, the general rule, only is applicable unless otherwise provided. A very broad provision to the contrary, effective whenever the security interest is unperfected, is found in UCC § 9-317. A series of narrower provisions to the contrary, applicable even though the security interest in question is perfected, is found in the priority rules of UCC §§ 9-319 through 9-323.

> **Example:** Priorities Dealer sells a washing machine to Buyer, a consumer, and retains by written agreement a security interest in the washer to secure payment of the purchase price. Dealer does not file a financing statement but, as explained in Example d, Dealer's interest is automatically perfected. To what extent is Dealer protected against potential claims to the property by third parties?

(a) Dealer's interest has priority over the claims of Buyer's general unsecured creditors regardless of whether Dealer's interest is perfected. *See* UCC § 9-201.

(b) As a perfected security interest, Dealer's interest has priority over the claims of Buyer's lien creditors. *See* UCC §§ 9-201, 9-317(a)(2).

(c) As a perfected purchase money security interest, Dealer's interest will be prior to virtually all competing secured parties. *See* UCC § 9-322.

(d) Unless Dealer agrees to the disposition of the washer by Buyer free of the security interest, Dealer will have priority over most purchasers from Buyer. *See* UCC § 9-201; *cf.* UCC § 9-320. Dealer's interest is cut off, however, if Buyer sells to another consumer who does not know about the security interest. Only by filing is Dealer protected from this possibility. *See* UCC § 9-320.

2. Priority Rules—Types of Third Party Claimants—Impact on Priority Status

We next identify different types of third party claimants and the priority status for each type of claimant under Article 9.

a. An Unsecured Creditor vs. Debtor

The unsecured creditor has no interest in debtor's assets. The general rule of UCC § 9-201 will give the secured party priority whether the unsecured creditor's interest arose before or after the security interest attached.

b. Judgment Creditor vs. Debtor

With the exception of several jurisdictions, the judgment creditor will have no interest in the judgment debtor's personal property. The judgment creditor, therefore, in most jurisdictions is no better off than the unsecured creditor without a judgment.

c. Lien Creditor vs. Unperfected Security Interest

A creditor can obtain a lien on the debtor's personal property through judicial process, usually after judgment is entered into against the debtor. This lien is not an Article 9 security interest because a judicial lien is not consensual. *See* UCC §§ 9-102(a)(73), 1-201(b)(3), 1-201(b)(35), 9-109. The lien does, however, give the creditor (lien creditor) an interest in debtor's personal property that competes with a secured party's security interest in the same property. The lien is governed by state law, but this law is not uniform. When a lien arises, therefore, varies from jurisdiction to jurisdiction. As a general rule, a lien creditor's lien will have priority over a security interest if the lien arises before the security interest is perfected. UCC § 9-317(a)(2). Note: there can be other statutory liens under state law arising by statute. Generally, Article 9 does not deal with these. *But see* UCC §§ 9-333, 9-322. *See* Problem 4-6, *infra*.

Problem 4-5: Lien Creditor vs. Unperfected Security Interest. On March 15, Samuel Clemens borrows $50,000 and gives Steady State Bank a secured interest in existing and after acquired collateral but does not file a financing statement. On April 15, Acme Office Equipment obtains a judgment against Clemens in the amount of $50,000. Acme has a writ of execution issued against Samuel Clemens. Will Acme have priority over Steady State Bank? UCC §§ 9-201, 9-317(a)(2).

d. Debtor's Trustee in Bankruptcy—Priority vs. Unperfected Security Interest

The trustee is assimilated to the lien creditor under state law and will therefore have priority over an unperfected security interest. *See* Bankr. Code § 544(a)(1); *see also* UCC §§ 9-317(a)(2), 9-102(a)(52). As will be discussed later, the trustee may also be able to "avoid" a security interest if it is preferential or fraudulent. *See* Bankr. Code §§ 547, 548.

The trustee in bankruptcy is the most feared of these potential claimants. Bankruptcy provides an "acid test" for security interests. To mix metaphors, a trustee may use the "strong arm" to strike down a security interest if it is unperfected but not if the interest is perfected. The strong-arm clause of the Bankruptcy Code is § 544(a)(1). That clause states:

(a)   The trustee shall have, as of the commencement of the case, and without regard to any knowledge of the trustee or of any creditor, the rights and powers of, or may avoid any transfer of property of the debtor or any obligation incurred by the debtor that is voidable by—

(1)   a creditor that extends credit to the debtor at the time of the commencement of the case, and that obtains, at such time and with respect to such credit, a judicial lien on all property on which a creditor on a simple contract could have obtained such a judicial lien, whether or not such a creditor exists . . . .

In other words, the Bankruptcy Code gives a trustee in bankruptcy the rights of a lien creditor under state law, which will often be UCC Article 9 which includes:

". . . a trustee in bankruptcy from the date of the filing of the petition; . . ." in its definition of "lien creditor." UCC § 9-102(a)(52) confirms this. As a result, a trustee will look to UCC §§ 9-201 and 9-317(a)(2), which, as we have seen, subordinate unperfected security interests to the lien of a lien creditor. Therefore, even though the financer of a retail appliance dealership will not prevail over a buyer in the ordinary course, the holder of the perfected security interest in retail inventory nevertheless prevails over the trustee in bankruptcy.

Problem 4-6: Trustee in Bankruptcy vs. Unperfected Security Interest. On January 15, Steady State Bank extends a loan of $50,000 to Samuel Clemens and takes a security interest in his existing and after-acquired equipment but does not file a financing statement. On July 15, a petition in bankruptcy against Samuel Clemens is issued. Does the trustee in bankruptcy have priority in the office equipment over Steady State Bank? *See* UCC §§ 9-102(a)(52), 9-201, 9-317(a)(2); *see also* Bankr. Code § 544(a).

e. First to File or Perfect Rule

The general rule as between secured parties is that the first to perfect or to file a financing statement will have priority. *See* UCC § 9-322. The principal exceptions to this first in time rule involve purchase money security interests as those interests are defined in UCC § 9-103. *See* UCC § 9-324.

Problem 4-7: Filing of Financing Statement Preceding Perfection. On January 15, Clemens executes a security agreement giving Steady State Bank a security interest in a mobile x-ray machine as security for any loans which Steady State Bank, in its discretion, thereafter makes to Clemens. Steady State Bank files appropriate financing statements on February 5 but does not make a loan to

Clemens until February 25. In the meantime, on February 20, Clemens obtains a loan from Acme Bank, duly signs a security agreement and gives Acme Bank possession of the mobile x-ray machine to secure repayment of the loan. Which bank has priority with respect to the mobile x-ray machine? Would the result be different if Steady State Bank on January 15 had made a binding promise to extend a $40,000 loan to Clemens on February 25? Would the result be different if Acme Bank had filed a financing statement on February 20 covering its security interest in the x-ray machine rather than taking possession thereof? *See* UCC §§ 9-322(a)(1), 9-102(a)(68), 9-308, 9-310.

f. Creditor with a Lien that Arises by Operation of Law

State laws frequently give a statutory lien to persons who render services or furnish materials in the ordinary course of their business. The lien is a nonconsensual interest in a debtor's personal property to secure the debtor's promise to pay for the services or materials. These state lien laws are not uniform; they may be statutory or common law liens. The lien is prior to the security interest unless the lien arises under a statute that provides otherwise. *See* UCC § 9-333. Such liens accorded to persons who supply goods and services to farmers are agricultural liens. (UCC § 9-102(a)(5)), and revised Article 9, but not the earlier version, also includes such liens primarily for purposes of perfection and priority. UCC § 9-109(a)(2)).

Problem 4-8: Repairman's Lien vs. Perfected Security Interest. Samuel Clemens buys a truck for use in his business. Steady State Bank extends a loan of $15,000 to finance this purchase and takes a security interest in the truck to secure payments of the loan. Steady State Bank perfects the security interest by noting its encumbrance on the certificate of title as required by UCC § 9-311(a)(2). As Clemens is driving the truck to work a few days after all this paperwork has been completed, he is involved in an intersection accident which causes $5,000 damage to the truck. Reliable Body Works, Inc. repairs the truck and when Clemens defaults on the repair bill, Reliable Body resells the truck to satisfy its $5,000 repair bill. Does the $5,000 claim of Reliable Body Works have priority over Steady State Bank for the $15,000 loan which remains unpaid?

g. Priority of Buyers of Collateral

Whether or not a security interest is perfected, it will be cut off if the secured party authorized the sale of the collateral free of the interest or if the sale is of goods from inventory other than farm products. UCC §§ 9-315(a)(1), 9-320(a).

UCC 9-320(a) provides that a "buyer in ordinary course of business" (UCC § 1-201(b)(9)) "takes free of a security interest created by his seller even though the security interest is perfected and even though the buyer knows of its existence." See similar provisions for licensees and lessees. UCC § 9-321.

Lawyers or students involved in an initial exposure to the UCC may have difficulty visualizing the applicability of this provision. It essentially gives priority to a buyer who buys in ordinary course from the inventory of a dealer, over claims of creditors who have a prior perfected security interest created by the dealer in the dealer's inventory.

To reach this level of understanding, we first refer to UCC § 1-201(b)(9) of the Code which provides that "buyer in ordinary course of business" means a person who:

(a)   in good faith,

(b)   without knowledge that the sale to him is in violation of the rights of a third party in the goods,

(c)   buys in ordinary course,

(d)   from a person other than a pawnbroker in the business of selling goods of that kind.

UCC § 9-320 gives a priority to the "buyer in ordinary course of business" over the prior perfected security interest even though the buyer knew of the prior perfected security interest. Note the difference between knowing of the interest and knowing of a violation; the latter is the second of the four requirements listed in UCC § 1-201(b)(9) for a "buyer in ordinary course of business."

There is a sound policy reason for this priority rule. Buyers would not be inclined to buy goods out of inventory if they were subject to claims of creditors who have financed such inventory and the lender is in a better position to see that its claim is satisfied than is a buyer. This in turn would make it difficult for sellers to sell their inventory to obtain funds with which to repay creditors who had financed the inventory.

i.   Priority of a Buyer in the Ordinary Course (i.e., Buyers Out of Inventory) with Knowledge Over a Perfected Security Interest in Inventory[5]

ACTUAL TEXT
§ 1-201 GENERAL DEFINITIONS

(9) "Buyer in ordinary course of business" means a person that buys goods in good faith, without knowledge that the sale violates the rights of another person in the goods, and in the ordinary course from a person, other than a pawnbroker, in the business of selling goods of that kind. A person buys goods in the ordinary course if the sale to the person comports with the usual or customary practices in the kind of business in which the seller is engaged

SIMPLIFIED VERSION

(9) "Buyer in ordinary course of business" means a person that buys goods
(i) in good faith,
(ii) without knowledge that the sale violates the rights of another person in the goods, and
(iii) in the ordinary course from a person, other than a pawnbroker, in the business of selling goods of that kind.

---

[5] The classification of the different types of "investment property" collateral is noted at Chapter 2, Section D.1., *supra*.

ACTUAL TEXT

or with the seller's own usual or customary practices. A person that sells oil, gas, or other minerals at the wellhead or minehead is a person in the business of selling goods of that kind. A buyer in ordinary course of business may buy for cash, by exchange of other property, or on secured or unsecured credit, and may acquire goods or documents of title under a preexisting contract for sale. Only a buyer that takes possession of the goods or has a right to recover the goods from the seller under Article 2 may be a buyer in ordinary course of business. "Buyer in ordinary course of business" does not include a person that acquires goods in a transfer in bulk or as security for or in total or partial satisfaction of a money debt.

SIMPLIFIED VERSION

In connection with the definition of buyer in ordinary course of business, the following provisions shall apply:

(A) Ordinary Course. A person buys goods in the ordinary course if the sale to the person comports with the usual or customary practices in the kind of business in which the seller is engaged or with the seller's own usual or customary practices.

(B) Sales at Wellhead or Minehead. A person that sells oil, gas, or other minerals at the wellhead or minehead is a person in the business of selling goods of that kind.

(C) Buying and Acquiring Goods or Documents of Title. A buyer in ordinary course of business may:

> (i) buy for cash, by exchange of other property, or on secured or unsecured credit, and

> (ii) may acquire goods or documents of title under a preexisting contract for sale.

(D) Possessory status or right to recover goods requirement. Only a buyer that takes possession of the goods or has a right to recover the goods from the seller under Article 2 may be a buyer in ordinary course of business.

(E) Bulk Transferees and Creditors. A person that acquires goods in a transfer in bulk or as security for or in total or partial satisfaction of a money debt is not a buyer in the ordinary course of business.

Problem 4-9: Priority of a Buyer in Ordinary Course (i.e., Buyers Out of Inventory) With Knowledge Over a Perfected Security Interest in Inventory. Clemens also runs a retail appliance dealership. Steady State Bank extended a loan of $300,000, taking a security interest in Clemens' existing and after-acquired inventory of appliances and duly filed a financing statement. John Smith buys a television set for cash from Clemens. Will John Smith take the television set free of Steady State Bank's prior perfected security interest even though at the time he buys the set he has knowledge of Steady State Bank's prior perfected security interest? *See* UCC § 9-320(a) and Simplified Version of § 1-201(b)(9) in Appendix A. Must Smith take delivery of the set to prevail? *See* Revised UCC § 9-320 cmt. 8.

ii. Priority of a Consumer Buyer From a Consumer Seller Over an Automatically Perfected Purchase Money Security Interest

Subsection (b) of UCC § 9-320 creates another class of buyers who take free of a perfected security interest in the property. A buyer who buys goods from a consumer seller takes free of any security interest if the buyer buys the goods:

(1) without knowledge of the security interest;

(2) for value;

(3) for the buyer's own personal use; and

(4) prior to the filing of a financing statement covering such goods.

Note the exception to the filing requirement which permits a purchase money security interest in consumer goods to be perfected "automatically" without filing. *See* UCC § 9-309(1).

The creditor who elects to use this automatic perfection procedure is protected against the buyer-debtor's trustee in bankruptcy, subsequent buyers and creditors, and the world in general. However, UCC § 9-320 gives a priority over such a creditor to the consumer buyer who meets the requirements set forth therein. This result involves a balancing of equities of sellers and consumer buyers. For sellers of relatively low price, high volume merchandise, it would be impractical to incur the cost of filing numerous financing statements for low priced items. On the other hand, unsophisticated buyers of the consumer goods without knowledge of the security interest have no way of discovering the encumbrance if a financing statement has not been filed.

While sellers of low priced, high volume items may choose not to file, a counseling caveat for sellers of high priced, low volume items (such as a diamond necklace for $100,000) is in order at this point. In such cases, it obviously is worth the comparatively low cost of filing a financing statement to achieve protection even against the possible emergence of a consumer-buyer otherwise protected by UCC § 9-320(b).

Problem 4-10: Priority of a Consumer Buyer From a Consumer Seller Over an Automatically Perfected Purchase Money Security Interest. Clemens buys an expensive stereo for his personal use and finances it with a loan from Steady

State Bank which takes a purchase money security interest (UCC § 9-103) in the set but does not file a financing statement to perfect, choosing instead to acquire automatic perfection status under UCC § 9-309(1). Without knowledge of the Bank's security interest, Harry buys the set from Clemens for his personal use. Does Steady State Bank or Harry have priority to the set? *See* UCC § 9-320.

Would the result be different if Clemens had originally purchased the stereo to provide background music in the office of his printing business? *See* UCC §§ 9-102(a)(33), 9-320(b).

Would the result be different if Clemens had bought the set for his personal use and Harry had bought it to resell it in a used appliance business which he owned?

Would the result be different if Clemens had bought the set for his personal use, and then used it as collateral to secure repayment of a $200 loan which Harry had extended to him?

h.   Priorities in Chattel Paper Collateral

We categorize chattel paper as semi-intangible collateral in our inventory of types of Article 9 collateral (*see* chart in Chapter 2, Section D.1., *supra*). To assist in visualizing the definition of chattel paper contained in § 9-102(a)(11), here we reproduce the actual text and the simplified version of the actual text side by side. The chattel paper is either a Purchase Money Security Interest (PMSI) or lease of goods by themselves or with associated software.

ACTUAL TEXT	SIMPLIFIED VERSION
§ 9-102(a)	
(11) "Chattel paper" means a record or records that evidence both a monetary obligation and a security interest in specific goods, a security interest in specific goods and software used in the goods, a security interest in specific goods and license of software used in the goods, a lease of specific goods, or a lease of specific goods and license of software used in the goods. In this paragraph, "monetary obligation" means a monetary obligation secured by the goods or owned under a lease of the goods and includes a monetary obligation with respect to software used in the goods. The term does not include (i) charters or other contracts involving the use of hire of a vessel or (ii) records that evidence a right to payment arising out of	(11) "Chattel Paper" (A) means a record or records that evidence both a monetary obligation and: (i) 1. a security interest in specific goods 2. a security interest in specific goods and software used in the goods [or] 3. a security interest in specific goods and license of software used in the goods; or (ii) 1. a lease of specific goods or 2. a lease of specific goods and license of software used in the goods (B) The term does not include: (i) charters or other contracts involving the use of hire of a

ACTUAL TEXT	SIMPLIFIED VERSION
the use of a credit or charge card or information contained on or for use with the card. If a transaction is evidence by records that include an instrument or series of instruments, the group of records taken together constitutes chattel paper.	vessel or (ii) records that evidence a right to payment arising out of the use of a credit or charge card or information contained on or for use with the card (C) If a transaction is evidence by records that include an instrument or series of instruments, the group of records taken together constitutes chattel paper.

NOTE

By creating "chattel paper" as a type of Article 9 collateral, the UCC significantly expands types of assets which can be used as collateral, thereby enhancing the availability of credit and facilitating achievement of a basic Article 9 policy. Not only can the debtor's inventory be used as collateral, but in addition, the paper or electronic record generated by sale of the inventory makes available an additional type of assets which can be encumbered. Beyond this, the definition of chattel paper also makes possible use by the debtor of the hard copy or electronic record of leases and associated software as an additional type of assets that can be encumbered.

Section 9-312 permits perfection of a security interest in chattel paper by filing a financing statement. Section 9-313 permits perfection of a security interest in chattel paper by taking possession of the chattel paper. Permissive use of either method further facilitates chattel paper based financing by giving creditors flexibility on deciding which method best serves their needs. Creditors who perfect a security interest in chattel paper by filing normally leave to the debtor the task of collecting installments (i.e. payments due from the "account debtor" (*see* § 9-201(a)(3)) on the PMSI or lease agreements). Creditors who take possession of the chattel paper in order to perfect normally collect the installment payment directly from the account debtors.

Retention of possession by the debtor of chattel paper creates a situation in which subsequent creditors extending additional credit to the debtor on a basis of using the retained chattel paper as collateral, or buyers of the chattel paper from the debtor may rely on the apparent ownership of the chattel paper by the debtor. Section 9-330 gives priority to purchasers (*see* definitions § 1-201(a)(29)(30)) who perfect by taking possession over a creditor who opts to perfect by filing unless the first creditor notes on the chattel paper that it has been assigned to a named creditor.

Problem 4-11: Chattel Paper (Purchase Money Security Interest Contract) Priority of Secured Creditor Who Perfects By Possession Over Secured Creditor Who Perfects By Filing. Dealer, a retail vendor of appliances, has its customers sign conditional sales contracts. Lender A extends a line of credit, takes a security interest in Dealer's existing and after acquired conditional sales contracts, and then files a financing statement covering its security interest in the conditional sales contracts. Lender A permits Dealer to collect the installment payments from the customers. However, Dealer is required to remit monthly payments due on its loan from these proceeds.

Needing additional cash, Dealer subsequently takes a second loan from Lender B. Lender B also takes a security interest in Dealer's existing and after acquired conditional sales contracts and takes physical possession of them instead of filing a financing statement.

When Dealer defaults on both loans, does Lender B have priority over Lender A? *See* UCC §§ 9-102(a)(11), 9-330.

Problem 4-12:   Chattel Paper—Sale or Encumbrance of Lease of Goods Contracts. Universal, Inc., is in the business of leasing heavy industrial equipment. On December 1, it had a total of ten million dollars of outstanding leases. Jones, the president of Universal Inc., seeks your advice regarding possible financing for an eight million dollar expansion program. He would like to encumber or sell to Universal Inc. interest in the leases.

Would the encumbrance of the leases be subject to Article 9? *See* UCC §§ 9-102(a)(11), 1-201(35)(a), 9-109(a)(1).

Would the proposed sale of outstanding leases be subject to Article 9? *See* UCC §§ 9-102(a)(11), 9-109(a)(3).

i.   Priority of Purchase Money Security Interests (PMSI)

Section 9-204 authorizes creditors to take an interest in after-acquired property (i.e., property acquired after the security agreement is executed). This facilitates "floating lien" financing by permitting the parties to specify in their security agreement and financing statement that existing and after-acquired collateral is covered, thereby making possible an addition to the secured pool of collateral without having to execute a new security agreement and financing statement each time new collateral is added to the pool.

Frequently, the debtor, for various reasons (i.e., inventory is held by a retailer or wholesaler), may wish to finance after-acquired collateral through creditors other than the first creditor. It obviously would be difficult for the debtor to obtain credit from a second creditor, if the first creditor is given priority. This would be true if the Code failed to provide an appropriate exception to the first to file or perfect rule of § 9-322. Accordingly, to balance the first creditor's right to priority to the after-acquired collateral with the interest of the debtor in possibly financing after-acquired collateral through creditors other than the first creditor, the UCC makes an exception by granting special priority to a Purchase Money Security Interest (i.e., PMSI)[6] in the pool of collateral if certain conditions are met.

---

[6] Recall that under § 9-103, a PMSI includes "an obligation . . . incurred as all or part of the price of the collateral or the value given to enable the debtor to acquire rights in or the use of the collateral if the value is in fact so used."

If the collateral is non-inventory or non-livestock collateral, the second creditor with the PMSI will prevail merely by perfecting the PMSI within twenty days after the debtor receives the collateral. (*See* § 9-324(a)).

If the collateral is inventory or livestock collateral, the PMSI creditor must, *inter alia*, perfect her security interest and also give notice to the first creditor that she "has or expects to acquire a PMSI in inventory of the debtor and describes the inventory,"[7] *see* § 9-324(b)(4), before the debtor receives possession of the collateral. *See* §§ 9-102(a)(23), 9-103, 9-324.

Problem 4-13:   Priority of PMSI in Non-Inventory Collateral Over Prior Perfected Security. Interest Steady State Bank finances Clemens' acquisition of a new $50,000 machine and takes a security interest in the machine. The machine is delivered on November 5. Steady State Bank filed its financing statement on November 6. Steady State Bank gave no notice to Finance Company. Finance Company had previously perfected a security interest in Clemens' existing and after-acquired equipment by filing a financing statement. Does Steady State Bank nevertheless have priority over Finance Company? *See* UCC §§ 9-102(a)(33), 9-103, 9-324(a).

Problem 4-14:   Priority of PMSI in Inventory Over Prior Perfected Security Interest. Steady State Bank advises Finance Company in writing that it plans to finance the acquisition of new raw leather for Clemens, who now decides to manufacture shoes. Finance Company had previously filed a financing statement covering Clemens' existing and after acquired raw leather. A new supply of leather was delivered to Clemens on November 3. Steady State Bank files its financing statement the next day on November 4. Does Steady State Bank prevail over Finance Company? When should Steady State Bank have filed its financing statement? *See* UCC §§ 9-102(a)(48), 9-103, 9-324(b).

E.   WHERE TO FILE

1.   Conflict of Law—In Which State Do I File?

a.   Non-Possessory Security Interests—Filing Required in the State Where Debtor is Located

Location of collateral and debtor in different states and movement of collateral, debtor's residence, or place of business from one state to another raise issues of determining in which state the filing should occur, or how long perfection in a state (i.e., the origin state) is effective in the destination state to which the collateral or debtor moves.

One of the most important changes under revised Article 9 is the simplification of the rules governing the jurisdiction in which filings occur. Under UCC § 9-301(1) of the revision, all filings subject to the stated exceptions, are to be made in the jurisdiction where the debtor is located as defined and discussed in § 9-307 for

---

[7] For analogous treatment of livestock collateral, *see* § 9-324(d)(4).

"individuals," "organizations," and "registered organizations." This rule replaces the pre-revision law under which the secured party had to file in the state where tangible collateral was physically located. The debtor's location controlled under the pre-revision law only where the collateral was intangible, such as accounts and general intangibles, or the collateral was "mobile goods." The revised rule simplifies compliance and reduces transaction costs and legal risk by generally enabling the secured party holding a non-possessory security interest to combine all types of collateral into a single filing—in the state where the debtor is located.

i. Definition of "Location of Debtor" for "Individuals," "Organizations," and "Registered Organizations"

Under Revised UCC § 9-307(b)(1), an "individual" debtor is located at his or her principal residence.

A debtor that is an "organization" and has only one place of business is located at its place of business (§ 9-307(b)(2)). A debtor that is an organization and has more than one place of business is located at its chief executive office (§ 9-307(b)(2)). "Organization" is defined as a "person other than an individual" (§ 1-201(b)(5)). "Place of business" means "a place where a debtor conducts its affairs" (§ 9-307(1)).

"Registered organization" is defined as "an organization organized solely under the law of a single State or the United States and as to which the State or the United States must maintain a public record showing the organization to have been organized" (§ 9-102(a)(70) (1998)). "State" means a "State of the United States, District of Columbia, Puerto Rico or any territory subject to the jurisdiction of the United States" (§ 9-102(a)(76) (1998) and § 9-102(a)(77) (2010)).

The definition of "registered organization" was changed in the 2010 amendments to Article 9 to provide the following amended definition. Additions are underlined and deletions show words struck through.

> (71) "Registered organization" means an organization formed or organized solely under the law of a single State or the United States and as to which the State or the United States must maintain a public record showing the organization to have been organized by the filing of a public organic record with, the issuance of a public organic record by, or the enactment of legislation by the State or the United States. The term includes a business trust that is formed or organized under the law of a single State if a statute of the State governing business trusts requires that the business trust's organic record be filed with the State.

The 2010 amendments also added a new definition of "public organic record", a term referred to in the definition of "registered organization":

> (68) "Public organic record" means a record that is available to the public for inspection and is:
>
> (A) a record consisting of the record initially filed with or issued by a State or the United States to form or organize an organization and any

record filed with or issued by the State or the United States which amends or restates the initial record;

(B) an organic record of a business trust consisting of the record initially filed with a State and any record filed with the State which amends or restates the initial record, if a statute of the State governing business trusts requires that the record be filed with the State; or

(C) a record consisting of legislation enacted by the legislature of a State or the Congress of the United States which forms or organizes an organization, any record amending the legislation, and any record filed with or issued by the State or the United States which amends or restates the name of the organization.

A registered organization that is organized under the laws of a State is located in that State. (UCC § 9-307(e)). For a corporation, limited partnership, limited liability company, statutory trust or under the 2010 amendments, if there is a filing requirement referred to in the last sentence of the definition of "registered organization" in UCC § 9-102(a)(71), common law business trust, the place to file is the entity's state of organization. The state of organization for a registered organization is more certain than the former chief executive office standard. If the debtor reincorporates in another state, perfection will generally lapse after four months. Rev. UCC § 9-316.

A foreign debtor that would otherwise be located in a foreign jurisdiction without a public filing system is deemed to be located in Washington, D.C. UCC § 9-307(c). The new rule would allow a domestic filing for a non-U.S. debtor by choice-of-law provision. The same is generally true of entities organized under federal law. UCC § 9-307(f).

b. Exceptions to Location of Debtor Rule for Non-Possessory Security Interests

The § 9-301(1) "location of debtor" rule for non-possessory security interests is subject to the exceptions which follow:

i. Possessory Security Interests—Location of Collateral

For possessory security interests, the Revised Code provides that the local law of the jurisdiction in which the collateral is located governs perfection, the effect of perfection or nonperfection, and priority. UCC § 9-301(2); *see also* vi. Non-Possessory Security Interests in Tangible or Semi-Intangible Collateral—Location of Collateral Priority Rule, *infra*.

ii. Fixture Filings—Location of Goods

UCC § 9-301(3)(A) of the Revised Code provides that for fixture filings, the local law of the jurisdiction in which the goods are located governs perfection. UCC § 9-301(3)(A).

iii.   Timber To Be Cut—Location of Timber

Under the Revised Code, the local law of the jurisdiction in which timber to be cut is located governs perfection of the security interest in the timber. UCC § 9-301(3)(B).

iv.   As Extracted Collateral (Collateral To Be Extracted)—Location of the Wellhead or Minehead

The Revised Code provides that the local law of the jurisdiction in which the wellhead or minehead is located governs perfection, the effect of perfection and nonperfection, and the priority of a security interest in as-extracted collateral. UCC §§ 9-102(a)(6), 9-301(4).

v.   Other Exceptions Pertaining to Goods Covered by a Certificate of Title or Collateral Subject to Perfection by Control

Other exceptions to the "Location of Debtor" rule are provided for goods covered by Certificates of Title (UCC§ 9-303), Deposit Accounts (UCC § 9-304), Investment Property (UCC § 9-305), and Letter of Credit Rights (UCC § 9-306).

vi.   Non-Possessory Security Interests in Tangible or Semi-Intangible Collateral—Location of Collateral Priority Rule

Section 9-301(3)(C) further provides that the effect of perfection or non-perfection and priority of a non-possessory security interest in tangible and intangible collateral (other than as extracted collateral) is governed by the law of the location of the collateral.

To facilitate immediate reference the Actual Text and Simplified Version of Actual Text of § 9-301[8] follows:

---

[8] This text is also available in Appendix A but reproduced here for ease of reference.

ACTUAL TEXT	SIMPLIFIED VERSION

Part 3

Perfection and Priority

Subpart 1. Law Governing Perfection and Priority

Section 9-301. Law Governing Perfection and Priority of Security Interests.

Except as otherwise provided in Sections 9-303 through 9-306, the following rules determine the law governing perfection, the effect of perfection or nonperfection, and the priority of a security interest in collateral:

(1) Except as otherwise provided in this section, while a debtor is located in a jurisdiction, the local law of that jurisdiction governs perfection, the effect of perfection or nonperfection, and the priority of a security interest in collateral.

(2) While collateral is located in a jurisdiction, the local law of that jurisdiction governs perfection, the effect of perfection or nonperfection, and the priority of a possessory security interest in that collateral.

(3) Except as otherwise provided in paragraph (4), while negotiable documents, goods, instruments, money, or tangible chattel paper is located in a jurisdiction, the local law of that jurisdiction governs:

(A) perfection of a security interest in the goods by filing a fixture filing;

(B) perfection of a security interest in timber to be cut; and

(C) the effect of perfection or nonperfection and the priority of a nonpossessory security interest in the collateral.

§ 9-301. Law Governing Perfection and Priority of Security Interests

(a) Non-Possessory Security Interest—Location of Debtor. Except as otherwise provided in subsection (b) through (g), while a debtor is located in a jurisdiction, the local law of that jurisdiction governs perfection, the effect of perfection or nonperfection, and the priority of a security interest in collateral.

(b) Possessory Security Interests—Location of Collateral. While collateral is located in a jurisdiction, the local law of that jurisdiction governs perfection, the effect of perfection or nonperfection, and the priority of a possessory security interest in that collateral.

(c) Priority of Non-Possessory Tangible and Intangible Property Security Interests. Except as otherwise provided in subsections (d), (e), and (f), while negotiable documents, goods, instruments, money, or tangible chattel paper is located in a jurisdiction, the local law of that jurisdiction governs the effect of perfection or nonperfection and the priority of a nonpossessory security interest.

(d) Fixture Filings—Location of Goods. While goods are located in a jurisdiction, the local law of that jurisdiction governs perfection, the effect of perfection or nonperfection, and the priority of a security interest in the goods by filing a fixture filing.

ACTUAL TEXT	SIMPLIFIED VERSION

(4) The local law of the jurisdiction in which the wellhead or minehead is located governs perfection, the effect of perfection or nonperfection, and the priority of a security interest in as-extracted collateral.

(e) Timber to be Cut—Location of the Timber. The local law of the jurisdiction in which timber to be cut is located governs perfection, the effect of perfection or nonperfection, and the priority of a security interest in the timber.

(f) Collateral to be Extracted—Location of Wellhead or Minehead. The local law of the jurisdiction in which the wellhead or minehead is located governs perfection, the effect of perfection or nonperfection, and the priority of a security interest in as-extracted collateral.

(g) Other Exceptions. Subsection (a) is subject to:

    (1) Section 9-303 (Certificates of Title).

    (2) Section 9-304 (Deposit Accounts).

    (3) Section 9-305 (Investment Property).

    (4) Section 9-306 (Letter- of-Credit Rights).

2. Problems on Non-Possessory and Possessory Security Interests

Problem 4-15(a): Non-Possessory Security Interests—In Which State Do I File?—Conflicts of Law Issues. Assume that Clemens is incorporated in Delaware as the Apex Printing Company. His principal place of business is in Texas. He utilizes a printing press at his Texas plant as collateral to obtain a loan from Steady State Bank. Steady State Bank files a financing statement in the State of Delaware. Has Steady State Bank perfected its security interest? *See* UCC §§ 9-308, 9-310, 9-301(1), 9-307(e), 9-102(a)(70), (76).

If Apex Company moves the printing press from Texas to Arizona, will this move have an effect on the perfected status of the security interest?

Would the law of Texas or Delaware be applicable to resolve priority issues if Apex Printing Company defaults on its loan and Bank forecloses on the printing press? *See* UCC § 9-301(3)(C).

Assume that in Problem 4-11, Clemens is not incorporated but is instead operating as an individually-owned business. In the above loan transaction, is the filing required in Texas or in Delaware in order to perfect the security interest? *See* §§ 9-301(1), 9-307(b).

Problem 4-15(b): Possessory Security Interest—Conflict of Law Issues.
Supposing as collateral for its secured loan to Apex, Bank takes physical possession
of a replica on display at its Texas plant of the printing press invented by
Guttenberg. Is the law of Texas applicable in determining perfection, the effect of
perfection or non-perfection and the priority of a possessory security interest in the
collateral? *See* UCC § 9-301(2).

**Problem 4-15(c): Non-Possessory Security Interests—Certificate of Title
Considerations.**

Debtor, a resident of Missouri, buys a snowmobile in Wisconsin and grants the
seller a security interest in the snowmobile to secure payment of the purchase price.
Debtor uses the snowmobile exclusively in Minnesota, where his brother lives. The
certificate of title statute in Minnesota covers snowmobiles; the certificate of title
statutes in Wisconsin and Missouri do not cover snowmobiles. What law governs the
perfection of the Wisconsin seller's security interest?

NOTE

Noting that the debtor resided in Missouri, bought the snowmobile in Wisconsin,
and used it in Minnesota, the court at the outset resolved the conflict of laws issue
citing § 9-301(1), which provides that the law of the jurisdiction where the debtor is
located governs perfection of a non-possessory security interest. *In re Lance*, 2006
Bankr. LEXIS 4293 (W.D. Mo., Mar. 20, 2006) Section 9-307 in turn provides that
an individual is "located" for purposes of the UCC in his or her place of principal
residence. Missouri law was therefore applicable.

Perfection of a purchase money security interest in a snowmobile which qualifies
as consumer goods and is not a motor vehicle is automatic and requires no filing or
other step to perfect. UCC §§ 9-309, 9-311.

So ruling, the court next decided that the snowmobile qualified as a "consumer
good" under § 9-102(a)(23), which defines "consumer goods" as "goods that are
used or bought for use primarily for personal, family, or household purposes."

The court then ruled that the snowmobile did not qualify as a "motor vehicle,"
which under applicable Missouri law and UCC §§ 9-310(b)(3) and 9-311 requires
that the perfection be under the state's certificate of title statute, rather than by
the Article 9 filing of a financing statement. Under the Missouri statute, "motor
vehicle" is defined as "any self-propelled vehicle not operated exclusively upon
tracks except farm tractors." "Vehicle" in turn is defined as "any mechanical device
on wheels, designed primarily for use, or used on highways, except motorized
bicycles, vehicles propelled or drawn by horses or human power or vehicles used
exclusively on fixed rails or tracks, or cotton trailers or motorized wheelchairs
operated by handicapped persons." Since the snowmobile is not operated on
wheels, it did not qualify as a motor vehicle.

Except as otherwise provided, UCC § 9-310 requires filing of a financing
statement to perfect a security interest in goods. Section 9-309(1) (combined with
§ 9-311(a)) provides that no filing or other step is required to perfect a purchase-
money security interest in consumer goods, other than goods, such as automobiles,

that are subject to a statute or treaty requiring notation of an encumbrance on a certificate of title or registration in a specified registry. Since the snowmobile was not a motor vehicle, Creditor's security interest in the snowmobile was automatically perfected. The court accordingly denied the Bankruptcy Trustee's motion to compel turnover of the snowmobile under Bankruptcy Code § 544(a) and UCC § 9-317(a)(2).

3. In Which Registry Do I File?

Place of filing requirements within the jurisdiction in which a filing must be made must also be clearly stated if the filing system is to provide effective public notice of encumbrances which might exist against particular personal property. UCC § 9-501 sets forth specific rules regarding the place for filing a financing statement in order for the secured creditor to give proper notice to the public of the encumbrance against collateral. As we will shortly see, the place of filing requirements continues to depend on the type of collateral which is involved. However, the 2001 Amendments as discussed below greatly simplify the filing process. If the financing statement is not filed or is filed in the wrong place, a subsequent correct filing by another creditor covering the same collateral will usually give the second creditor priority over the creditor who failed to file or filed improperly.

Under Revised UCC § 9-501, all filings are to be in the central registry except fixture filings and filings covering as-extracted minerals (UCC § 9-102(a)(6)) or timber to be cut. Usually a security interest in fixtures is perfected by filing locally. An alternative way to perfect a security interest in fixtures is to do a filing that is not a fixture filing. However, a failure to make a local fixture filing means that the secured party cannot claim purchase-money priority over real estate interests in the fixtures. UCC § 9-334.

Minerals and timber are treated differently. A filing in the office where a real estate mortgage would be recorded perfects a security interest in as-extracted collateral such as oil and gas. The filing continues to be effective after extraction. Timber to be cut, however, may be goods before it is cut. Once cut, the filing in the real estate office ceases to be effective. At that point, the timber is subject to the central filing rules governing inventory. In addition, once timber is cut, the state of filing is the state of the debtor's location, not where the timber is located.

Problem 4-16: Place of Filing a Financing Statement. Mr. Clemens returns the financing statement to Steady State Bank. The bank loan officer now asks you for advice on where to file the completed financing statement. Advise her. *See* UCC § 9-501.

Problem 4-17: Movement Within the State. Assume that three years after entering into the prototype transaction, Samuel Clemens moves his printing business into new premises elsewhere in Dallas. If Steady State Bank agrees to the move, must it file a new financing statement in order to have a continuing perfected security interest? *See* UCC § 9-501.

F. WHAT TO FILE

1. Contents of Financing Statement

a. Description of Collateral

Problem 4-18: Contents of Financing Statement. In the security agreement he signed, Samuel Clemens agrees to "join with Bank in executing a financing statement in form satisfactory to Bank." Steady State Bank asks him to complete the financing statement set out in Chapter 2, Section A.1., *supra*. Mr. Clemens asks you to help him complete the form. Advise him, paying particular attention to the appropriate description of the collateral. *See* UCC §§ 9-502, 9-504.

Note: The form in Chapter 2, Section A.1., *supra*, had been drafted by a task force of the Article 9 drafting committee as a national form in consultation with state filing officers in connection with the 1998 revisions of Article 9. The text of a slightly amended form is included in the 2010 amendments to Article 9. The form itself is being updated to reflect the 2010 amendments.

Problem 4-19: Effectiveness of a Financing Statement. Assume Steady State Bank mails a properly completed financing statement to the correct office on September 3 (i.e., two days after Mr. Clemens signed the security agreement). The financing statement is accompanied by a check made properly payable in the amount of the filing fee. The filing officer receives the financing statement at 10:25 a.m. on September 5 but does not record the financing statement until 3:06 p.m. on September 5. When is the financing statement effectively filed? *See* UCC §§ 9-516(a), 9-102(a)(18). How long will the financing statement be effective? *See* UCC § 9-515. When was the security interest perfected? *See* UCC § 9-308.

b. Issues Regarding the Debtor's Name

i. Registered Organizations—Minor and Seriously Misleading Errors in the Financing Statement

HOST AMERICA CORPORATION v. COASTLINE FINANCIAL, INC.
United States District Court, District of Utah
2006 U.S. Dist. LEXIS 35727 (May 39, 2006)

Host America Corporation filed this action seeking a declaration that its security interest in goods owned by K.W.M. Electronics Corporation ("KWM") has priority over Coastline Financial, Inc.'s lessor's lien, which attached to the same goods. Host America moved for summary judgment, claiming that its interest is superior to Coastline's because either (1) Host America's security interest was perfected before Coastline's lessor's lien, or (2) Host America has perfected its security interest, while Coastline has yet to perfect its lessor's lien.

Coastline opposed Host America's summary judgment motion and moved for partial summary judgment on the issue of perfection. Coastline argues that it perfected its lessor's lien no later than the fall of 2006 and that the security interest upon which Host America relies was not perfected at that time because the financing statement filed in connection with that security interest listed an incorrect debtor's name, rendering the financing statement "seriously misleading" and precluding perfection.

As detailed below, the undisputed material facts establish that the initial financing statement filed in connection with Host America's security interest was seriously misleading. Although Host America has since attempted to correct the initial financing statement in an effort to ensure perfection of its security interest, the court concludes that Coastline perfected its lessor's lien before Host America undertook its corrective actions. Accordingly, the court concludes that Coastline's lessor's lien has priority over Host America's security interest.

UNDISPUTED FACTS

KWM, a manufacturer and assembler of electronic goods, leased space for its corporate facilities from Coastline. In late spring of 2001, KWM entered into a financing arrangement with Washington Mutual Bank. Pursuant to that agreement, KWM provided Washington Mutual with two security interests in certain collateral. Washington Mutual assigned those security interests to Coastline in the fall of 2002.

Desiring to wind up the financing obligations represented by the Coastline security interests, KWM sought alternative financing. Around the same time, KWM granted Burton M. Sack a security interest in certain collateral. On May 12, 2003, Mr. Sack filed a financing statement to provide notice of his security interest and to perfect that interest. The financing statement listed the debtor as "K W M Electronics Corporation."

In the late summer of 2004, Coastline initiated an unlawful detainer action against KWM in the Third District Court for the State of Utah. Coastline initiated the action after KWM failed to pay rent. Coastline sought a writ of attachment, which it received on September 30, 2004, and ultimately obtained a default judgment against KWM on November 19, 2004. Coastline's lessor's lien attached to the goods identified as collateral in Mr. Sack's financing statement.

On December 9, 2005, Host America acquired the debt and the security interest held by Mr. Sack. On December 22, 2005, Host America filed a financing statement in connection with that debt and security interest, listing the debtor as "K. W. M. Electronics Corporation." On January 3, 2006, Host America filed the present action, claiming that its recently acquired security interest has priority over any lien held by Coastline. Two days later, Host America filed an additional financing statement in connection with the debt and security interest it acquired from Mr. Sack. That financing statement listed the debtor as "K.W.M. Electronics Corporation."

The key issue in the motions presently before the court is whether the security interest that Host America acquired from Mr. Sack has priority over Coastline's lessor's lien.

ANALYSIS

Host America argues that Mr. Sack perfected his security interest when he filed the May 2003 financing statement. Because Mr. Sack's financing statement was filed well before Coastline attempted to foreclose on its lessor's lien, Host America contends that the security interest it acquired from Mr. Sack has priority.

The court concludes that the Financing statement filed by Mr. Sack in May of 2003 failed to sufficiently list the name of the debtor. Additionally, the court concludes that the financing statement was seriously misleading because a search of the state's records, conducted using filing office's standard search logic, would not have revealed the financing statement. As a result, the financing statement filed by Mr. Sack failed to perfect his security interest.

I. Mr. Sack's May 2003 Financing Statement Was Seriously Misleading

Host America concedes that the financing statement Mr. Sack filed in May of 2003 did not provide KWM's correct name. The question before the court is whether the failure to list KWM's correct name on the financing statement rendered that statement "seriously misleading." If so, Mr. Sack's security interest remained unperfected until well after the time Coastline foreclosed its lessor's lien.

"The purpose behind the filing provisions is to provide notice to subsequent creditors in a manner which will give such creditors confidence that they are aware of any prior security interests in the collateral that may be superior to their own interest." *Pearson v. Salina Coffee House, Inc.*, 831 F.2d 1531, 1536 (10th Cir. 1987). If a financing statement fails to provide adequate notice to subsequent creditors, the Utah Uniform Commercial Code will not allow the security interest evidenced by that filing to have priority over a subsequently perfected security interest. See *Diversified Holdings, L.C. v. Turner*, 2002 UT 129, P42, 63 P.3d 686. "Because notice of a secured interest in property is accomplished by searching the debtor's name, the requirement that a financing statement provide the debtor's name is particularly important." *Clark v. Deere & Co. (In re Kinderknecht)*, 308 B.R. 71, 74 (10th Cir. B.A.P. 2004). Given the importance of the debtor's name, it should come as no surprise that a failure to adequately provide that name will render a financing statement "seriously misleading." *See* Utah Code Ann. § 70A-9a-506.

Two sections of the Utah Uniform Commercial Code are relevant to determining whether Mr. Sack's May 2003 financing statement was seriously misleading: Utah Code section 70A-9a-503 and section 70A-9a-506. The statutes are, in all relevant aspects, identical to revisions proposed by the National Conference of Commissioners on Uniform State Laws in 1998. See *In re Kinderknecht*, 308 B.R. at 74. The revisions "require more accuracy in filings, and place less burden on the searcher to seek out erroneous filings." *In re Summit Staffing Polk County, Inc.*, 305 B.R. 347, 354 (M.D. Fla. 2003). "Prior to that time, courts struggled with whether names, such as trade names, in a financing statement sufficiently provided the name of the debtor. [The revisions were] meant to 'clarify when a debtor's name is correct and when an incorrect name is insufficient.'" *In re Kinderknecht*, 308 B.R. at 74–75 (quoting Official Uniform Commercial Code Comment 4.h).

When interpreting statutes, the court's "primary goal . . . is to give effect to the legislative intent, as evidenced by the plain language, in light of the purpose the statute was meant to achieve." *Foutz v. City of S. Jordan*, 2004 UT 74 P11, 100 P.3d 1171 (internal quotation omitted). Accordingly, the court first turns to the plain language of the relevant statutes.

Section 70A-9a-503(1) provides that "[a] financing statement sufficiently provides the name of the debtor: (a) if the debtor is a registered organization, *only* if the financing statement provides the name of the debtor indicated on the public record of the debtor's jurisdiction of organization . . . ." Utah Code Ann. § 70A-9a-503(1)(a) (emphasis added). Section 70A-9a-506 states that, "[e]xcept as provided in Subsection (3), a financing statement *that fails sufficiently to provide the name of the debtor in accordance with Subsection 70A-9a-503(1) is seriously misleading.*" § 70A-9a-506(2) (emphasis added).

Subsection (3) of the same statute provides an "escape hatch" for creditors that fail to strictly comply with the Utah Code's requirement that the creditor of a registered organization list the name of that organization as it appears on the public record:

> If a search of the records of the filing office under the debtor's correct name, using the filing office's standard search logic, if any, would disclose a financing statement that fails sufficiently to provide the name of the debtor in accordance with Subsection, 70A-9a-503(1), the name provided does not make the financing statement seriously misleading.

§ 70A-9a-506(3).

Interestingly, the parties do not agree on KWM's correct name and therefore diverge on the question of what name would need to be listed on the financing statement to satisfy section 70A-9a-503(1). Host America contends that the public record lists KWM as "K. W. M. Electronics Corporation," with spaces between the periods; Coastline asserts that KWM's correct name is "K.W.M. Electronics Corporation," with no spaces between the periods. But the parties' dispute is immaterial because the financing statement filed by Mr. Sack failed to use any periods at all, and instead listed the debtor as "K. W M Electronics Corporation." As mentioned, Host America concedes that by failing to indicate the presence of periods, Mr. Sack's financing statement did not comply with the requirements of section 70A-9a-503(1) of the Utah Code.

The plain language of section 70A-9a-506(2) dictates that Mr. Sack's failure to comply with the requirements of section 70A-9a-503(1) rendered his financing statement "seriously misleading" unless saved by the escape hatch provision of subsection (3). In other words, if a search under KWM's correct name, using the filing office's standard search logic, would have revealed Mr. Sack's security interest, then the Utah Code would not consider Mr. Sack's financing statement "seriously misleading." *See id.*; § 70A-9a-506(3).

The parties provided the court with extensive information about the search logic used by the state's filing office, including multiple declarations from Kathy Berg, the director of the Division of Corporations and Commercial Code. The evidence is undisputed that a search under KWM's correct name using the filing office's standard search logic would not have revealed Mr. Sack's security interest at any point in time before Coastline seized the goods as part of its foreclosure activities. As a result, the conclusion seems foregone that the escape hatch provision of subsection (3) is not available to Host America.

What complicates that conclusion is that, until recently, the filing office's standard search logic was not capable of compensating for even minor errors in a debtor's name. As a result, Host America claims that the escape hatch provided by subsection (3) was completely illusory at the time Mr. Sack filed his financing statement. In essence, Host America argues that the limitations of the state filing office's search logic improperly eviscerated a creditor protection that the legislature intended to provide.

Although sympathetic with Host America's position, the court concludes that the historical limitations of the state's filing office—though severe indeed—do not excuse Mr. Sack's failure to comply with section 70A-9a-503(1). The plain language of section 70A-9a-506(3) establishes an escape hatch to creditors who list an improper debtor name only to the extent that the state's standard search logic can compensate for that error. By necessity, the breadth of the safe haven provided by section 70A-9a-506(3) will either expand or contract as the capabilities of the state's standard search logic change over time. The escape hatch provision is expressly tied to the state's search logic and allows no leeway for financing statements that remain undiscovered due to a creditor's failure to comply with section 70A-9a-503(1).

This is so even when, as here, a search under the debtor's correct name, using the filing office's standard search logic, fails to retrieve financing statements with relatively minor errors. The Utah Uniform Commercial Code, as it now stands, provides this court with no guidance on how to determine if a debtor's name is seriously misleading, other than referencing the filing office's standard search logic. *Cf. Clark*, 308 B.R. at 75 ("The intent to clarify when a debtor's name is sufficient shows a desire to foreclose fact-intensive tests, such as those that existed under the former Article 9 of the UCC, inquiring into whether a person conducting a search would discover a filing under any given name. Requiring a financing statement to provide a debtor's legal name is a clear cut test that is in accord with that intent.") In short, the legislature elected to leave the fate of those creditors that fail to comply with the strict naming requirement of section 70A-9a-503(1) in the hands of those that develop and manage the filing office's search logic. *See* Meghan M. Sercombe, *Note, Good Technology and Bad Law: How Computerization Threatens Notice Filing Under Revised Article 9*, 84 Tex. L. Rev. 1065, 1068 (March 2006) ("[T]he drafters of the revised Article 9 opted for a bright-line rule, rejecting any language that would have measured validity against principles of fairness or equity.").

Following the plain language of the relevant statutes, the court concludes that Mr. Sack's May financing statement was seriously misleading and that his security interest was therefore unperfected at the time Coastline began foreclosing on its lessor's lien.

CONCLUSION

The financing statement filed by Mr. Sack in May of 2003 was seriously misleading because it failed to provide the correct name of the debtor and a search under the debtor's correct name, using the filing office's standard search logic, would not have revealed the financing statement. Coastline perfected its lessor's lien before Host America took steps to remedy the deficiency of Mr. Sack's financing statement. Accordingly, Coastline's lessor's lien has priority over Host America's security interest. Therefore, Host America's Motion for Summary Judgment is DENIED, Coastline's Motion for Partial Summary Judgment is GRANTED.

IN RE TYRINGHAM, INC.
(TYRINGHAM, INC. v. SUNA BROS. INC.)
United States Bankruptcy Court, Eastern District of Virginia
354 B.R. 363 (2006)

Trial was held on November 13, 2006, on plaintiff's complaint to determine the validity, priority, or extent of a lien under a consignment held by defendant Suna Bros. Inc. The issue is whether Suna's financing statement was seriously misleading because it was not filed under the correct name of the debtor. For the reasons set forth below, the court finds that the financing statement is seriously misleading. Therefore, the defendant's lien is unperfected, and plaintiff may sell the collateral free and clear of any lien or interest of Suna.

FINDINGS OF FACT

Pursuant to a consignment agreement dated October 18, 2004, debtor Tyringham Holdings, Inc., held a number of pieces of jewelry inventory consigned to it by Suna. Suna held a security interest in the consigned inventory and attempted to perfect the security interest by filing a financing statement with the Virginia State Corporation Commission on June 10, 2005. The financing statement covered 65 pieces of jewelry totaling $310,925.00 worth of consigned inventory.

The financing statement was filed by Suna on June 10, 2005, and listed the debtor's name as "Tyringham Holdings." The debtor is a Virginia Corporation and is listed as "Tyringham Holdings, Inc." on the public records of the Virginia State Corporation Commission.

An official UCC search certified by the State Corporation Commission revealed a search conducted under the name "Tyringham Holdings, Inc.," which did not reveal the Suna financing statement.

DISCUSSION AND CONCLUSIONS OF LAW

Where a filed financing statement is required to perfect a security interest, it must substantially satisfy the requirements of a financing statement. Generally, the name of a corporate debtor, as indicated on the public record of the debtor's jurisdiction of organization, must be listed on the financing statement for it to be valid. Va. Code Ann. § 8.9A-503(a)(1) (2006). Where the requirements are substantially satisfied, a financing statement "is effective, even if it has minor errors or omissions, unless the errors or omissions make the financing statement seriously misleading." Va. Code Ann. § 8.9A-506(a). By law, "[e]xcept as otherwise provided in subsection (c), a financing statement that fails sufficiently to provide the name of the debtor in accordance with § 8.9A-503(a) is seriously misleading." Va. Code Ann. § 8.9A-506(b). There is no question in this case that the name of the debtor in the Suna financing statement, "Tyringham Holdings," was not the same corporate name as that on the public record for the state of Virginia, "Tyringham Holdings, Inc." Therefore, unless excepted by Va. Code Ann. § 8.9A-506(c), the financing statement is seriously misleading and is ineffective to perfect Suna's security interest.

The exception in subsection (c) represents a shift between the previous version of Article 9 and Revised Article 9 in dealing with errors on financing statements. Prior to the revisions enacted in 2001, Virginia's version of Article 9 had no equivalent to subsections (b) and (c). Instead, the governing principle for financing statement sufficiency was a diligent searcher standard. Subsection (c) now provides a more concrete rule for determining if errors are seriously misleading, providing that:

> If a search of the records of the filing office under the debtor's correct name, using the filing office's standard search logic, if any, would disclose a financing statement that fails sufficiently to provide the name of the debtor in accordance with *§ 8.9A-503(a)*, the name provided does not make the financing statement seriously misleading.

Va. Code Ann. § 8.9A-506(c) (emphasis added).

According to the statute, the appropriate standard by which to judge a search is the filing office's standard search logic for a search under the debtor's correct name, in the filing office's database. *See, e.g.*, Va. Code Ann. § 8.9A-506 Official Comment 2 (stating that "a financing statement that is seriously misleading under this section is ineffective even if it is disclosed by (i) using a search logic other than that of the filing office to search the official records, or (ii) using the filing office's standard search logic to search a data base other than that of the filing office"). Several cases in other jurisdictions, applying parallel provisions in their respective Uniform Commercial Codes, emphasize that the filing office's standard search logic is the governing factor in determining whether a financing statement is seriously misleading. *See Pankratz Implement Co. v. Citizens National Bank*, 281 Kan. 209, 130 P.3d 57 (Kan. 2006) (finding a financing statement seriously misleading where the official search conducted by the Kansas secretary of state under the proper name did not reveal the financing statement); *Receivables Purchasing Co., Inc., v. R&R Directional Drilling, LLC*, 263 Ga. App. 649, 588 S.E.2d 831 (Ga. Ct. App. 2003) (explaining that case law under the previous version of Article 9 was no longer applicable and finding a financing statement seriously misleading where a search under the debtor's correct name did not reveal the financing statement); *All Bus. Corp. v. Choi*, 280 Ga. App. 618, 634 S.E.2d 400 (Ga. Ct. App. 2006) (following *Receivables Purchasing Co.* and holding that regardless of private searches done with incomplete stems of the proper debtor name, the law required a search through the clerk's office with the correct name). Therefore, it is clear in these jurisdictions that the filing office's standard search logic governs.

In the time period between filing of the financing statement and the trial in this Adversary Proceeding, a number of UCC searches were performed by private search companies such as Corporation Service Company, Access Information Services, Inc., and UCC Retrievals, Inc. Each of these searches disclosed the existence of the Suna financing statement. No evidence was presented as to the underlying methodology behind the Corporation Service Company or Access Information Services, Inc., searches. At trial, a witness for Suna testified that she had conducted the search by UCC Retrievals, Inc., under the name "Tyringham Holdings." Her search disclosed the existence of the Suna financing statement. Her rationale for searching under the name "Tyringham Holdings" rather than the correct "Tyringham Holdings, Inc.," was that she considered the term "Inc." to be a "noise word." Noise words for these purposes are words that are removed or ignored in the process of performing an electronic database search for financing statements. The witness classified "Inc." as a noise word because it is one of such words on a list promulgated by the International Association of Corporation Administrators (IACA). Other abbreviations on the IACA "noise word" list include "Corporation," "Corp," "Company," "Co," "Limited," and "Ltd."

Suna repeatedly emphasizes that these private searches used "standard search logic" to disclose the Suna financing statement. Suna would have this court readout the portion of the statute that specifies whose "standard search logic" is employed in the analysis. The relevant standard is clearly no longer the diligent searcher's standard search logic nor a private search organization's standard search logic, but it is instead the filing office's standard search logic.

The Virginia State Corporation Commission has promulgated filing rules in 5 Va. Admin. Code 5-30-70(E) (2006) that describe the standard search logic employed by the commission when conducting a search. Search results are produced by the application of standardized search logic to the name presented to the filing officer, along with several additional requirements, including the following subsection 4:

> "Noise words" include, but are not limited to, "an," "and," "for," "of," and "the." The word "the" always will be disregarded and other noise words appearing anywhere except at the beginning of an organization name will be disregarded. Certain business words are modified to a standard abbreviation: company to "co," corporation to "corp," limited to "ltd," incorporated to "inc."

5 Va. Admin. Code 5-30-70(E)(4). The State Corporation Commission has not adopted the full list of noise words promulgated by the IACA.

Plaintiff called as a witness an employee of the Virginia State Corporation Commission, who described the coding of the UCC search program utilized by the Corporation Commission in its official UCC searches. As explained by the witness, the search logic modifies a given entry by removing certain items from the name entered by a searcher, including punctuation, spaces, and the five noise words listed in the State Corporation Commission Rules. This creates a search key which is then matched to names on filed financing statements, which have likewise been modified in accordance with the same standards.

No evidence was presented to show that the private searches were conducted in accordance with the Virginia State Corporation Commission's standard search logic on the debtor's correct name. The only private search supported by additional evidence at trial was the one conducted by UCC Retrievals, Inc. This search was conducted using the State Corporation Commission's website, but only after the witness truncated the name, "Tyringham Holdings, Inc." to "Tyringham Holdings," based solely on her own belief that "Inc." was a noise word in the state of Virginia. The searcher entered "Tyringham Holdings" into the search field and retrieved the Suna financing statement. No evidence was presented that the searcher ever entered "Tyringham Holdings, Inc.," into the search field and recovered the Suna financing statement.

Suna attempts to argue that the State Corporation Commission's search logic is faulty because it does not filter out "Inc." as a noise word, even though the IACA considers it as such. According to Plaintiff's witness, the State Corporation Commission is in the process of revising its list of noise words and changing the search logic to include terms such as "inc." However, the standard in place at all times relevant to this case did not include "Inc." as a noise word; at present, the underlying search engine code filters out only five articles as noise words. Suna makes much of the fact that noise words in the filing rules contained at 5 Va. Admin. Code 5-30-70(E)(4) "include, but are not limited to" the five articles filtered out by the search engine. Suna essentially argues that the search engine improperly employs the search methodology prescribed by the statute, because it in fact filters out only the five articles and thus is "limited to" those words only. Regardless of whether this argument makes logical sense, the court cannot conclude on the basis of the statutory language that "Inc." should be considered a noise word. The third sentence of subsection 4 says that "Certain business words are modified to a standard abbreviation . . . ," the last of which is "incorporated" to "inc." 5 Va. Admin. Code 5-30-70(E)(4). If "inc" is a standard abbreviation, it cannot simultaneously be a disregarded noise word according to the State Corporation Commission's standard search logic as embodied by this statute and the search engine code utilizing it. As a result, it is clear that "Inc." is not a noise word for purposes of a Virginia UCC search, and the State Corporation Commission's search logic is functioning as it was presently intended to function in this respect.

None of the cases cited by Suna support its proposition that the language of § 8.9A-503(c) does not mean what it says regarding the use of the filing office's standard search logic. The closest Suna comes is in its discussion of *Planned Furniture Promotions*, 374 F. Supp. 2d 1227 (M.D. Ga. 2005), where the United States District Court for the Middle District of Georgia ruled that a party's omission of "Inc" from the end of the debtor's name was not seriously misleading because a search "would almost assuredly turn up a financing statement . . . ," and "a diligent creditor searching the filing records under the name Benjamin S. Youngblood, Inc. would be put on notice to inquire into the interests of a debtor listed as Benjamin Scott Youngblood." *Id.* at 1234. This case essentially ignores the provisions of the Georgia UCC referring to the filing office's standard search logic and appears to rest on pre-revised Article 9 law dealing with the diligent searcher standard. Further, the 2006 Georgia Court of Appeals case, *All Bus. Corp.*, calls into question the U.S. District Court's 2005 ruling in *Planned Furniture Promotions* by reaffirming the defunct status of the diligent searcher rule under Georgia law, whose UCC sections are identical to those at issue in this Virginia case. This court finds the logic of *Planned Furniture Promotions* inapplicable to the present case and finds persuasive the number of cases that apply the plain language of the UCC, requiring a search using the filing office's standard search logic. Thus, a search using the correct debtor name under the filing office's standard search logic—as embodied by any relevant statute and search engine programming that implements the search logic—must reveal the financing statement filed under the incorrect name or it will be deemed seriously misleading.

While application of the filing office's standard search logic may lead to situations where it appears that a relatively minor error in a financing statement leads to a security interest becoming unperfected, it is not that difficult to ensure that a financing statement is filed with the correct name of the debtor. Little more is asked of a creditor than to accurately record the debtor's name, and according to the statute, failure to perform this action clearly dooms the perfected status of a security interest.

The official search certified by the State Corporation Commission, under the correct name, "Tyringham Holdings, Inc.," fails to disclose the Suna financing statement. Thus, the only search which used the correct name under the standard search logic actually employed by the State Corporation Commission did not disclose the Suna financing statement. As a result, the court must conclude that the financing statement is seriously misleading and is insufficient to perfect Suna's security interest in the collateral. Therefore, Suna's security interest in the collateral is unperfected and the collateral may be sold free and clear of any lien held by Suna.

Accordingly, IT IS ORDERED that judgment is entered for plaintiff and the defendant's lien claim is denied.

ii. Individual or Organization Name—Minor and Seriously Misleading Errors in the Financing Statement

Problem 4-20(a): Errors in Individual Debtor's Name in the Financing Statement. A bank secretary types "Samuel Clements" rather than "Samuel Clemens" when completing the financing statement. If the filing officer accepts the financing statement, is the filing effective in a hard copy system? In an electronic system? *See* UCC §§ 9-506, 1-201(a)(25)(27).

What if the Debtor, an individual, is named "Terrance Joseph Kinderknecht" but is known as "Terry Kinderknecht"? See *In re Terrance Joseph Kinderknecht*, 308 B.R. 71 (2004), holding that the filing under "Terry Kinderknect" was ineffective. *See* UCC §§ 9-503(a)(4)(A) (1998), 9-506, 1-201(a)(25)(27).

It is one thing for the secretary to make an error in typing Samuel Clemens' name. It is another for Bank to be sure that its debtor's name is actually "Samuel Clemens." The 2010 amendments to Article 9 tried to achieve greater certainty for a secured party to know under which name to search, and what name should be provided on a financing statement, when the debtor is an individual.

Edwin E. Smith, *A Summary of the 2010 Amendments to Article 9 of the Uniform Commercial Code*
42 U.C.C. L.J. 345, 350 (2010)[9]

Name of Individual Debtor on Financing Statement

Some courts have struggled with the question of what name a financing statement must provide for an individual debtor in order for the debtor's name on the financing statement to be sufficient. The problem arises because an individual does not typically have a single name. The individual's name on his or her birth certificate, driver's license, passport, tax return or bankruptcy petition may all be different. Moreover, the debtor may be known in his or her community by a name that is not reflected on any official document. It would appear that most cases decided under the 1998 revisions to Article 9 and finding the individual debtor's name provided on the financing statement to be insufficient have involved the secured party making a filing error rather than being uncertain as to the debtor's actual name. Nevertheless, the cases have created a level of uncertainty that has led secured parties to search and file financing statements under multiple names.

To provide greater guidance, the amendments offer to each state one of two alternatives for the name of an individual debtor provided on a financing statement to be sufficient. If Alternative A is in effect in the state in which the financing statement is filed, and if the debtor holds a driver's license that has not expired and that has been issued by the state, then the name of the debtor that must be provided on the financing statement is the name of the debtor as it appears on the driver's license. This is the so-called "only if" rule, i.e., the debtor's name on the financing statement will be sufficient "only if" the name provided is the name on the driver's license.

Of course, the name on the driver's license cannot be followed slavishly. The financing statement written form or electronic template will require that the financing statement set forth the surname and first personal name of the debtor. The secured party will need to determine which name on the driver's license is the debtor's surname and which is the debtor's first personal name. This would normally be an easy task. For example, if the name on the driver's license is Lester Henry Smith, it would appear obvious that the debtor's surname is Smith and that the debtor's first personal name is Lester. Henry would then be inserted in the financing statement block for "additional names." In other cases, determining from the driver's license which name is the debtor's surname and which name is the debtor's first personal name may not be as easy and may require the secured party to perform additional investigation.

Under Alternative A, if the debtor does not hold a driver's license issued by the state in which the financing statement is filed, then either of the following names for the debtor would be sufficient as the debtor's name on the financing statement: (1) the individual name of the debtor, as under current Article 9, or (2) the debtor's surname and first personal name.

---

[9] Reprinted with permission.

Under Alternative B, any of the following names for the debtor would be sufficient as the debtor's name on the financing statement: (1) the debtor's name as shown on the debtor's driver's license if the debtor holds an unexpired driver's license issued by the state, (2) the individual name of the debtor, as under current Article 9, or (3) the debtor's surname and first personal name. Alternative B has been called the "safe harbor" approach, in contrast to the "only if" approach reflected in Alternative A.

Under either Alternative A or Alternative B, if the debtor holds two driver's licenses issued by the state, the most recently issued driver's license is the one to which reference should be made to determine the debtor's name to be provided on the financing statement.

In some states, the same office of the state that issues a driver's license also issues an identification card for an individual who does not hold a driver's license, and the state or office does not permit an individual to hold both a driver's license and a non-driver's license identification card at the same time. A Legislative Note to amended section 9-503 suggests that, regardless of which alternative is adopted, these states should refer to the non-driver's license identification card as an alternative of equal dignity with the driver's license.

The rationale for choosing the driver's license name as the name of the debtor to be provided in order for the debtor's name on the financing statement to be sufficient is that in most cases an individual debtor holds a driver's license that is offered as a form of identification when the debtor seeks to obtain secured financing. For lenders that extend credit on a volume basis, procedures can easily be established for the lender to search the records of the filing office under the driver's license name and to file in the filing office a financing statement providing that name as the name of the debtor.

To be sure, a rule that contemplates use of the debtor's driver's license name is not without risk. The driver's license may expire, or the debtor may exchange the current driver's license for a new driver's license. Either event could constitute a change in the name that Article 9 requires to be provided for the debtor. This may be the case if the debtor's name on an expired driver's license is different from a name that would be sufficient for the name of the debtor to be provided on a financing statement in the absence of a driver's license name or if the name of the debtor on the new driver's license is different than the name of the debtor as it appeared on the old driver's license.

If a search under the new name required to be provided for the debtor, following the filing office's standard search logic, does not disclose the financing statement filed under the expired or original driver's license name, the financing statement would become seriously misleading. In that case, the normal rules for a name change under section 9-507(c) would apply. The financing statement would remain effective for collateral in existence on the date of the name change and for collateral acquired by the debtor during the four-month period after the date of the name change. For the financing statement to be effective for collateral acquired by the debtor after the end of the four-month period, the secured party would need to amend the financing statement within the four-month period to provide the debtor's new name.

The observers from the lending community felt that, under either the "only if" rule of Alternative A or the "safe harbor" rule of Alternative B, the risk that debtor name changes may be more likely to occur than under current law was more than offset by the greater certainty of being able to look to the debtor's driver's license name.

Problem 4-20(b): Errors in Individual Debtor's Name in the Financing Statement—2010 Amendments. Mr. Clemens resides in a state that has adopted Alternative A to UCC § 9-503 (2010). A bank secretary types "Samuel Clemens" when completing the financing statement rather than "Samuel T. Clemens", the name on Mr. Clemens' driver's license issued by the state. If the filing officer accepts the financing statement, is the filing effective? *See* UCC §§ 9-503(a)(4) (Alternative A) (2010), 9-506(c).

Problem 4-20(c): Errors in Organization Debtor's Name in the Financing Statement. Suppose Samuel Clemens is doing business as a partnership with his brother, John Clemens, under the partnership name "Apex Printing." Does the filing have to be under "Apex Printing" or the individual or the individual partners names (i.e., Samuel Clemens and John Clemens)? *See* UCC §§ 9-503(a)(4)(B) (1998); 9-503(a)(6)(B) (Alternative A) (2010), 9-503(a)(5)(B) (Alternative B) (2010), 9-503(b)(2), 9-506, 1-201(a)(25)(27).

Problem 4-20(d): Errors in Organization Debtor's Name in the Financing Statement—2010 Amendments. Suppose Samuel Clemens' business is conducted as a limited liability company under the name "Apex Printing and Distribution Company" as reflected on the certificate of organization filed with the Secretary of State's office. But the Secretary of State's data base from which it issues legal existence certificates shows the name as "Apex Printing and Dist. Co." Does the filing have to be under "Apex Printing and Distribution Company" or can it be under "Apex Printing and Dist. Co."? *See* UCC §§ 9-503(a)(1) (2010), 9-506, 9-102(a)(68) (2010).

Edwin E. Smith, *A Summary of the 2010 Amendments to Article 9 of the Uniform Commercial Code*
42 U.C.C. L.J. 345, 350 (2010)[10]

Name of registered corporation in the Financing Statement

Some concern in practice has been expressed that, in determining the name of a debtor that is a registered organization for the purpose of providing the debtor's name on a financing statement, there may be more than one name of a registered organization reflected on a state's public record. This circumstance could arise when the state maintains a searchable data base of the names of registered organizations but where the data base uses abbreviations or has limited field codes. In that case, for example, the name of a corporation reflected in its charter

------

[10] Reprinted with permission.

document in a public file with the state and the name reflected on the state's publicly available data base may differ. If the secured party is to file a financing statement providing the corporation's name as debtor or to search for the debtor's name in the state's filing office records, the secured party may be uncertain as to whether the name should be the name on the corporation's charter document or the name in the searchable data base.

The amendments clarify that, for a financing statement to be sufficient, the name of the registered organization debtor to be provided on the financing statement is the name reflected on the "public organic record" of the registered organization. In most cases, a registered organization's "public organic record" is the publicly available record filed with the state to form or organize the registered organization. . . .

Accordingly, in the example above of the corporation with a name on its publicly available charter document that is different than the name on the state's publicly searchable data base, the debtor's name to be provided on the financing statement should be the debtor's name as reflected on the charter document.

If the name of the debtor on a public organic record is amended, the name of the debtor to be provided on a financing statement is the name as so amended. If otherwise there is more than one public organic record stating the debtor's name, the debtor's name is that provided on the most recently filed public organic record as the debtor's name.

iii.   Trade Name Ineffective

Problem 4-21:   Trade Name in Financing Statement Ineffective. The bank files a financing statement with the trade name, Apex Printing, rather than "Samuel Clemens." If the filing officer accepts the financing statement, is the filing effective? *See* UCC §§ 9-503(a)(4), (c), 9-506.

Texas, like most states, has an Assumed Business or Professional Name Act that would require Samuel Clemens and the partnership to file a statement setting out the assumed name and the full name and residence of each proprietor or partner. TEX. BUS. & COM. CODE §§ 36.01–36.26 (Vernon's Supp. 1996–1997). Relevant?

iv.   Changes in Form of Debtor

Problem 4-22:   Change in Form of Debtor: Partnership. Assume that Samuel Clemens agrees to create a general partnership with his brother, Mark, to run the printing business. The partnership would continue the printing business under the trade name, Apex Printing. If Steady State Bank agrees to the change, must it file a new financing statement in order to have a continuing perfected security interest? *See* UCC §§ 9-503(a)(4) (1998), 9-503(a)(6) (Alternative A) (2010), 9-503(a)(5) (Alternative B) (2010), 9-503(c), 9-507.

Problem 4-23:   Change in Form of Debtor: Corporation. Assume that instead of forming a partnership, Samuel and Mark Clemens incorporate the printing business under the name "Apex Printing Co., Inc." Samuel Clemens transfers the assets of the sole proprietorship in return for 100 shares in the new corporation. If

Steady State Bank agrees to the change, must it file a new financing statement in order to have a continuing perfected security interest? *See* UCC §§ 9-102(a)(56), 9-203(d), 9-507, 9-508.

c.   Obtaining Further Information

Problem 4-24:   Further Information. Assume that two years after entering into the prototype transaction with Steady State Bank, Samuel Clemens approaches Southwest Finance Company for a loan to purchase additional equipment. By filing with the Texas Secretary of State's office a prescribed form requesting copies of all financing statements on which Samuel Clemens is listed as debtor, the finance company discovers Steady State Bank's financing statement. The finance company writes a letter to the bank requesting information about the present status of the loan to Clemens and asking for a copy of the security agreement. The bank's loan officer asks you whether she must comply with this request. Advise her. *See* UCC §§ 9-210, 9-523.

d.   Procedure for Continuing Perfected Status in Proceeds

Problem 4-25:   Perfected Security Interest in Proceeds. In addition to his work as a printer, Samuel Clemens is an amateur photographer. In the October after he entered into the secured loan agreement with Steady State Bank, Mr. Clemens prints and publishes a picture calendar with his own photographs. He sells individual copies of the calendar from his printing shop. Some customers pay cash, some pay by check, some pay part of the purchase price by exchanging the new picture calendars for used books, supplemented by cash proceeds. Mr. Clemens immediately deposits these payments into the sole proprietorship checking account at the bank. Mr. Clemens also sells 500 copies to a local real estate/insurance agency on open account. Does the bank have a perfected security interest in the inventory of calendars or the proceeds of their sale? *See* UCC §§ 9-203(b)(3)(F), 9-315, 9-102(a)(33), (48), (29), 9-109(d)(13).

NOTE ON SECURITY INTEREST IN PROCEEDS

When a debtor sells or exchanges collateral, the security interest continues in both the original collateral and identifiable proceeds including collections received by the debtor unless the disposition was authorized free of the security interest by the secured party. *See* UCC § 9-315(a)(1).

A security interest in proceeds is automatically perfected for 20 days without filing or possession. *See* UCC § 9-315(c)–(e). The security interest in the proceeds will continue beyond 20 days if:

1.   A financing statement has been filed covering the original collateral and the proceeds are collateral in which a security interest may be perfected by filing in the same office where the financing statement has been filed; and if the proceeds are purchased with cash proceeds, the financing statement covering the original collateral describes the type of property acquired with the proceeds, UCC § 9-315(d); or

2.   The proceeds are identifiable cash proceeds, UCC § 9-315(d); or

3.   The security interest in the proceeds is perfected before the expiration of the 20 day period. UCC § 9-315(d).

Note that under (1) and (3) if proceeds are collateral that cannot be perfected by filing in the same office or offices where the financing statement covering the original collateral has been filed, a financing statement must be filed within 20 days covering the proceeds in order to retain a continuing perfected security interest in the proceeds. The purpose of this additional filing requirement is to aid creditors and buyers searching for encumbrances. For example, sale of inventory subject to a security interest is likely to generate cash and check proceeds which the Debtor is likely to deposit in his deposit account. In order to continue to have a perfected security interest in the proceeds, creditor would have to obtain "control" of the deposit account within the twenty days after the security interest attached to the account. (Section 9-315(c)).

2.   Assets Subject to a Certificate-of-Title Law

Revised Article 9, like its predecessor, looks to the perfection provisions of state certificate-of-title statutes for security interests in certain assets, such as motor vehicles and the like. UCC §§ 9-310(b)(3), 9-311(a)(2), 9-311(b). When such a statute applies, the filing of a financing statement is neither necessary nor effective to perfect a security interest, but compliance with the requirements of the statute is the equivalent of filing. Note that UCC § 9-303(a) permits the secured party to perfect under a certificate-of-title statute in a state that bears no relation to the goods or to the debtor. Comment 1 to UCC § 9-303 indicates that this comports with the modern practice in the trucking industry. Note also that the certificate-of-title method of perfection does not apply if the collateral is inventory held for sale or lease by a person that deals in goods of the kind. Thus, a bank that is "floor-planning" a dealer's inventory of cars need only file an ordinary financing statement to perfect its security interest. Do you see the rationale for this exception?

The law of the jurisdiction under whose certificate-of-title statute the secured party first proceeds governs perfection, the effect of perfection or nonperfection, and priority from the time the goods "become covered" until they "cease to be covered." UCC § 9-303(c). Goods "become covered" when a valid application and fee are delivered to the appropriate authority as designated by the certificate-of-title statue, and they "cease to be covered" at the time the certificate of title ceases to be effective under the law of the issuing jurisdiction (e.g., when the secured indebtedness is fully paid) or when they "become covered" in another jurisdiction.

Example 1: Debtor buys a car on credit and grants Bank a security interest. Bank delivers an application and fee to the proper office in State A requesting that a certificate of title be issued showing its lien. The goods have "become covered" in State A, and that means that the law of State A determines whether perfection has occurred, the effects of perfection or nonperfection, and the priority of Bank's security interest. The certificate-of-title law of State A may provide that delivery of the application and fee result in perfection of the security interest, or it may provide that delivery of the application and fee are conditions to perfection but that perfection occurs when the certificate is issued. All UCC § 9-303 tells us is that the law of State A answers our questions. (A legislative note appended to UCC § 9-311 indicates that the revision's rules contemplate that perfection will occur upon receipt by the appropriate state official of a properly tendered application, without relation back to an earlier time. The note suggests that statutes that provide for perfection at a different time or that contain a relation-back provision be amended. The repeal of relation-back provisions should cause secured parties to consider whether an alternative method of perfection is available between the time the security interest attaches and the time the application is tendered.)

Example 2: Debtor now moves to State B and on January 15 registers the car for the purpose of obtaining license plates but does not apply for a State B certificate of title. The law of State A continues to govern because the car has not ceased to be covered by its certificate. There is no requirement that Bank take any steps to perfect in State B. Why, theoretically, should that not be misleading to potential purchasers?

Example 3: Debtor now moves to State C and on June 15 registers the car for the purpose of obtaining license plates. State C also requires that Debtor apply for a certificate of title, and on June 15 Debtor submits an application and fee. At this time, the car ceases to be covered by State A's certificate of title. UCC § 9-303(b). What law now governs perfection, the effect of perfection or nonperfection, and priority? *See* UCC § 9-303(c).

Once we determine that the governing law has shifted from one jurisdiction to another, we must look at UCC § 9-316 to appreciate fully the effect of the shift. We begin with UCC § 9-316(d), which contains a general savings provision that preserves the advantages gained by perfection in State A.

Example 4: Even though the law of State C now governs, UCC § 9-316(d) as enacted in State C defers to the law of State A to determine whether the security interest is perfected. Other issues—the effect of perfection or nonperfection and priority—are determined by the law of State C. Thus, Bank continues its perfected status.

UCC 9-316(e) limits the effect of UCC § 9-316(d). Under that subsection, Bank's security interest becomes both prospectively and retroactively unperfected as against purchasers for value if Bank does not take the appropriate steps to perfect its security interest under State C's certificate-of-title statute before the expiration of four months after the goods became covered by the laws of State C.

Example 5: If Bank takes whatever steps are required to perfect its security interest in State C within four months after June 15, there will be no gap in its perfection. If State C's law requires that a certificate actually be issued for perfection to occur, Bank must make certain that it applies and pays its fee in time for the certificate to be issued before the four months lapses.

Note that under UCC § 9-316(e), Bank can take possession of the car and thereby perfect in State C. See UCC § 9-313(b) and the cross-reference to § 9-313 in § 9-316(e). This is an exception to the normal rule that compliance with a state's certificate-of-title law is the exclusive method for perfecting assets covered by that law.

> **Example 6:** Suppose Bank does not perfect under State C's certificate-of-title law. On October 10, Bank discovers that Debtor has moved to State C but doesn't know whether Debtor has applied for a certificate from State C. Its security agreement provides that a permanent move to another state is an event of default, so Bank repossesses the car on October 14. It has perfected under State C's law within the four-month grace period and there is no gap in its perfection. If Bank had repossessed on October 20, it would have been perfected prospectively as of that date but would have been deemed unperfected as against a prior purchaser for value.

Note that the rule on lapse of perfection in this context is different from the other lapse rules in Article 9. When a financing statement lapses at the end of five years, the security interest becomes prospectively unperfected against all third parties but retroactively unperfected only against purchasers for value. UCC § 9-515(c) (last sentence). Similarly, when perfection by filing lapses four months after a debtor changes location or one year after a transferee located in another jurisdiction acquires an interest in the collateral, the security interest becomes prospectively unperfected against all third parties but retroactively unperfected only against purchasers for value. UCC § 9-316(a), (b). Under UCC § 9-316(e), however, upon lapse the security interest becomes both prospectively and retroactively unperfected only against purchasers for value.

> **Example 7:** Suppose Bank fails to perfect under State C's certificate-of-title statute. On November 1, Debtor files a petition in bankruptcy. Is Bank's perfection in State A still effective against the trustee as lien creditor?

METZGER v. AMERICREDIT FINANCIAL SERVICES, INC.
Georgia Court of Appeals
615 S.E.2d 120 (2005)

OPINION BY: BERNES

. . .

FACTS

The underlying facts are not in dispute. On or about October 1, 2002, Americredit repossessed a 1997 Ford Taurus from Metzger, who had purchased the vehicle from a used car dealership in March 2002. Metzger did not realize that Americredit had a prior lien on the vehicle or that it had been repossessed. As a result, she reported the vehicle as stolen to the police.

Metzger later learned that Americredit had obtained a security interest in the vehicle in 1998, when the company financed James Strong's purchase of the vehicle in the State of New York. The New York certificate of title issued to Strong reflected Americredit's security interest in the vehicle.

Strong later moved from New York to Georgia and submitted a "MV1Z" application form, along with the existing title and the required fee, to the Cobb County tag agent for the Georgia Department of Motor Vehicles ("DMV") in order to convert the existing New York certificate of title to a Georgia one. The DMV processed the application, but as a result of a clerical data entry error, the DMV issued a Georgia certificate of title that did not reflect Americredit's security interest in the vehicle.

Strong later transferred the vehicle to an automobile dealer owner, and the vehicle thereafter passed through a nondealer owner and additional dealer owners before Metzger purchased it in March 2002. None of the subsequent Georgia certificates of title issued for the vehicle in connection with these transfers reflected Americredit's security interest.

After Metzger purchased the vehicle and registered it with the DMV, Americredit, having finally located the vehicle, repossessed it from Metzger's residence and sold it at auction. Once she learned from the police department that her vehicle had been repossessed rather than stolen, Metzger filed suit against Americredit in the Superior Court of Clayton County. She contended that Americredit wrongfully repossessed her vehicle and kept her personal belongings contained therein, and, as a consequence, should be held liable for conversion, negligence, deceptive trade practices, breach of the peace, breach of good faith, racketeering, unjust enrichment, and breach of sale.

Metzger subsequently filed a motion seeking partial summary judgment on her claim of conversion. Americredit filed its response and a cross-motion for summary judgment on all of Metzger's claims. The superior court denied Metzger's motion for partial summary judgment and granted summary judgment in favor of Americredit on Metzger's conversion claim only. The superior court concluded that Americredit had a perfected security interest in the vehicle that it could enforce against Metzger. Metzger now appeals from that order.

. . . .

GEORGIA MOTOR VEHICLE CERTIFICATE OF TITLE ACT

"[I]n construing [Georgia statutes], we apply the fundamental rules of statutory construction that require us to construe a statute according to its terms, to give words their plain and ordinary meaning, and to avoid a construction that makes some language mere surplusage." (Citation omitted.) *Slakman v. Continental Cas. Co.*, 277 Ga. 189, 191 (587 SE 2d 24) (2003). *See also City of Atlanta v. Yusen Air & Sea Svc. Holdings*, 263 Ga. App. 82, 84 (1) (587 SE 2d 230) (2003). With these rules in mind, we turn to the Motor Vehicle Certificate of Title Act, OCGA § 40-3-1 et seq. (the "Act"), which provides the exclusive procedure for perfecting a security interest in a motor vehicle in Georgia. *Staley v. Phelan Finance Corp.*, 116 Ga. App. 1, 1–2 (156 SE 2d 201) (1967).

Under the *Act*, a security interest in a motor vehicle is perfected, at the latest, on the date when the application documents for obtaining a certificate of title are delivered to the DMV or local tag agent, so long as the application documents properly reflect the existence of the security interest:

(b)(1) A security interest is perfected by delivery to the commissioner or to the county tag agent of the county in which the seller is located, of the county in which the sale takes place, of the county in which the vehicle is delivered, or of the county wherein the vehicle owner resides, of the required fee and:

(A) The existing certificate of title, if any, and an application for a certificate of title containing the name and address of the holder of a security interest; or

(B) A notice of security interest on forms prescribed by the commissioner.

OCGA § 40-3-50. Perfection occurs on that date, irrespective of whether the certificate of title subsequently issued by the DMV fails to reflect the security interest:

(b)(2) The security interest is perfected as of the time of its creation if the initial delivery of the application or notice to the commissioner or local tag agent is completed within 20 days thereafter, regardless of any subsequent rejection of the application or notice for errors; otherwise, as of the date of the delivery to the commissioner or local tag agent. The local tag agent shall issue a receipt or other evidence of the date of filing of such application or notice. When the security interest is perfected as provided for in this subsection, it shall constitute notice to everybody of the security interest of the holder.

Id. "Compliance with the filing requirements of the *Act* has the effect of imputing constructive notice to all who may subsequently acquire an interest in or lien against the property." (Citation and punctuation omitted.) *Cobb Center Pawn & Jewelry Brokers, Inc. v. Gordon*, 242 Ga. App. 73, 75 (2) (529 S.E.2d 138) (2000).

Based on this statutory language and case law, it might appear that because Strong delivered proper application forms reflecting Americredit's security interest to the Cobb County tag agent, Americredit could enforce its security interest against Metzger, who under OCGA § 40-3-50(b)(2) would have constructive notice of the security interest despite the clerical error contained in the Georgia certificate of title that was later issued. However, OCGA § 40-3-50 contains three statutory exceptions:

(a) *Except as provided in Code Sections 11-9-303, 11-9-316, and 11-9-337,* the security interest in a vehicle of the type for which a certificate of title is required shall be perfected and shall be valid against subsequent creditors of the owner, subsequent transferees, and the holders of security interests and liens on the vehicle by compliance with this chapter.

UCC § 9-337

Significantly, one of those exceptions, OCGA § 11-9-337, states:

If, *while a security interest in goods is perfected by any method under the law of another jurisdiction*, this state issues a certificate of title that does not show that the goods are subject to the security interest or contain a statement that they may be subject to security interests not shown on the certificate:

(1) *A buyer of the goods, other than a person in the business of selling goods of that kind, takes free of the security interest if the buyer gives value and receives delivery of the goods after issuance of the certificate and without knowledge of the security interest.*

(Emphasis supplied.)[11] An explanation of this provision is set forth in Comment 2 to Uniform Commercial Code § 9-337:

This section affords protection to certain good-faith purchasers for value who are likely to have relied on a "clean" certificate of title, i.e., one that neither shows that the goods are subject to a particular security interest nor contains a statement that they may be subject to security interests not shown on the certificate. Under this section, a buyer can take free of, and the holder of a conflicting security interest can acquire priority over, a security interest that is perfected by any method under the law of another jurisdiction.

UCC § 9-337 cmt. 2.[12]

In the present case, the undisputed evidence of record shows that the six requirements of the statutory exception contained in OCGA § 11-9-337(1) have been met. First, the parties agree that, at the time that Strong filed his application for a Georgia certificate of title with the Cobb County tag agent, Americredit had previously perfected its security interest in the vehicle under New York law, and the security interest remained perfected. Second, the certificate of title issued by the DMV to Strong failed to show that the vehicle was subject to a security interest. Third, Metzger is not a person in the business of selling automobiles. Fourth, Metzger gave value for the vehicle. Fifth, Metzger received delivery of the vehicle after issuance of the Georgia certificate of title by the DMV erroneously omitting reference to Americredit's security interest. Sixth, and finally, Metzger was without knowledge of the security interest that Americredit held in the vehicle. Thus, Metzger was entitled to invoke OCGA § 11-9-337(1). It necessarily follows that Metzger took the vehicle free of Americredit's security interest.

---

[11] [2] OCGA § 11-9-337 was enacted by the Georgia legislature as part of the revisions to Article 9 of the Uniform Commercial Code made in 2001. *See* Ga. L. 2001, p. 362, § 1. *See also id*. at § 32 (substituting "Sections 11-9-303, 11-9-316, and 11-9-337" for "Section 11-9-103, relating to accounts, contract rights, general intangibles, and equipment governed by the laws of another jurisdiction, and incoming goods already subject to a security interest" in *subsection (a)* of OCGA § 40-3-50). Because the priority of claims as between Americredit and Metzger could not have been established until after Metzger purchased the vehicle in March 2002, the 2001 version of *Article 9* applies in this case to determine priority rather than earlier versions. *See* OCGA § 11-9-709(a).

[12] [3] In order to determine the meaning and purpose behind the enactment of a Georgia Commercial Code provision that is taken verbatim from the UCC, we turn to the UCC Official Comments for assistance. *Gerber & Gerber, P.C. v. Regions Bank*, 266 Ga. App. 8, 11 (2), n. 1 (596 S.E.2d 174) (2004).

UCC §§ 9-303 & 9-316

However, Americredit contends that two additional statutes found in Georgia's Uniform Commercial Code, OCGA §§ 11-9-303 and 11-9-316, indicate that Metzger took the vehicle subject to the security interest. Based on these two statutes, Americredit argues that the special good faith purchaser rule set forth in OCGA § 11-9-337(1) has no application in this case, because its perfected security interest in Metzger's vehicle was no longer governed by New York law once the proper application documents and required fee for a Georgia certificate of title were submitted to the Georgia DMV by James Strong. Thus, in Americredit's view, OCGA § 11-9-337(1) does not apply under the circumstances here because the erroneous Georgia certificate of title was not issued "*while*" its security interest in the vehicle was perfected "under the law of another jurisdiction."

Americredit's statutory argument is based on a strained reading of the interplay between OCGA §§ 11-9-303, 11-9-316(d) and (e), and 11-9-337. OCGA § 11-9-303, entitled "Law governing perfection and priority of security interests in goods covered by a certificate of title," is a choice of law provision, as its title suggests. OCGA § 11-9-303(b) provides that:

> Goods become covered by a certificate of title when a valid application for the certificate of title and the applicable fee are delivered to the appropriate authority. Goods cease to be covered by a certificate of title at the earlier of the time the certificate of title ceases to be effective under the law of the issuing jurisdiction or the time the goods become covered subsequently by a certificate of title issued by another jurisdiction.

OCGA § 11-9-303(c) then provides that "[t]he local law of the jurisdiction under whose certificate of title the goods are covered governs perfection."[13] These provisions indicate that even when a security interest in goods has been perfected in another state, Georgia law determines perfection and priority issues once the goods become "covered" by a Georgia certificate of title, which occurs when a valid application and fee are submitted to the DMV.

Once it becomes clear that Georgia law governs because the goods are covered by a Georgia certificate of title, the next question is whether the security interest previously perfected in another state remains perfected. That issue is addressed by

---

[13] [4] OCGA § 11-9-303 provides in full:

(a) *Applicability of Code section.* This Code section applies to goods covered by a certificate of title, even if there is no other relationship between the jurisdiction under whose certificate of title the goods are covered and the goods or the debtor.

(b) *When goods covered by certificate of title.* Goods become covered by a certificate of title when a valid application for the certificate of title and the applicable fee are delivered to the appropriate authority. Goods cease to be covered by a certificate of title at the earlier of the time the certificate of title ceases to be effective under the law of the issuing jurisdiction or the time the goods become covered subsequently by a certificate of title issued by another jurisdiction.

(c) *Applicable law.* The local law of the jurisdiction under whose certificate of title the goods are covered governs perfection, the effect of perfection or nonperfection, and the priority of a security interest in goods covered by a certificate of title from the time the goods become covered by the certificate of title until the goods cease to be covered by the certificate of title.

OCGA § 11-9-316, entitled "Continued perfection of security interest following change in governing law," specifically *subsections (d)* and *(e)*, which deal with certificates of title.[14] These subsections set forth the general rules for when a security interest perfected in another state remains perfected in Georgia, once the goods are "covered" by a Georgia certificate of title.

"A statute must be construed in relation to other statutes of which it is a part, and all statutes relating to the same subject-matter, briefly called statutes *in pari materia*, are construed together, and harmonized wherever possible, so as to ascertain the legislative intendment and give effect thereto." (Punctuation omitted.) *City of Buchanan v. Pope*, 222 Ga. App. 716, 717 (1) (476 S.E.2d 53) (1996). When read *in pari materia* with OCGA §§ 11-9-303 and 11-9-316(d) and (e), OCGA § 11-9-337(1) gives protection to a good faith purchaser for value who is not "in the business of selling goods of that kind," when there is continued perfection of the security interest under OCGA § 11-9-316(d) and (e), but the Georgia certificate of title fails to reflect the security interest. Consequently, in the present case, although Americredit's security interest in the vehicle remained perfected at the time that Metzger purchased the vehicle, that security interest could not be enforced as against Metzger, a good faith purchaser as that term is defined in OCGA § 11-9-337(1), since the security interest was not properly reflected on the Georgia certificate of title.

Furthermore, "a specific statute will prevail over a general statute, absent any indication of a contrary legislative intent, to resolve any inconsistency between them." (Citation, punctuation and emphasis omitted.) *Hooks v. Cobb Center Pawn & Jewelry Brokers Inc.*, 241 Ga. App. 305, 309(6) (527 SE 2d 566) (1999). OCGA § 11-9-316 (d) and (e) are general statutory provisions addressing continued perfection of an out-of-state security interest once goods become covered by a Georgia certificate of title. In contrast, OCGA § 11-9-337(1) sets forth a more specific rule addressing what occurs in the unique circumstance where the Georgia certificate of title that covers the goods erroneously fails to reflect the security interest originally perfected in another state. Because OCGA § 11-9-337(1) is the more specific statute, it controls, even if there were a perceived inconsistency

---

[14] [5] OCGA § 11-9-316(d) and (e) provide:

> (d) *Goods covered by certificate of title from this state.* Except as otherwise provided in subsection (e) of this Code section, a security interest in goods covered by a certificate of title which is perfected by any method under the law of another jurisdiction when the goods become covered by a certificate of title from this state remains perfected until the security interest would have become unperfected under the law of the other jurisdiction had the goods not become so covered.

> (e) *When subsection (d) of this Code section security interest becomes unperfected against purchasers.* A security interest described in subsection (d) of this Code section becomes unperfected as against a purchaser of the goods for value and is deemed never to have been perfected as against a purchaser of the goods for value if the applicable requirements for perfection under subsection (b) of Code Section 11-9-311 or Code Section 11-9-313 are not satisfied before the earlier of:

> (1) The time the security interest would have become unperfected under the law of the other jurisdiction had the goods not become covered by a certificate of title from this state; or

> (2) The expiration of four months after the goods had become so covered.

between the various statutory provisions. Accordingly, Americredit's statutory interpretation argument is unavailing.

Finally, we conclude that the superior court erred by relying on OCGA § 40-3-31(4)[15] and our decision in *Strother Ford, Inc. v. First Nat. Bank of Maryland*, 132 Ga. App. 268, 208 S.E.2d 25, instead of OCGA § 11-9-337(1). OCGA § 40-3-31 by its terms only applies when a certificate of title has been "lost, stolen, mutilated, or destroyed or becomes illegible" (OCGA § 40-3-31(a)), and none of those circumstances occurred here. Furthermore, *Strother* is distinguishable from the instant action. The certificate of title at issue in that case failed to reflect a security interest on the vehicle due to fraud by the party that submitted the application to the DMV (*see Strother*, 132 Ga. App. at 268, 272 (2)), whereas here the certificate omitted the security interest information as a result of clerical error, not intentional wrongdoing. Moreover, at the time *Strother* was decided in 1974, Georgia statutory law did not yet contain an exception to its priority statutes akin to OCGA § 11-9-337 for security interests on automobiles perfected in another state but not reflected in a later issued Georgia certificate of title. *See* GA. CODE ANN. § 68-421a (Supp. 1974). Thus, the superior court improperly relied on OCGA § 40-3-31(4) and *Strother* as a basis for its decision in this case.

For these reasons, we reverse the partial grant of summary judgment in favor of Americredit. We remand to the superior court to enter summary judgment in favor of Metzger on her conversion claim. *Judgment reversed and case remanded with direction. Blackburn, P. J., and Miller, J., concur.*

G. FIXTURES, ACCESSIONS, AND COMMINGLED GOODS

1. Fixtures

a. Holders of Security Interests in Fixtures Versus Owners or Mortgagees of Real Estate Whose Interest Extends to Fixtures

The UCC law on fixtures addresses priority issues between creditors who have a security interest in fixtures annexed to the real estate and owners or mortgagees of the real estate whose interest in the real estate extends to the same fixtures. UCC § 9-334 states rules of priority applicable to these conflicting interests in fixtures. Resolution of such disputes requires us to preliminarily distinguish goods

---

[15] [6] OCGA § 40-3-31, entitled "Lost, stolen, mutilated, or destroyed certificates," provides in part:

If a certificate of title is *lost, stolen, mutilated, or destroyed or becomes illegible*, the owner or the legal representative of the owner named in the certificate, as shown by the records of the commissioner or the commissioner's duly authorized county tag agent, shall promptly make application for and may obtain a replacement, upon furnishing information satisfactory to the commissioner or authorized county tag agent. . . .

(4) If two or more innocent persons are the victims of the fraud or mistake of another and none of the victims could have reasonably taken steps to detect or prevent the fraud or mistake, the victim who first acquired an interest in a vehicle through any certificate of title shall have such victim's interest protected.

(Emphasis supplied.)

(i.e., movables), realty (i.e., immovables) and fixtures.

The UCC provides that "fixtures" means "goods that have become so related to particular real property that an interest in them arises under real property law." UCC § 9-102(a)(41). This incorporation of each UCC enacting state's definition of "fixtures" is limited by UCC § 9-334(a), which further provides that "[a] security interest under this article may be created in goods that are fixtures or may continue in goods that become fixtures. A security interest does not exist under this Article in ordinary building materials incorporated into an improvement on land." Accordingly, while each state is free to develop its own definition of "fixtures," bricks, lumber and mortar, which start out as personal property and are subsequently incorporated into a permanent structure, lose their identity and become part of the real estate and may not be considered as fixtures.

Apart from this uniform "ordinary building materials" limitation, there is substantial disparity in the case law of the various states in classifying property as goods, fixtures or realty. In the absence of a statutory definition, applicable state case law must be consulted. While courts of the various states agree on: (1) the degree of annexation, (2) the use of property attached to the real estate, and (3) the intent of the parties as criteria to be used in determining whether specific collateral is to be classified as goods or fixtures or real estate, the results under the case law in the fifty states in classifying property as a fixture are not always uniform or predictable.

b.   Attachment to the Property

IN RE FLORES DE NEW MEXICO, INC.
United States Bankruptcy Court, District of New Mexico
151 B.R. 571 (1993)

McFEELEY, CHIEF JUDGE.

* * *

Flores was organized as a floriculture operation with its facilities in Las Cruces, New Mexico. It subleased twenty-eight acres from the New Mexico State University Foundation, Inc., (the "University") and placed ten of those acres under greenhouse. Flores' primary product was cut roses. It also produced other types of cut flowers, as well as container grown plants. As a rose producer, Flores had approximately 60,000 rose bushes contained in three of the greenhouses. The rose bushes were planted in the ground and had relatively extensive root systems. The remaining seven greenhouses were used for growing other types of cut flowers and for the production of container grown plants.

* * *

[On or about March 8, 1988, Flores entered into an agreement with Banda Negra whereby Banda Negra loaned $1,100,000 to Flores. The loan was to be secured by Flores' assets. Flores executed and delivered to Banda Negra a loan agreement and a security agreement, to secure the debt. The security agreement and UCC financing statement naming Fores as debtor and Banda Negra as secured party, and listing the collateral *inter alia* as equipment and accounts receivable and proceeds of such collateral was duly filed.]

* * *

Flores duly filed a voluntary petition under Chapter 11 of the Bankruptcy Code and subsequently filed motions to sell property outside the ordinary course of business free and clear of liens and other interests, and this court entered its order authorizing the sale at auction of certain of the Debtor's assets. Liens, claims and encumbrances were to attach to the same extent and with the same validity to the proceeds of the sale, subject to later determination by this Court. . . .

* * *

Flores, in its capacity as debtor in possession, later filed its Second Amended Complaint Objecting To Secured Claim And Seeking Valuation. In that complaint . . . Flores further alleged that Banda Negra had not validly perfected its security interest in the rose bushes . . . . [The complaint listed several additional items of dispute.]

DISCUSSION

This case presents the Court with the competing claims of Banda Negra, a secured creditor of the Debtor, and the bankruptcy estate which, under the Bankruptcy Code, has "the rights and powers of . . . a creditor that extends credit at the debtor at the time of the commencement of the case, and that obtains . . . a judicial lien on all property on which a creditor on a simple contract could have obtained such a judicial lien . . . ." 11 U.S.C. § 544(a).

* * *

[The court finds that the rose bushes were not consumer goods (§ 9-102(a)(23))[16] farm products (§ 9-102(a)(34)) or inventory (§ 9-102(a)(48)), and therefore would be equipment under § 9-102(33).]

* * *

The distinction is whether the tenant plants seeds (or very young plants), raises them, and harvests the entire plant, in which case they constitute crops, [§ 9-102(a)(34)(A)] or whether the fruit of the plant is harvested. In the latter case, the plant is not a crop, and therefore must constitute equipment under UCC § 9-109(a)(33), as any item which does not fit into the other categories is defined as equipment. Here, the rose bushes produced successive crops of blooms, which were periodically harvested. The rose bushes had a life expectancy of seven to eight years and testimony at trial showed that there was no intent to remove the bushes until they ceased producing adequate crops of cut roses. Thus, the rose bushes must be equipment under UCC § 9-102(a)(33).

---

[16] [For pedagogical reasons, the Pre-Revision Article 9 citations in the court's decision are replaced with the Revised Article 9 citations.—Eds.]

If, however, the rose bushes had become so related to the real estate that an interest in them arose under real estate law, they are fixtures within the meaning of UCC § 9-102(41). The Defendant asserts that as a matter of law the rose bushes are personalty because the lease agreement between Flores and the University, the owner of the real estate, provides that the "corporation personalty" will remain the property of Flores and may be removed by Flores at the end of the lease period.

* * *

In the instant case, the evidence shows that the rose bushes were not intended for eventual sale. Testimony at trial showed that it was the intent of Flores to continue to produce cut roses for the useful life of the rose bushes. Testimony further showed that the useful productive life of the rose bushes was between seven and eight years.

* * *

In New Mexico, intent, adaptation, and annexation are the three relevant factors in determining whether personal property has become so attached to real estate that an interest in that property arises under real estate law. *Kerman v. Swafford*, 101 N.M. 241, 680 P.2d 622 (1984). Adaptation and annexation are principally relevant as indicators of intent, which is the controlling consideration and the chief fixture test. *Id.* at 243. Courts have historically been concerned with apparent or objective intent, rather than the actual state of mind of the owner or installer of the purported fixture. *Southwestern Public Service Co. v. Chaves County*, 85 N.M. 313, 512 P.2d 73 (1973). Where a court finds objectively manifested intent, a fixture may be presumed or inferred from the circumstances. *Kerman*, 680 P.2d at 625.

No New Mexico court has addressed the question of whether growing plants, planted directly in the earth, become fixtures and I have found only one case from another jurisdiction, *First Wisconsin National Bank of Milwaukee v. Federal Land Bank of St. Paul*, 849 F.2d 284 (7th Cir. 1988), which addresses this question. In that case, the court held that cranberries [sic] plants, planted in a cranberry bog, had become so related to the real estate that an interest in them arose under real estate law and that they were thus fixtures. *Id.* at 287. The court based its holding on the same three part test used in New Mexico, finding that the roots of the cranberries were embedded in the soil thus affixing the vines to the realty. The planting of the vines in the bog constituted a "use or purpose to which the realty is devoted" which met the test for adaptation. And finally, that "it is the presumed intention of a hypothetical ordinary reasonable person that when a cranberry vine is planted in a cranberry bog such vine will remain a permanent accession to the real estate." *Id.* at 287.

In the instant case, no showing has been made that Flores had the subjective intent that the rose bushes remain personal property. Defendant asserts that the lease with the University demonstrates that intent. As previously discussed, however, this Court has found the lease to be ambiguous in its treatment of the rose bushes.

The evidence shows that the rose bushes were planted directly into the earth, and that each bush has a root system that extends three or four feet into the earth.

Thus, the bushes were affixed to the realty. The evidence further shows that Flores intended to produce successive crops of cut roses from these bushes for a period of seven to eight years, at which time the bushes would be in need of replacement and that Flores had gone to substantial expense to erect a series of greenhouses specifically designed for the production of cut roses. Thus, the requirement of adaptation of the realty is met. Finally, the evidence shows that Flores had no intent to sell or dispose of the rose bushes and that Flores planned to be a long term producer of cut roses. This Court therefore finds that the rose bushes had become so attached to the real estate than an interest in them arose under real estate law, and that they became fixtures.

*   *   *

The rose bushes are fixtures under UCC § 9-102(a)(41) and thus, a fixture filing under UCC § 9-334 was required to perfect a security interest in them. Such a filing was not made by Banda Negra . . . .

NOTE AND QUESTIONS

Note the court's emphasis on the following three factors in determining whether the rose bushes had become so attached to the real property that an interest arose under real property law:

(1)   objective intent

(2)   annexation

(3)   adaptation.

Are any of these three factors more relevant than the others? *See Bank of Valley v. United States National Bank of Omaha*, 37 U.C.C. Rep. Serv. (CBC) 994, 341 N.W.2d 592 (Neb. 1998) (finding intention to be the controlling consideration). However, is objective intent not demonstrated through one's taking steps to annex and adapt particular personal property to the reality?

c.   Perfection of a Security Interest in Fixtures—"Fixture Filing"

"Fixture Filing" Concept. UCC § 9-502(a) & (b) require a creditor to file a "fixture filing" in order to perfect a security interest in goods which are or are to become fixtures. UCC § 9-102(a)(40) defines a "fixture filing" as the "filing of a financing statement covering goods that are to become fixtures and satisfying UCC § 9-502(a) and (b)." The general rule regarding sufficiency of the financing statement found in UCC § 9-502(a) requires that the statement:

(1)   provide the name of the debtor;

(2)   provide the name of the secured party or a representative of the secured party; and

(3)   indicate the collateral covered.

UCC § 9-502(b) adds that if the financing statement is filed as a "fixture filing and covers goods that are or are to become fixtures," the financing statement must, in addition to the above requirements found in UCC § 9-502(a):

(1)   indicate that it covers this type of collateral,

(2)   indicate that it is to be filed [for record] in the real property records;

(3)   provide a description of the real property to which the collateral is related [sufficient to give constructive notice of a mortgage under the law of this State if the description were contained in a record of the mortgage of the real property]; and

(4)   if the debtor does not have an interest of record in the real property, provide the name of a record owner.

UCC § 9-501(a)(1)(B) provides that a fixture filing must be filed in the office designated for the filing or recording of a record of a mortgage on the related real property. UCC § 9-301(3)(A) requires the fixture filing to be filed in the state in which the fixture is located.

These provisions are designed to give creditors easier access to information concerning encumbrances on fixtures. A search of the real estate records will normally suffice to disclose whether fixtures attached to specific real estate are subject to a creditor's security interest.

d. Priority Issues

i. General Priority of Real Estate Interest

UCC § 9-334(c) states that in cases not otherwise provided for an interest in the real estate takes priority over a security interest in fixtures.

An important exception provides that a security interest that is perfected in fixtures before the interest of the real estate interest is recorded has priority over the real estate interest. *See* UCC § 9-334(e).

Problem 4-26: General Priority of Real Estate Interest. Real Estate Owner encumbered Blackacre with a real estate mortgage of $100,000 on January 2 in favor of Bank 1 covering the real estate and "all fixtures currently or hereafter a part of" the real estate. This mortgage was properly recorded in the real estate records on January 3.

Real Estate Owner obtains a loan of $10,000 from Bank 2 a year later in January. To secure this $10,000 loan, Bank 2 takes a security interest in air conditioning equipment which Owner had previously purchased for cash. This equipment was subsequently installed in February as a fixture in Blackacre. Bank 2 files a fixture filing in the real estate record on January 20 covering its interest in the fixtures. Does Bank 1 or 2 have priority to the fixtures? *See* UCC §§ 9-334(e)(1), 9-103(b), 9-502(b), 9-501(a)(1)(B) provides that a fixture filing must be filed in the office designated for the filing or recording of a record of a mortgage on the related real property.

ii.　Purchase Money Security Interest in Fixtures—20-Day Grace Period

UCC § 9-334(d) states that a purchase money secured creditor (UCC § 9-103) of goods which are or are to become fixtures has priority with respect to the goods if the creditor perfects by a fixture filing before the goods become fixtures or within twenty days thereafter. *See* UCC § 9-313(4)(a) (1972).

Problem 4-27: Purchase Money Security Interests. What difference would result in the priority of Bank 1 and Bank 2 if Owner had borrowed money from Bank 2 to buy air conditioners to be installed as fixtures in its property instead of using air conditioners Owner already owned? *See* UCC §§ 9-102(a)(40), 9-334(d), 9-502(c), 9-103(b).

iii.　Readily Removable Factory or Office Machines or Equipment, or Readily Removable Replacements of Domestic Appliances—"Perfection by Any Method"

It is generally understood that one of the main problems encountered in complying with the fixture provisions of the Uniform Commercial Code is the difficulty of determining whether or not a particular item is a fixture. The difficulties the court had in *Flores* (the rose bush case) *supra*, is relatively *de minimis* in comparison to difficulties courts have with cases involving *readily removable* machines or equipment and cases involving buildings or other structures attached to the real estate.

Consider this quote from an article by Professor Robert M. Lloyd, *Article 9 and Real Estate Law: Practical Solutions for Some Bothersome Problems*, 29 IDAHO L. REV. 583, 617 (1993).

> There is no question that it is very difficult to predict in advance whether a court will determine a particular item to be a fixture or pure personal property. There is also no question that standards vary greatly from jurisdiction to jurisdiction. Commentators love to cite *First National Bank of Mount Carmel v. Reichneder*,[17] in which the irrepressible Justice Musmanno[18] pointed out that under the majority's interpretation of Pennsylvania's "integrated industrial plant doctrine," a real estate mort-

---

[17] [195] 91 A.2d 277 (Pa. 1952). . . .

[18] [196] Justice Michael A. Musmanno, who sat for many years on the Pennsylvania Supreme Court, is one of the most colorful figures in American legal history. He is noted not only for this florid prose, but also for his vigorous exposition of his strongly held opinions. In one notable case, he went to a trial court to obtain a writ of mandamus to compel the reporter of decisions to print his (Musmanno's) dissenting opinion in a case where the Chief Justice had ordered it not be reported. *Musmanno v. Eldredge*, 1 Pa. D. & C. 2d 535 (1955). After the writ was denied, *id.*, Musamanno appealed to the supreme court, making a motion that all of his brother justices disqualify themselves. He lost on both the motion and the merits. *Musmanno v. Eldredge*, 114 A.2d 511 (Ps. 1955). *See also* Karl M. ZoBell, *Division of Opinion in the Supreme Court: A History of Judicial Disintegration*, 44 CORNELL L.Q. 186, 209–10 n. 120 (1959). Unfazed, Musmanno published a law review article in which he argued the merits of his position. Michale A. Musmanno, *Dissenting Opinions*, 60 DICK. L. REV. 139 (1956).

gage of a brewery covered the empty kegs and bottles in the plant, to the exclusion of a chattel mortgage expressly claiming those items.[19] Going in the opposite direction, the Nebraska Supreme Court held that a five bedroom house was personal property and not a fixture because the house was built on leased land and the lease gave the lessee the right to remove it.[20] In a tax case, a California court held that the ocean liner Queen Mary became a fixture when moored in Long Beach Harbor to serve as a floating museum.[21]

In *Voorhis v. Freeman*, 37 Am. Dec. 490 (1841), the Pennsylvania Supreme Court, seeking to increase the collateral available for loan purposes in financing new manufacturing enterprises, created the "integrated industrial plant doctrine" by stating:

> Whether fast or loose . . . all the machinery of a manufactory which is necessary to constitute it, and without which it would not be a manufactory at all, must pass for part of the freehold. This is no more than an enlargement of the principle of constructive attachment.

Pennsylvania Courts subsequently seeking to increase the collateral available for loan purposes in financing new enterprises other than manufacturing expanded the Industrial Plant Doctrine to include in the concept of "Industrial Establishment" non-manufacturing commercial establishments such as laundromats and other service businesses. *N. Side Laundry Co. v. Bd. of Prop. Assessment*, 366 Pa. 636 (1951); *see also* Robert M. Lloyd, *Article 9 and Real Estate Law: Practical Solutions for Some Bothersome Problems*, 29 IDAHO L. REV. 583 (1993).

In the context of these difficulties and complications, the drafters sought to achieve predictability. Accordingly, UCC § 9-334(e)(2) provides:

> (e) [Priority of security interest in fixtures over interests in real property.]
>
> . . .
>
> (2) Before the goods become fixtures, the security interest is perfected by any method permitted by this article and the fixtures are readily removable:
>
> > (A) factory or office machines;
> >
> > (B) equipment that is not primarily used or leased for use in the operation of the real property; or
> >
> > (C) replacements of domestic appliances that are consumer goods;
>
> . . .

Comment 8 to UCC § 9-334 gives the reason for including this section. The Comment states, "[t]his rule is made necessary by the confusion of the law as to

---

[19] [197] *First Nat'l Bank*, 91 A.2d at 282 (Musmanno, J., dissenting).

[20] [198] *Bank of Valley v. United States Nat'l Bank of Omaha*, 341 N.W.2d 592, 596 (Neb. 1983).

[21] [199] *Specialty Restaurants Corp. v. County of Los Angeles*, 136 Cal. Rptr. 904, 915 (Ct. App. 1977).

whether certain machinery and appliances become fixtures." If these items are not fixtures under state law, the real estate interest does not reach them. If they are deemed to be fixtures, the security interest has priority over the real estate interest if the security interest is perfected "by any method" before the goods become fixtures. For example, a purchase money security interest in such consumer goods, which is automatically perfected without filing or possession under § UCC 9-309(1), will have priority over a conflicting interest in the real estate even if state law defines the goods as fixtures. Comment 8 to UCC § 9-334 also clarifies the application of subsection (e)(2) to appliances. The Comment states that the rule is limited to readily removable replacements, not original installations, of appliances which are consumer goods in the hands of the debtor.

Problem 4-28:   Readily Removable Factory and Office Machines. Manufacturer gives Bank a security interest in readily removable factory and office machines to be installed in a factory and its office in a state which treats such machines as fixtures. Before the machines are installed, Bank files a financing statement in the chattel records but does not make a fixture filing. Will bank have priority over persons having interests in the real estate? *See* UCC §§ 9-334(e)(2), 9-313(4)(c).[22]

iv.   Liens on the Real Estate Obtained by Legal or Equitable Proceedings

UCC § 9-334(e)(3) provides that a security interest in fixtures has priority over liens on the real estate that are obtained by legal or equitable proceedings after the security interest has been perfected. The security interest may be perfected by any method permitted in Article 9.

Problem 4-29:   Lien Creditors, Including Bankruptcy Trustees. Owner gives Bank a security interest in fixtures already installed in his building. Bank files a fixture filing in the real estate records in the office where real estate records are kept. Thereafter, a creditor of Owner obtains a judgment lien on the building and Owner then files a bankruptcy petition. Does Bank have priority over the judgment creditor or Owner's trustee in bankruptcy? Would the result change if Bank had filed a financing statement in the chattel records rather than making a fixture filing? *See* UCC § 9-334(e)(3); § 544(a) of Bankruptcy Act.

---

[22] *See generally Voorhis v. Freeman*, 37 Am. Dec. 490 (1841) (Court created the Industrial Plant Doctrine by stating "Whether fast or loose . . . all the machinery of a manufactory which is necessary to constitute it, and without which it would not be a manufactory at all, must pass for part of the freehold. This is no more than an enlargement of the principle of constructive attachment."); *see also N. Side Laundry Co. v. Bd. of Prop. Assessment*, Appeals and Review, 366 Pa. 636 (1951) (where the court found commercial laundromats to be an industrial establishment.); Andrew H. Schuster, *Furnishing, Fixtures, and the Functional Unit*, SH053 ALI-ABA 333 (2003) (Summarizing the use of the Industrial Plant Doctrine in determining what constitutes a fixture.); Robert M. Lloyd, *Article 9 and Real Estate Law: Practical Solutions for Some Bothersome Problems*, 29 IDAHO L. REV. 583 (1993). *But see BFC Hardwoods Inc. v. Bd. of Assessment Appeals of Crawford County*, 565 Pa. 65, 771 A.2d 759 (2001) (Stating the Pennsylvania General Assembly "Abolish[ed] this doctrine of inclusion in favor of a prescription which expressly required the exclusion of attached or unattached machinery or equipment for purposes of local real estate valuation and assessment.").

v. Consent of the Owner or Encumbrancer to an Interest in Fixtures; Debtor's Right to Remove Fixtures

UCC § 9-334(f) states that the person with a security interest in fixtures has priority over the owner or encumbrancer of land if the owner or encumbrancer has consented in writing to the security interest or has disclaimed an interest in the goods or fixtures, or if the debtor has rights to remove the goods as against the encumbrancer or owner. The consent procedure will be particularly helpful to a creditor seeking to use as collateral fixtures which are already a part of the real estate.

Problem 4-30: Debtor's Right to Remove Fixtures. Tenant businessman decided to accommodate his customers by purchasing and installing a large air conditioning unit in his bookstore. Acme Air Conditioning retained a security interest in the unit but did not file the appropriate fixture financing statement. Instead it chose to rely on a clause in Tenant's lease giving Tenant the right to remove such fixtures when the lease expired. Shortly thereafter, Landlord obtained a loan by giving Lending Bank a real estate mortgage on the business property. Does Acme Air Conditioning prevail over Lending Bank? *See* UCC § 9-334(f).

vi. Construction Mortgagee's Priority Over Purchase Money Security Interest

"Construction mortgage" is defined by UCC § 9-334(h), which states, "a mortgage is a 'construction mortgage' to the extent that it secures an obligation incurred for the construction of an improvement on land including the acquisition cost of the land," if the recorded record of the mortgage so indicates.

Usually a construction mortgage is recorded before delivery of construction materials. UCC § 9-334, cmt. 11. Under a first-in-time, first-in-right rule, the construction mortgage should have priority over a security interest in fixtures. *See* UCC § 9-334, cmt. 11. By exempting construction contracts from the application of UCC § 9-334(d), UCC § 9-334(h) assures this priority even as against creditors perfecting a purchase money security interest within 20 days after the goods become fixtures. UCC § 9-334(h) gives a construction mortgage priority over a security interest in fixtures if: (1) the construction mortgage is recorded before the goods become fixtures; and (2) the goods become fixtures before the construction is finished.

Problem 4-31: Priority of Construction Mortgage over Purchase Money Security Interest. Owner is constructing a building with funds advanced by First Bank under a recorded construction mortgage. The owner of the real estate obtains a loan from Second Bank and uses the proceeds to purchase air conditioning equipment. The owner gives Second Bank a security interest in the equipment, and a financing statement is filed in the real estate records. Thereafter, within the construction period the equipment is installed and becomes a fixture to the building. Which bank has priority with respect to the equipment? *See* UCC § 9-334(h). How can Second Bank avoid taking a second lien on the air conditioning units? *See* UCC § 9-334(f).

vii.   Liability for Damage to Real Estate

UCC § 9-604(c) gives the secured creditor with a priority the right to remove his collateral from the real estate. If the creditor removes the fixtures, he must promptly reimburse any encumbrancer or owner of the real property rather than the debtor, for the cost of repair of any physical injury caused by the removal. UCC § 9-604(d).

2.   Accessions

UCC § 9-102(a)(1) provides that "accession" means "goods that are physically united with other goods in such a manner that the identity of the original goods is not lost." For example, a new motor added to a tractor or new tires placed on an automobile are accessions. The secured transaction problem that arises results from the fact that the tractor, or the automobile, may have been used as collateral by a creditor whose security interest covers the tractor or automobile and also any property thereafter annexed to the tractor or automobile. If a second secured creditor finances the motor or the tires in the two hypotheticals posed, the question arises as to whether first creditor who financed the whole will have superior rights over the claim of the second creditor who financed only the accession.

UCC § 9-335(a) provides that a security interest may be created in an accession and continues in collateral that becomes an accession. UCC § 9-335(b) provides that if a security interest is perfected when the collateral becomes an accession, the security interest remains perfected in the collateral. UCC § 9-335(c) provides that except for situations involving a Certificate of Title statute, the other priority rules of Article 9 determine the priority of a security interest in an accession. Where the security interest in the whole was perfected by compliance with requirements of a certificate of title statute (*see* UCC §§ 9-308, 9-310(b)(3), 9-311(b)), UCC § 9-335(d) provides a special priority rule by making the security interest in the accession subordinate to a security interest in the whole.

Accordingly, in the above tractor hypothetical, depending on whether Creditor 1 (who took a security interest in the whole) or Creditor 2 (who took a security interest only in the motor which was subsequently annexed to the tractor) filed or perfected first, the first to file or perfect rule of UCC § 9-322(a)(1) would be applicable.

The exception for automobile Certificate of Title transactions would be illustrated by our second hypothetical, where Creditor 1 took a security interest in the automobile and property subsequently annexed to it as an accession and the owner of the automobile subsequently purchased tires which were annexed to the automobile as an accession and financed through a loan provided by a second lender. The first to file or perfect rule and even the purchase money security interest special priority rules would be inapplicable since UCC § 9-335(d) provides that perfection by compliance with the requirements of the Certificate of Title statute gives priority to the creditor who so perfected over the claims of the creditor who only perfected a security interest in the tires which became an accession to the automobile.

UCC § 9-335(e) further gives the secured party the right to remove an accession from other goods if the security interest in the accession has priority over the claims of other persons interested in the whole. UCC § 9-335(f) provides for reimbursement of persons having an interest in the whole for damages which result when the secured party removes an accession from the whole.

3. Commingled Goods

UCC § 9-336(a) provides that "commingled goods" means "goods that are physically united with other goods in such a manner that their identity is lost in a product or mass." Comment 1 to UCC § 9-336 states that this definition includes not only goods whose identity is lost through manufacture or production, such as flour that has become part of baked goods, but also includes goods such as ball bearings whose identity is lost by commingling with other goods from which they cannot be distinguished.

UCC § 9-336(b) and (c) provide that a security interest does not exist in commingled goods but that the security interest may attach to a product or mass that results when goods become commingled goods. Where the security in collateral is perfected before the collateral becomes commingled goods, the security interest that attaches to the product or mass is perfected. UCC § 9-336(d).

If more than one security interest attaches to the product or mass, a security interest that is perfected has priority over a security interest that is unperfected at the time the collateral becomes commingled goods. If more than one security interest is perfected in the commingled mass, the security interests rank equally in proportion to the value of the collateral at the time it became commingled goods. UCC § 9-336(f).

Problem 4-32:   Priorities in Commingled or Processed Goods. Cambel Foods bought cans for use in its food processing on credit from Containers Inc. In exchange for a loan of $50,000 to cover the purchase price, Cambel Foods granted Containers Inc. a security interest in its existing and after acquired inventory and promptly filed a financing statement covering the collateral. Cambel Foods subsequently bought $2,000,000 worth of vegetables from Acme Farms and gave Acme Farms a security interest in the vegetables in exchange for the $2,000,000 loan it had obtained to cover the purchase price. Acme Farms promptly filed its financing statement covering the collateral.

Cambel Foods defaults on both loans. Does Containers Inc. have priority of Cambel Foods inventory of canned vegetables because it filed its financing statement first? Acme Farms claims a pro rata share of the value of the inventory. Who prevails? *See* UCC §§ 9-322(a)(1), 9-336(d), 9-336(f)(1). Would the result be different if Containers Inc. had filed its financing statement after the vegetables had become a part of the finished canned vegetable?

Suppose that instead of taking a security interest in Cambel Foods existing and after acquired inventory to secure its $50,000 loan, Containers Inc. had taken a security interest in the cans it was selling to Cambel Foods and promptly filed a financing statement covering its collateral. Would Acme Farms be entitled to a pro rata share in the value of the inventory if Cambel Foods defaults on both loans? *See* UCC §§ 9-322(a)(1), 9-326(b), 9-336(f)(1).

Chapter 5

THE EFFECTS OF BANKRUPTCY

A. BANKRUPTCY GENERALLY

The filing of a petition under the federal Bankruptcy Code has two important and immediate effects: it creates an estate, and it imposes a stay on the collection acts of creditors. Subject to certain statutory exceptions, the estate consists of "all legal or equitable interests of the debtor in property as of the commencement of the case." Bankr. Code § 541(a)(1). The estate also includes in limited circumstances assets acquired by the debtor within 180 days after the filing of the petition (*i.e.*, assets acquired by bequest or devise, through a divorce settlement or decree, or as beneficiary of a life insurance policy or death benefit plan). Bankr. Code § 541(a)(5).

In a case filed under Chapter 7 of the Bankruptcy Code, sometimes called a liquidation case, the assets of the estate are sold and the proceeds are used to repay the claims of creditors. In exchange, the debtor is granted a discharge from most of its debts. Bankr. Code § 727. The estate is managed by an official called the bankruptcy trustee, who generally distributes assets in one of the following ways: 1) abandonment of property that secures a debt equal to or greater than the value of the property (§ 554(a)); 2) abandonment of property claimed by the debtor as exempt (§ 554(a)) (the right to claim exemptions facilitates a fresh start by the debtor); and 3) sale of assets (§ 363) and distribution of the proceeds to pay administrative expenses (the expenses incurred in administering the estate) and the claims of creditors (§ 726).

In a reorganization case (*i.e.*, a case filed under Chapter 11, 12, or 13), the estate typically remains in the debtor's control, subject to the court's supervision. In a Chapter 11 case involving a corporation or other business entity, creditors often receive new claims or interests in the reorganized business. In a Chapter 11 involving an individual or in a Chapter 12 or 13 case, creditors are paid with, among other things, income generated by the debtor after the filing. Bankr. Code §§ 1115, 1207(a), 1306. The role of the trustee differs depending upon the type of case. In a Chapter 11 case, a trustee will not be appointed except in unusual circumstances. Bankr. Code § 1104(a). Instead, the debtor itself, acting as "debtor-in-possession" (DIP), exercises the powers and carries out the responsibilities of the trustee. Bankr. Code § 1107(a). In a Chapter 12 or 13 case, the trustee collects the debtor's disposable post-bankruptcy income and distributes it to creditors according to a plan of reorganization approved by the court. Bankr. Code §§ 1202(b); 1302(b).

In any case filed under the Bankruptcy Code, whether a Chapter 7, 11, 12 or 13 case, the trustee or DIP may be entitled to set aside ("avoid") the security interest of an Article 9 secured party and to treat the Article 9 secured party as a general unsecured creditor for the amount of its claim. If the security interest cannot be avoided, the secured party's claim will remain secured by the collateral, and the secured party will generally be entitled to be paid from its collateral ahead of unsecured creditors. The trustee or DIP has a number of statutory powers, however, that can be invoked to avoid the security interest. The avoidance powers are discussed below.

If the secured party is undersecured, § 506(a) bifurcates the secured party's claim into a secured claim equal to the value of the collateral and an unsecured claim for the deficiency. For example, suppose that Debtor owes Bank $25,000 and Bank has an unavoidable security interest in Debtor's equipment. If the equipment has a value of $20,000, Bank will hold a secured claim of $20,000 and an unsecured claim of $5,000. The secured claim will be fully satisfied from the collateral or otherwise paid in full, but the unsecured claim will be paid ratably from the funds available for distribution to general unsecured creditors, usually in an amount less than the full amount of the claims. Section 507 creates a multi-tiered system of priorities for unsecured claims, and all higher ranking claims must be paid before any lower ranking claims are paid. An ordinary lender with an unsecured claim will not be entitled to priority and thus will share *pro rata* with other general unsecured creditors after all secured claims, all administrative expenses and all unsecured claims entitled to priority are fully satisfied.

Disputes frequently arise over the valuation of collateral for the purpose of calculating a secured claim. Amendments made by the Bankruptcy Abuse and Prevention and Consumer Protection Act of 2005 to the Bankruptcy Code codified the replacement valuation method used by the Supreme Court in *Associates Commercial Corp. v. Rash*, 520 U.S. 953 (1997), for an individual debtor in a Chapter 7 or 13 case. *See* Bankr. Code § 506(a)(2).

B. THE AUTOMATIC STAY

The filing of a bankruptcy petition automatically results in a stay that prevents creditors from using the remedies that would ordinarily be available to collect their debts. Under § 362(a), a creditor cannot, *inter alia*, commence or continue to prosecute a legal proceeding based on a prepetition claim; enforce a prepetition judgment; take any action to obtain possession of or control over property of the estate; take any action to create, perfect, or enforce a security interest against property of the estate; take any action to create, perfect, or enforce a security interest in property of the debtor (*i.e.*, assets acquired after the filing of a bankruptcy petition that may not be included in the bankruptcy estate) to secure a prepetition claim; or take any other action to collect, assess, or recover against the debtor a prepetition claim.

Problem 5-1. Based on the provisions of § 362, please answer the following questions:

    a.   Assets are divided into property of the estate and property of the debtor. All acts by prepetition creditors are stayed, and all acts against property of the estate are stayed. Nothing stays postpetition creditors from reaching assets of the debtor. Do you see why?

b.   After the filing of a petition in bankruptcy, may a creditor send a dunning letter to a debtor? May a secured party repossess collateral? If a secured party has already repossessed collateral prior to bankruptcy, may it proceed with an Article 9 disposition? In *In re Whiting Pools, Inc.*, 674 F.2d 144 (2d Cir. 1982), *aff'd sub nom. United States v. Whiting Pools, Inc.*, 462 U.S. 198 (1983), the United States Supreme Court held that a seized asset in which a debtor retains a right of redemption constitutes property of the estate and that, while the creditor is not a custodian required to deliver the property to the trustee under § 543(b), it can be ordered by the bankruptcy court to turn it over to the trustee pursuant to § 542(a). Although *Whiting Pools* involved assets seized by the IRS, the same rationale applies to collateral repossessed by an Article 9 secured party until such time as the debtor's right to redeem the collateral is cut off. *See* UCC § 9-623(c).

Would the rationale of *Whiting Pools* require a secured party to account to the trustee for the proceeds of a completed foreclosure sale? Could a secured party be ordered to turn over collateral after the completion of a strict foreclosure?

c.   What happens if a secured party violates the automatic stay? As a rule, any action taken is considered void. *See, e.g., In re Smith*, 876 F.2d 524 (6th Cir. 1989) (disposition of collateral by secured party held void). Is the secured party also subject to monetary liability? *See* Bankr. Code § 362(h).

d.   How long does the stay remain in effect? *See* Bankr. Code § 362(c). If a secured party's security interest is perfected by the filing of a financing statement at the time of a bankruptcy filing and the financing statement is about to lapse, may the secured party, while the stay is in effect, file a continuation statement to maintain its perfected status? *See* Bankr. Code § 362(b)(3).

e.   Procedurally, what must a secured party do to obtain relief from the stay so that it can proceed against its collateral? *See* Bankr. Code § 362(e).

Problem 5-1(e) refers to the procedural requirements for obtaining relief from the stay. The grounds for obtaining relief from the stay are set forth in § 362(d). In a Chapter 7 case, the ground that will be relevant is § 362(d)(2)(A). Section 362(d)(2)(B) is not applicable since in a Chapter 7 case no reorganization is contemplated. If the debtor has equity in the collateral, the secured party will usually not be granted relief from the stay. Instead, the trustee will typically sell the asset under § 363(f)(3) free of the security interest, pay the secured claim in full from the proceeds, and retain the excess for distribution to other claimants. If the debtor does not have equity in the collateral, the asset is worthless to the estate and the stay will usually be lifted. Indeed, the trustee may even abandon the collateral or acquiesce in the lifting of the stay. In a reorganization case, lack of equity is not enough—as contemplated by § 362(d)(2)(b)—the debtor must also not need the collateral for an effective reorganization. For example, suppose a wage-earner in a Chapter 13 proceeding owns a car subject to a security interest and has no equity in the car. What argument would the debtor make in opposition to the secured party's motion to lift the stay?

Under § 362(d)(1), the automatic stay may also be lifted "for cause, including the lack of adequate protection of an interest in property of such party in interest." Who is the "party in interest" in this situation?

The concept of "lack of adequate protection" can be illustrated by the following example. Suppose Bank is owed $500,000 and has a perfected security interest in Debtor's cargo plane, which is worth roughly the amount of the debt. Debtor, which is a small corporation, files for bankruptcy under Chapter 11. The plane is Debtor's only significant asset. Could Bank obtain relief from the stay under § 362(d)(2)? What risks might cause the secured party's position to deteriorate during the pendency of the bankruptcy proceeding? Assume that, when Debtor files its petition, Debtor will cease making payments to Bank until Debtor's plan of reorganization is approved by the court and becomes effective. Of course, if a plan of reorganization is not approved or does not become effective, the case may be converted to a Chapter 7 case.

If the court concludes that there is cause for lifting the stay, are there any strategies that the Debtor can employ to prevent the stay from being lifted? *See* Bankr. Code § 361. To provide adequate protection under § 361, the trustee or DIP must ensure that the collateral's value is preserved or that the secured party is otherwise protected against the risk of depreciation. Adequate protection may consist of cash payments, replacement liens on other property, or any other relief that will provide the secured party with the "indubitable equivalent" of its security interest (discussed further *infra*).

Even if Bank's secured claim is otherwise adequately protected, the stay may cause it to suffer lost opportunity costs. After all, but for the stay, Bank could foreclose on its security interest and then reinvest the proceeds of the foreclosure disposition applied to the claim. If the secured party is oversecured, the adverse effect of the automatic stay is mitigated by § 506(b). That provision permits secured creditors to recover postpetition interest on their secured claims up to the value of the collateral (the excess value of the collateral over the secured claim is sometimes referred to as an "equity cushion"). What about undersecured creditors, however? Not only can they not recover postbankruptcy interest on their secured claims, but also they cannot even assert an unsecured claim for such interest. Bankr. Code § 502(b)(2). Does this lost opportunity cost constitute "cause" for lifting the automatic stay?

The United States Supreme Court answered the foregoing question in the negative in *United Savings Ass'n of Texas v. Timbers of Inwood Forest Associates, Ltd.*, 484 U.S. 365 (1988). In a unanimous opinion, Justice Scalia concluded as follows:

> Since [§ 506(b)] permits postpetition interest to be paid only out of the "security cushion," the undersecured creditor, who has no such cushion, falls within the general rule disallowing postpetition interest. If the Code had meant to give the undersecured creditor, who is thus denied interest on his claim, interest on the value of his collateral, surely [§ 506(b)] is where that disposition would have been set forth, and not obscured within the "adequate protection" provision of § 362(d)(1).

Although lost opportunity costs do not constitute grounds for lifting the stay, lack of adequate protection for a secured claim does. A secured claim is adequately protected under the indubitable-equivalent test if there is an equity cushion sufficient to absorb post-bankruptcy interest and to protect against depreciation. *See In re Investment Company of the Southwest, Inc.*, 341 B.R. 298, 318-27 (10th. Cir. B.A.P. 2006); *In re Castle Ranch of Ramona*, 3 B.R. 45 (S.D. Cal. 1980). If the equity cushion is insufficient for those purposes, the stay should be lifted unless adequate protection in another form is provided (*e.g.*, cash payments or a replacement lien).

C.   AVOIDANCE POWERS—THE TRUSTEE AS HYPOTHETICAL LIEN CREDITOR (THE "STRONG-ARM" CLAUSE)

Section 544(a)(1) permits the trustee to avoid any transfer made by the debtor that could have been avoided by a lien creditor with an interest arising at the time the bankruptcy petition is filed. This power, sometimes referred to as the "strong-arm" power, is used to defeat secured parties with unperfected security interests. Note that § 544(a)(1) does not itself provide a sufficient basis for avoiding an unperfected security interest; instead, it gives the trustee the "rights and powers" of a lien creditor under state law. For our purposes, the state law in question is Article 9, which gives a lien creditor priority over an unperfected security interest. *See* UCC § 9-317(a)(2). Note that § 544(a)(1) gives the trustee the rights and powers of a lien creditor "whether or not such a creditor exists." For this reason, the trustee is sometimes referred to as a "hypothetical" lien creditor. If the security interest is avoided under § 544(a)(1), the secured party is treated as a general unsecured creditor. The following problems explore the trustee's strong-arm power in more detail:

Problem 5-2.

a.   On May 1, Bank lends Debtor $5,000 and takes a security interest in Debtor's equipment. On May 10, Debtor files a bankruptcy petition. On May 11, Bank files a financing statement. Can the trustee avoid Bank's security interest under § 544(a)(1)? Would your answer be different if Bank had filed on May 9?

b.   On May 1, Seller sells a piece of equipment to Buyer on credit and retains a security interest in the equipment. The equipment is delivered to Buyer on May 5. On May 10, Buyer files a bankruptcy petition, and on May 23, Seller files a financing statement. Can the trustee avoid Seller's security interest under § 544(a)(1)? To answer this question, you should consult UCC § 9-317(e). You must also consider whether Seller's filing is void as a violation of the automatic stay. This requires that you consider § 362(b)(3) and § 546(b). What does the phrase "generally applicable law" mean in § 546(b)?

Note that § 362(b)(3) also contains an exception to the stay for a perfecting act that is accomplished within the period provided in § 547(e)(2)(A). This exception relates to the trustee's power to avoid preferential transfers and is discussed further below.

c.   On May 1, Seller sells a big-screen TV set to Buyer on credit for use in Buyer's home and retains a security interest in the set. The set is delivered to Buyer on May 5. On May 10, Buyer files a bankruptcy petition. Can the trustee avoid Seller's security interest under § 544(a)(1) if Seller fails to file a financing statement (or take possession of the set) by May 25? *See* UCC § 9-309(1).

D.   AVOIDANCE POWERS—PREFERENTIAL TRANSFERS

1. Preferential Transfers Generally

Outside bankruptcy (and subject to the law governing fraudulent transfers discussed below), a debtor is free to prefer one creditor over another. For example, if Debtor owes two unsecured trade creditors $5,000 each and has only $5,000 in assets, Debtor is free to pay one creditor in full even though that means that the other will receive nothing. Bankruptcy, by contrast, is a collective debt-resolution process that treats similarly situated creditors similarly, and Debtor's preference of one creditor over another circumvents that fundamental principle.

As a Debtor's financial condition deteriorates, the common law's tolerance of preferential transfers creates an incentive for a race among creditors to reach the debtor's assets. If there are insufficient assets to go around, one creditor's success in this race inevitably reduces the assets available for other creditors. Once a petition in bankruptcy is filed, the race is ended by the automatic stay, but by then the damage has been done. Section 547 of the Bankruptcy Code seeks to discourage the race in the first place by creating a mechanism for forcing creditors to disgorge preferential transfers received on the eve of bankruptcy and to be treated in the bankruptcy as if the transfers had not been made. Preferential transfers can be voluntary, or they can be involuntary and effectuated by way of legal process or statutory lien. Bankr. Code §§ 101(36), (53), 545. State created priorities are also ineffective. Bankr. Code § 507.

The trustee can avoid any transfer, defined in § 101(54) to mean "every mode, direct or indirect, absolute or conditional, voluntary or involuntary, of disposing of or parting with property or an interest in property," and therefore including the creation of an Article 9 security interest that meets all of the following characteristics, as specified in § 547(b).

a. The Transfer Must Be Made of an Interest of the Debtor in Property

The law of preferences is not concerned with transfers that are not of an interest in property of the debtor. Recoveries by creditors of the debtor are not diluted by transfers that are not of an interest of the debtor in property.

b.   The Transfer Must Be Made to or for the Benefit of a Creditor

The law of preferences is not concerned with transfers, such as gifts, that do not benefit creditors by reducing their claims. The transfer need not, however, be made directly to the creditor. For example, a transfer by a corporation to one of its creditors might indirectly benefit a shareholder who guaranteed the debt. In such an "indirect preference" case, the trustee can recover the transfer from either the creditor or from the guarantor (assuming all the other elements of § 547(b) are present). Bankr. Code § 550(a)(1). Note that under § 550(c) a transfer made between 90 days and one year prior to bankruptcy cannot be recovered from an initial transferee that is not an insider merely because it benefits a guarantor that is an insider. Section 550(c) became effective as part of the Bankruptcy Reform Act of 1994. The section was later amended further as part of the Bankruptcy Abuse Prevention and Consumer Protection Act of 2005. The two amendments together reversed the result of the infamous case of *Levit v. Ingersoll Rand Financial Corp.*, 874 F.2d 1186 (7th Cir. 1989) (commonly known as the *DiPrizio* case).

c.   The Transfer Must Be Made for or on Account of an Antecedent Debt

The term "antecedent debt" is not defined, but the term "new value" is defined in § 547(a)(2)). An antecedent debt is any indebtedness that does not qualify as new value. The Bankruptcy Code is concerned only with transfers that have a deleterious effect on unsecured creditors. A transfer that is made in exchange for new value does not have such an effect as the new value substitutes *pro tanto* for the property transferred. Accordingly, a security interest granted to secure a new debt or a future debt would not be a transfer on account of antecedent debt.

d.   The Debtor Must Have Been Insolvent at the Time of the Transfer

If the debtor is solvent at the time of the transfer, there is less suspicion that the creditor was seeking to improve its position over other creditors of the debtor. Insolvency is defined in § 101(32). Note the difference between this definition and the definition of insolvent in UCC § 1-201(b)(23) [§ 1-201(23)]. Under § 547(f), the debtor is presumed to have been insolvent during the 90 days prior to the filing of the bankruptcy petition.

e.   The Transfer Must Take Place Within 90 Days Prior to the Filing of the Bankruptcy Petition (Or Within One Year Prior to Filing if the Creditor is an "Insider")

Transfers made within 90 days prior to bankruptcy are inherently suspicious and may be set aside if all the other elements of a preference are met. Note that the 90-day period coincides with the period during which the debtor is presumed to be insolvent. In the case of a transfer to a creditor who is an officer or director of the debtor or other insider (defined in § 101(31)), there is a concern that the creditor has an earlier warning of the upcoming bankruptcy and might also have the power to manipulate the timing of the bankruptcy filing. Thus, the preference period for insider transferees is extended to one year. In an action against an insider to avoid a transfer occurring between one year and 90 days prior to bankruptcy, the trustee would not have the benefit of the presumption of insolvency.

f. The Transfer Must Not Place the Creditor in a Better Position Than It Would Have Occupied Had the Transfer Not Occurred and Had the Creditor Asserted Its Claim in a Chapter 7 Liquidation Proceeding

In our example of two trade creditors, each of whom is owed $5,000, the payment (transfer) of $5,000 to one creditor puts it in an advantageous position. Had the transfer not occurred, the creditor would have had a general unsecured claim in bankruptcy and, if there had been $5,000 available for distribution to such creditors, would have received $2,500 in a Chapter 7 liquidation case. The other creditor would also have received the other $2,500.

Suppose, on the other hand, that the creditor had been fully secured from the time when the debt was first incurred by a perfected Article 9 security interest in the debtor's assets and had received a payment a few days before bankruptcy. Because the creditor party would have received the economic benefit of the collateral up to the amount of the debt in a Chapter 7 case, the payment would not have placed the creditor in a better position than it otherwise would have occupied in the absence of the transfer.

Problem 5-3.   Based on the foregoing factors, please determine which of the following transfers is voidable under § 547(b):

a.   On June 1, SP takes and perfects a security interest in a piece of equipment as collateral for a $5,000 loan made to D that same day. D files a petition in bankruptcy on August 1.

b.   On June 1, SP loans $5,000 to D on an unsecured basis. On July 1, SP takes and perfects a security interest in a piece of equipment as collateral for the loan. On December 1, D files a petition in bankruptcy. Would your answer change if D was a corporation and SP was its president?

c.   On June 1, SP takes and perfects a security interest in a piece of equipment as collateral for a $5,000 loan made to D that same day. The equipment is at all relevant times worth more than $5,000. On July 1, D pays the loan in full. D files a petition in bankruptcy on August 1.

d.   On June 1, SP loans $5,000 to D on an unsecured basis. On July 1, SP takes and perfects a security interest in a piece of equipment as collateral for the loan. On September 15, D files a petition in bankruptcy.

e.   On June 1, SP takes and perfects a security interest in a piece of equipment as collateral for a $5,000 loan made to D that same day. The equipment is at all relevant times worth $2,500. On July 1, D pays the loan in full. D files a petition in bankruptcy on August 1.

Note that in this instance, § 506(b) bifurcates SP's claim into a secured claim of $2,500 and an unsecured claim of $2,500.

f.   On June 1, SP takes and perfects a security interest in Debtor's gold bar as collateral for a $5,000 loan made to D that same day. The gold bar is worth $2,500 on June 1. On August 1, D files a petition in bankruptcy. On that day, because the price of gold has risen, the gold bar is worth $3,500.

2.   The Timing of the Transfer

Establishing the date of the transfer is critical for purposes of determining whether the transfer is for or on account of an antecedent debt and for determining whether the transfer occurred during the preference period.

As a general rule, a transfer takes effect for purposes of § 547(b) at the same time it takes effect between the parties under non-bankruptcy law. Section 547(e), however, contains a series of special timing rules that can modify the date of a transfer for purposes of § 547(b). Key to understanding how the timing rules work with respect to personal property is § 547(e)(1)(B), which tells us when the transfer is "perfected." A transfer is perfected when creditor of the transferor on a simple contract cannot acquire a judicial lien on the transferred property that is superior to the rights of the transferee. If the transfer is the grant of a security interest, the security interest will not be "perfected" under § 547(e)(1)(B) unless the security will be senior to the lien of a judicial lien creditor, *i.e.*, unless the security interest is perfected under Article 9 at or before the time when the judicial lien arises. *See* UCC § 9-317(a)(2).

To work the following problems, you should first identify the possible preferential transfer. Then determine when the transfer occurred under § 547(e). Finally, determine whether the transfer is for an antecedent debt and within the preference period.

Problem 5-4.

a.   On June 1, SP lends $100,000 to D and takes and perfects a security interest in all D's present and after-acquired equipment. On that date, D owns two items of equipment worth $25,000 each. On July 1, D uses its own funds to buy a new piece of equipment worth $25,000, and on August 1, D again uses its own funds to buy a new piece of equipment, also worth $25,000. On October 15, D files a petition in bankruptcy. Assume that all equipment values in this problem remain static at all relevant times and that SP has received no payments on the loan since June 1. To what extent can the trustee avoid SP's security interest in the four pieces of equipment? *See* Bankr. Code § 547(e)(3).

b.   On June 1, SP takes a security interest in a piece of equipment as collateral for a $5,000 loan made to D that same day. On June 25, SP files a financing statement covering the equipment. On August 1, D files a petition in bankruptcy. *See* Bankr. Code § 547(e)(2)(A).

c.   On June 1, SP loans $5,000 to D on an unsecured basis. On July 1, SP takes a security interest in a piece of D's equipment as collateral for the loan. On

July 25, SP files a financing statement covering the equipment. On August 1, D files a petition in bankruptcy.

d. On June 1, SP takes a security interest in a piece of equipment as collateral for a $5,000 loan made to D that same day. On July 15, SP file a financing statement covering the equipment. On September 1, D files a petition in bankruptcy. *See* Bankr. Code § 547(e)(2)(B). Would your answer change if D had filed the petition on November 1?

e. On June 1, Merchant sells an item of equipment to Buyer for $5,000 on credit and Buyer immediately takes possession. The contract of sale states that Merchant retains title to the equipment until Buyer makes payment in full. *See* UCC § 1-201(b)(35) [§ 1-201(37)]. On June 25, Merchant files a financing statement covering the equipment. On September 5, D files a petition in bankruptcy. *See* Bankr. Code §§ 547(e)(2)(A) and 547(c)(3)(B).

f. On June 1, SP takes a security interest in a piece of equipment as collateral for a $5,000 loan made to D that same day. On June 5, D files a petition in bankruptcy. On June 18, SP files a financing statement covering the equipment. Does the filing violate the automatic stay? *See* Bankr. Code § 362(b)(3). May the trustee avoid the transfer under § 547(b)? May the trustee avoid the transfer under § 544(a)?

g. On June 1, SP takes a security interest in a piece of equipment as collateral for a $5,000 loan made to D that same day. On August 1, D files a petition in bankruptcy. SP never perfects its security interest. What is the date of the transfer for purposes of § 547(b). *See* Bankr. Code § 547(e)(2)(C). Why is that section necessary?

3. Exceptions to the Trustee's Power to Avoid Preferences Generally

There are a number of transfers that meet all the elements of § 547(b) but ought not be avoided because they do not improperly favor the creditor transferee. Section 547(c) was adopted to shield these transfers from the trustee's avoidance power. As an analytical matter, though, you should first determine whether a transfer meets the requirements of § 547(b). Only if it does should you determine whether any of the exceptions (sometimes referred to as "defenses") in § 547(c) apply to the transfer.

The following notes and problems explore some of the more important provisions of § 547(c) (other than § 547(c)(5), which will be dealt with separately).

Problem 5-5.

a. On June 1, D enters into a contract to buy a car from SP, a dealer, on secured credit. When D drops by to pick up the car, SP advises him that the paperwork is not yet ready. SP gives the car to D, who needs it that day, and asks him to drop by the next morning to sign the security agreement. D does so and then files a petition in bankruptcy the next week. Assuming that SP promptly perfected its security interest, can the trustee avoid the security interest? *See* Bankr. Code § 547(c)(1).

Suppose that a secured party delays more than 30 days in perfecting its security interest and a petition in bankruptcy is then filed within 90 days after the date of perfection. Can the transfer be protected from avoidance under § 547(c)(1) notwithstanding the timing rule of § 547(e)(2)(A)? Before the Bankruptcy Abuse Prevention and Consumer Protection Act of 2005 became effective, the 30-day periods in § 547(e)(2) were 10-day periods. *Compare In re Arnett*, 731 F.2d 358 (6th Cir. 1984) (transfer not substantially contemporaneous as a matter of law unless perfected within the 10-day period set forth in § 547(e)(2)(A)), *with In re Dorholt*, 224 F.3d 871 (8th Cir. 2000) (transfer may be substantially contemporaneous even though perfection occurs after expiration of 10-day period).

b.   On the morning of June 1, a sales clerk at SP's store advises D that he can purchase a computer for home use on unsecured credit. D agrees to the terms and takes the computer home. That afternoon, SP's manager learns what has happened and fires the clerk. She then calls D, explains that the clerk made a mistake, and asks D to drop by the store and sign a security agreement. D does so the next morning and then files a petition in bankruptcy the next week. Can the trustee avoid the security interest?

c.   Two years ago, D has purchased a computer on secured credit from SP's store for D's personal use. D was required to make monthly payments of interest and principal to SP over a three-year period. D faithfully made all of the payments on time before filing for bankruptcy. By that time, though, and for the 90-day period before the bankruptcy petition was filed, the computer had declined so much in value so that it was worth at all times during the 90 day period far less than the loan from SP then outstanding. Can the trustee avoid the payments made to SP during the preference period? *See* § 547(c)(2).

There are countless situations in which a payment of money is technically a preferential transfer, yet avoidance of such payments would be inordinately disruptive of normal commercial activity. For example, without § 547(c)(2) every utility payment or credit card payment made within the preference period would be voidable. Note carefully that § 547(c)(2) applies only to the payment of money, not to the creation of a security interest. Note also the likely application of § 547(c)(8) to this problem even if the § 547(c)(2) defense was not available to SP.

d.   Assume that C is a trade creditor who sells supplies to D on unsecured credit. D gets behind in her payments. On June 1, C calls D and states that her purchasing rights will be suspended unless she pays the balance of her account, which is $5,000, in full. D makes the requested payment on June 10. On June 15, C ships supplies worth $3,000 to D on unsecured credit, and on July 1, D files a petition in bankruptcy. To what extent may the trustee recover the June 10 payment from C? *See* Bankr. Code § 547(c)(4). Would your answer be different if C had taken the precaution of retaining and perfecting a security interest in the June 15 shipment of supplies?

4.   Exceptions to the Trustee's Power to Avoid Preferences—Floating Liens on Inventory and Receivables

The timing rule of § 547(e)(3) creates problems for secured parties with liens that "float" over inventory, receivables (as defined in § 547(a)(3)), or the proceeds of either. In these instances, the secured party relies on a revolving pool of collateral—the pool is reduced as inventory is acquired by buyers in the ordinary course of business and as receivables are collected; it is increased as the debtor acquires inventory and generates receivables. The level of indebtedness also changes as the secured party advances funds for the acquisition of inventory or the generation of receivables and receives payments as inventory is sold and receivables are collected.

Under § 547(e)(3), a transfer that consists of the creation of a security interest in an asset cannot occur until the debtor acquires rights in the asset. Consider the effect of this rule on an inventory financier. Each time the debtor acquired new inventory a transfer consisting of the attachment of a security interest in the new inventory would occur. Because the new inventory would secure the existing indebtedness, the transfer would inevitably be on account of an antecedent debt. Of course, a new advance might be made based on the new inventory. This is a process not uncommon in inventory and accounts financing. But usually the new advance is not for the entire value of the new inventory (an advance of 50% of the value of the new inventory is typical). Unless the secured party was fully secured at the time the debtor acquired the new inventory or could establish that the new inventory was in substitution for the release of the lien in old inventory of no lesser value (an exercise that requires extensive records and is often not practical to be done), its security interest in the new inventory would be voidable if bankruptcy occurred within the preference period. Without amelioration of the effects of § 547(e)(3), secured parties could not rely on floating liens; yet such liens are a highly efficient means by which business is conducted and do not offend the policies that underlie the law of preferences.

Section 547(c)(5) provides an exception for perfected security interests in inventory, receivables, and the proceeds of either. The exception does not override § 547(e)(3) but does ameliorate its effects by valuing the collateral in the aggregate and permitting avoidance only to the extent that the secured party's overall position improves during the preference period. To determine the amount that the trustee can avoid, § 547(c)(5) requires a calculation of the extent to which, during the preference period, the aggregate of all transfers to the secured party (including a payment of money and the attachment of a security interest to a particular item acquired by the debtor) "caused a reduction, as of the date of the filing and to the prejudice of other creditors holding unsecured claims, of any amount by which the debt secured by such security interest exceeded the value of all security interests for such debt on" a measuring date that is the later of 1) 90 days before the filing of the petition or one year before the filing in the case of an insider, or 2) the date on which new value was first given by the secured party. The calculation permits a comparison of what the secured party's position would have been had the petition been filed on the measuring date and what its actual position is on the date of filing. Its security interest is voidable to the extent its position improves to the detriment of unsecured creditors.

The calculations required by § 547(c)(5) are not complex and can be accomplished as follows:

1.   The first step is to determine the outstanding indebtedness and the value of the collateral (all inventory, receivables, and the proceeds of either subject to a perfected security interest) on the measuring date. If the collateral's value is equal to or greater than the indebtedness, there is no need to go further—a fully secured party cannot receive a transfer that is voidable as a preference. If the collateral's value is less than the indebtedness, the secured party would have asserted a secured claim for the value of the collateral and an unsecured claim for the remainder of the indebtedness if bankruptcy had occurred on the measuring date.

2.   Perform the same calculation as of the petition date. This determines the amount of the secured and unsecured claims that the secured party will assert if none of the transfers is avoided.

3.   Compare the unsecured claim as of the measuring date with the unsecured claim as of the petition date. If that number has remained static or has increased, the trustee may not avoid any of the transfers that occurred during the preference period. If that number has decreased, the secured party's position has improved to the detriment of creditors with unsecured claims. The trustee can avoid the transfers to the extent necessary to offset the improvement.

While the calculations are not difficult, determining the value of the pool of collateral at any given point in time is complicated. The trustee will naturally argue for the lowest possible value (*e.g.*, liquidation or foreclosure sale value), while the secured party will argue for the highest possible value (*e.g.*, the retail value of inventory and the face amount of receivables). Section 506 provides in part that in determining the amount of a secured claim the value of the collateral "shall be determined in light of the purpose of the valuation and of the proposed disposition or use of such property." Thus, in *In re Clark Pipe and Supply Co., Inc.*, 893 F.2d 693 (5th Cir. 1990), the debtor was in the process of liquidating its inventory during the preference period and the court properly used a liquidation value. By contrast, in a Chapter 11 rehabilitation proceeding in which it is anticipated that the inventory will be sold at retail, use of a retail or replacement value would be more appropriate.

Try applying § 547(c)(5) to the following problem.

Problem 5-6.

a.   SP's floating lien on D's inventory and receivables antedates the start of the preference period. As of the 90th day prior to the filing of a petition in bankruptcy, the collateral has a value of $150,000 and the indebtedness is $200,000. On the date of the petition, the debt has been reduced to $175,000 and the collateral's value has risen to $160,000. To what extent may the trustee avoid transfers that occurred during the preference period?

b. Same facts as Problem 5-6(a), except the value of the collateral on the date of the petition has fallen to $110,000.

c. Suppose the numbers on the 90th day prior to the date of the petition had been reversed—that is, the debt had been $150,000 and the collateral had a value of $200,000. On the date of the petition, the debt had risen to $170,000 and the value of the collateral had fallen to $160,000.

E. AVOIDANCE POWERS—FRAUDULENT TRANSFERS

The bankruptcy trustee may also avoid transfers by the debtor that are fraudulent as to the debtor's creditors. These transfers are different than preferences, which merely prefer one creditor to other creditors of the debtor. A fraudulent transfer is fraudulent as to the debtor's creditors as a group.

Fraudulent transfer law is derived in large part from the Statute of Elizabeth referred to in *Clow v. Woods* discussed in Chapter 1. The statute addressed a common scheme when taxes were levied based on the number of sheep owned by a farmer. Before the tax collector arrived to count the sheep, the farmer moved a large number of his sheep to his neighbor's farm. When the tax collector left, the sheep would be moved back. As Justice Gibson stated in *Clow*, the statute "renders void all conveyances made to the end, purpose, and intent of defrauding creditors."

Today, most states have adopted the Uniform Fraudulent Transfer Act (the "UFTA") or its predecessor, the Uniform Fraudulent Conveyance Act (the "UFCA"). Both the UFTA and the UFCA permit creditors of a debtor to set aside a transfer or the incurrence of an obligation made by a debtor with an actual intent to hinder, delay or defraud the debtor's creditors. *See* UFTA § 4(a)(1) and UCFA § 7.

Problem 5-7. Debtor owns a car with a value of $5,000 and has other non-exempt assets worth $500. Debtor owes her creditors $10,000. Debtor has lost her job and has no source of income other than unemployment benefits. She gives her car to her brother, because, as she claims, she loves her brother, and her brother needs a car. Does Debtor have an actual intent to hinder, delay or defraud her creditors? How does one prove actual intent? *See* UFTA § 4(b).

Because of the evidentiary problem that often arises in proving the actual intent of the debtor, both the UFTA and the UFCA permit actual intent to be presumed in certain circumstances: when the debtor receives in exchange for the transfer less than "reasonably equivalent value" in the case of the UFTA or less than "fair consideration" in the case of the UCTA, and afterwards the debtor is left insolvent or, in the case of business debtor, with insufficient capital to run its business. *See* UFTA § 5(a) and UFCA § 4. Accordingly, if the UFTA or the UFCA were applicable in the above problem, it would not be necessary for a creditor to prove actual intent by Debtor to hinder, delay or defraud her creditors. It would be enough to show that the transaction was a gift, for which Debtor received no reasonably equivalent value or fair consideration, and that Debtor had insufficient assets to pay her liabilities after giving effect to the gift.

Both the UFTA and the UFCA have their own definitions "reasonably equivalent value" or "fair consideration" and their own rules for determining insolvency. Generally, though, a payment on, or the creation or perfection of a security interest to secure, antecedent debt is reasonably equivalent value or fair consideration. *See* UFTA § 3(a), UFCA § 3(a). These definitions distinguish a fraudulent transfer from a preference. The only exception is in § 5(b) of the UFTA which makes certain transfers to an insider on account of antecedent debt a fraudulent transfer. Also, as a general matter, a debtor is insolvent if the fair value of the debtor's assets is less than the debtor's liabilities. *See* UFTA § 2(a), UFCA § 2(1).

Problem 5-8.

a. Debtor is a corporation owned by A and B. Debtor has cash on hand of $50,000 and owns other assets worth $100,000. Debtor owes $200,000 to its creditors. Debtor uses the cash to redeem A's stock in Debtor, leaving B as the sole shareholder. Is the redemption of A's stock a fraudulent transfer under the UFTA?

b. C, a judgment creditor of Debtor, is owed $10,000. If the redemption is a fraudulent transfer under the UFTA, what remedies are available to C under the UFTA? *See* UFTA § 7.

c. Section 544(b)(1) of the Bankruptcy Code generally permits the trustee to avoid the transfer of any property of the debtor, or the incurrence by the debtor of any obligation, that a creditor of the debtor outside of bankruptcy can set aside under applicable non-bankruptcy law. If Debtor filed for bankruptcy soon after the redemption of A's stock, would Debtor's trustee be able to use § 544(b)(1) to avoid the redemption?

d. By the time of Debtor's bankruptcy, C is the only creditor who had a claim against Debtor at the time of the redemption and whose claim remains unpaid. If Debtor's trustee uses § 544(b)(1) to avoid the redemption, how much of the redemption should the trustee be able to avoid—the $10,000 owed to C or the entire $50,000 redemption? The case of *Moore v. Bay*, 284 U.S. 4 (1931), written by Justice Holmes, is widely cited for the proposition that the trustee may avoid the entire $50,000. Does it make sense that the trustee may assert rights greater than an actual creditor of the debtor may assert against the debtor under non-bankruptcy law?

e. What if, by the time of Debtor's bankruptcy, all creditors of Debtor who were creditors at the time of the redemption had been paid? Could the trustee use § 544(b) to set aside the redemption? If not, could the trustee use the Bankruptcy Code's own federally-created fraudulent transfer statute, § 548?

f. What if Debtor did not have the $50,000 in cash to make the redemption but rather borrowed the $50,000 from Bank and granted to Bank a security interest, which Bank promptly perfected by filing, in Debtor's machine worth $60,000? Do you see any argument that the trustee might make to set aside the loan obligation or the security interest as a fraudulent transfer either under § 544(b)(1) and the UFTA or under § 548? *Compare United States v. Tabor Court Realty Corp.*, 803 F.2d 1288 (3d Cir. 1986), *with In re*

Greenbrook Carpet Co., 722 F.2d 659 (11th Cir. 1984).

F. OTHER EFFECTS OF BANKRUPTCY

The materials set forth above do not by any means exhaust the potential effects of bankruptcy on Article 9 security interests—indeed, they just scratch the surface. The following problems shed light on just a few of the other provisions that might be relevant.

Problem 5-9.

a. Finance Company makes a $2,500 loan to Debtor and takes and perfects a security interest in Debtor's piano. Subsequently, Debtor files a petition in bankruptcy and seeks to claim the piano as exempt (assume that without the security interest Debtor would be entitled to the exemption). As a rule, the existence of a security interest precludes exemption claims except as to any equity. Can Debtor nevertheless avoid Finance Company's security interest and claim the piano as exempt? *See* Bankr. Code § 522(f)(1)(B).

b. Bank takes and perfects a security interest in all Debtor's present and after-acquired equipment. Subsequently, Debtor files a Chapter 11 petition and continues to run its business as debtor-in-possession. If Debtor acquires new equipment, will Bank's security interest attach? *See* Bankr. Code § 552(a). Would your answer change if Bank could prove that the after-acquired equipment was a proceed of equipment owned by Debtor prior to bankruptcy? *See* Bankr. Code § 552(b).

c. Bank has a perfected security interest in Debtor's car at the time Debtor files a Chapter 7 petition. The car has a value of $5,000 and the outstanding balance of the loan is $7,000. Because the car is worthless to the estate, the trustee has abandoned it (§ 554(a)) and Bank is seeking relief from the stay in order to commence foreclosure proceedings. Is there anything Debtor can do to avoid losing the car? *See* Bankr. Code § 722. Will Debtor be allowed to use assets of the estate to redeem the car?

Chapter 6

INTRODUCTION TO INTERNATIONAL SECURED TRANSACTIONS

A. HARMONIZATION THROUGH TREATIES AND DOMESTIC LAWS

When U.S. businesses trade with foreign enterprises or invest abroad, attorneys advising them must consider the possibility that Article 9 of the UCC will not govern the attachment, perfection, priority or enforcement of security interests. Consider, for example, the case of a U.S. lender who lends to an English borrower and who wants the borrower to grant a security interest in equipment located in England.

The Code itself provides limited guidance for these "multiple state" transactions. As previously discussed, UCC §§ 9-301 to 9-307 set out mandatory choice-of-law rules governing perfection, the effect of perfection or non-perfection, and the priority of security interests and agricultural liens.[1] In our English Borrower hypothetical, these rules instruct the U.S. lender as to whether the UCC or English law governs. If English law governs, the lender must comply with English law in order to have the equivalent of a "perfected" security interest. UCC § 9-301's choice-of-law rules, however, only tell the lender which jurisdiction's law governs issues of perfection and the effect of perfection or non-perfection and priority. For choice-of-law rules on other issues, such as these pertaining to the validity of the security interest, the lender must consult UCC § 1-301 [§ 1-105]. Under that section, the lender and the borrower may choose for these other issues to have the law of a state *or nation* govern if the chosen law bears a reasonable relation to the transaction. If the lender and the borrower choose English law, again the UCC will not apply to those other issues. Moreover, if they choose U.S. law, an English court will not necessarily be bound by their agreement or even by the mandatory choice of law rules of Article 9: neither UCC § 9-301 nor UCC § 1-310 [§ 1-105] is the law of England. The UCC, in other words, cannot provide complete and definitive rules for multinational secured transactions.[2]

However, the rest of the world has not enacted secured transactions laws similar to UCC Article 9. Most Canadian provinces and New Zealand have adopted personal property security acts that resemble—and even improve—Article 9, but

---

[1] *See* Chapter 4; UCC § 1-301(g) [§ 1-105(2)].

[2] For a more detailed discussion of how UCC Article 9 addresses international transactions, *see* Neil B. Cohen & Edwin E. Smith, *International Secured Transactions and Revised UCC Article 9*, 74 CHICAGO-KENT L. REV. 1191 (1999).

English law bears little resemblance to Article 9 or to pre-Code security devices in the United States. Indeed, under the laws of many common law countries and most civil law countries, many of the concepts taken for granted under Article 9 for security interests in personal property are absent or dramatically different, including:

- A single set of rules governing security interests regardless of the form of the transaction

- Security devices being available to all classes of creditors rather than merely to certain classes such as licensed banks

- Recognition of non-possessory security interests

- The possibility of describing collateral in a security agreement by general description (e.g., "all equipment") instead of by specific description (e.g., "drill press with serial number 1234")

- Permitting a security interest to attach to future assets by virtue of an "after-acquired property" clause in a security agreement

- Having clear perfection and priority rules generally based on a notice filing system by which notices of security interests (financing statements) are filed in a recording office at a nominal cost and by which the notices are accessible to a quick simple low-cost search by the public

- The possibility for a lender financing a debtor's purchase of goods, by taking certain steps, to obtain a "super priority" status for its security interest in the goods

- The security interest automatically attaching to proceeds of the collateral

- Having clear and flexible market-oriented rules for enforcement of security interests

- Having clear conflict of laws rules that determine under which jurisdiction's laws the above matters are governed.[3]

As international trade has increased, the uncertainty described above, as well as the problem of subjection to an unfamiliar legal regime, has led increasingly to the negotiation of international conventions in the commercial law area. Today, there are international conventions on sales of goods,[4] leasing,[5] negotiable instruments,[6]

---

[3] *See, e.g.* HARRY C. SIGMAN & EVA-MARIA KIENINGER (EDS.), CROSS-BORDER SECURITY OVER TANGIBLES (2007).

[4] Reference is made to the United Nations Convention on Contracts for the International Sale of Goods, also known as the Vienna Convention. This convention was signed in 1980 and has been ratified by 70 countries so far. The Vienna Convention entered into force on January 1, 1988. For the complete text of the Vienna Convention go to: http://www.uncitral.org/pdf/english/texts/sales/cisg/CISG.pdf

[5] Reference is made to the Unidroit Convention on International Financial Leasing adopted in Ottawa on May 28, 1988. This convention has been ratified by 10 countries so far and entered into force on May 1, 1995. For the complete text of the Unidroit Convention on international Financial Leasing go to: http://www.unidroit.org/english/conventions/1988leasing/1988leasing-e.htm

[6] Reference is made to the United Nations Convention on International Bills of Exchange and

funds transfers,[7] and letters of credit.[8] Such conventions, when ratified by and entered into force in the United States under the federal Constitution, become federal law, and, if the convention is self-executing or is accompanied by implementing federal legislation, supersede state law, such as the Uniform Commercial Code. To date, only the sales convention and the convention on international security interests in mobile equipment, discussed below, have this status in the United States, but consideration of the other efforts is underway.

To address non-uniformity in the area of secured transactions, several international bodies have recently undertaken to draft uniform or model rules. In 1980, the United Nations Commission on International Trade Law (UNCITRAL) concluded that worldwide unification of secured transactions law was unattainable. Not only would it be difficult to adjust existing secured transactions laws, but, in the view of the Commission, it would also be necessary to harmonize closely-related areas of the law, such as bankruptcy.[9] More recently, however, the United Nations has offered to countries a treaty—the United Nations Convention on the Assignment of Receivables in International Trade—that provides uniform rules on receivables financing.[10] The Receivables Convention builds on the 1988 Convention on International Factoring,[11] a text prepared by the Institute for the Unification of Private Law (commonly known as "UNIDROIT"). UNIDROIT itself has prepared a companion 1988 convention, the Convention on International Financial Leasing,[12] and has promulgated a Convention on International Security Interests in Mobile Equipment which is discussed later in these materials.[13] A third international body, European Bank for Reconstruction and Development (EBRD), has completed drafting a Model Law on Secured Transactions.[14] The EBRD now provides advice to countries in Eastern Europe and the former Soviet Union that are preparing new national legislation.[15] In addition, UNCITRAL has recently adopted the UNICI-

International Promissory Notes adopted in New York on December 9, 1988. It has been ratified by 5 countries and requires ratification by other 5 countries to enter into force. For the complete text of this convention go to: http://www.uncitral.org/pdf/english/texts/payments/billsnotes/X_12_e.pdf

[7] Reference is made to the Uncitral Model Law on International Credit Transfers adopted on May 15, 1992. For the complete text of this convention go to: http://www.uncitral.org/pdf/english/texts/payments/transfers/ml-credittrans.pdf

[8] Reference is made to the United Nations Convention on Independent Guarantees and Stand-by Letters of Credit adopted on December 11, 1995. This convention has been ratified by 8 countries and entered into force on January 1, 2000. For the complete text of the convention go to: http://www.uncitral.org/pdf/english/texts/payments/guarantees/guarantees.pdf.

[9] *See* XI [1980] UNCITRAL Y.B. 10-11.

[10] An overview of this Convention, including a comparison of the Convention to UCC Article 9, is found in Harry C. Sigman & Edwin E. Smith. *Toward Facilitating Cross-Border Financing and Securitization: an Analysis of the United Nations Convention on the Assignment of Receivables in International Trade*, 57 Bus. Law. No. 2 (Feb. 2002).

[11] *See* 27 I.L.M. 943 (1988) (entered into force on May 1, 1995 among France, Italy, and Nigeria).

[12] 21 I.L.M. 943 (1988) (entered into force on May 1, 1995 among France, Italy, and Nigeria).

[13] Ronald C.C. Cuming, *The Registry System of the Convention on International Interests in Mobile Equipment (Draft) and the Aircraft Equipment Protocol (Draft)*, 34 UCC L.J. 81 (2001).

[14] *See* EBRD Model Law on Secured Transactions (1994).

[15] John Simpson, *Ten Years of Secured Transactions Reform*, E.B.R.D. L. Transition 20 (Autumn 2000); Duncan Fairgrieve, *Securing Progress in Collateral Law Reform: The E.B.R.D.'s Regional Survey*

TRAL Legislative Guide on Secured Transactions to assist countries in implementing a modern secured transactions law based on many of the principles found in Article 9.[16]

The EBRD Model Law and the UNCITRAL Legislative Guide on Secured Transactions promote uniformity in much the same way that the U.S. Commissioners on Uniform State Laws promote uniformity of domestic law: each country or state may adopt the model law with or without amendments. The UNCITRAL and UNIDROIT treaty projects, on the other hand, promote uniformity through multilateral conventions which will allow few reservations. These convention rules are more closely analogous to federal legislation in the United States. If widely adopted, the draft conventions provide greater assurance of uniformity.

Many countries are not waiting for completion of the international projects to reform their domestic secured transactions laws. These countries are under pressure from the World Bank, the EBRD, and other international development banks, not to mention the international capital market itself. By adopting new legislation or reforming existing legislation, these countries hope to signal their readiness to receive investments and to honor trading contracts. Draft legislation has advanced significantly in Eastern Europe, including such countries as Hungary and Poland.[17] On the Pacific Rim, drafts have been submitted to drafting committees in Indonesia and Vietnam, while in Latin America, Argentina and Bolivia are considering proposals for legislation.

Most of these countries have sought the advice of foreign experts. A number of different governmental and other bodies in the United States and Europe provided advisers. No one has prepared a comprehensive list of these bodies, let alone a list of the projects presently under way. For Eastern Europe, the Institutional Reform and Informal Sector (IRIS) of the University of Maryland has focused on developing "pledge" laws in such countries as Albania, Bulgaria, Lithuania, and Poland. Also, in 2004, IRIS helped the Ministry of Finance and the Central Bank of Russia in establishing a secured finance system and worked with local authorities in the drafting of a secured financing law which "addresses the creation, registration and enforcement of secured interests in movable property."[18] Both the Commercial Law Development Program for Central and Eastern Europe in the U.S. Department of Commerce and the American Bar Association's Central and Eastern European Law Initiative (CEELI) program have provided advisers and sponsored programs that touch on secured financing. The Washington, D.C., Center for Economic Analysis of Law (CEAL), whose director and associates are consultants to the World Bank and other international financial institutions, presently has

---

of Secured Transactions Laws, E.B.R.D. L. TRANSITION 28 (Autumn 2000).

[16] The legislative guide was adopted at UNICITRAL's fortieth session held in Vienna in 2007. For the complete text of the legislative guide, *see* http://www.uncitral.org/uncitral/en/uncitral_texts/payments/Guide_securedtrans.html. This text is the final copy submitted for publication subject to final corrections of typographical and similar errors.

[17] John Simpson, *Ten Years of Secured Transactions Reform*, E.B.R.D. L. TRANSITION 20 (Autumn 2000); Tomasz Slawecki, *Secured Transactions in Poland: Coping with the Traditional Thinking and the New Challenges for Central and Eastern Europe*, 32 UCC L.J. 25 (1999).

[18] For further information, go to http://www.iris.umd.edu/Reader.aspx?TYPE=PROJECT&ID=b7dfbc6e-e2b0-44e8-87cc-491ab9bfdbf9.

projects in several countries including Argentina, Bolivia, Colombia, Ecuador and Nicaragua. CEAL has also completed projects in Bangladesh, Bulgaria, Colombia, Costa Rica, Dominican Republic, Ecuador, India, Indonesia, Mexico, Nepal, Poland, Romania, Thailand, Uruguay, Venezuela and Vietnam. Guatemala, Mexico, Peru and Rumania have already modernized their legislation on secured transactions after having worked with CEAL in the past.

Another important entity that has made significant contributions to the modernization and reform of Latin American laws on secured transaction is the Organization of American States (OAS). On February 8, 2002, the OAS adopted the Model Inter-American Law on Secured Transactions.[19] This model law was the object of a detailed analysis made by Boris Kozolchyk, Professor of Law at the University of Arizona and president of the National Law Center for International Trade, and Dale Beck Furnish, Professor of Law at Arizona State University. According to their study paper,

> The rules, concepts, and principles of interpretation found in the OAS Model Law embody those secured lending practices successfully tested in most active secured credit marketplaces of the financial world. Although the OAS Model Law rules, concepts and principles of interpretation were thoroughly and painstakingly tropicalized to make them acceptable within Latin American legal systems, they were inspired by Article 9 of the Uniform Commercial Code of the United States, by Canada's Personal Property Security Act and by drafts of the United Nations Convention on the Assignment of Accounts Receivable in International Trade . . .[20]

Countries such as Mexico, Guatemala, El Salvador, Peru, and Chile have either adopted or are in the process of adopting secured transactions laws inspired by the OAS Model Law.

Driven by many of the same causes, bankruptcy law reform is also being seriously considered. Privatization has forced reexamination of national insolvency policies and procedures. UNCITRAL developed a model law containing rules encouraging cooperation between insolvency authorities in different countries.[21] In May 2002, the European Union's Regulation on Insolvency Proceedings[22] became effective. The Regulation seeks to harmonize insolvency proceedings among the European Union states. UNCITRAL also issued in 2004 its Legislative Guide on Insolvency Law to assist countries in developing and enacting modern insolvency laws.

We have noted above that presently there are two conventions that have been recently completed in relation to the subject matter of UCC Article 9. One, the Convention on International Interests in Mobile Equipment (hereinafter the

---

[19] *See* the complete text of the Model Inter-American Law on Secured Transactions on: http://www.oas.org/DIL/CIDIP-VI-securedtransactions_Eng.htm

[20] Boris Kozolchyk & Dale Beck Furnish, *The OAS Model Law on Secured Transactions: A Comparative Analysis*, 12 Sw. J. L. & Trade in the Americas 101 (2006).

[21] UNCITRAL Model Law on Cross-Border Insolvency (1977). The model law has been substantially adopted by the United States in Chapter 15 of the Bankruptcy Code.

[22] Council Regulation No. 44/2001 of Dec. 22, 2000, Official Journal 2001 L 12/1.

CIIME), is focused on certain high priced mobile goods. The other, the United Nations Convention on the Assignment of Receivables on International Trade, focuses on assignments, whether security interests securing obligations or sales, of receivables consisting of contractual rights to the payment of money. At the current time, only the CIIME has been adopted by the United States.

The following article by Ronald C.C. Cuming and the attached problems provide an introductory overview to the CIIME.

Ronald C.C. Cuming, *Overview of the Convention on International Interests in Mobile Equipment, 2001*
35 UCC L.J. 1 (2002)[23]

INTRODUCTION

The Convention on International Interests in Mobile Equipment, 2001 (hereafter the "Convention") and an associated Protocol on Matters Specific to Aircraft Equipment (hereafter the "Aircraft Protocol") was adopted at a diplomatic conference in November of 2001. When it comes into force, it will provide an international regime within which secured financing and leasing of high-value mobile equipment will occur.

The basic structures of the Convention and Aircraft Protocol were developed by committees of the International Institute on Unification of Private Law (UNIDROIT) with the participation of the Legal Committee of the International Civil Aviation Organization (ICAO) during the later stages.

The Convention and associated protocols were designed to address the problem of refusal by national courts to recognize the validity, priority or enforceability of secured party, seller or lessor interests in mobile equipment created under the law of other states.[24]

The Convention is unprecedented in that it provides for a regime that in substantial measure will displace the municipal law of the Contracting States that would otherwise govern the types of transactions to which the Convention applies. It will implement a priority regime based on a single, world-wide registry system designed to reduce dramatically the legal risk associated with acquiring interests in property to which the Convention applies. It will enable the parties to a secured financing transaction to use forms of agreements not recognized by the municipal law of many States. The result will be that persons located in Contracting States will have available to them a system of international law for the creation and

---

[23] Prepared by Professor Ronald C.C. Cuming, University of Saskatchewan, Saskatoon, Canada. Professor Cuming was the originator of the proposal for the Convention. Copyright 2002. Reprinted by permission.

[24] [1] *See generally* Cuming, R.C.C., *International Regulation of Aspects of Security Interests in Mobile Equipment* UNIFORM LAW REVIEW 64, 77–89 (1990–91), and Shilling, *Some European Decisions on Non-possessory Security Rights in Private International Law*, 34 INTERNATIONAL AND COMPARATIVE LAW QUARTERLY 87 (1985).

regulation of rights even though the municipal law of these States does not provide for transactions of this kind.

SCOPE

1. Types of Equipment

The Convention has been designed to apply to a range of different types of mobile equipment.[25] However, because of the early participation of an Aviation Working Group, formed by representatives of a wide range of organizations involved in the sale, financing and use of commercial aircraft, it was possible to develop the Convention and an accompanying aircraft protocol in tandem and adopt both of them at the diplomatic conference in South Africa.

2. Types of Financing Transactions

The Convention employs both a functional and a formal approach to the identification of transactions falling within its scope. A functional test is used to identify transactions that create international security interests. Article 2(2)(a) provides that the Convention applies to a "security agreement" defined in Article 1(ii) in generic terms. However, this approach was not applied universally. Article 2(2) of the Convention includes two additional types of agreements solely by reference to their form: a title reservation agreement (defined in Article 1(ll)) and a leasing agreement (defined in Article 1(q)). A very limited concept of "proceeds" is recognized. *See* Articles 1(w) and 2(5).

3. Characterization of Transactions

Article 2(4) refers characterization of transactions falling within the scope of the Convention to the "applicable law" which, under Article 5(3), is the domestic law applicable by virtue of the rules of private international law of the forum. The separate recognition of three types of transactions should create no difficulties for legal systems that rely heavily on formalism when categorizing transactions. These include most national systems. However, a more complex approach is required in the context of the secured financing systems of the United States and the common law jurisdictions of Canada that focus on function and reject formalism as a factor in characterizing transactions as security agreements, leases or conditional sales contracts.

The secured financing law of these jurisdictions defines conditional sales contracts as security agreements and not as transactions under which the conditional seller has ownership and the conditional buyer only possession with a

---

[25] [2] Article 2(3) of the Convention lists three categories of equipment to which it will apply: aircraft objects (airframes, aircraft engines and helicopters), railway rolling stock and space assets. Resolution No. 3 of the Final Act of the Diplomatic Conference provides for early completion of protocols dealing with railway rolling stock and space assets and expedited procedures leading up to diplomatic conferences at which they are adopted. Article 51 provides for the development of additional protocols dealing with other types of high-value mobile equipment.

contractual right to become owner upon fulfilling specified conditions. Under this approach, the conditional buyer is the owner of the goods and the conditional seller has a security interest or charge on those goods. Recognizing that, functionally, leases are frequently used as secured financing devices in the United States and Canadian common law systems, the secured financing law of these jurisdictions attaches little importance to form in the determination as to whether a particular transaction is a true lease or a security agreement in the form of a lease.

Consequently, a transaction in the form of a title reservation agreement would be viewed very differently if the applicable law were the secured financing regime of the United States or a common law province of Canada than it would be if the applicable law were that of most other jurisdictions in the world. A transaction in the form of a lease that would be characterized as a lease in a jurisdiction that employs a formal test could be a security agreement under the law of a jurisdiction that applies a functional test.

The result is that whether a transaction is viewed, on the one hand, as a security agreement, or, on the other, as a title reservation agreement will depend upon the forum in which the issue arises. While the characterization of a particular transaction as a security agreement rather than a lease or title reservation agreement does not affect the application of the priority rules of the Convention or its registration requirements, it does affect the remedies of a defaulting chargor, lessee or buyer. Under Article 9, the remedies of a lessor or conditional seller are those of an owner: simple recovery of the leased or sold object is permitted. Under Articles 7 and 8, the remedies of a chargee are those of a secured party. These remedies are designed to provide protection to the chargor's interest in the object.

4. Nonconsensual Rights and Interests

The Convention also provides for the extension of the registration and priority rules to a "non-consensual right or interest," such as repairers' or suppliers' liens, tax liens and wage liens, that a contracting State in its declaration elects to treat as consensual international interest. The term "non-consensual right or interest" is defined in Article 1(s) as a right or interest conferred by law to secure the performance of an obligation, including an obligation to a State or State entity. Under Article 40, a State may declare that specified non-consensual rights or interests are to be treated as interests to which the Convention applies with the result that they will be subject to the registration requirements and priority rules of the Convention and Protocol. An alternative approach is offered by Article 39. It provides that a State may make a declaration setting out a list of non-consensual rights or interests having priority under the national law of that State and that will have priority under the Convention. These rights or interests will not be subject to the registration requirement or priority regime of the Convention. The list of such interests will be kept on record at the International Registry. *See* Article 23.

5. Assignments

The effect of Chapter IX (Articles 31–38) is to bring assignments of "associated rights" within the scope of the Convention. However, in order for the Convention to apply, the international interest and at least some of the payment rights associated with it must be transferred together. Article 32(3) provides that the Convention does not apply to an assignment of associated rights that is not accompanied by the transfer of the related international interest. Article 32(3) provides that an assignment of an international interest created under a security agreement is not valid unless some or all related associated rights are assigned. The term "associated rights" is defined in Article 1(c) as "all rights to payment or other performance by a debtor under an agreement which are secured by or associated with" equipment to which the Convention applies. This definition is in effect limited by Article 36(2) that restricts application of the priority rules of the Convention to situations in which the competing assignments involve specified kinds of payment rights.

6. Sales of Aircraft Objects

The effect of Article III of the Aircraft Protocol and Article 40 of the Convention is to bring within the priority and registration provisions of the Convention sales of aircraft and aircraft engines. While this feature will not provide a title registration system for these items, it will have this effect with respect to aircraft and engines purchased from manufacturers after the Convention and Protocol come into effect. A potential buyer will be able to search the "chain of ownership" from the manufacturer to the seller. A person who buys on the strength of this information will take free from an intervening transfer of ownership that has not been registered.

THE INTERNATIONAL ELEMENT

The location of the chargor, lessee or buyer in a Contracting State at the time of execution of the security agreement, lease or conditional sale is the factor that invokes application of the Convention. *See* Articles 3 and 4. *See also* Article III, Aircraft Protocol. The location of the secured party, lessor or seller is not relevant. Article IV of the Aircraft Protocol provides, however, that the Convention will apply to a transaction involving an aircraft (but not to an aircraft engine)[26] or helicopter if the aircraft or helicopter is registered in a Contracting State or an agreement exits that the aircraft will be registered in a Contracting State.

The Convention applies to what in other contexts would be a transaction governed by national law because all or most of the factors relating to the agreement and the equipment are located in a single State. However, a limited exception is allowed. Under Article 50, a Contracting State is entitled to declare that the Convention will not apply to "an internal transaction" (defined in Article 1(n)). However, the effect of such a declaration will be limited since it will not exempt the transaction from the registration and priority rules of the Convention. *See* Article 50(2)–(3).

---

[26] [3] The Aircraft Protocol distinguishes between an aircraft airframe and the aircraft engines. This feature reflects the fact that only airframes (and helicopters) are registered under the Chicago Convention on International Civil Aviation, 1944.

THE PRIORITY STRUCTURE

The priority structure of the Convention is dependent upon an international registry for international interests and registerable non-consensual interests. The priority rules of the Convention are very simple. Competing registered interests will rank in order of their registration,[27] and a registered interest will have priority over an unregistered interest (Article 29(1)). Knowledge of a prior unregistered interest will not affect the priority status of a holder of a registered interest (Article 29(2)). Similarly, an unregistered international interest will be subordinate to the interest of a person who buys the property subject to an international interest from the chargor, lessee or conditional buyer. This is so whether or not the buyer's interest was acquired with or without actual knowledge of the unregistered international interest (Article 29(3)–(4)). A registered international interest will have priority over a trustee in bankruptcy and execution or attaching creditors. Otherwise, an international interest will have the same priority in insolvency proceedings that it has under the law applicable to the proceedings (Article 30). If, under that law, the interest is valid against the trustee or administrator without registration, the lack of registration in the international registry will not be relevant.

POST DEFAULT RIGHTS AND REMEDIES

Articles 8-15 of the Convention provide a regime of post-default *in rem* rights and remedies of secured parties that bears close resemblance to secured transactions laws of most North American jurisdictions. However, the Articles contain qualifications designed to accommodate approaches to enforcement employed elsewhere in the world and to address what are perceived to be special needs. Article 15 provides that the parties may agree in writing to derogate from or vary most of the rights and obligations specified by the Convention. Article 11 provides that the parties may agree to additional remedies not inconsistent with its mandatory provisions.

The remedies given to secured parties, lessors and title retention sellers under the Convention must be read in light of Article 14, which makes it clear that the procedural laws of the place of exercise of the remedy must be followed.[28] In addition, Article 54(2) empowers a Contracting State to declare that enforcement rights may be exercised only with leave of a court.

INSOLVENCY

An issue that caused great difficulty for the drafters of the Convention and Aircraft Protocol was the interface between national insolvency law

---

[27] [4] As to priority in the case of competing buyers, *see* Protocol, Article XIV(1)–(2). The Convention does not affect the rights of a person in an item held prior to its installation on property to which the Convention applies if under the applicable law those rights continue after installation. Nor does it prevent the creation of rights recognized under the applicable law in such an item when it is installed. *See* Convention, Article 29(7).

[28] [5] The Aircraft Protocol also modifies and supplements the remedial structure of the Convention. *See, e.g.*, Articles IX and X.

(reorganization) and the rights of secured parties in the event of default by debtors. One group of States wanted to have the Aircraft Protocol specify the right of a secured party, lessor or seller to have an aircraft object surrendered by the debtor or insolvency administrator in possession within a very short period of time after default unless, within that time, the default has been remedied. This concept, while well-known in United States law,[29] is not a feature of the insolvency law of many States. Another group of States wanted a "softer" rule that would give the insolvency administrator greater flexibility. The issue was addressed in Article XI of the Protocol. A Contracting State that is a "primary insolvency jurisdiction" (defined in Article 1(2)(n)) may make a declaration as to which of two alternative approaches set out in the Protocol will be applied. Under Article XI, Alternative A, the aircraft object must be surrendered to the creditor as provided in the security agreement following the occurrence of an insolvency related event (defined in Article I(m)) unless the default that gave rise to the event is remedied immediately. Under Article XI, Alternative B, the insolvency administrator can be given a longer period of time (specified in the declaration of the Contracting State) to cure the default that resulted in the opening of the bankruptcy proceedings.

THE INTERNATIONAL REGISTRY

1. Introduction

The following description of the proposed International Registry is based on the provisions of the Convention and the Aircraft Protocol. However, it cannot be definitive because the details were yet to be finalized when this paper was prepared.[30]

---

[29] [6] Article 1110 United States Bankruptcy Code, 11 United States Code.

[30] [7] The following is an excerpt from Resolution No. 2 of the Final Act of the Diplomatic Conference:

The Conference RESOLVES:

TO INVITE ICAO to accept the functions of Supervisory Authority upon the entry into force of the Convention and the Protocol;

TO INVITE ICAO to establish a Commission of Experts consisting of not more than 15 members appointed by the ICAO Council from among persons nominated by the Signatory and Contracting States to the Convention and to the Protocol, having the necessary qualifications and experience, with the task of assisting the Supervisory Authority, upon the entry into force of the Convention and the Protocol;

TO SET UP, pending the entry into force of the Convention and the Protocol, a Preparatory Commission to act with full authority as Provisional Supervisory Authority for the establishment of the International Registry, under the guidance and supervision of the ICAO Council. Such Preparatory Commission shall be composed of persons, having the necessary qualifications and experience, nominated by the following States: Argentina, Brazil, Canada, China, Cuba, Egypt, France, Germany, India, Ireland, Kenya, Nigeria, Russian Federation, Senegal, Singapore, Switzerland, South Africa, Tonga, United Arab Emirates, and United States.

TO DIRECT the Preparatory Commission to carry out, under the guidance and supervision of the ICAO Council, the following functions:

(1) to ensure that the international registration system be set up, in accordance with an objective, transparent and fair selection process, and that it become ready to be operated with a target date of one year from the adoption of the Convention and the Protocol, and at the latest by the time of the entry into force of the Convention and the Protocol;

2. The Administrative Structure

The Convention and Aircraft Protocol provide for a single registry for the registration of all international interests and registerable non-consensual interests in aircraft objects. There will be no direct reliance on or coordination with existing national registries.[31] All registration information will be communicated directly to a single registry location.

3. The Supervisory Authority and Registrar

Since the Registry will not be under the administrative control of any national government, it was necessary to provide for a body that will make policy decisions and regulations that address the details of the system. The Convention and Aircraft Protocol provide for the designation of a Supervisory Authority that will be an international entity with powers and responsibilities paralleling those of a government department responsible for establishing and maintaining a registry (Convention Article 17 and Protocol Article XVII). ICAO will become or will create the Supervisory Authority as one of its branches.[32] ICAO is the arm of the United Nations with a mandate to regulate many aspects of civil aviation; it has international legal personality and an established bureaucracy.

Article 17 of the Convention gives to the Supervisory Authority responsibility for a wide range of matters relating to the Registry, including establishing it, appointing the Registrar, making regulations for the operation of the Registry, providing guidance to the Registrar, setting Registry fees and addressing complaints of users. More generally, it is required to "do all things necessary to ensure that an efficient, notice-based electronic registration system exists to implement the objectives of the" Convention and Protocol. While not precluded from doing so, the Convention assumes that the Supervisory Authority will not

---

(2) to ensure the necessary liaison and co-ordination with private industry which will be users of the International Registry; and

(3) to work on such other matters relating to the International Registry as may be required with a view to ensuring the establishment of the International Registry.

[31] [8] Article 18(5) of the Convention and Article XIX of the Protocol permit a contracting State to designate an entity or entities in its territory as an alternative or the exclusive conduit through which registration data are transmitted to the International Registry. Almost all States currently have a recording office operated by a civil aviation authority as required by the Chicago Convention on International Civil Aviation, 1944 at which aircraft airframes and helicopters are registered as to nationality. States that are party to the Geneva Convention on the International Recognition of Rights in Aircraft, 1948 use these offices as registries for interests recognized by that Convention. In addition, some States have central national or regional registries for interests in aircraft and aircraft engines created under domestic law. These existing facilities could be designated under the Aircraft Protocol as exclusive or non-exclusive transmitters of registration data. However, the designation can apply only with respect to international interests in, or sales of, helicopters or airframes and registerable non-consensual interests. It cannot include international interest in or sales of aircraft engines. Similarly, the national agency will not be the conduit for discharges, amendments or subordinations of registrations.

[32] [9] On the recommendation of the Legal Committee, the Council of ICAO has given its preliminary support for ICAO accepting the role of Supervisory Authority. *See* Summary of Council decision (C-DEC 161/9, 24/11/00). Resolution No. 3 of the Final Act provides for this. *See also, supra,* note 7.

operate the International Registry. The day-to-day operations of the Registry will be under the management of a Registrar retained under contract with the Supervisory Authority for this purpose.

The Registrar appointed by the Supervisory Authority could be a private company or an agency of a national or sub-national government that has expertise and facilities to operate a modern electronic registry. Canada, Ireland and Singapore have indicated preliminary interest in hosting the International Registry. In the Canadian context, every province has a modern, efficient remote-access registry for security interests in personal property that could be adapted to accommodate the International Registry. The location of ICAO headquarters in Montreal, Canada would suggest that, all other things being equal, it would be logical to ask the Registre de droits personnels et réels mobiliers to act as Registrar for the International Registry. It is one of the most modern and technologically sophisticated registries in the World with adequate capacity to handle the small volume of registrations that will be made in the International Registry.

4. Guarantee of Reliability

An important feature of a modern registry of legal rights is protection of users against structural or operational deficiencies in its operation. Without this protection, a registry loses much of its value. The amounts involved in aircraft financing are very large and deficiencies in the system can be very costly to its users. Consequently, reliability of the Registry has been a central theme in its development.

Article 28 of the Convention and Article XX(5)–(6) of the Aircraft Protocol require the Registrar to provide insurance or a financial guarantee covering the Registrar's liability. Since it is unlikely that the Registrar, whether a private company or a national or sub-national government agency, will be prepared to assume this liability, external insurance will be obtained. The International Registry must be financially self-supporting (*see* Aircraft Protocol, Article XX(3)); consequently, the cost of liability insurance must be recovered in the fees charged for registry services.

Article 28 of the Convention provides that the Registrar shall "be liable for compensatory damages for loss suffered by a person directly resulting from an error or omission of the Registrar and its officers and employees or from a malfunction of the international registry system." However, exceptions are recognized. There is no liability where the malfunction of the registry is "caused by an event of an inevitable and irresistible nature which could not be prevented by using the best practices in current use in the field of electronic registry design and operation." Nor is the registrar liable for factual inaccuracy of registration information or acts or circumstances for which the Registrar is not responsible and arising prior to receipt of registration information at the International Registry.

5. Notice Registration

The International Registry will provide for notice, not document registration. What will be entered into the database of the system will be minimal information relating to an existing or potential interest. Apart from the description of the property that is subject to the international interest,[33] the Convention and Aircraft Protocol leave to the regulations the types of data that will constitute a registration. If the pattern of most modern North American registries is followed, all that will be required to effect a registration will be identification of the type of transaction, the names and addresses of the debtor, buyer or lessee, assignor or transferor and the secured party, conditional seller, lessor, assignee or transferee, as the case may be, and a description of the property affected by the interest. No additional details of the transaction giving rise to the international interest will be required or permitted.[34] This approach represents the conclusion that it is not the function of the system to provide the details of the contract between the parties to the contract creating the interest.[35] This information must come from the party who has effected the registration through direct inquiry or indirectly through the debtor, buyer or lessee, assignor or transferor, as the case may be.

6. Pre-Agreement Registration

Article 16(1)(a) and Article 19(4) of the Convention provides for registration of a "prospective international interest" (defined in Article 1(y)) and a "prospective assignment" (defined in Article 1(x)). As is the case under the Canadian Personal Property Security Acts and Article 9 of the United States Uniform Commercial Code, it will be possible to effect a registration relating to an aircraft object before the transaction creating an interest in that object has been executed. The priority of this interest dates from the date of the registration of it as a prospective interest and not from the date the interest arises.

7. Date of Effectiveness and Duration of a Registration

A registration will be valid only when it is searchable (Article 19(2)). The effect of this provision is to put on the registering party not only the risk of delay in transmission of registration data to the International Registry but also any risk of delay that results from temporary suspension of registry facilities. However, management of this risk will not be difficult. A registering party will transmit the

---

[33] [10] A description that allows the equipment to be specifically identified is necessary since this will be the factor (registration-search criterion) used to store registration data in and retrieve them from the registry database. *See* Aircraft Protocol, Article XX(1).

[34] [11] A feature of the Convention that dictates a minimalists approach to registration data is provision for registrations relating to a "prospective international interest." *See* Articles 16(1)(a) and 18(3). This term is defined in Article 1(y). By definition, a registration relating to a prospective international interest cannot contain details of an agreement since no agreement may exist at the time the registration is effected.

[35] [12] Article 20 of the Convention requires the consent of the affected party when a registration is effected, amended or discharged. However, the Registry has no duty to inquire as to whether or not the requisite consent has been obtained.

registration data and shortly thereafter request a search result from the International Registry. If the search result is not available or does not indicate the registration, it is clear that some aspect of the transmission or reception and storage of the data is non-functional. The facility to register a prospective international interest or a prospective assignment of an international interest will be very important in this context. Pre-agreement registration not only allows the registering party to determine what its priority status will be if it executes the proposed agreement, but in addition, its use provides a warning with respect to problems with the functioning of the Registry that will delay establishing that priority position.

8. Compulsory Discharge

Article 25 of the Convention requires discharge of a registration relating to an international interest arising under a security agreement or title retention sale, or a registration relating to a prospective interest or an assignment of a prospective interest when the obligations protected by the interest have been performed or where no such obligations were created.[36] As a result of Article 44, when the person who effected the registration fails to discharge the registration, the aggrieved party must seek a remedy in a court having the power to enforce compliance against that person. This order can be enforced by the court of the place in which the Registrar has its centre of administration. However, where the person who effected the registration cannot be found or has ceased to exist, this court has original jurisdiction to order discharge of the registration.

9. Transition

An important issue that must be addressed any time a new registration system is put into operation is whether or not interests created under contracts governed by prior law will be required to be registered in the new system in order to have priority over new interests created after the system comes into effect.

As a result of Article 60, the Convention does not apply to a pre-existing right or interest. However, a Contacting State may apply the Convention to these rights and interests. It may by declaration specify a date, not earlier than 3 years after the date the declaration comes into effect, when the Convention is effective for the purposes of determining priority issues involving pre-existing rights and interests arising under an agreement made at the time when the debtor is situated in that State when the Convention enters into effect.

The merit in the approach contained in Article 60 is that, unless a declaration is made, holders of prior interests will have priority (if they had priority under the applicable law)[37] without incurring the costs of registration. The supporters of this

---

[36] [13] Under Article 21 of the Convention, a registration is effective until discharged or until expiry of the period specified in the registration. Under Article V(3) of the Aircraft Protocol, registration of a contract of sale of an aircraft object remains effective indefinitely.

[37] [14] The difficulty in determining whether this is the case may induce many holders of these interests to register the interests in the International Registry. However, registration would not bring

approach argue that the costs of having to identify and register all pre-existing interests would be prohibitive, particularly in the context of aircraft financing which tends to be multi-tiered and complex. However, there is a major weakness in this approach. The purpose of the Registry is to allow persons who deal with property falling within the scope of the Convention and Protocol to reduce the legal risk that there may be prior interests in the property to which they would be subject. Under Article 60, this policy is substantially frustrated since it results in giving priority to prior undisclosed interests. The result is that some of the risk the international registration of interests is supposed to eliminate remains for many years after the Convention comes into effect.

SUMMARY

The Convention on International Interests in Mobile Equipment 2001 has been designed to provide an international regime for the creation and perfection of security interests and interests arising under other financing devices. If a large number of countries become contracting states, there will be a significant reduction in financial and legal risks associated with financing of very high-priced mobile goods that are used in more than one country. The primary beneficiaries of the system will be users of this equipment that do not have sources of low cost financing.

John Atwood, *The Status of the Mobile Equipment (Cape Town) Convention—Arrival of an International Registration System*
39 UCC L.J. 1, Art. 3 (2006)[38]

[UPDATE ON THE INTERNATIONAL REGISTRY]

The International Registry formally commenced operations upon the entry into force of the Aircraft Protocol on 1 March 2006. In fact, it had commenced operations prior to that date for the limited purpose of enabling registration of registry users. Although based in Dublin, the International Registry is a fully electronic registry that is available on-line for all 24 hours of every day.

The Convention provides for the International Registry to provide a notice-based electronic registration system.[39] The International Registry provides public notice of the existence of an international interest, but contracts and other transaction documents are not registered on the International Registry, and registration of an international interest on the International Registry cannot be taken as proof that the international interest was validly created. Only minimal identifying information is required to effect a registration, as detailed in Section 5 of the Regulations. For example, Section 5.3 of the Regulations provides that the

---

the interests to the priority regime of the Convention. Consequently, there is little to be gained from registration.

[38] Reprinted by permission.

[39] [23] Convention Article 17(2)(i).

information required to effect registration of an international interest in an aircraft object is:

- the identity and electronic signature of the registering person and a statement on whose behalf that person is acting;

- the identity of the named parties;

- the type of aircraft object, the manufacturer's name, the manufacturer's generic model designation and the manufacturer's serial number assigned to the aircraft object;

- information about the State of Registry for nationality purposes and aircraft nationality and registration marks assigned pursuant to the Chicago Convention;

- the duration of the registration (if the registration is to lapse prior to the filing of a discharge);

- the consent of the named parties given under an authorization;

- the names and electronic addresses of the persons to whom the Registrar is required to send information notices under the Regulations.

Of these items of registration information, the most critical for the purposes of conducting searches of the International Registry are the manufacturer's name, the manufacturer's generic model designation and the manufacturer's serial number assigned to the aircraft object. This is because these are the 3 criteria prescribed by Section 7.1 of the Regulations as the criteria against which searches of the International Registry may be performed. The additional criteria of the State of Registry and the nationality or registration mark are relevant criteria in the case of airframes and helicopters.

Once a registration has been effected, the Registrar is required to provide prompt electronic confirmation to all named parties and the registering person, advising of all the registered information and the date and time of registration.[40] Although the electronic confirmation is prima facie proof of the facts recited therein, including the date and time of registration, it does not indicate whether any other interests are registered against the aircraft object. In order to confirm the priority status of a particular registered international interest, it is necessary to conduct a "priority search" of the particular object and to obtain a "priority search certificate," which lists all registered information both in chronological order and in a manner that indicates the transactional history of each registered interest.[41]

Another important type of search prescribed in Section 7 of the Regulations is a "Contracting State Search," which indicates all declarations and designations, and withdrawals thereof, made under the Convention and Aircraft Protocol by a Contracting State. A Contracting State Search results in a Contracting State Search Certificate which indicates in chronological order all declarations and

---

[40] [24] Convention Article 22(2)(a); Regulations Section 6.2.

[41] [25] Regulations Section 7.2, Section 7.4.

designations by the Contracting State and the effective date of ratification or accession, and includes an electronic copy of all instruments deposited by the Contracting State.[42] This type of search is particularly important in light of the ability of a Contracting State to make declarations affecting the application of some provisions of the Convention and Aircraft Protocol.

Accessing the International Registry

Access to the International Registry is not limited to those who are party to transactions giving rise to an international interest. The Convention itself provides that no person shall be denied access to the registration and search facilities of the International Registry on any ground other than failure to comply with the procedures prescribed by Chapter V of the Convention.[43]

Pursuant to the Regulations, use of and access to the International Registry for purposes other than searches is limited to those who have made previous arrangements with the Registry to become registered as authorised registry users. The regulations provided for a number of different categories of users, including:

- "transacting user/transacting user entity"—a person or entity intending to be a named party in a registration;

- "professional user/professional user entity"—a firm, or a member of a firm providing professional services for a party to a transaction subject to registration; (The term "registry user/registry user entity" covers any person or entity in either of these 2 categories)

- "Administrator"—a person with authority to act on behalf of a registry user entity on administrative matters in dealings with the International Registry.[44]

. . .

Once access to the International Registry has been obtained, the registry itself is very easy to navigate through. Further, the use of drop-down menus wherever possible has reduced the prospects of users making inadvertent errors when entering search information. Anyone familiar with using an existing on-line registry system should have little difficulty in using the International Registry. In the event that problems do arise, the Procedures provide for a help desk and technical support facility to be provided: this is currently provided on the International Registry through an email link to the help desk which operates in English, French and Spanish.[45]

---

[42] [26] Regulations Section 7.5.

[43] [27] Chapter V of the Convention includes Article 18(1), which provides for a protocol and regulations to specify requirements for effecting a registration and for making searches.

[44] [28] Regulations Section 2.1.1.

[45] [29] Procedures Section 9.

Harold S. Burman,[46] *2007 Luxembourg Protocol on International Rail Equipment Concluded at Luxembourg February 23, 2007*
http://67.159.80.145/cicl/pdf/burman.pdf[47]

Overview

The "Luxembourg Protocol" on international finance of railroad equipment was concluded at a Diplomatic Conference in February 2007[48] as the second Protocol to the 2001 Cape Town Convention on mobile equipment finance.[49] The Conference was organized by UNIDROIT, the Rome-based intergovernmental body,[50] which initiated the Cape Town treaty system for the new concept of "international interests" (contractually created liens or security interests) in high-value mobile equipment, and OTIF, the Intergovernmental Organization for International Carriage by Rail, based in Berne, Switzerland.[51] By validating the new concept of international secured interests in railway rolling stock (mobile assets such as locomotives, freight cars, passenger cars and other equipment) and providing for the registration of such interests in a new global computer system, the Luxembourg Protocol can have a significant effect on lowering costs and increasing exports of rail equipment, prompting regional cross-border transportation, and modernizing commercial law in various parts of the world.

. . .

[Conference Dynamics]

The dynamics of bringing the Rail Protocol into force also are likely to differ from those of the Aircraft Protocol. The economics of aircraft finance meant that without early US participation, the new aircraft registry system might not for some time have had sufficient volume to be viable, whereas in rail finance, early participation by some EU states and/or large developing country markets can provide the needed volume. EU states have had a track record in post-WWII years

---

[46] [i] Office of Legal Adviser, Department of State and co-head of US Delegation for the negotiation of the Luxembourg Protocol. Steven Harris, co-reporter for Uniform Commercial Code Article 9 Revised, and Professor of law, Chicago Kent-IIT Law School, was a member of the delegation and contributed to this introduction. Other contributors were co-head of delegation Peter Bloch, Department of Transportation Office of General Counsel, and Louis Emery, member of the delegation, US Export-Import Bank, Office of General Counsel.

[47] Reprinted with permission.

[48] [ii] www.unidroit.org/eng/adopted texts/conventions/Luxembourg Protocol.

[49] [iii] The Cape Town Convention came into force April 1, 2004. www. Unidroit.org/eng/conventions. The United States ratified the Convention and the Aircraft Protocol in November 2004. *See* Senate Treaty Doc. 108-10, 108th Congress, UNIDROIT in 1964.

[50] [iv] Established 1926 as an auxiliary body of the League of Nations, formally the International Institute for the Unification of Private Law, later reconstituted as an independent multilateral body. The United States joined UNIDROIT in 1964.

[51] [v] Established May 1, 1985 by multilateral agreement. 42 member states (the United States is not a party). www.otif.org.

of more significant public investment in rail infrastructure than has been the case in the US. With the growth of integrated markets under the EU system, EU states are seeking to further integrate EU rail systems and rail finance, an integration that has already been largely accomplished in North America. Also relevant was the fact that while rail equipment exporters, including US manufacturers, can benefit from the Protocol, rail operators, unlike airline companies, are often more territorially focused. This plus the fact that rail car equipment involves tens of thousands of pieces of equipment will pose challenges for a future interface between existing US and North American registry practices and those that may be required for a new international system. On the other hand, the Rail Protocol offers an opportunity for a number of regions to further integrate their rail services, which may become one of the significant results of the Protocol.

Establishing the treaty framework for implementation of the Aircraft Protocol drew substantially on the lead role of the International Civil Aviation Organization (ICAO), established by the 1944 Chicago Convention and headquartered in Montreal, which operates as a specialized UN agency.[52] No comparable intergovernmental rail body exists. Organizational rail interests at the Conference revolved around OTIF, which is largely European based (none of the NAFTA states are a party), with some member states coming from the Near East and North Africa,[53] although membership might be expected to increase as a result of its role on the Luxembourg Protocol.

The Government of Luxembourg, host state of the Conference and an important financial center for rail finance, will be the host state of the new international finance registry for rail equipment.[54]

. . .

Path forward

In order to fast-track implementation of the Rail Protocol, Luxembourg, selected by the Diplomatic Conference as the host state for the new international rail registry, together with OTIF and UNIDROIT in July 2007 convened in Berne, Switzerland the first meeting of the 20-state Preparatory Commission which will draw up draft regulations and technical parameters for a global computer registration system. The process can be relatively short (possibly one year), since it would draw on many solutions already developed for the international aircraft registry. Conclusion of that process and assessment of costs and options for implementation will allow consideration of possible ratification by the United States. U.S. ratification would affect costs of exporting or importing such

---

[52] [xi] www.icao.org. ICAO joined the UNIDROIT-initiated process and hosted multilateral meetings on the draft Convention and Aircraft Protocol.

[53] [xii] 42 states are currently members, primarily those of the European Union, including eastern European EU states but, with the exception of the Ukraine not other prior states of the Soviet Union, and four Near-Eastern and three North African states. There are at present no broad multilateral bodies for rail transportation that include the NAFTA states or all principal geographic regions.

[54] [xiii] A factor that may facilitate approval by the European Council for EU member states to adopt the Protocol, subject to whatever conditions are laid down by the Council.

equipment, but would not require participation of the North American rail registration system, absent its consent. Once the rail registry is operational, ratifications would be expected to increase.[55]

B. COMPARISON OF THE SCOPE OF THE CONVENTION ON INTERNATIONAL INTERESTS IN MOBILE EQUIPMENT (HEREAFTER CIIME) AND UCC ARTICLE 9

In his article, Ronald Cuming notes that the CIIME uses a "functional" and a "formal" approach in identifying transactions to which it applies. The "functional" approach refers to an agreement in which a creditor is given an interest in the collateral in the form of a right to repossess it in the event of default by the debtor. The "formal" approach identifies three types of transactions subject to the Convention that create security interests merely on the basis of the form of the agreement as a lease agreement, conditional sales contract, or outright sale of personal property.

The problems which follow illustrate the broader types of transactions covered by the CIIME in comparison to the coverage of Article 9 on Secured Transactions.[56] However, application of these broader types of transactions is limited to a single type of personal property (*i.e.*, mobile equipment, *see* Problem 6-5, *infra*) in contrast with the expansive list of different types of personal property covered by Article 9. *See* Chapter 2, Section A.1., *supra*.

Reasons for differences between the CIIME Convention and Article 9 of the UCC in scope and applicability can be understood by the difference in the *raison d'etre* of the two systems. Only mobile equipment is subject to the Convention. The limited coverage of the CIIME to this single type of collateral meets the needs of "a wide range of organizations involved in the sale, financing and use of commercial aircraft." (Cuming, *supra*.) Conversely, Article 9 of the UCC provides a secured transactions system covering many types of personal property. Pervasive needs of the general public across the industrial, commercial, agricultural and consumer segments of the economy are addressed by Article 9. The CIIME has a much smaller constituency. It addresses needs of organizations involved in the sale, financing, leasing and use of high-value mobile equipment. Both systems share the task of providing a legal framework for creation of security interests, determining priority of interests, establishing a procedure for public disclosure of interests, and providing procedures for enforcement after default.

---

[55] [xv] Having concluded the rail equipment Protocol, negotiation under UNIDROIT auspices will resume on a third protocol governing international interests in satellites and other space assets, a substantially different challenge since, unlike rail transportation which is grounded on a variety of national laws and some regional legal frameworks, commercial activity in outer space has a minimal legal structure and limited application of national law. www.unidroit.org/eng/work in progress/intern interests in mobile equipment. A fourth protocol in the initial stage of consideration, supported by the United States, would cover agricultural, construction and mining equipment.

[56] The text of the CIIME is attached as Appendix 2, *infra*. The text of the Aircraft Protocol is attached as Appendix 3, *infra*. These texts are also available at http://www.unidroit.org.

The problems which follow illustrate the manner in which this difference in coverage is achieved by the two systems.

Problem 6-1: Applicability to "Functional" Security Interests. Does the CIIME "functionally identify" transactions within its scope? (*See* Cuming, *supra.*)

Article 2(2)(a) provides that the CIIME applies to a "security agreement" which is defined in Article 1(ii) as "an agreement by which a chargor grants or agrees to grant to a chargee an interest in or over an object to secure the performance of an existing or future obligation of the chargor . . . ."

Does UCC Article 9 functionally identify transactions within its scope?

UCC § 9-109(a)(1) provides that subject to stated exceptions "this article applies to (1) a transaction regardless of its form that creates a security interest in personal property or fixtures by contract . . . ." The first sentence of UCC § 1-201(b)(35) further provides that "security interest" means "an interest in personal property . . . which secures payment or performance of an obligation" by a "debtor" to a "secured party."

Problem 6-2: Applicability to Conditional Sales Contracts. Does the CIIME apply to a conditional sales contract?

Article 2(2)(b) provides that the CIIME applies to an interest "vested in a person who is the conditional seller under a title reservation agreement; . . ."

Does UCC Article 9 apply to a conditional sales contract?

UCC § 9-109(a)(1) provides that subject to stated exceptions "this article applies to (1) a transaction, regardless of its form that creates a security interest in personal property or fixtures by contract; . . ." UCC § 1-201(b)(35) [§ 1-201(37)] *inter alia* provides in its fifth sentence that "[t]he retention or reservation of title by seller of goods notwithstanding shipment or delivery to the buyer (Section 2-401) is limited in effect to a reservation of a 'security interest.' "

Problem 6-3: Applicability to True Leases and "Leases" Which Actually Create a Security Interest. Does the CIIME apply to a true lease as well as a "lease" which actually creates a security interest?

Article 2(2)(c) provides that the CIIME applies to an interest "vested in a person who is the lessor under a leasing agreement." It further defines "leasing agreement" in Article 1(q) to mean "an agreement by which a lessor grants a right to possession or control of an object (with or without an option to purchase) to a lessee in return for a rental or other payment; . . ."

Does UCC Article 9 apply to a true lease as well as a "lease" which actually creates a security interest?

UCC § 9-109(a)(1) as noted above provides that Article 9 applies to "a transaction . . . that creates a security interest in personal property . . . by contract." The security interest definition (UCC § 1-203 provides in part that whether a transaction creates a lease or is merely in the form of a lease but actually creates a security interest is determined by the facts of each case. It then provides criteria for making this determination. (See Chapter 2, *supra*, for a discussion of these criteria).

Problem 6-4: Applicability to Sales. Does the CIIME apply to the sale of personal property?

Article 41 of Chapter XI entitled "Application of the Convention to Sales" provides that "This Convention shall apply to the sale or prospective sale of an object as provided for in the protocol with any modifications therein." Article III of the Aircraft Protocol lists articles of the Cape Town Convention that should be read as if they referred to sale rather than creation of an international interest. These provisions articles would then cover the sale of "aircraft objects" (airframes, aircraft engines and helicopters). Aircraft Protocol art. I(2)(c).

Does UCC Article 9 apply to a "sale" of "personal property"?

UCC § 9-109(a)(1) provides that Article 9 applies to "a transaction . . . that creates a security interest in personal property" and in UCC § 9-109(a)(3) provides that it applies to "a sale of accounts, chattel paper, payment intangibles, or promissory notes . . . ." These latter four types of collateral do not include sale of tangible personal property such as the mobile equipment to which the CIIME applies. For consideration of the types of tangible personal to which CIIME applies, see the discussion in Problem 6-5.

Problem 6-5: Types of Personal Property Covered. What types of property does the CIIME cover by its provisions? Article 2(2) of the CIIME provides that the international interest in mobile equipment is an interest "in a uniquely identifiable object of a category of such objects listed in paragraph 3 . . . ." Paragraph 3 specifies that the categories referred to are:

(a)   airframes, aircraft engines and helicopters;

(b)   railway, rolling stock; and

(c)   space assets.

Compare UCC § 9-109(a)(1), which provides that Article 9 applies to "a transaction, . . . that creates a security interest in *personal property* . . ." (emphasis supplied). As noted previously (*see* Chapter 2, *supra*), Article 9 does not include a general definition of "personal property." However, a long list of types of tangible, semi-intangible, and intangible personal property are addressed by various provisions of Article 9. In addition, Article 9 includes a residual type of category entitled "General Intangibles" which is defined as "any personal property, including things in action, other than accounts, chattel paper, commercial tort claims, deposit accounts, documents, goods, instruments, investment property, letter of credit rights, letters of credit, money, and oil, gas or other minerals before extraction. The term includes payment intangibles and software." UCC § 9-102(a)(42).

Problem 6-6: Differences in Coverage. The CIIME covers true leases as well as "leases" in form only which are actually intended to create a security interest (*see* Problem 6-3, *supra*) and outright sales of mobile equipment (*see* Problem 6-4, *supra*). UCC Article 9 does not cover either one of these types of transactions. (*See* Problems 6-3 & 6-4, *supra*.) Why does the CIIME cover a broader range of types of transactions than the UCC Article 9?

The CIIME applies only to security interests created in the three categories of mobile equipment set forth in Article 2(3), while UCC Article 9 applies to a much broader lengthy list of types of personal property (*see* Problem 6-5, *supra*). Why is the UCC coverage of personal property security interests broader than the types of personal property covered by the CIIME?

C. TERRITORIAL APPLICABILITY, FILING AND PRIORITY UNDER THE CONVENTION ON INTERNATIONAL INTERESTS IN MOBILE EQUIPMENT AND THE AIRCRAFT EQUIPMENT PROTOCOL

In Problems 6-7, 6-8, and 6-9, below, assume that the CIIME has been ratified by the United States, Canada, and the requisite number of other states required to make it operative. Assume also that a registry office has been created and is in operation in Montreal, Canada, under the terms of the Convention and the Aircraft Protocol. (CIIME Art. 16; Protocol Art. XVII.) Counsel Chicago Bank as to its rights and duties in the following transactions.

Problem 6-7:   Territorial Applicability of CIIME—Filing Requirement—Priority Issues. Chicago Bank extends a loan of one hundred million dollars to Canada Airlines and takes a security interest in a 747 aircraft purchased by Canada Airlines from Boeing Aircraft. Chicago Bank is headquartered in Illinois and incorporated in Delaware. Canada Airlines is incorporated and headquartered in Ottawa, Canada. Is the CIIME Aircraft Protocol System applicable? (CIIME Arts. 3, 4.) What are the filing requirements which Chicago Bank must follow? (*See* CIIME arts. 7, 18, 19 & 20; Aircraft Protocol Art. VII.)

After Chicago Bank extends its loan and files its documents in the Dublin Registry of the Aircraft Protocol, Chase Bank (headquartered in New York and incorporated in Delaware) extends a loan of fifty million dollars to Canada Airlines. Who has priority if Chase Bank files its documents in the Montreal Registry subsequent to Chicago Bank? (CIIME Art. 29(1)).

Problem 6-8:   Territorial Applicability—Debtor and Creditor in the Same State. Assume the same facts as Problem 6-7 above, except that the loan is extended by Chicago Bank to Midland Airlines covering the same aircraft. Midland Airlines is headquartered and incorporated in Illinois. Is the CIIME Aircraft Protocol System applicable? (CIIME Arts. 7, 3, 50, 1(n), and 1(r); Aircraft Protocol, Art. IV.) Is Chicago Bank's interest a "national interest"? What is the effect of so classifying the creditor's rights on registration and priority rules? On enforcement rules?

Problem 6-9:   Applicability Limited to Mobile Equipment. Assume that Chicago Bank finances an inventory of four passenger Piper Cub planes for Aircraft, Inc., a vendor of small aircraft incorporated and headquartered in Toronto, Canada. Is the CIIME Aircraft Protocol system applicable to this transaction? (CIIME Arts. 2(1), (2) and (3); Aircraft Protocol Art. II(1), Art. I(2)(c) and (e)). Would the result be different if Chicago Bank financed an inventory of 20 passenger Piper Cub planes for Aircraft, Inc.?

D. COMPLIANCE WITH THE FEDERAL AVIATION ACT OR THE CRIIE AIRCRAFT PROTOCOL SYSTEM?

Would the *Sanders* case which follows be decided in the same fashion if the United States had ratified the CIIME and Aircraft Protocol and both were operative because the requisite number of ratifications had occurred? Is the result affected if the inventory financed consisted of 20 passenger Piper Cub planes rather than four passenger Piper Cub planes?

SANDERS v. M.D. AIRCRAFT SALES, INC.
United States Court of Appeals, Third Circuit
575 F.2d 1086 (1978)

OPINION OF THE COURT

GIBBONS, CIRCUIT JUDGE.

This case involves a dispute over title to an airplane. The appellant, Charles J. Sanders, purchased the airplane in the ordinary course of business from M.D. Aircraft Sales, Inc. (Aircraft Sales), a dealer in aircraft. The appellee, General Electric Credit Corp. (GECC), is a finance company which lent money to Aircraft Sales on the security of inventory. On cross-motions for summary judgment, the district court awarded title to GECC. We agree with the district court and the parties that the facts are not in dispute, but we reverse with directions to enter judgment for Sanders.

Aircraft Sales is located in Latrobe, Pennsylvania. On June 13, 1974, it executed and delivered to GECC at Pittsburgh, Pennsylvania, an agreement creating a security interest in all its new and used inventory and in the proceeds of sale or other disposition of such inventory. The inventory covered by the agreement included a 1970 Piper Arrow PA 28R airplane (Federal Registration number N 4964S). The agreement provides:

> So long as [Aircraft Sales] is not in default under any of its obligations to you hereunder or otherwise, [Aircraft Sales] shall have the right to sell all inventory financed by you in the normal course of its business and undersigned will notify you promptly of any sale of any item of such inventory and pay you therefor in accordance with paragraph 2 hereof. To the extent that [Aircraft Sales] may become obligated to repay any advance to you upon the sale of any unit of inventory by it, undersigned agrees that it will hold all proceeds of the sale of such unit in trust for you.

* * *

Upon . . . default, all indebtedness secured hereby shall become immediately due and payable at your option without notice to [Aircraft Sales], and you may proceed to enforce payment of same and to exercise any or all of the rights and remedies afforded to you by the Uniform Commercial Code, as in effect in [Aircraft Sales']

State, or otherwise possessed by you.

Thus, the agreement afforded Aircraft Sales an express power of sale of inventory, including the Piper Arrow, in the normal course of its business. The agreement further provided that GECC's lien would apply to the proceeds of such sale. If Aircraft Sales defaulted by failing to hold the proceeds of sale in trust, GECC, according to the agreement, had the rights and remedies provided by the Pennsylvania Uniform Commercial Code.

GECC recorded the security agreement with the Federal Aviation Administration Aircraft Registry in Oklahoma City, Oklahoma, on June 18, 1974. Aircraft Sales sold the Piper Arrow airplane to Sanders on July 12, 1974, in the normal course of its business. Aircraft Sales did not, however, hold the proceeds in trust for GECC. When the default was discovered, GECC notified Sanders that it was asserting a lien on the aircraft superior to his title. Sanders then brought the instant action for declaratory and injunctive relief. GECC answered his complaint and filed its own counterclaim.

The district court held that the GECC lien was superior to Sander's title by virtue of § 503 of the Federal Aviation Act of 1958.[57] The court reasoned that Congress's adoption of the federal lien registration system for aircraft totally preempted state law. The court conceded that, if the Uniform Commercial Code applied, Section 9.307(1) would protect Sanders, a buyer in the ordinary course of business. But the court held that § 503 totally displaced state law.

But counsel had not briefed the district court, or this court, on the possible application of § 506 of Pub.L. No. 88-346, 78 Stat. 236, which, as codified at 49 U.S.C. § 1406, provides:

> The validity of any instrument the recording of which is provided for by section 1403 of this title [§ 503] shall be governed by the laws of the State, District of Columbia, or territory or possession of the United States in which such instrument is delivered, irrespective of the location or the place of delivery of the property which is the subject of such instrument.

Senate Commerce Committee Report No. 1060, which accompanied the bill that became Pub.L. No. 88-346, explained that while Title V of the Federal Aviation Act of 1958 had adopted a federal recording system, it had left to state law the legal effect of a recorded instrument. In doing so, however, Title V had left unresolved serious choice of law questions with respect to liens on chattels so mobile as aircraft. Section 506 answered these questions. Explaining the purpose of what is now 49 U.S.C. § 1406, the Senate Report states:

> The rule would apply to all instruments subject to the recording provisions of § 503 of the Federal Aviation Act. Included would be various instruments executed for security purposes such as conveyances, leases, mortgages, equipment trusts, conditional sales contracts, etc. Assignments, amendments, and supplements to such instruments would similarly be covered. To determine the validity of such an instrument, one need only to

---

[57] [1] Pub.L. No. 85-726, tit. V, § 503, 72 Stat. 772 (codified at 49 U.S.C. § 1403).

look to the substantive law of the particular State in which the instrument was delivered.[58]

Thus, there has been preemption by federal law only to the limited extent that Congress has sensibly federalized choice of law, thereby freeing aircraft financing from the forum shopping which the rule of *Klaxon Co. v. Stentor Elec. Mfg. Co.*, 313 U.S. 487 (1941), might otherwise produce.

In this case, the security agreement was delivered in Pennsylvania. The federal recording statute establishes that Sanders had notice of the security interest. But Pennsylvania law determines the validity of the lien against him.[59] Indeed the very text of the security agreement, by referring to the Uniform Commercial Code in the dealer's state, acknowledges as much. GECC does not suggest that under Pennsylvania law a holder of a floor plan lien can prevail over a purchaser in the ordinary course of business. In fact, under Pennsylvania law a purchaser in the ordinary course of business prevails even if the security agreement does not contain an express power of sale. PA. STAT. ANN. tit. 12A, § 9-307(1). Where, as here, the agreement does contain an express power of sale, it is an a fortiori case.

Moreover, even if Congress had intended totally to preempt the state law of aircraft liens, a federal court would still be required to choose an appropriate federal rule as to the effect of a security agreement creating a floor plan lien but containing a power of sale. The only appropriate rule, we think, would be to give effect to the very terms of the security agreement. According to those terms, the GECC lien was transferred to the proceeds of sale, and Sanders took free and clear title to the aircraft.

The judgment appealed from will be reversed and the case remanded for the entry of judgment in favor of Sanders.

---

[58] [2] S.REP. No. 1060, 88th Cong., 2d Sess., *reprinted in* [1964] U.S. Code Cong. & Admin. News, pp. 2319, 2320.

[59] [3] *See, e.g., Idabel National Bank v. Tucker*, 544 P.2d 1287 (Okla. App. 1976); Annot., *Construction and Effect of 49 U.S. Code § 1403, Governing Recordation of Ownership, Conveyance, and Encumbrances of Aircraft*, 22 A.L.R.3d 1270, 1275 (1968).

Appendix A

ACTUAL TEXT AND SIMPLIFIED VERSION OF SELECTED PROVISIONS OF THE UCC PERTAINING TO SECURED TRANSACTIONS

SIMPLIFICATION OF STATUTES: MAKING ARTICLE 9 MORE UNDERSTANDABLE AND USER FRIENDLY

Students and practitioners first encountering Article 9 of the UCC will encounter difficulties reading and understanding its text. In particular, some of the provisions are written in a "paragraph format" that makes it difficult to separate the factors or components contained within the provision. An illustration of the paragraph format is found in the Actual Text of § 1-201, *infra*. In the paragraph format, a series of categories are run horizontally across the page, making it difficult to separate the categories and relate modifying language to the appropriate categories. Compare the Actual Text with the Simplified Version, *infra*, in which each category is vertically lettered and listed, making the text more user-friendly and more easily understandable.

In order to facilitate understanding and produce a more user-friendly context, selected sections of Article 9, as well as sections from other Articles relating to Article 9, are reproduced in an ACTUAL TEXT format alongside a SIMPLIFIED VERSION of the actual text utilizing simplification techniques such as:

- Vertical listing of categories,

- Shortened paragraphs

- Use of captions for subsections, and as necessary, for paragraphs,[1] and

- Statement of the general rule, followed by exceptions

For more information regarding the simplification of Article 9, see Del Duca, et al., *Applying Plain English Techniques in Revising the UCC*, 29 UCC L.J. 428, 428 (1997); Del Duca, et al., *Revisiting the Application of Plain English in Revising the UCC — Current Practice Among the Fifty States on Use of Captions in Legislation*, 30 UCC L.J. 167, 167-68 (1997); Del Duca, et al., *Simplification in Drafting — The Uniform Commercial Code Article 9 Experience*, 74 CHI.-KENT L. REV. 1309 (1999); Weise, *"Plain English" Will Set the UCC Free*, 28 LOY L.A. L. REV. 317 (1994).

---

[1] Article 9 includes headings for the subsections as an aid to readers. Unlike section captions, which are part of the UCC, *see* § 1-109, subsection headings are not part of the official text itself and have not been approved by the sponsors. Each jurisdiction in which this Article is introduced may consider whether to adopt the headings as part of the statute and whether to adopt a provision by clarifying the effect, if any, to be given to the headings. (§ 9-101(3)).

Selected Article 1 Provisions Relevant to Secured Transactions

Side-by-Side Actual and Simplified Versions

§ 1-201. GENERAL DEFINITIONS.

ACTUAL TEXT

(9) "Buyer in ordinary course of business" means a person that buys goods in good faith, without knowledge that the sale violates the rights of another person in the goods, and in the ordinary course from a person, other than a pawnbroker, in the business of selling goods of that kind. A person buys goods in the ordinary course if the sale to the person comports with the usual or customary practices in the kind of business in which the seller is engaged or with the seller's own usual or customary practices. A person that sells oil, gas, or other minerals at the wellhead or minehead is a person in the business of selling goods of that kind. A buyer in ordinary course of business may buy for cash, by exchange of other property, or on secured or unsecured credit, and may acquire goods or documents of title under a pre-existing contract for sale. Only a buyer that takes possession of the goods or has a right to recover the goods from the seller under Article 2 may be a buyer in ordinary course of business. A "buyer in ordinary course of business" does not include a person that acquires goods in a transfer in bulk or as security for or in total or partial satisfaction of a money debt.

SIMPLIFIED VERSION

(9) **"Buyer in ordinary course of business"** means a person that buys goods:

(i) in good faith,

(ii) without knowledge that the sale violates the rights of another person in the goods, and

(iii) in the ordinary course from a person, other than a pawnbroker, in the business of selling goods of that kind.

In connection with the definition of buyer in ordinary course of business, the following provisions shall apply:

(A) **Ordinary course;** A person buys goods in the ordinary course if the sale to the person comports with the usual or customary practices in the kind of business in which the seller is engaged or with the seller's own usual or customary practices.

(B) **Sales at wellhead or minehead;** A person that sells oil, gas, or other minerals at the wellhead or minehead is a person in the business of selling goods of that kind.

(C) **Buying and acquiring goods or documents of title;** A buyer in ordinary course of business may:

(i) buy for cash, by exchange of other property, or on secured or unsecured credit, and

(ii) acquire goods or documents of title under a pre-existing contract for sale.

(D) **Possessory status or right to recover goods requirement;** Only a buyer that takes possession of the goods or has a right to recover the goods from the seller under Article 2 may be a buyer in ordinary course of business.

ACTUAL TEXT	SIMPLIFIED VERSION
	(E) **Bulk transferees and creditors;** a "buyer in ordinary course of business" does not include a person that acquires goods in a transfer in bulk or as security for or in total or partial satisfaction of a money debt.

§ 1-201(35). DEFINITIONS AND INDEX OF DEFINITIONS.

(a) Unless the context otherwise requires, words or phrases defined in this section, or in the additional definitions contained in other articles of [the Uniform Commercial Code] that apply to particular articles or parts thereof, have the meanings stated.

(a) Unless the context otherwise requires, words or phrases defined in this section, or in the additional definitions contained in other articles of [the Uniform Commercial Code] that apply to particular articles or parts thereof, have the meanings stated.

(b) Subject to definitions contained in other articles of [the Uniform Commercial Code] that apply to particular articles or parts thereof:

(b) Subject to definitions contained in other articles of [the Uniform Commercial Code] that apply to particular articles or parts thereof:

. . .

. . .

(35) **"Security interest"** means an interest in personal property or fixtures which secures payment or performance of an obligation. "Security interest" includes any interest of a consignor and a buyer of accounts, chattel paper, a payment intangible, or a promissory note in a transaction that is subject to Article 9. "Security interest" does not include the special property interest of a buyer of goods on identification of those goods to a contract for sale under Section 2-505, the right of a seller or lessor of goods under Article 2 or 2A to retain or acquire possession of the goods is not a "security interest", but a seller or lessor may also acquire a "security interest" by complying with Article 9. The retention or reservation of title by a seller of goods notwithstanding shipment or delivery to the buyer under Section 2-401 is limited in effect to a reservation of a "security interest." Whether a transaction in the form of a lease creates a "security interest" is determined pursuant to Section 1-203.

(35) **"SECURITY INTEREST"** means an interest in personal property or fixtures which secures payment or performance of an obligation.

(A) "Security interest" includes any interest of a consignor and a buyer of accounts, chattel paper, a payment intangible, or a promissory note in a transaction that is subject to Article 9.

(B) "Security interest" does not include the special property interest of a buyer of goods on identification of those goods to a contract for sale under Section 2-505.

(C) The right of a seller or lessor of goods under Article 2 or 2A to retain or acquire possession of the goods is not a "security interest", but a seller or lessor may also acquire a "security interest" by complying with Article 9.

(D) The retention or reservation of title by a seller of goods notwithstanding shipment or delivery to the buyer under Section 2-401 is limited in effect to a reservation of a "security interest."

ACTUAL TEXT

SIMPLIFIED VERSION

(E) Whether a transaction in the form of a lease creates a "security interest" is determined pursuant to Section 1-203.

§ 1-203. LEASE DISTINGUISHED FROM SECURITY INTEREST

ACTUAL TEXT

SIMPLIFIED VERSION

(a) Whether a transaction in the form of a lease creates a lease or security interest is determined by the facts of each case.

(a) **Determination is one of fact.** Whether a transaction in the form of a lease creates a lease or security interest is determined by the facts of each case.

(b) A transaction in the form of a lease creates a security interest if the consideration that the lessee is to pay the lessor for the right to possession and use of the goods is an obligation for the term of the lease and is not subject to termination by the lessee, and:

(b) **Factors which create a security interest.** A transaction in the form of a lease creates a security interest if the consideration that the lessee is to pay the lessor for the right to possession and use of the goods is an obligation for the term of the lease and is not subject to termination by the lessee, and:

(1) the original term of the lease is equal to or greater than the remaining economic life of the goods;

(1) *Length of original term of the lease.* The original term of the lease is equal to or greater than the remaining economic life of the goods;

(2) the lessee is bound to renew the lease for the remaining economic life of the goods or is bound to become the owner of the goods;

(2) *Lessee's obligation to renew the lease or become owner.* The lessee is bound to renew the lease for the remaining economic life of the goods or is bound to become the owner of the goods;

(3) the lessee has an option to renew the lease for the remaining economic life of the goods for no additional consideration or for nominal additional consideration upon compliance with the lease agreement; or

(3) *Renewal option for no additional or nominal consideration.* The lessee has an option to renew the lease for the remaining economic life of the goods for no additional consideration or for nominal additional consideration upon compliance with the lease agreement; or

(4) the lessee has an option to become the owner of the goods for no additional consideration or for nominal additional consideration upon compliance with the lease agreement

(4) *Lessee's option to become owner of the goods for no additional or nominal consideration.* The lessee has an option to become the owner of the goods for no additional consideration or for nominal additional consideration upon compliance with the lease agreement.

(c) A transaction in the form of a lease does not create a security interest merely because:

(c) **Leases that are not security interests.** A transaction in the form of a lease does not create a security interest merely because:

ACTUAL TEXT

(1) the present value of the consideration the lessee is obligated to pay the lessor for the right to possession and use of the goods is substantially equal to or is greater than the fair market value of the goods at the time the lease is entered into;

(2) the lessee assumes risk of loss of the goods;

(3) the lessee agrees to pay, with respect to the goods, taxes, insurance, filing, recording, or registration fees, or service or maintenance costs;

(4) the lessee has an option to renew the lease or to become the owner of the goods;

(5) the lessee has an option to renew the lease for a fixed rent that is equal to or greater than the reasonably predictable fair market rent for the use of the goods for the term of the renewal at the time the option is to be performed; or

(6) the lessee has an option to become the owner of the goods for a fixed price that is equal to or greater than the reasonably predictable fair market value of the goods at the time the option is to be performed.

(d) Additional consideration is nominal if it is less than the lessee's reasonably predictable cost of performing under the lease agreement if the option is not exercised. Additional consideration is not nominal if:

SIMPLIFIED VERSION

(1) *Present value of lessee's consideration to pay.* The present value of the consideration the lessee is obligated to pay the lessor for the right to possession and use of the goods is substantially equal to or is greater than the fair market value of the goods at the time the lease is entered into;

(2) *Assumption of risk of loss.* The lessee assumes risk of loss of the goods;

(3) *Lessee agrees to pay certain costs.* The lessee agrees to pay, with respect to the goods, taxes, insurance, filing, recording, or registration fees, or service or maintenance costs;

(4) *Lessee's option to renew the lease or acquire ownership of the goods.* The lessee has an option to renew the lease or to become the owner of the goods;

(5) *Lessee's option to renew the lease for a fixed rent.* The lessee has an option to renew the lease for a fixed rent that is equal to or greater than the reasonably predictable fair market rent for the use of the goods for the term of the renewal at the time the option is to be performed; or

(6) *Lessee's option to become owner of the goods for a fixed price.* The lessee has an option to become the owner of the goods for a fixed price that is equal to or greater than the reasonably predictable fair market value of the goods at the time the option is to be performed.

(d) **Additional consideration being nominal.** Additional consideration is nominal if it is less than the lessee's reasonably predictable cost of performing under the lease agreement if the option is not exercised.

Additional consideration is not nominal if:

ACTUAL TEXT

(1) when the option to renew the lease is granted to the lessee, the rent is stated to be the fair market rent for the use of the goods for the term of the renewal determined at the time the option is to be performed; or

(2) when the option to become the owner of the goods is granted to the lessee, the price is stated to be the fair market value of the goods determined at the time the option is to be performed.

(e) The "remaining economic life of the goods" and "reasonably predictable" fair market rent, fair market value, or cost of performing under the lease agreement must be determined with reference to the facts and circumstances at the time the transaction is entered into.

SIMPLIFIED VERSION

(1) *Fair market rent for the use of the goods.* When the option to renew the lease is granted to the lessee, the rent is stated to be the fair market rent for the use of the goods for the term of the renewal determined at the time the option is to be performed; or

(2) *Fair market value of the goods.* When the option to become the owner of the goods is granted to the lessee, the price is stated to be the fair market value of the goods determined at the time the option is to be performed.

(e) **Determination of "remaining economic life of the goods" and "reasonably predictable" fair market rent.** The "remaining economic life of the goods" and "reasonably predictable" fair market rent, fair market value, or cost of performing under the lease agreement must be determined with reference to the facts and circumstances at the time the transaction is entered into.

Selected Article 9 Provisions

Side-by-Side Actual and Simplified Versions

§ 9-102. DEFINITIONS AND INDEX OF DEFINITIONS.

ACTUAL TEXT

(a) [**Article 9 definitions.**] In this article:

. . .

(2) "Account," except as used in "account for," means a right to payment of a monetary obligation, whether or not earned by performance, (i) for property that has been or is to be sold, leased, licensed, assigned, or otherwise disposed of, (ii) for services rendered or to be rendered, (iii) for a policy of insurance issued or to be issued, (iv) for a secondary obligation incurred or to be incurred, (v) for energy provided or to be provided, (vi) for the use or hire of a vessel under a charter or other contract, (vii) arising out of the use of a credit or charge card or information contained on or for use with the card, or (viii) as winnings in a lottery or other game of chance operated or sponsored by a State, governmental unit of a State, or person licensed or authorized to operate the game by a State or governmental unit of a State. The term includes health-care-insurance receivables. The term does not include (i) rights to payment evidenced by chattel paper or an instrument, (ii) commercial tort claims, (iii) deposit accounts, (iv) investment property, (v) letter-of-credit rights or letters of credit, or (vi) rights to payment for money or funds advanced or sold, other than rights arising out of the use of a credit or charge card or information contained on or for use with the card.

SIMPLIFIED VERSION

(a) [**Article 9 definitions.**] In this article:

. . .

(2) "**ACCOUNT,**" except as used in "**account for**":

(A) means a right to payment of a monetary obligation, whether or not earned by performance:

(i) for property that has been or is to be sold, leased, licensed, assigned, or otherwise disposed of,

(ii) for services rendered or to be rendered,

(iii) for a policy of insurance issued or to be issued,

(iv) for a secondary obligation incurred or to be incurred,

(v) for energy provided or to be provided,

(vi) for the use or hire of a vessel under a charter or other contract,

(vii) arising out of the use of a credit or charge card or information contained on or for use with the card, or

(viii) as winnings in a lottery or similar game operated or sponsored by a State, governmental unit of a State, or person licensed or authorized to operate the game by a State or governmental unit of a State;

(B) "Account" includes a health-care-insurance receivables;

(C) "Account" does not include:

(i) rights to payment evidenced by chattel paper or an instrument,

(ii) commercial tort claims,

(iii) deposit accounts,

(iv) investment property,

ACTUAL TEXT

(11) "Chattel paper" means a record or records that evidence both a monetary obligation and a security interest in specific goods, a security interest in specific goods and software used in the goods, a security interest in specific goods and license of software used in the goods, a lease of specific goods, or a lease of specific goods and license of software used in the goods. In this paragraph, "monetary obligation" means a monetary obligation secured by the goods or owned under a lease of the goods and includes a monetary obligation with respect to software used in the goods.

The term does not include (i) charters or other contracts involving the use of hire of a vessel or (ii) records that evidence a right to payment arising out of the use of a credit or charge card or information contained on or for use with the card. If a transaction is evidence by records that include an instrument or series of instruments, the group of records taken together constitutes chattel paper.

(42) "General intangible" means any personal property, including things in action, other than accounts, chattel paper, commercial tort claims, deposit accounts, documents, goods, instruments, investment property, letter-of-credit rights, letters of credit, money, and oil, gas, or other minerals before extraction. The terms includes payment intangibles and software.

SIMPLIFIED VERSION

(11) "CHATTEL PAPER"

(A) means a record or records that evidence both a monetary obligation and:

(i)

1. a security interest in specific goods

2. a security interest in specific goods and software used in the goods [or]

3. a security interest in specific goods and license of software used in the goods; or

(ii)

1. a lease of specific goods or

2. a lease of specific goods and license of software used in the goods

(B) The term does not include:

(i) charters or other contracts involving the use of hire of a vessel or

(ii) records that evidence a right to payment arising out of the use of a credit or charge card or information contained on or for use with the card

(C) If a transaction is evidence by records that include an instrument or series of instruments, the group of records taken together constitutes chattel paper.

(42) **"GENERAL INTANGIBLE"**

(A) means any personal property, including things in action, other than:

(i) accounts,

(ii) chattel paper,

(iii) commercial tort claims,

(iv) deposit accounts,

(v) documents,

(vi) goods,

(vii) instruments,

(viii) investment property,

(ix) letter-of-credit rights,

(x) letters of credit,

(xi) money, and

ACTUAL TEXT

SIMPLIFIED VERSION

(xii) oil, gas, or

(xiii) other minerals before extraction

(B) The term "General intangible" includes payment intangibles and software

(44) "Goods" means all things that are movable when a security interest attaches. The term includes (i) fixtures, (ii) standing timber that is to be cut and removed under a conveyance or contract for sale, (iii) the unborn young of animals, (iv) crops grown, growing, or to be grown, even if the crops are produced on trees, vines or bushes, and (v) manufactured homes. The terms also includes a computer program embedded in goods and any supporting information provided in connection with a transaction relating to the program if (i) the program is associated with the goods in such a manner that it customarily is considered part of the goods, or (ii) by becoming the owner of the goods, a person acquires a right to use the program in connection with the goods. The term does not include a computer program embedded in goods that consist solely of the medium in which the program is embedded. The term also does not include accounts, chattel paper, commercial tort claims, deposit accounts, documents, general intangibles, instruments, investment property, letter-of-credit rights, letters of credit, money, oil or gas, or other minerals before extraction

(44) **"GOODS"** means all things that are movable when a security interest attaches.

(A) The term includes:

(i) fixtures,

(ii) standing timber that is to be cut and removed under a conveyance or contract for sale,

(iii) the unborn young of animals

(iv) crops grown, growing, or to be grown, even if the crops are produced on trees, vines, or bushes, and

(v) manufactured in homes

(B) The term also includes a computer program embedded in goods and any supporting information provided in connection with a transaction relating to the program if:

(i) the program is associated with the goods in such a manner that it customarily is considered part of the goods, or

(ii) by becoming the owner of the goods, a person acquires a right to use the program in connection with the goods. The term does not include a computer program embedded in goods that consist solely of the medium with which the program is embedded.

(C) The terms does not include accounts, chattel paper, commercial tort claims, deposit accounts, documents, general intangibles, instruments, investment property, letter-of-credit rights, letters of credit, money, or oil, gas, or other minerals before extraction.

ACTUAL TEXT

(47) "Instrument" means a negotiable instrument or any other writing that evidences a right to the payment of a monetary obligation, is not itself a security agreement or lease, and is of a type that in ordinary course of business is transferred by delivery with any necessary indorsement or assignment. The terms does not include (i) investment property, (ii) letters of credit, or (iii) writings that evidence a right to payment arising out of the use of a credit or charge card or information contained on or for use with the card.

SIMPLIFIED VERSION

(47) "**INSTRUMENT**":

(A) means a negotiable instrument, or

(B) any other writing that:

(i) evidences a right to the payment of a monetary obligation,

(ii) is not itself a security agreement of lease, and

(iii) is of a type that in ordinary course of business is transferred by delivery with any necessary indorsement or assignment

(C) The terms "instrument" does not include:

(i) investment property,

(ii) letters of credit, or

(iii) writings that evidence a right to payment arising out of the use of a credit or charge card or information contained on or for use with the card

(49) "Investment property" means a security, whether certificated or uncertificated, security entitlement, securities account, commodity contract, or commodity account.

(49) "**INVESTMENT PROPERTY**":

(A) a security, whether certificated or uncertificated,

(B) security entitlement,

(C) securities account,

(D) commodity contract, or

(E) commodity account

§ 9-301. LAW GOVERNING PERFECTION AND PRIORITY OF SECURITY INTERESTS

ACTUAL TEXT

Except as otherwise provided in Sections 9-303 through 9-306, the following rules determine the law governing perfection, the effect of perfection or nonperfection, and the priority of a security interest in collateral:

(1) Except as otherwise provided in this section, while a debtor is located in a jurisdiction, the local law of that jurisdiction governs perfection, the effect of perfection or nonperfection, and the priority of a security interest in collateral.

SIMPLIFIED VERSION

(a) **Non-Possessory Security Interest — Location of Debtor.** Except as otherwise provided in subsection (b) through (g), while a debtor is located in a jurisdiction, the local law of that jurisdiction governs perfection, the effect of perfection or nonperfection, and the priority of a security interest in collateral.

ACTUAL TEXT	SIMPLIFIED VERSION
(2) While collateral is located in a jurisdiction, the local law of that jurisdiction governs perfection, the effect of perfection or nonperfection, and the priority of a possessory security interest in that collateral.	**(b) Possessory Security Interests — Location of Collateral.** While collateral is located in a jurisdiction, the local law of that jurisdiction governs perfection, the effect of perfection or nonperfection, and the priority of a possessory security interest in that collateral.
(3) Except as otherwise provided in paragraph (4), while negotiable documents, goods, instruments, money, or tangible chattel paper is located in a jurisdiction, the local law of that jurisdiction governs:	**(c) Priority of Non-Possessory Security Interests In Tangible and Semi-tangible Property.** Except as otherwise provided in subsections (d), (e), and (f), while negotiable documents, goods, instruments, money, or tangible chattel paper is located in a jurisdiction, the local law of that jurisdiction governs the effect of perfection or nonperfection and the priority of a nonpossessory security interest.
(A) perfection of a security interest in the goods by filing a fixture filing;	**(d) Perfection of A Fixture Filing — Location of Goods.** While goods are located in a jurisdiction, the local law of that jurisdiction governs perfection, the effect of perfection or nonperfection, and the priority of a security interest in the goods by filing a fixture filing.
(B) perfection of a security interest in timber to be cut; and (C) the effect of perfection or nonperfection and the priority of a nonpossessory security interest in the collateral.	**(e) Perfection of A Security Interest In Timber To Be Cut — Location of the Timber.** The local law of the jurisdiction in which timber to be cut is located governs perfection, the effect of perfection or nonperfection, and the priority of a security interest in the timber.
4) The local law of the jurisdiction in which the wellhead or minehead is located governs perfection, the effect of perfection or nonperfection, and the priority of a security interest in as-extracted collateral.	**(f) Collateral to be Extracted — Location of Wellhead or Minehead.** The local law of the jurisdiction in which the wellhead or minehead is located governs perfection, the effect of perfection or nonperfection, and the priority of a security interest in as-extracted collateral. **(g) Other Exceptions.** Subsection (a) is subject to: (1) Section 9-303 (Certificates of Title). (2) Section 9-304 (Deposit Accounts). (3) Section 9-305 (Investment Property). (4) Section 9-306 (Letter-of-Credit Rights).

Appendix B

DETAILED MODEL SECURITY AGREEMENT

SECURITY AGREEMENT

This is a security agreement ("Security Agreement") made September 1, 2000, between Samuel Clemens and Mark T. Clemens, d/b/a Apex Printing, 3412 Milton Ave., University Park, Texas, ("Debtor") and Steady State Bank, 6518 Hillcrest Ave., University Park, Texas ("Secured Party").

This Security Agreement is entered into with respect to:

(i) a loan (the "Loan") made by Secured Party to Debtor pursuant to a Loan Agreement (the "Loan Agreement") dated the same date as this Security Agreement, and evidenced by a note dated September 1, 2000;

(ii) the sale by Debtor and the purchase by Secured Party of Accounts, and

(iii) the sale by Debtor and the purchase by Secured Party of Chattel Paper.

Secured Party and Debtor agree as follows:

1. Definitions.

1.1 "Collateral." The Collateral consists of one ABM printing press, Model #3142, Serial #76458; two Xerox photocopy machines, Model #5042, with attachments; one automated Miti binder/stapler; one Dell desktop computer with HP laser printer, and the following property of Debtor, wherever located, and now owned or hereafter acquired:

(i) Accounts, including all amounts owed to Debtor for the licensing of intellectual property rights;

(ii) Chattel paper, including equipment leases and conditional sales agreements;

(iii) Inventory, including property held for sale or lease and raw materials;

(iv) Equipment, including property used in the Debtor's business, machinery and production machines, and including any fixtures;

(v) Instruments, including negotiable instruments and negotiable certificates of deposit;

(vi) Fixtures;

(vii) General intangibles;

(viii) Additions, accessions and substitutions and rights ancillary to, or arising in any way in connection with, any of the foregoing, including security agreements securing any of the foregoing, guaranties guarantying any of the foregoing, documents, notes and drafts representing any of the foregoing, the right to returned goods, warranty claims with respect to any of the foregoing, amounts owed in connection with the short term use or licensing of any of the foregoing, government payments in connection with the purchase or agreement not to produce any of the foregoing;

(ix) Books and records pertaining to the foregoing and the equipment containing the books and records; and

(x) Money, deposit accounts, goods, insurance proceeds and other tangible or intangible property received upon the sale or other disposition of the foregoing.

1.2 "Obligations." This Security Agreement secures the following:

(i) Debtor's obligations under the Loan, the Loan Agreement, and this Security Agreement;

(ii) All other amounts now or in the future owed by Debtor to Secured Party; whether or not of the same kind or class as the other obligations owed by Debtor to Secured Party;

(iii) The repayment of (a) any amounts that Secured Party may advance or spend for the maintenance or preservation of the Collateral and (b) any other expenditures that Secured Party may make under the provisions of this Security Agreement or for the benefit of Debtor;

(iv) All amounts owed under any modifications, renewals or extensions of any of the foregoing obligations; and

(v) Any of the foregoing that arises after the filing of a petition by or against Debtor under the Bankruptcy Code, even if the obligations due do not accrue because of the automatic stay under Bankruptcy Code § 362 or otherwise.

This Security Agreement does not secure any obligation described above which is secured by a consensual lien on real property.

1.3 UCC. Any term used in the Uniform Commercial Code ("UCC") and not defined in this Security Agreement has the meaning given to the term in the UCC.

2. Grant of Security Interest.

Debtor grants a security interest in the Collateral to Secured Party to secure the payment or performance of the Obligations.

3. Perfection of Security Interest.

3.1 Filing of financing statement.

(i) Debtor, by signing this Security Agreement, authorizes Secured Party to file a financing statement (the "Financing Statement") describing the Collateral, and any amendment.

(ii)   Secured Party shall receive prior to the Closing an official report from the appropriate filing office(s) of each Collateral State, and the Chief Executive Office State, (each as defined below) (the "SOS Reports") indicating that Secured Party's security interests are prior to all other security interests or other interests reflected in the report.

3.2 Possession.

(i)   Debtor shall have possession of and full title to the Collateral, except where expressly otherwise provided in this Security Agreement or where Secured Party chooses to perfect its security interests by possession.

(ii)   Where Collateral is in the possession of a third party, Debtor will join with Secured Party in notifying the third party of Secured Party's security interest.

4.   Post-Closing Covenants and Rights Concerning the Collateral.

4.1 Inspection. The parties to this Security Agreement may inspect any Collateral in the other party's possession, at any time upon reasonable notice.

4.2 Personal Property. The Collateral shall remain personal property at all times. Debtor shall not affix any of the Collateral to any real property in any manner which would change its nature from that of personal property to real property or to a fixture.

4.3 Secured Party's collection rights. Secured Party shall have the right at any time to notify any account debtors and any obligors under instruments to make payments directly to Secured Party. Secured Party may at any time judicially enforce Debtor's rights against the account debtors and obligors.

4.4 Limitations on obligations concerning maintenance of collateral.

(i)   Risk of loss. Debtor has the risk of loss of the Collateral. Secured Party shall not be responsible for any injury to, loss to, or loss in value of, the Collateral, or any part thereof, arising from any act of nature, flood, fire or any other cause beyond the control of Secured Party.

(ii)   No collection obligation. Secured Party has no duty to collect any income accruing on the Collateral or to preserve any rights relating to the Collateral.

4.5 No disposition of collateral. Except as to inventory held for sale or lease in ordinary course of business, Debtor has no right to sell, lease or otherwise dispose of any of the Collateral. Any failure of Secured Party to object to an unauthorized disposition does not modify or waive any rights of Secured Party.

5.   Debtor's Representations and Warranties.

Debtor warrants and represents that:

5.1 Title to and transfer of Collateral. Its title to the Collateral is free of all adverse claims, liens, security interests and restrictions on transfer or pledge except as created by this Security Agreement.

5.2 Location of Collateral. All collateral consisting of goods is located solely in the States (the "Collateral States") listed in Exhibit C.

5.3 Location of Debtor. Debtor's chief executive office is located in the State (the "State") identified in Exhibit B.

6.   Debtor's Covenants.

Until the Obligations are paid in full, Debtor agrees that it will:

6.1 preserve its current business structure and not, in one transaction or a series of related transactions, merge into or consolidate with any entity, or sell all or substantially all of its assets;

6.2 not change the State where Collateral or the Debtor is located; and

6.3 not change any name without providing Secured Party with 30 days' prior written notice.

7.   Events of Default.

The occurrence of any of the following, at the option of Secured Party, notice of the exercise of which need not be given to Debtor, shall be an Event of Default:

7.1 Any default by Debtor or Event of Default (as defined) under the Loan Agreement or any of the other Obligations;

7.2 Debtor's failure to comply with any of the provisions of, or the incorrectness of any representation or warranty contained in, this Security Agreement, the Note, or in any of the other Obligations;

7.3 Transfer or disposition of any of the Collateral, except as expressly permitted by this Security Agreement;

7.4 Attachment, execution or levy on any of the Collateral;

7.5 Debtor voluntarily or involuntarily becoming subject to any proceeding under (a) the Bankruptcy Code or (b) any similar remedy under state statutory or common law;

7.6 Debtor failing to comply with, or becoming subject to any administrative or judicial proceeding under any federal, state or local (a) hazardous waste or environmental law, (b) asset forfeiture or similar law which can result in the forfeiture of property, or (c) other law, where noncompliance may have any significant effect on the Collateral;

7.7 Any default by Debtor in any obligation owed to another person;

7.8 The Debtor's death; or

7.9 Any other event that occurs or fails to occur which the Secured Party deems a risk to payment of the Obligations or to the Collateral.

8.   Default Costs.

8.1 Should an Event of Default occur, Debtor will pay to Secured Party all costs reasonably incurred by the Secured Party for the purpose of enforcing its rights hereunder, including:

(i)   costs of foreclosure;

(ii)   costs of obtaining money damages; and

(iii) a fee charged for the services of attorneys employed by Secured Party for any purpose related to this Security Agreement or the Obligations, including consultation, drafting documents, sending notices or instituting, prosecuting or defending litigation or arbitration.

9.   Remedies Upon Default.

9.1 General. Upon any Event of Default, Secured Party may pursue any remedy available at law (including those available under the provisions of the UCC), or in equity to collect, enforce or satisfy any Obligations then owing, whether by acceleration or otherwise.

9.2 Conformer remedies. Upon any Event of Default, Secured Party shall have the right to pursue any of the following remedies separately, successively or simultaneously:

(i)   File suit and obtain judgment and, in conjunction with any action, Secured Party may seek any ancillary remedies provided by law, including levy of attachment and garnishment.

(ii)   Take possession of any Collateral if not already in its possession without demand and without legal process. Upon Secured Party's demand, Debtor will assemble and make the Collateral available to Secured Party as it directs. Debtor grants to Secured Party the right, for this purpose, to enter into or on any premises where Collateral may be located and also to take possession of any personal property located in the Collateral, which property upon demand will be returned to Debtor.

(iii) Without taking possession, sell, lease or otherwise dispose of the Collateral at public or private sale in accordance with the UCC.

10.   Foreclosure Procedures.

10.1 No waiver. No delay or omission by Secured Party to exercise any right or remedy accruing upon any Event of Default shall: (a) impair any right or remedy, (b) waive any default or operate as an acquiescence to the Event of Default, or (c) affect any subsequent default of the same or of a different nature. Acceptance of late payments does not modify the Debtor's duty to perform on time or impose a notification duty on Secured Party before strict enforcement.

10.2 Notices. Secured Party shall give Debtor such notice of any private or public sale as may be required by the UCC. Secured Party shall have no obligation to give a notice to any other person, except as required by law under the circumstances.

10.3 No obligation to pursue others. Secured Party has no obligation to attempt to satisfy the Obligations by collecting them from any other person liable for them and Secured Party may release, modify or waive any collateral provided by any other person to secure any of the Obligations, all without affecting Secured Party's rights against Debtor.

10.4 Warranties. Secured Party may sell the Collateral without giving any warranties as to the Collateral. This procedure will not be considered adversely to affect the commercial reasonableness of any sale of the Collateral.

10.5 Purchases by Secured Party. In the event Secured Party purchases any of the Collateral being sold, Secured Party may pay for the Collateral by crediting some or all of the Obligations of the Debtor.

10.6 No marshaling. Secured Party has no obligation except as required by law to marshal any assets in favor of Debtor, or against or in payment of:

    (i)   the Note,

    (ii)   any of the other Obligations, or

    (iii)   any other obligation owed to Secured Party by Debtor or any other person.

11.   Miscellaneous.

11.1 Assignment.

    (i)   *Binds assignees.* This Security Agreement shall bind and shall inure to the benefit of the heirs, legatees, executors, administrators, successors and assigns of Debtor and Secured Party.

    (ii)   *No assignments by Debtor.* Secured Party does not consent to any assignment by Debtor except as expressly provided in this Security Agreement.

    (iii)   *Secured Party assignments.* Secured Party may assign its rights and interests under this Security Agreement. If an assignment is made, Debtor shall render performance under this Security Agreement to the assignee. Debtor will not assert against any assignee any claims, defenses or set-offs which Debtor could assert against Secured Party except defenses which cannot be waived.

11.2 Severability. Should any provision of this Security Agreement be found to be void, invalid or unenforceable by a court or panel of arbitrators of competent jurisdiction, that finding shall only affect the provisions found to be void, invalid or unenforceable and shall not affect the remaining provisions of this Security Agreement.

11.3 Notices. Any notices required by this Security Agreement shall be deemed to be delivered when (a) deposited in any United States postal box if postage is prepaid, and the notice properly addressed to the intended recipient, (b) received by telecopy, (c) received through the Internet, or (d) when personally delivered.

11.4 Headings. Section headings used in this Security Agreement are for convenience only. They are not a part of this Security Agreement and shall not be used in construing it.

11.5 Governing law. This Security Agreement is being executed and delivered and is intended to be performed in the State of Texas and shall be construed and enforced in accordance with the laws of the State of Texas, except to the extent that the UCC provides for perfection under the law of another state.

11.6 Rules of construction.

(i)   No reference to "proceeds" in this Security Agreement authorizes any sale, transfer, or other disposition of the Collateral by the Debtor.

(ii)   "Includes" and "including" are not limiting.

(iii)   "Or" is not exclusive.

(iv)   "All" includes "any" and "any" includes "all."

11.7 Integration and modifications.

(i)   This Security Agreement is the entire agreement of the Debtor and Secured Party concerning its subject matter.

(ii)   Any modification to this Security Agreement must be made in writing and signed by the party adversely affected.

11.8 Waiver. Any party to this Security Agreement may waive the enforcement of any provision to the extent the provision is for its benefit.

11.9 Further assurances. Debtor agrees to execute any further documents, and to take any further actions, reasonably requested by Secured Party to evidence or perfect the security interest granted herein, to maintain the first priority of the security interests, or to effectuate the rights granted to Secured Party herein.

The Debtor has signed this Security Agreement on the day and year indicated above.

"DEBTOR"

_____

Samuel Clemens

_____

Mark T. Clemens

QUESTIONS

1. Would you make any changes in this agreement due to the enactment of Revised Article 9? Any changes to improve it? *See A Comparison of a Security Agreement Under the Former Article 9 and the New Article 9, in* SELECTED COMMERCIAL STATUTES 1336 (2001) (or later edition).

2. Other law besides the UCC may be applicable, particularly if the loan were not for use in the individuals' business but rather was for a personal, family, or household purpose. What other laws in that context included in SELECTED COMMERCIAL STATUTES (2001) (or later edition) do you believe might apply? One law not contained there is a consumer deceptive practices statute; most states have one. What changes in the security agreement would be necessary under Article 9 itself in the consumer context?

Appendix C

CONVENTION ON INTERNATIONAL INTERESTS IN MOBILE EQUIPMENT

THE STATES PARTIES TO THIS CONVENTION,

AWARE of the need to acquire and use mobile equipment of high value or particular economic significance and to facilitate the financing of the acquisition and use of such equipment in an efficient manner,

RECOGNISING the advantages of asset-based financing and leasing for this purpose and desiring to facilitate these types of transaction by establishing clear rules to govern them,

MINDFUL of the need to ensure that interests in such equipment are recognised and protected universally,

DESIRING to provide broad and mutual economic benefits for all interested parties,

BELIEVING that such rules must reflect the principles underlying asset-based financing and leasing and promote the autonomy of the parties necessary in these transactions,

CONSCIOUS of the need to establish a legal framework for international interests in such equipment and for that purpose to create an international registration system for their protection,

TAKING INTO CONSIDERATION the objectives and principles enunciated in existing Conventions relating to such equipment,

HAVE AGREED upon the following provisions:

Chapter I
Sphere of Application and General Provisions

Article 1 — Definitions

In this Convention, except where the context otherwise requires, the following terms are employed with the meanings set out below:

a. "agreement" means a security agreement, a title reservation agreement or a leasing agreement;

b. "assignment" means a contract which, whether by way of security or otherwise, confers on the assignee associated rights with or without a transfer of the related international interest;

c. "associated rights" means all rights to payment or other performance by a debtor under an agreement which are secured by or associated with the object;

d. "commencement of the insolvency proceedings" means the time at which the insolvency proceedings are deemed to commence under the applicable insolvency law;

e. "conditional buyer" means a buyer under a title reservation agreement;

f. "conditional seller" means a seller under a title reservation agreement;

g. "contract of sale" means a contract for the sale of an object by a seller to a buyer which is not an agreement as defined in (a) above;

h. "court" means a court of law or an administrative or arbitral tribunal established by a Contracting State;

i. "creditor" means a chargee under a security agreement, a conditional seller under a title reservation agreement or a lessor under a leasing agreement;

j. "debtor" means a chargor under a security agreement, a conditional buyer under a title reservation agreement, a lessee under a leasing agreement or a person whose interest in an object is burdened by a registrable non-consensual right or interest;

k. "insolvency administrator" means a person authorised to administer the reorganisation or liquidation, including one authorised on an interim basis, and includes a debtor in possession if permitted by the applicable insolvency law;

l. "insolvency proceedings" means bankruptcy, liquidation or other collective judicial or administrative proceedings, including interim proceedings, in which the assets and affairs of the debtor are subject to control or supervision by a court for the purposes of reorganisation or liquidation;

m. "interested persons" means:

   i   the debtor;

   ii any person who, for the purpose of assuring performance of any of the obligations in favour of the creditor, gives or issues a suretyship or demand guarantee or a standby letter of credit or any other form of credit insurance;

   iii any other person having rights in or over the object;

n. "internal transaction" means a transaction of a type listed in Article 2(2)(a) to (c) where the centre of the main interests of all parties to such transaction is situated, and the relevant object located (as specified in the Protocol), in the same Contracting State at the time of the conclusion of the contract and where the interest created by the transaction has been registered in a national registry in that Contracting State which has made a declaration under Article 50(1);

o.   "international interest" means an interest held by a creditor to which Article 2 applies;

p.   "International Registry" means the international registration facilities established for the purposes of this Convention or the Protocol;

q.   "leasing agreement" means an agreement by which one person (the lessor) grants a right to possession or control of an object (with or without an option to purchase) to another person (the lessee) in return for a rental or other payment;

r.   "national interest" means an interest held by a creditor in an object and created by an internal transaction covered by a declaration under Article 50(1);

s.   "non-consensual right or interest" means a right or interest conferred under the law of a Contracting State which has made a declaration under Article 39 to secure the performance of an obligation, including an obligation to a State, State entity or an intergovernmental or private organisation;

t.   "notice of a national interest" means notice registered or to be registered in the International Registry that a national interest has been created;

u.   "object" means an object of a category to which Article 2 applies;

v.   "pre-existing right or interest" means a right or interest of any kind in or over an object created or arising before the effective date of this Convention as defined by Article 60(2)(a);

w.   "proceeds" means money or non-money proceeds of an object arising from the total or partial loss or physical destruction of the object or its total or partial confiscation, condemnation or requisition;

x.   "prospective assignment" means an assignment that is intended to be made in the future, upon the occurrence of a stated event, whether or not the occurrence of the event is certain;

y.   "prospective international interest" means an interest that is intended to be created or provided for in an object as an international interest in the future, upon the occurrence of a stated event (which may include the debtor's acquisition of an interest in the object), whether or not the occurrence of the event is certain;

z.   "prospective sale" means a sale which is intended to be made in the future, upon the occurrence of a stated event, whether or not the occurrence of the event is certain;

aa. "Protocol" means, in respect of any category of object and associated rights to which this Convention applies, the Protocol in respect of that category of object and associated rights;

bb. "registered" means registered in the International Registry pursuant to Chapter V;

cc. "registered interest" means an international interest, a registrable non-consensual right or interest or a national interest specified in a notice of a national interest registered pursuant to Chapter V;

dd. "registrable non-consensual right or interest" means a non-consensual right or interest registrable pursuant to a declaration deposited under Article 40;

ee. "Registrar" means, in respect of the Protocol, the person or body designated by that Protocol or appointed under Article 17(2)(b);

ff. "regulations" means regulations made or approved by the Supervisory Authority pursuant to the Protocol;

gg. "sale" means a transfer of ownership of an object pursuant to a contract of sale;

hh. "secured obligation" means an obligation secured by a security interest;

ii. "security agreement" means an agreement by which a chargor grants or agrees to grant to a chargee an interest (including an ownership interest) in or over an object to secure the performance of any existing or future obligation of the chargor or a third person;

jj. "security interest" means an interest created by a security agreement;

kk. "Supervisory Authority" means, in respect of the Protocol, the Supervisory Authority referred to in Article 17(1);

ll. "title reservation agreement" means an agreement for the sale of an object on terms that ownership does not pass until fulfilment of the condition or conditions stated in the agreement;

mm. "unregistered interest" means a consensual interest or non-consensual right or interest (other than an interest to which Article 39 applies) which has not been registered, whether or not it is registrable under this Convention; and

nn. "writing" means a record of information (including information communicated by teletransmission) which is in tangible or other form and is capable of being reproduced in tangible form on a subsequent occasion and which indicates by reasonable means a person's approval of the record.

Article 2 — The international interest

1. This Convention provides for the constitution and effects of an international interest in certain categories of mobile equipment and associated rights.

2. For the purposes of this Convention, an international interest in mobile equipment is an interest, constituted under Article 7, in a uniquely identifiable object of a category of such objects listed in paragraph 3 and designated in the Protocol:

   (a) granted by the chargor under a security agreement;

    (b)   vested in a person who is the conditional seller under a title reservation agreement; or

    (c)   vested in a person who is the lessor under a leasing agreement.

An interest falling within sub-paragraph (a) does not also fall within sub-paragraph (b) or (c).

3.   The categories referred to in the preceding paragraphs are:

    (a)   airframes, aircraft engines and helicopters;

    (b)   railway rolling stock; and

    (c)   space assets.

4.   The applicable law determines whether an interest to which paragraph 2 applies falls within sub-paragraph (a), (b) or (c) of that paragraph.

5.   An international interest in an object extends to proceeds of that object.

Article 3 — Sphere of application

1.   This Convention applies when, at the time of the conclusion of the agreement creating or providing for the international interest, the debtor is situated in a Contracting State.

2.   The fact that the creditor is situated in a non-Contracting State does not affect the applicability of this Convention.

Article 4 — Where debtor is situated

1.   For the purposes of Article 3(1), the debtor is situated in any Contracting State:

    a.   under the law of which it is incorporated or formed;

    b.   where it has its registered office or statutory seat;

    c.   where it has its centre of administration; or

    d.   where it has its place of business.

2.   A reference in sub-paragraph (d) of the preceding paragraph to the debtor's place of business shall, if it has more than one place of business, mean its principal place of business or, if it has no place of business, its habitual residence.

Article 5 — Interpretation and applicable law

1.   In the interpretation of this Convention, regard is to be had to its purposes as set forth in the preamble, to its international character and to the need to promote uniformity and predictability in its application.

2.   Questions concerning matters governed by this Convention which are not expressly settled in it are to be settled in conformity with the general principles on which it is based or, in the absence of such principles, in conformity with the applicable law.

3. References to the applicable law are to the domestic rules of the law applicable by virtue of the rules of private international law of the forum State.

4. Where a State comprises several territorial units, each of which has its own rules of law in respect of the matter to be decided, and where there is no indication of the relevant territorial unit, the law of that State decides which is the territorial unit whose rules shall govern. In the absence of any such rule, the law of the territorial unit with which the case is most closely connected shall apply.

Article 6 — Relationship between the Convention and the Protocol

1. This Convention and the Protocol shall be read and interpreted together as a single instrument.

2. To the extent of any inconsistency between this Convention and the Protocol, the Protocol shall prevail.

Chapter II

Constitution of an International Interest

Article 7 — Formal requirements

An interest is constituted as an international interest under this Convention where the agreement creating or providing for the interest:

a. is in writing;

b. relates to an object of which the chargor, conditional seller or lessor has power to dispose;

c. enables the object to be identified in conformity with the Protocol; and

d. in the case of a security agreement, enables the secured obligations to be determined, but without the need to state a sum or maximum sum secured.

Chapter III

Default Remedies

Article 8 — Remedies of chargee

1. In the event of default as provided in Article 11, the chargee may, to the extent that the chargor has at any time so agreed and subject to any declaration that may be made by a Contracting State under Article 54, exercise any one or more of the following remedies:

   a. take possession or control of any object charged to it;

   b. sell or grant a lease of any such object;

    c.   collect or receive any income or profits arising from the management or use of any such object.

2.   The chargee may alternatively apply for a court order authorising or directing any of the acts referred to in the preceding paragraph.

3.   Any remedy set out in sub-paragraph (a), (b) or (c) of paragraph 1 or by Article 13 shall be exercised in a commercially reasonable manner. A remedy shall be deemed to be exercised in a commercially reasonable manner where it is exercised in conformity with a provision of the security agreement except where such a provision is manifestly unreasonable.

4.   A chargee proposing to sell or grant a lease of an object under paragraph 1 shall give reasonable prior notice in writing of the proposed sale or lease to:

    a.   interested persons specified in Article 1(m)(i) and (ii); and

    b.   interested persons specified in Article 1(m)(iii) who have given notice of their rights to the chargee within a reasonable time prior to the sale or lease.

5.   Any sum collected or received by the chargee as a result of exercise of any of the remedies set out in paragraph 1 or 2 shall be applied towards discharge of the amount of the secured obligations.

6.   Where the sums collected or received by the chargee as a result of the exercise of any remedy set out in paragraph 1 or 2 exceed the amount secured by the security interest and any reasonable costs incurred in the exercise of any such remedy, then unless otherwise ordered by the court the chargee shall distribute the surplus among holders of subsequently ranking interests which have been registered or of which the chargee has been given notice, in order of priority, and pay any remaining balance to the chargor.

Article 9   — Vesting of object in satisfaction; redemption

1.   At any time after default as provided in Article 11, the chargee and all the interested persons may agree that ownership of (or any other interest of the chargor in) any object covered by the security interest shall vest in the chargee in or towards satisfaction of the secured obligations.

2.   The court may on the application of the chargee order that ownership of (or any other interest of the chargor in) any object covered by the security interest shall vest in the chargee in or towards satisfaction of the secured obligations.

3.   The court shall grant an application under the preceding paragraph only if the amount of the secured obligations to be satisfied by such vesting is commensurate with the value of the object after taking account of any payment to be made by the chargee to any of the interested persons.

4.   At any time after default as provided in Article 11 and before sale of the charged object or the making of an order under paragraph 2, the chargor or any interested person may discharge the security interest by paying in full

the amount secured, subject to any lease granted by the chargee under Article 8(1)(b) or ordered under Article 8(2). Where, after such default, the payment of the amount secured is made in full by an interested person other than the debtor, that person is subrogated to the rights of the chargee.

5. Ownership or any other interest of the chargor passing on a sale under Article 8(1)(b) or passing under paragraph 1 or 2 of this Article is free from any other interest over which the chargee's security interest has priority under the provisions of Article 29.

Article 10 — Remedies of conditional seller or lessor

In the event of default under a title reservation agreement or under a leasing agreement as provided in Article 11, the conditional seller or the lessor, as the case may be, may:

a. subject to any declaration that may be made by a Contracting State under Article 54, terminate the agreement and take possession or control of any object to which the agreement relates; or

b. apply for a court order authorising or directing either of these acts.

Article 11 — Meaning of default

1. The debtor and the creditor may at any time agree in writing as to the events that constitute a default or otherwise give rise to the rights and remedies specified in Articles 8 to 10 and 13.

2. Where the debtor and the creditor have not so agreed, "default" for the purposes of Articles 8 to 10 and 13 means a default which substantially deprives the creditor of what it is entitled to expect under the agreement.

Article 12 — Additional remedies

Any additional remedies permitted by the applicable law, including any remedies agreed upon by the parties, may be exercised to the extent that they are not inconsistent with the mandatory provisions of this Chapter as set out in Article 15.

Article 13 — Relief pending final determination

1. Subject to any declaration that it may make under Article 55, a Contracting State shall ensure that a creditor who adduces evidence of default by the debtor may, pending final determination of its claim and to the extent that the debtor has at any time so agreed, obtain from a court speedy relief in the form of such one or more of the following orders as the creditor requests:

    a. preservation of the object and its value;

    b. possession, control or custody of the object;

    c. immobilisation of the object; and

    d. lease or, except where covered by sub-paragraphs (a) to (c), management of the object and the income therefrom.

2. In making any order under the preceding paragraph, the court may impose such terms as it considers necessary to protect the interested persons in the event that the creditor:

   a. in implementing any order granting such relief, fails to perform any of its obligations to the debtor under this Convention or the Protocol; or

   b. fails to establish its claim, wholly or in part, on the final determination of that claim.

3. Before making any order under paragraph 1, the court may require notice of the request to be given to any of the interested persons.

4. Nothing in this Article affects the application of Article 8(3) or limits the availability of forms of interim relief other than those set out in paragraph 1.

Article 14   — Procedural requirements

Subject to Article 54(2), any remedy provided by this Chapter shall be exercised in conformity with the procedure prescribed by the law of the place where the remedy is to be exercised.

Article 15   — Derogation

In their relations with each other, any two or more of the parties referred to in this Chapter may at any time, by agreement in writing, derogate from or vary the effect of any of the preceding provisions of this Chapter except Articles 8(3) to (6), 9(3) and (4), 13(2) and 14.

Chapter IV

The International Registration System

Article 16   — The International Registry

1. An International Registry shall be established for registrations of:

   a. international interests, prospective international interests and registrable non-consensual rights and interests;

   b. assignments and prospective assignments of international interests;

   c. acquisitions of international interests by legal or contractual subrogations under the applicable law;

   d. notices of national interests; and

   e. subordinations of interests referred to in any of the preceding sub-paragraphs.

2. Different international registries may be established for different categories of object and associated rights.

3. For the purposes of this Chapter and Chapter V, the term "registration" includes, where appropriate, an amendment, extension or discharge of a registration.

Article 17 — The Supervisory Authority and the Registrar

1. There shall be a Supervisory Authority as provided by the Protocol.

2. The Supervisory Authority shall:

   a. establish or provide for the establishment of the International Registry;

   b. except as otherwise provided by the Protocol, appoint and dismiss the Registrar;

   c. ensure that any rights required for the continued effective operation of the International Registry in the event of a change of Registrar will vest in or be assignable to the new Registrar;

   d. after consultation with the Contracting States, make or approve and ensure the publication of regulations pursuant to the Protocol dealing with the operation of the International Registry;

   e. establish administrative procedures through which complaints concerning the operation of the International Registry can be made to the Supervisory Authority;

   f. supervise the Registrar and the operation of the International Registry;

   g. at the request of the Registrar, provide such guidance to the Registrar as the Supervisory Authority thinks fit;

   h. set and periodically review the structure of fees to be charged for the services and facilities of the International Registry;

   i. do all things necessary to ensure that an efficient notice-based electronic registration system exists to implement the objectives of this Convention and the Protocol; and

   j. report periodically to Contracting States concerning the discharge of its obligations under this Convention and the Protocol.

3. The Supervisory Authority may enter into any agreement requisite for the performance of its functions, including any agreement referred to in Article 27(3).

4. The Supervisory Authority shall own all proprietary rights in the data bases and archives of the International Registry.

5. The Registrar shall ensure the efficient operation of the International Registry and perform the functions assigned to it by this Convention, the Protocol and the regulations.

Chapter V
Other Matters Relating to Registration

Article 18 — Registration requirements

1. The Protocol and regulations shall specify the requirements, including the criteria for the identification of the object:

   a. for effecting a registration (which shall include provision for prior electronic transmission of any consent from any person whose consent is required under Article 20);

   b. for making searches and issuing search certificates, and, subject thereto;

   c. for ensuring the confidentiality of information and documents of the International Registry other than information and documents relating to a registration.

2. The Registrar shall not be under a duty to enquire whether a consent to registration under Article 20 has in fact been given or is valid.

3. Where an interest registered as a prospective international interest becomes an international interest, no further registration shall be required provided that the registration information is sufficient for a registration of an international interest.

4. The Registrar shall arrange for registrations to be entered into the International Registry data base and made searchable in chronological order of receipt, and the file shall record the date and time of receipt.

5. The Protocol may provide that a Contracting State may designate an entity or entities in its territory as the entry point or entry points through which the information required for registration shall or may be transmitted to the International Registry. A Contracting State making such a designation may specify the requirements, if any, to be satisfied before such information is transmitted to the International Registry.

Article 19 — Validity and time of registration

1. A registration shall be valid only if made in conformity with Article 20.

2. A registration, if valid, shall be complete upon entry of the required information into the International Registry data base so as to be searchable.

3. A registration shall be searchable for the purposes of the preceding paragraph at the time when:

   a. the International Registry has assigned to it a sequentially ordered file number; and

   b. the registration information, including the file number, is stored in durable form and may be accessed at the International Registry.

4. If an interest first registered as a prospective international interest becomes an international interest, that international interest shall be treated as registered from the time of registration of the prospective international interest provided that the registration was still current immediately before the international interest was constituted as provided by Article 7.

5. The preceding paragraph applies with necessary modifications to the registration of a prospective assignment of an international interest.

6. A registration shall be searchable in the International Registry data base according to the criteria prescribed by the Protocol.

Article 20 — Consent to registration

1. An international interest, a prospective international interest or an assignment or prospective assignment of an international interest may be registered, and any such registration amended or extended prior to its expiry, by either party with the consent in writing of the other.

2. The subordination of an international interest to another international interest may be registered by or with the consent in writing at any time of the person whose interest has been subordinated.

3. A registration may be discharged by or with the consent in writing of the party in whose favour it was made.

4. The acquisition of an international interest by legal or contractual subrogation may be registered by the subrogee.

5. A registrable non-consensual right or interest may be registered by the holder thereof.

6. A notice of a national interest may be registered by the holder thereof.

Article 21 — Duration of registration

Registration of an international interest remains effective until discharged or until expiry of the period specified in the registration.

Article 22 — Searches

1. Any person may, in the manner prescribed by the Protocol and regulations, make or request a search of the International Registry by electronic means concerning interests or prospective international interests registered therein.

2. Upon receipt of a request therefor, the Registrar, in the manner prescribed by the Protocol and regulations, shall issue a registry search certificate by electronic means with respect to any object:

   a. stating all registered information relating thereto, together with a statement indicating the date and time of registration of such information; or

b.   stating that there is no information in the International Registry relating thereto.

3.   A search certificate issued under the preceding paragraph shall indicate that the creditor named in the registration information has acquired or intends to acquire an international interest in the object but shall not indicate whether what is registered is an international interest or a prospective international interest, even if this is ascertainable from the relevant registration information.

Article 23   — List of declarations and declared non-consensual rights or interests

The Registrar shall maintain a list of declarations, withdrawals of declaration and of the categories of non-consensual right or interest communicated to the Registrar by the Depositary as having been declared by Contracting States in conformity with Articles 39 and 40 and the date of each such declaration or withdrawal of declaration. Such list shall be recorded and searchable in the name of the declaring State and shall be made available as provided in the Protocol and regulations to any person requesting it.

Article 24   — Evidentiary value of certificates

A document in the form prescribed by the regulations which purports to be a certificate issued by the International Registry is prima facie proof:

a.   that it has been so issued; and

b.   of the facts recited in it, including the date and time of a registration.

Article 25   — Discharge of registration

1.   Where the obligations secured by a registered security interest or the obligations giving rise to a registered non-consensual right or interest have been discharged, or where the conditions of transfer of title under a registered title reservation agreement have been fulfilled, the holder of such interest shall, without undue delay, procure the discharge of the registration after written demand by the debtor delivered to or received at its address stated in the registration.

2.   Where a prospective international interest or a prospective assignment of an international interest has been registered, the intending creditor or intending assignee shall, without undue delay, procure the discharge of the registration after written demand by the intending debtor or assignor which is delivered to or received at its address stated in the registration before the intending creditor or assignee has given value or incurred a commitment to give value.

3.   Where the obligations secured by a national interest specified in a registered notice of a national interest have been discharged, the holder of such interest shall, without undue delay, procure the discharge of the registration after written demand by the debtor delivered to or received at its address

stated in the registration.

4.   Where a registration ought not to have been made or is incorrect, the person in whose favour the registration was made shall, without undue delay, procure its discharge or amendment after written demand by the debtor delivered to or received at its address stated in the registration.

Article 26   — Access to the international registration facilities

No person shall be denied access to the registration and search facilities of the International Registry on any ground other than its failure to comply with the procedures prescribed by this Chapter.

Chapter VI

Privileges and Immunities of the Supervisory Authority and the Registrar

Article 27   — Legal personality; immunity

1.   The Supervisory Authority shall have international legal personality where not already possessing such personality.

2.   The Supervisory Authority and its officers and employees shall enjoy such immunity from legal or administrative process as is specified in the Protocol.

   a.   The Supervisory Authority shall enjoy exemption from taxes and such other privileges as may be provided by agreement with the host State.

   b.   For the purposes of this paragraph, "host State" means the State in which the Supervisory Authority is situated.

3.   The assets, documents, data bases and archives of the International Registry shall be inviolable and immune from seizure or other legal or administrative process.

4.   For the purposes of any claim against the Registrar under Article 28(1) or Article 44, the claimant shall be entitled to access to such information and documents as are necessary to enable the claimant to pursue its claim.

5.   The Supervisory Authority may waive the inviolability and immunity conferred by paragraph 4.

Chapter VII

Liability of the Registrar

Article 28   — Liability and financial assurances

1.   The Registrar shall be liable for compensatory damages for loss suffered by a person directly resulting from an error or omission of the Registrar and its officers and employees or from a malfunction of the international

registration system except where the malfunction is caused by an event of an inevitable and irresistible nature, which could not be prevented by using the best practices in current use in the field of electronic registry design and operation, including those related to back-up and systems security and networking.

2.   The Registrar shall not be liable under the preceding paragraph for factual inaccuracy of registration information received by the Registrar or transmitted by the Registrar in the form in which it received that information nor for acts or circumstances for which the Registrar and its officers and employees are not responsible and arising prior to receipt of registration information at the International Registry.

3.   Compensation under paragraph 1 may be reduced to the extent that the person who suffered the damage caused or contributed to that damage.

4.   The Registrar shall procure insurance or a financial guarantee covering the liability referred to in this Article to the extent determined by the Supervisory Authority, in accordance with the Protocol.

Chapter VIII
Effects of an International Interest as Against Third Parties

Article 29 — Priority of competing interests

1.   A registered interest has priority over any other interest subsequently registered and over an unregistered interest.

2.   The priority of the first-mentioned interest under the preceding paragraph applies:

   a.   even if the first-mentioned interest was acquired or registered with actual knowledge of the other interest; and

   b.   even as regards value given by the holder of the first-mentioned interest with such knowledge.

3.   The buyer of an object acquires its interest in it:

   a.   subject to an interest registered at the time of its acquisition of that interest; and

   b.   free from an unregistered interest even if it has actual knowledge of such an interest.

4.   The conditional buyer or lessee acquires its interest in or right over that object:

   a.   subject to an interest registered prior to the registration of the international interest held by its conditional seller or lessor; and

b. free from an interest not so registered at that time even if it has actual knowledge of that interest.

4. The priority of competing interests or rights under this Article may be varied by agreement between the holders of those interests, but an assignee of a subordinated interest is not bound by an agreement to subordinate that interest unless at the time of the assignment a subordination had been registered relating to that agreement.

5. Any priority given by this Article to an interest in an object extends to proceeds.

6. This Convention:

a. does not affect the rights of a person in an item, other than an object, held prior to its installation on an object if under the applicable law those rights continue to exist after the installation; and

b. does not prevent the creation of rights in an item, other than an object, which has previously been installed on an object where under the applicable law those rights are created.

Article 30 — Effects of insolvency

1. In insolvency proceedings against the debtor an international interest is effective if prior to the commencement of the insolvency proceedings that interest was registered in conformity with this Convention.

2. Nothing in this Article impairs the effectiveness of an international interest in the insolvency proceedings where that interest is effective under the applicable law.

3. Nothing in this Article affects:

a. any rules of law applicable in insolvency proceedings relating to the avoidance of a transaction as a preference or a transfer in fraud of creditors; or

b. any rules of procedure relating to the enforcement of rights to property which is under the control or supervision of the insolvency administrator.

Chapter IX

Assignments of Associated Rights and International Interests; Rights of Subrogation

Article 31 — Effects of assignment

1. Except as otherwise agreed by the parties, an assignment of associated rights made in conformity with Article 32 also transfers to the assignee:

a. the related international interest; and

    b.   all the interests and priorities of the assignor under this Convention.

2.   Nothing in this Convention prevents a partial assignment of the assignor's associated rights. In the case of such a partial assignment the assignor and assignee may agree as to their respective rights concerning the related international interest assigned under the preceding paragraph but not so as adversely to affect the debtor without its consent.

3.   Subject to paragraph 4, the applicable law shall determine the defences and rights of set-off available to the debtor against the assignee.

4.   The debtor may at any time by agreement in writing waive all or any of the defences and rights of set-off referred to in the preceding paragraph other than defences arising from fraudulent acts on the part of the assignee.

5.   In the case of an assignment by way of security, the assigned associated rights revest in the assignor, to the extent that they are still subsisting, when the obligations secured by the assignment have been discharged.

Article 32 — Formal requirements of assignment

1.   An assignment of associated rights transfers the related international interest only if it:

    a.   is in writing;

    b.   enables the associated rights to be identified under the contract from which they arise; and

    c.   in the case of an assignment by way of security, enables the obligations secured by the assignment to be determined in accordance with the Protocol but without the need to state a sum or maximum sum secured.

2.   An assignment of an international interest created or provided for by a security agreement is not valid unless some or all related associated rights also are assigned.

3.   This Convention does not apply to an assignment of associated rights which is not effective to transfer the related international interest.

Article 33 — Debtor's duty to assignee

1.   To the extent that associated rights and the related international interest have been transferred in accordance with Articles 31 and 32, the debtor in relation to those rights and that interest is bound by the assignment and has a duty to make payment or give other performance to the assignee, if but only if:

    a.   the debtor has been given notice of the assignment in writing by or with the authority of the assignor; and

    b.   the notice identifies the associated rights.

2. Irrespective of any other ground on which payment or performance by the debtor discharges the latter from liability, payment or performance shall be effective for this purpose if made in accordance with the preceding paragraph.

3. Nothing in this Article shall affect the priority of competing assignments.

Article 34 — Default remedies in respect of assignment by way of security

In the event of default by the assignor under the assignment of associated rights and the related international interest made by way of security, Articles 8, 9 and 11 to 14 apply in the relations between the assignor and the assignee (and, in relation to associated rights, apply in so far as those provisions are capable of application to intangible property) as if references:

a. to the secured obligation and the security interest were references to the obligation secured by the assignment of the associated rights and the related international interest and the security interest created by that assignment;

b. to the chargee or creditor and chargor or debtor were references to the assignee and assignor;

c. to the holder of the international interest were references to the assignee; and

d. to the object were references to the assigned associated rights and the related international interest.

Article 35 — Priority of competing assignments

1. Where there are competing assignments of associated rights and at least one of the assignments includes the related international interest and is registered, the provisions of Article 29 apply as if the references to a registered interest were references to an assignment of the associated rights and the related registered interest and as if references to a registered or unregistered interest were references to a registered or unregistered assignment.

2. Article 30 applies to an assignment of associated rights as if the references to an international interest were references to an assignment of the associated rights and the related international interest.

Article 36 — Assignee's priority with respect to associated rights

1. The assignee of associated rights and the related international interest whose assignment has been registered only has priority under Article 35(1) over another assignee of the associated rights:

   a. if the contract under which the associated rights arise states that they are secured by or associated with the object; and to the extent that the associated rights are related to an object.

2. For the purposes of sub-paragraph (b) of the preceding paragraph, associated rights are related to an object only to the extent that they consist of rights to payment or performance that relate to:

    a. a sum advanced and utilised for the purchase of the object;

    b. a sum advanced and utilised for the purchase of another object in which the assignor held another international interest if the assignor transferred that interest to the assignee and the assignment has been registered;

    c. the price payable for the object;

    d. the rentals payable in respect of the object; or

    e. other obligations arising from a transaction referred to in any of the preceding sub-paragraphs.

3. In all other cases, the priority of the competing assignments of the associated rights shall be determined by the applicable law.

Article 37   — Effects of assignor's insolvency

The provisions of Article 30 apply to insolvency proceedings against the assignor as if references to the debtor were references to the assignor.

Article 38   — Subrogation

1. Subject to paragraph 2, nothing in this Convention affects the acquisition of associated rights and the related international interest by legal or contractual subrogation under the applicable law.

2. The priority between any interest within the preceding paragraph and a competing interest may be varied by agreement in writing between the holders of the respective interests but an assignee of a subordinated interest is not bound by an agreement to subordinate that interest unless at the time of the assignment a subordination had been registered relating to that agreement.

Chapter X
Rights or Interests Subject to
Declarations by Contracting States

Article 39   — Rights having priority without registration

1. A Contracting State may at any time, in a declaration deposited with the Depositary of the Protocol declare, generally or specifically:

    a. those categories of non-consensual right or interest (other than a right or interest to which Article 40 applies) which under that State's law have priority over an interest in an object equivalent to that of the holder of a registered international interest and which shall have priority over a registered international interest, whether in or outside insolvency proceedings; and

b.   that nothing in this Convention shall affect the right of a State or State entity, intergovernmental organisation or other private provider of public services to arrest or detain an object under the laws of that State for payment of amounts owed to such entity, organisation or provider directly relating to those services in respect of that object or another object.

2.   A declaration made under the preceding paragraph may be expressed to cover categories that are created after the deposit of that declaration.

3.   A non-consensual right or interest has priority over an international interest if and only if the former is of a category covered by a declaration deposited prior to the registration of the international interest.

4.   Notwithstanding the preceding paragraph, a Contracting State may, at the time of ratification, acceptance, approval of, or accession to the Protocol, declare that a right or interest of a category covered by a declaration made under sub-paragraph (a) of paragraph 1 shall have priority over an international interest registered prior to the date of such ratification, acceptance, approval or accession.

Article 40   — Registrable non-consensual rights or interests

A Contracting State may at any time in a declaration deposited with the Depositary of the Protocol list the categories of non-consensual right or interest which shall be registrable under this Convention as regards any category of object as if the right or interest were an international interest and shall be regulated accordingly. Such a declaration may be modified from time to time.

Chapter XI
Application of the Convention to Sales

Article 41   — Sale and prospective sale

This Convention shall apply to the sale or prospective sale of an object as provided for in the Protocol with any modifications therein.

Chapter XII
Jurisdiction

Article 42   — Choice of forum

1.   Subject to Articles 43 and 44, the courts of a Contracting State chosen by the parties to a transaction have jurisdiction in respect of any claim brought under this Convention, whether or not the chosen forum has a connection with the parties or the transaction. Such jurisdiction shall be exclusive

unless otherwise agreed between the parties.

2. Any such agreement shall be in writing or otherwise concluded in accordance with the formal requirements of the law of the chosen forum.

Article 43 — Jurisdiction under Article 13

1. The courts of a Contracting State chosen by the parties and the courts of the Contracting State on the territory of which the object is situated have jurisdiction to grant relief under Article 13(1)(a), (b), (c) and Article 13(4) in respect of that object.

2. Jurisdiction to grant relief under Article 13(1)(d) or other interim relief by virtue of Article 13(4) may be exercised either:

   a. by the courts chosen by the parties; or

   b. by the courts of a Contracting State on the territory of which the debtor is situated, being relief which, by the terms of the order granting it, is enforceable only in the territory of that Contracting State.

3. A court has jurisdiction under the preceding paragraphs even if the final determination of the claim referred to in Article 13(1) will or may take place in a court of another Contracting State or by arbitration.

Article 44 — Jurisdiction to make orders against the Registrar

1. The courts of the place in which the Registrar has its centre of administration shall have exclusive jurisdiction to award damages or make orders against the Registrar.

2. Where a person fails to respond to a demand made under Article 25 and that person has ceased to exist or cannot be found for the purpose of enabling an order to be made against it requiring it to procure discharge of the registration, the courts referred to in the preceding paragraph shall have exclusive jurisdiction, on the application of the debtor or intending debtor, to make an order directed to the Registrar requiring the Registrar to discharge the registration.

3. Where a person fails to comply with an order of a court having jurisdiction under this Convention or, in the case of a national interest, an order of a court of competent jurisdiction requiring that person to procure the amendment or discharge of a registration, the courts referred to in paragraph 1 may direct the Registrar to take such steps as will give effect to that order.

4. Except as otherwise provided by the preceding paragraphs, no court may make orders or give judgments or rulings against or purporting to bind the Registrar.

Article 45 — Jurisdiction in respect of insolvency proceedings

The provisions of this Chapter are not applicable to insolvency proceedings.

Chapter XIII
Relationship with Other Conventions

Article 45 bis — Relationship with the United Nations Convention on the Assignment of Receivables in International Trade

This Convention shall prevail over the United Nations Convention on the Assignment of Receivables in International Trade, opened for signature in New York on 12 December 2001, as it relates to the assignment of receivables which are associated rights related to international interests in aircraft objects, railway rolling stock and space assets.

Article 46 — Relationship with the UNIDROIT Convention on International Financial Leasing

The Protocol may determine the relationship between this Convention and the UNIDROIT Convention on International Financial Leasing, signed at Ottawa on 28 May 1988.

Chapter XIV
Final Provisions

Article 47 — Signature, ratification, acceptance, approval, or accession

1. This Convention shall be open for signature in Cape Town on 16 November 2001 by States participating in the Diplomatic Conference to Adopt a Mobile Equipment Convention and an Aircraft Protocol held at Cape Town from 29 October to 16 November 2001. After 16 November 2001, the Convention shall be open to all States for signature at the Headquarters of the International Institute for the Unification of Private Law (UNIDROIT) in Rome until it enters into force in accordance with Article 49.

2. This Convention shall be subject to ratification, acceptance or approval by States which have signed it.

3. Any State which does not sign this Convention may accede to it at any time.

4. Ratification, acceptance, approval or accession is effected by the deposit of a formal instrument to that effect with the Depositary.

Article 48 — Regional Economic Integration Organisations

1. A Regional Economic Integration Organisation which is constituted by sovereign States and has competence over certain matters governed by this Convention may similarly sign, accept, approve or accede to this Convention. The Regional Economic Integration Organisation shall in that case have the rights and obligations of a Contracting State, to the extent that that Organisation has competence over matters governed by this Conven-

tion. Where the number of Contracting States is relevant in this Convention, the Regional Economic Integration Organisation shall not count as a Contracting State in addition to its Member States which are Contracting States.

2. The Regional Economic Integration Organisation shall, at the time of signature, acceptance, approval or accession, make a declaration to the Depositary specifying the matters governed by this Convention in respect of which competence has been transferred to that Organisation by its Member States. The Regional Economic Integration Organisation shall promptly notify the Depositary of any changes to the distribution of competence, including new transfers of competence, specified in the declaration under this paragraph.

3. Any reference to a "Contracting State" or "Contracting States" or "State Party" or "States Parties" in this Convention applies equally to a Regional Economic Integration Organisation where the context so requires.

Article 49   — Entry into force

1. This Convention enters into force on the first day of the month following the expiration of three months after the date of the deposit of the third instrument of ratification, acceptance, approval or accession but only as regards a category of objects to which a Protocol applies:

    a. as from the time of entry into force of that Protocol;

    b. subject to the terms of that Protocol; and

    c. as between States Parties to this Convention and that Protocol.

2. For other States this Convention enters into force on the first day of the month following the expiration of three months after the date of the deposit of their instrument of ratification, acceptance, approval or accession but only as regards a category of objects to which a Protocol applies and subject, in relation to such Protocol, to the requirements of sub-paragraphs (a), (b) and (c) of the preceding paragraph.

Article 50   — Internal transactions

1. A Contracting State may, at the time of ratification, acceptance, approval of, or accession to the Protocol, declare that this Convention shall not apply to a transaction which is an internal transaction in relation to that State with regard to all types of objects or some of them.

2. Notwithstanding the preceding paragraph, the provisions of Articles 8(4), 9(1), 16, Chapter V, Article 29, and any provisions of this Convention relating to registered interests shall apply to an internal transaction.

3. Where notice of a national interest has been registered in the International Registry, the priority of the holder of that interest under Article 29 shall not be affected by the fact that such interest has become vested in another person by assignment or subrogation under the applicable law.

Article 51 — Future protocols

1. The Depositary may create working groups, in co-operation with such relevant non-governmental organisations as the Depositary considers appropriate, to assess the feasibility of extending the application of this Convention, through one or more Protocols, to objects of any category of high-value mobile equipment, other than a category referred to in Article 2(3), each member of which is uniquely identifiable, and associated rights relating to such objects.

2. The Depositary shall communicate the text of any preliminary draft Protocol relating to a category of objects prepared by such a working group to all States Parties to this Convention, all member States of the Depositary, member States of the United Nations which are not members of the Depositary and the relevant intergovernmental organisations, and shall invite such States and organisations to participate in intergovernmental negotiations for the completion of a draft Protocol on the basis of such a preliminary draft Protocol.

3. The Depositary shall also communicate the text of any preliminary draft Protocol prepared by such a working group to such relevant non-governmental organisations as the Depositary considers appropriate. Such non-governmental organisations shall be invited promptly to submit comments on the text of the preliminary draft Protocol to the Depositary and to participate as observers in the preparation of a draft Protocol.

4. When the competent bodies of the Depositary adjudge such a draft Protocol ripe for adoption, the Depositary shall convene a diplomatic conference for its adoption.

5. Once such a Protocol has been adopted, subject to paragraph 6, this Convention shall apply to the category of objects covered thereby.

6. Article 45 bis of this Convention applies to such a Protocol only if specifically provided for in that Protocol.

Article 52 — Territorial units

1. If a Contracting State has territorial units in which different systems of law are applicable in relation to the matters dealt with in this Convention, it may, at the time of ratification, acceptance, approval or accession, declare that this Convention is to extend to all its territorial units or only to one or more of them and may modify its declaration by submitting another declaration at any time.

2. Any such declaration shall state expressly the territorial units to which this Convention applies.

3. If a Contracting State has not made any declaration under paragraph 1, this Convention shall apply to all territorial units of that State.

4. Where a Contracting State extends this Convention to one or more of its territorial units, declarations permitted under this Convention may be made

in respect of each such territorial unit, and the declarations made in respect of one territorial unit may be different from those made in respect of another territorial unit.

5. If by virtue of a declaration under paragraph 1, this Convention extends to one or more territorial units of a Contracting State:

    a. the debtor is considered to be situated in a Contracting State only if it is incorporated or formed under a law in force in a territorial unit to which this Convention applies or if it has its registered office or statutory seat, centre of administration, place of business or habitual residence in a territorial unit to which this Convention applies;

    b. any reference to the location of the object in a Contracting State refers to the location of the object in a territorial unit to which this Convention applies; and

    c. any reference to the administrative authorities in that Contracting State shall be construed as referring to the administrative authorities having jurisdiction in a territorial unit to which this Convention applies.

Article 53 — Determination of courts

A Contracting State may, at the time of ratification, acceptance, approval of, or accession to the Protocol, declare the relevant "court" or "courts" for the purposes of Article 1 and Chapter XII of this Convention.

Article 54 — Declarations regarding remedies

1. A Contracting State may, at the time of ratification, acceptance, approval of, or accession to the Protocol, declare that while the charged object is situated within, or controlled from its territory the chargee shall not grant a lease of the object in that territory.

2. A Contracting State shall, at the time of ratification, acceptance, approval of, or accession to the Protocol, declare whether or not any remedy available to the creditor under any provision of this Convention which is not there expressed to require application to the court may be exercised only with leave of the court.

Article 55 — Declarations regarding relief pending final determination

A Contracting State may, at the time of ratification, acceptance, approval of, or accession to the Protocol, declare that it will not apply the provisions of Article 13 or Article 43, or both, wholly or in part. The declaration shall specify under which conditions the relevant Article will be applied, in case it will be applied partly, or otherwise which other forms of interim relief will be applied.

Article 56 — Reservations and declarations

1. No reservations may be made to this Convention but declarations authorised by Articles 39, 40, 50, 52, 53, 54, 55, 57, 58 and 60 may be made in accordance with these provisions.

2. Any declaration or subsequent declaration or any withdrawal of a declaration made under this Convention shall be notified in writing to the Depositary.

Article 57 — Subsequent declarations

1. A State Party may make a subsequent declaration, other than a declaration authorised under Article 60, at any time after the date on which this Convention has entered into force for it, by notifying the Depositary to that effect.

2. Any such subsequent declaration shall take effect on the first day of the month following the expiration of six months after the date of receipt of the notification by the Depositary. Where a longer period for that declaration to take effect is specified in the notification, it shall take effect upon the expiration of such longer period after receipt of the notification by the Depositary.

3. Notwithstanding the previous paragraphs, this Convention shall continue to apply, as if no such subsequent declarations had been made, in respect of all rights and interests arising prior to the effective date of any such subsequent declaration.

Article 58 — Withdrawal of declarations

1. Any State Party having made a declaration under this Convention, other than a declaration authorised under Article 60, may withdraw it at any time by notifying the Depositary. Such withdrawal is to take effect on the first day of the month following the expiration of six months after the date of receipt of the notification by the Depositary.

2. Notwithstanding the previous paragraph, this Convention shall continue to apply, as if no such withdrawal of declaration had been made, in respect of all rights and interests arising prior to the effective date of any such withdrawal.

Article 59 — Denunciations

1. Any State Party may denounce this Convention by notification in writing to the Depositary.

2. Any such denunciation shall take effect on the first day of the month following the expiration of twelve months after the date on which notification is received by the Depositary.

3. Notwithstanding the previous paragraphs, this Convention shall continue to apply, as if no such denunciation had been made, in respect of all rights and

interests arising prior to the effective date of any such denunciation.

Article 60 — Transitional provisions

1. Unless otherwise declared by a Contracting State at any time, the Convention does not apply to a pre-existing right or interest, which retains the priority it enjoyed under the applicable law before the effective date of this Convention.

2. For the purposes of Article 1(v) and of determining priority under this Convention:

    a. "effective date of this Convention" means in relation to a debtor the time when this Convention enters into force or the time when the State in which the debtor is situated becomes a Contracting State, whichever is the later; and

    b. the debtor is situated in a State where it has its centre of administration or, if it has no centre of administration, its place of business or, if it has more than one place of business, its principal place of business or, if it has no place of business, its habitual residence.

3. A Contracting State may in its declaration under paragraph 1 specify a date, not earlier than three years after the date on which the declaration becomes effective, when this Convention and the Protocol will become applicable, for the purpose of determining priority, including the protection of any existing priority, to pre-existing rights or interests arising under an agreement made at a time when the debtor was situated in a State referred to in sub-paragraph (b) of the preceding paragraph but only to the extent and in the manner specified in its declaration.

Article 61 — Review conferences, amendments, and related matters

1. The Depositary shall prepare reports yearly or at such other time as the circumstances may require for the States Parties as to the manner in which the international regimen established in this Convention has operated in practice. In preparing such reports, the Depositary shall take into account the reports of the Supervisory Authority concerning the functioning of the international registration system.

2. At the request of not less than twenty-five per cent of the States Parties, Review Conferences of States Parties shall be convened from time to time by the Depositary, in consultation with the Supervisory Authority, to consider:

    a. the practical operation of this Convention and its effectiveness in facilitating the asset-based financing and leasing of the objects covered by its terms;

    b. the judicial interpretation given to, and the application made of the terms of this Convention and the regulations;

c.   the functioning of the international registration system, the performance of the Registrar and its oversight by the Supervisory Authority, taking into account the reports of the Supervisory Authority; and

d.   whether any modifications to this Convention or the arrangements relating to the International Registry are desirable.

3.   Subject to paragraph 4, any amendment to this Convention shall be approved by at least a two-thirds majority of States Parties participating in the Conference referred to in the preceding paragraph and shall then enter into force in respect of States which have ratified, accepted or approved such amendment when ratified, accepted, or approved by three States in accordance with the provisions of Article 49 relating to its entry into force.

4.   Where the proposed amendment to this Convention is intended to apply to more than one category of equipment, such amendment shall also be approved by at least a two-thirds majority of States Parties to each Protocol that are participating in the Conference referred to in paragraph 2.

Article 62   — Depositary and its functions

1.   Instruments of ratification, acceptance, approval or accession shall be deposited with the International Institute for the Unification of Private Law (UNIDROIT), which is hereby designated the Depositary.

2.   The Depositary shall:

a.   inform all Contracting States of:

i   each new signature or deposit of an instrument of ratification, acceptance, approval or accession, together with the date thereof;

ii   the date of entry into force of this Convention;

iii   each declaration made in accordance with this Convention, together with the date thereof;

iv   the withdrawal or amendment of any declaration, together with the date thereof; and

v   the notification of any denunciation of this Convention together with the date thereof and the date on which it takes effect;

b.   transmit certified true copies of this Convention to all Contracting States;

c.   provide the Supervisory Authority and the Registrar with a copy of each instrument of ratification, acceptance, approval or accession, together with the date of deposit thereof, of each declaration or withdrawal or amendment of a declaration and of each notification of denunciation, together with the date of notification thereof, so that the information contained therein is easily and fully available; and

d.   perform such other functions customary for depositaries.

IN WITNESS WHEREOF the undersigned Plenipotentiaries, having been duly authorised, have signed this Convention.

DONE at Cape Town, this sixteenth day of November, two thousand and one, in a single original in the English, Arabic, Chinese, French, Russian and Spanish languages, all texts being equally authentic, such authenticity to take effect upon verification by the Joint Secretariat of the Conference under the authority of the President of the Conference within ninety days hereof as to the conformity of the texts with one another.

Appendix D

PROTOCOL TO THE UNIDROIT CONVENTION ON INTERNATIONAL INTERESTS IN MOBILE EQUIPMENT ON MATTERS SPECIFIC TO AIRCRAFT EQUIPMENT

THE STATES PARTIES TO THIS PROTOCOL,

CONSIDERING it necessary to implement the *Convention on International Interests in Mobile Equipment* (hereinafter referred to as "the Convention") as it relates to aircraft equipment, in the light of the purposes set out in the preamble to the Convention,

MINDFUL of the need to adapt the Convention to meet the particular requirements of aircraft finance and to extend the sphere of application of the Convention to include contracts of sale of aircraft equipment,

MINDFUL of the principles and objectives of the *Convention on International Civil Aviation*, signed at Chicago on 7 December 1944,

HAVE AGREED upon the following provisions relating to aircraft equipment:

Chapter I
Sphere of Application and General Provisions

Article I — Defined terms

1. In this Protocol, except where the context otherwise requires, terms used in it have the meanings set out in the Convention.

2. In this Protocol the following terms are employed with the meanings set out below:

   a. "aircraft" means aircraft as defined for the purposes of the Chicago Convention which are either airframes with aircraft engines installed thereon or helicopters;

   b. "aircraft engines" means aircraft engines (other than those used in military, customs or police services) powered by jet propulsion or turbine or piston technology and:

      i   in the case of jet propulsion aircraft engines, have at least 1750 lb of thrust or its equivalent; and

      ii in the case of turbine-powered or piston-powered aircraft engines, have at least 550 rated take-off shaft horsepower or its equivalent, together with all modules and other installed, incorporated or attached accessories, parts and equipment and all data, manuals and records relating thereto;

c.   "aircraft objects" means airframes, aircraft engines and helicopters;

d.   "aircraft register" means a register maintained by a State or a common mark registering authority for the purposes of the Chicago Convention;

e.   "airframes" means airframes (other than those used in military, customs or police services) that, when appropriate aircraft engines are installed thereon, are type certified by the competent aviation authority to transport:

   i   at least eight (8) persons including crew; or

   ii   goods in excess of 2750 kilograms, together with all installed, incorporated or attached accessories, parts and equipment (other than aircraft engines), and all data, manuals and records relating thereto;

f.   "authorised party" means the party referred to in Article XIII(3);

g.   "Chicago Convention" means the *Convention on International Civil Aviation*, signed at Chicago on 7 December 1944, as amended, and its Annexes;

h.   "common mark registering authority" means the authority maintaining a register in accordance with Article 77 of the Chicago Convention as implemented by the Resolution adopted on 14 December 1967 by the Council of the International Civil Aviation Organization on nationality and registration of aircraft operated by international operating agencies;

i.   "de-registration of the aircraft" means deletion or removal of the registration of the aircraft from its aircraft register in accordance with the Chicago Convention;

j.   "guarantee contract" means a contract entered into by a person as guarantor;

k.   "guarantor" means a person who, for the purpose of assuring performance of any obligations in favour of a creditor secured by a security agreement or under an agreement, gives or issues a suretyship or demand guarantee or a standby letter of credit or any other form of credit insurance;

l.   "helicopters" means heavier-than-air machines (other than those used in military, customs or police services) supported in flight chiefly by the reactions of the air on one or more power-driven rotors on substantially vertical axes and which are type certified by the competent aviation authority to transport:

   i   at least five (5) persons including crew; or

    ii   goods in excess of 450 kilograms, together with all installed, incorporated or attached accessories, parts and equipment (including rotors), and all data, manuals and records relating thereto;

m.   "insolvency-related event" means:

    i   the commencement of the insolvency proceedings; or

    ii   the declared intention to suspend or actual suspension of payments by the debtor where the creditor's right to institute insolvency proceedings against the debtor or to exercise remedies under the Convention is prevented or suspended by law or State action;

n.   "primary insolvency jurisdiction" means the Contracting State in which the centre of the debtor's main interests is situated, which for this purpose shall be deemed to be the place of the debtor's statutory seat or, if there is none, the place where the debtor is incorporated or formed, unless proved otherwise;

o.   "registry authority" means the national authority or the common mark registering authority, maintaining an aircraft register in a Contracting State and responsible for the registration and de-registration of an aircraft in accordance with the Chicago Convention; and

p.   "State of registry" means, in respect of an aircraft, the State on the national register of which an aircraft is entered or the State of location of the common mark registering authority maintaining the aircraft register.

Article II — Application of Convention as regards aircraft objects

1.   The Convention shall apply in relation to aircraft objects as provided by the terms of this Protocol.

2.   The Convention and this Protocol shall be known as the Convention on International Interests in Mobile Equipment as applied to aircraft objects.

Article III — Application of Convention to sales

The following provisions of the Convention apply as if references to an agreement creating or providing for an international interest were references to a contract of sale and as if references to an international interest, a prospective international interest, the debtor and the creditor were references to a sale, a prospective sale, the seller and the buyer respectively:

Articles 3 and 4;

Article 16(1)(a);

Article 19(4);

Article 20(1) (as regards registration of a contract of sale or a prospective sale);

Article 25(2) (as regards a prospective sale); and

Article 30.

In addition, the general provisions of Article 1, Article 5, Chapters IV to VII, Article 29 (other than Article 29(3) which is replaced by Article XIV(1) and (2)), Chapter X, Chapter XII (other than Article 43), Chapter XIII and Chapter XIV (other than Article 60) shall apply to contracts of sale and prospective sales.

Article IV   — Sphere of application

1. Without prejudice to Article 3(1) of the Convention, the Convention shall also apply in relation to a helicopter, or to an airframe pertaining to an aircraft, registered in an aircraft register of a Contracting State which is the State of registry, and where such registration is made pursuant to an agreement for registration of the aircraft it is deemed to have been effected at the time of the agreement.

2. For the purposes of the definition of "internal transaction" in Article 1 of the Convention:

   a. an airframe is located in the State of registry of the aircraft of which it is a part;

   b. an aircraft engine is located in the State of registry of the aircraft on which it is installed or, if it is not installed on an aircraft, where it is physically located; and

   c. a helicopter is located in its State of registry, at the time of the conclusion of the agreement creating or providing for the interest.

3. The parties may, by agreement in writing, exclude the application of Article XI and, in their relations with each other, derogate from or vary the effect of any of the provisions of this Protocol except Article IX (2)–(4).

Article V   — Formalities, effects and registration of contract of sale

1. For the purposes of this Protocol, a contract of sale is one which:

   a. is in writing;

   b. relates to an aircraft object of which the seller has power to dispose; and

   c. enables the aircraft object to be identified in conformity with this Protocol.

2. A contract of sale transfers the interest of the seller in the aircraft object to the buyer according to its terms.

3. Registration of a contract of sale remains effective indefinitely. Registration of a prospective sale remains effective unless discharged or until expiry of

the period, if any, specified in the registration.

Article VI   — Representative capacities

A person may enter into an agreement or a sale, and register an international interest in, or a sale of, an aircraft object, in an agency, trust or other representative capacity. In such case, that person is entitled to assert rights and interests under the Convention.

Article VII   — Description of aircraft objects

A description of an aircraft object that contains its manufacturer's serial number, the name of the manufacturer and its model designation is necessary and sufficient to identify the object for the purposes of Article 7(c) of the Convention and Article V(1)(c) of this Protocol.

Article VIII   — Choice of law

1.   This Article applies only where a Contracting State has made a declaration pursuant to Article XXX(1).

2.   The parties to an agreement, or a contract of sale, or a related guarantee contract or subordination agreement may agree on the law which is to govern their contractual rights and obligations, wholly or in part.

3.   Unless otherwise agreed, the reference in the preceding paragraph to the law chosen by the parties is to the domestic rules of law of the designated State or, where that State comprises several territorial units, to the domestic law of the designated territorial unit.

Chapter II
Default Remedies, Priorities and Assignments

Article IX   — Modification of default remedies provisions

1.   In addition to the remedies specified in Chapter III of the Convention, the creditor may, to the extent that the debtor has at any time so agreed and in the circumstances specified in that Chapter:

   a.   procure the de-registration of the aircraft; and

   b.   procure the export and physical transfer of the aircraft object from the territory in which it is situated.

2.   The creditor shall not exercise the remedies specified in the preceding paragraph without the prior consent in writing of the holder of any registered interest ranking in priority to that of the creditor.

3.   Article 8(3) of the Convention shall not apply to aircraft objects. Any remedy given by the Convention in relation to an aircraft object shall be exercised in a commercially reasonable manner. A remedy shall be deemed to be exercised in a commercially reasonable manner where it is exercised in

conformity with a provision of the agreement except where such a provision is manifestly unreasonable.

4. A chargee giving ten or more working days' prior written notice of a proposed sale or lease to interested persons shall be deemed to satisfy the requirement of providing "reasonable prior notice" specified in Article 8(4) of the Convention. The foregoing shall not prevent a chargee and a chargor or a guarantor from agreeing to a longer period of prior notice.

5. The registry authority in a Contracting State shall, subject to any applicable safety laws and regulations, honour a request for de-registration and export if:

     a. the request is properly submitted by the authorised party under a recorded irrevocable de-registration and export request authorisation; and

     b. the authorised party certifies to the registry authority, if required by that authority, that all registered interests ranking in priority to that of the creditor in whose favour the authorisation has been issued have been discharged or that the holders of such interests have consented to the de-registration and export.

6. A chargee proposing to procure the de-registration and export of an aircraft under paragraph 1 otherwise than pursuant to a court order shall give reasonable prior notice in writing of the proposed de-registration and export to:

     a. interested persons specified in Article 1(m)(i) and (ii) of the Convention; and

     b. interested persons specified in Article 1(m)(iii) of the Convention who have given notice of their rights to the chargee within a reasonable time prior to the de-registration and export.

Article X   — Modification of provisions regarding relief pending final determination

1. This Article applies only where a Contracting State has made a declaration under Article XXX(2) and to the extent stated in such declaration.

2. For the purposes of Article 13(1) of the Convention, "speedy" in the context of obtaining relief means within such number of working days from the date of filing of the application for relief as is specified in a declaration made by the Contracting State in which the application is made.

3. Article 13(1) of the Convention applies with the following being added immediately after sub-paragraph (d):

"(e) if at any time the debtor and the creditor specifically agree, sale and application of proceeds therefrom,"

and Article 43(2) applies with the insertion after the words "Article 13(1)(d)" of the words "and (e)".

4. Ownership or any other interest of the debtor passing on a sale under the preceding paragraph is free from any other interest over which the creditor's international interest has priority under the provisions of Article 29 of the Convention.

5. The creditor and the debtor or any other interested person may agree in writing to exclude the application of Article 13(2) of the Convention.

6. With regard to the remedies in Article IX(1):

    a. they shall be made available by the registry authority and other administrative authorities, as applicable, in a Contracting State no later than five working days after the creditor notifies such authorities that the relief specified in Article IX(1) is granted or, in the case of relief granted by a foreign court, recognised by a court of that Contracting State, and that the creditor is entitled to procure those remedies in accordance with the Convention; and

    b. the applicable authorities shall expeditiously co-operate with and assist the creditor in the exercise of such remedies in conformity with the applicable aviation safety laws and regulations.

7. Paragraphs 2 and 6 shall not affect any applicable aviation safety laws and regulations.

Article XI — Remedies on insolvency

1. This Article applies only where a Contracting State that is the primary insolvency jurisdiction has made a declaration pursuant to Article XXX(3).

Alternative A

2. Upon the occurrence of an insolvency-related event, the insolvency administrator or the debtor, as applicable, shall, subject to paragraph 7, give possession of the aircraft object to the creditor no later than the earlier of:

    a. the end of the waiting period; and

    b. the date on which the creditor would be entitled to possession of the aircraft object if this Article did not apply.

3. For the purposes of this Article, the "waiting period" shall be the period specified in a declaration of the Contracting State which is the primary insolvency jurisdiction.

4. References in this Article to the "insolvency administrator" shall be to that person in its official, not in its personal, capacity.

5. Unless and until the creditor is given the opportunity to take possession under paragraph 2:

    a. the insolvency administrator or the debtor, as applicable, shall preserve the aircraft object and maintain it and its value in accordance with the agreement; and

    b.   the creditor shall be entitled to apply for any other forms of interim relief available under the applicable law.

6.   Sub-paragraph (a) of the preceding paragraph shall not preclude the use of the aircraft object under arrangements designed to preserve the aircraft object and maintain it and its value.

7.   The insolvency administrator or the debtor, as applicable, may retain possession of the aircraft object where, by the time specified in paragraph 2, it has cured all defaults other than a default constituted by the opening of insolvency proceedings and has agreed to perform all future obligations under the agreement. A second waiting period shall not apply in respect of a default in the performance of such future obligations.

8.   With regard to the remedies in Article IX(1):

    a.   they shall be made available by the registry authority and the administrative authorities in a Contracting State, as applicable, no later than five working days after the date on which the creditor notifies such authorities that it is entitled to procure those remedies in accordance with the Convention; and

    b.   the applicable authorities shall expeditiously co-operate with and assist the creditor in the exercise of such remedies in conformity with the applicable aviation safety laws and regulations.

9.   No exercise of remedies permitted by the Convention or this Protocol may be prevented or delayed after the date specified in paragraph 2.

10.   No obligations of the debtor under the agreement may be modified without the consent of the creditor.

11.   Nothing in the preceding paragraph shall be construed to affect the authority, if any, of the insolvency administrator under the applicable law to terminate the agreement.

12.   No rights or interests, except for non-consensual rights or interests of a category covered by a declaration pursuant to Article 39(1), shall have priority in insolvency proceedings over registered interests.

13.   The Convention as modified by Article IX of this Protocol shall apply to the exercise of any remedies under this Article.

Alternative B

1.   Upon the occurrence of an insolvency-related event, the insolvency administrator or the debtor, as applicable, upon the request of the creditor, shall give notice to the creditor within the time specified in a declaration of a Contracting State pursuant to Article XXX(3) whether it will:

    a.   cure all defaults other than a default constituted by the opening of insolvency proceedings and agree to perform all future obligations, under the agreement and related transaction documents; or

b.   give the creditor the opportunity to take possession of the aircraft object, in accordance with the applicable law.

2.   The applicable law referred to in sub-paragraph (b) of the preceding paragraph may permit the court to require the taking of any additional step or the provision of any additional guarantee.

3.   The creditor shall provide evidence of its claims and proof that its international interest has been registered.

4.   If the insolvency administrator or the debtor, as applicable, does not give notice in conformity with paragraph 2, or when the insolvency administrator or the debtor has declared that it will give the creditor the opportunity to take possession of the aircraft object but fails to do so, the court may permit the creditor to take possession of the aircraft object upon such terms as the court may order and may require the taking of any additional step or the provision of any additional guarantee.

5.   The aircraft object shall not be sold pending a decision by a court regarding the claim and the international interest.

Article XII   — Insolvency assistance

1.   This Article applies only where a Contracting State has made a declaration pursuant to Article XXX(1).

2.   The courts of a Contracting State in which an aircraft object is situated shall, in accordance with the law of the Contracting State, co-operate to the maximum extent possible with foreign courts and foreign insolvency administrators in carrying out the provisions of Article XI.

Article XIII   — De-registration and export request authorisation

1.   This Article applies only where a Contracting State has made a declaration pursuant to Article XXX(1).

2.   Where the debtor has issued an irrevocable de-registration and export request authorisation substantially in the form annexed to this Protocol and has submitted such authorisation for recordation to the registry authority, that authorisation shall be so recorded.

3.   The person in whose favour the authorisation has been issued (the "authorised party") or its certified designee shall be the sole person entitled to exercise the remedies specified in Article IX(1) and may do so only in accordance with the authorisation and applicable aviation safety laws and regulations.

Such authorisation may not be revoked by the debtor without the consent in writing of the authorised party. The registry authority shall remove an authorisation from the registry at the request of the authorised party.

4.   The registry authority and other administrative authorities in Contracting States shall expeditiously co-operate with and assist the authorised party in

the exercise of the remedies specified in Article IX.

Article XIV — Modification of priority provisions

1. A buyer of an aircraft object under a registered sale acquires its interest in that object free from an interest subsequently registered and from an unregistered interest, even if the buyer has actual knowledge of the unregistered interest.

2. A buyer of an aircraft object acquires its interest in that object subject to an interest registered at the time of its acquisition.

3. Ownership of or another right or interest in an aircraft engine shall not be affected by its installation on or removal from an aircraft.

4. Article 29(7) of the Convention applies to an item, other than an object, installed on an airframe, aircraft engine or helicopter.

Article XV — Modification of assignment provisions

Article 33(1) of the Convention applies as if the following were added immediately after sub-paragraph (b):

"and (c) the debtor has consented in writing, whether or not the consent is given in advance of the assignment or identifies the assignee."

Article XVI — Debtor provisions

1. In the absence of a default within the meaning of Article 11 of the Convention, the debtor shall be entitled to the quiet possession and use of the object in accordance with the agreement as against:

   a. its creditor and the holder of any interest from which the debtor takes free pursuant to Article 29(4) of the Convention or, in the capacity of buyer, Article XIV(1) of this Protocol, unless and to the extent that the debtor has otherwise agreed; and

   b. the holder of any interest to which the debtor's right or interest is subject pursuant to Article 29(4) of the Convention or, in the capacity of buyer, Article XIV(2) of this Protocol, but only to the extent, if any, that such holder has agreed.

2. Nothing in the Convention or this Protocol affects the liability of a creditor for any breach of the agreement under the applicable law in so far as that agreement relates to an aircraft object.

Chapter III
Registry Provisions Relating to International Interests in Aircraft Objects

Article XVII — The Supervisory Authority and the Registrar

1. The Supervisory Authority shall be the international entity designated by a Resolution adopted by the Diplomatic Conference to Adopt a Mobile Equipment Convention and an Aircraft Protocol.

2. Where the international entity referred to in the preceding paragraph is not able and willing to act as Supervisory Authority, a Conference of Signatory and Contracting States shall be convened to designate another Supervisory Authority.

3. The Supervisory Authority and its officers and employees shall enjoy such immunity from legal and administrative process as is provided under the rules applicable to them as an international entity or otherwise.

4. The Supervisory Authority may establish a commission of experts, from among persons nominated by Signatory and Contracting States and having the necessary qualifications and experience, and entrust it with the task of assisting the Supervisory Authority in the discharge of its functions.

5. The first Registrar shall operate the International Registry for a period of five years from the date of entry into force of this Protocol. Thereafter, the Registrar shall be appointed or reappointed at regular five-yearly intervals by the Supervisory Authority.

Article XVIII — First regulations

The first regulations shall be made by the Supervisory Authority so as to take effect upon the entry into force of this Protocol.

Article XIX — Designated entry points

1. Subject to paragraph 2, a Contracting State may at any time designate an entity or entities in its territory as the entry point or entry points through which there shall or may be transmitted to the International Registry information required for registration other than registration of a notice of a national interest or a right or interest under Article 40 in either case arising under the laws of another State.

2. A designation made under the preceding paragraph may permit, but not compel, use of a designated entry point or entry points for information required for registrations in respect of aircraft engines.

Article XX   — Additional modifications to Registry provisions

1. For the purposes of Article 19(6) of the Convention, the search criteria for an aircraft object shall be the name of its manufacturer, its manufacturer's serial number and its model designation, supplemented as necessary to ensure uniqueness. Such supplementary information shall be specified in the regulations.

2. For the purposes of Article 25(2) of the Convention and in the circumstances there described, the holder of a registered prospective international interest or a registered prospective assignment of an international interest or the person in whose favour a prospective sale has been registered shall take such steps as are within its power to procure the discharge of the registration no later than five working days after the receipt of the demand described in such paragraph.

3. The fees referred to in Article 17(2)(h) of the Convention shall be determined so as to recover the reasonable costs of establishing, operating and regulating the International Registry and the reasonable costs of the Supervisory Authority associated with the performance of the functions, exercise of the powers, and discharge of the duties contemplated by Article 17(2) of the Convention.

4. The centralised functions of the International Registry shall be operated and administered by the Registrar on a twenty-four hour basis. The various entry points shall be operated at least during working hours in their respective territories.

5. The amount of the insurance or financial guarantee referred to in Article 28(4) of the Convention shall, in respect of each event, not be less than the maximum value of an aircraft object as determined by the Supervisory Authority.

6. Nothing in the Convention shall preclude the Registrar from procuring insurance or a financial guarantee covering events for which the Registrar is not liable under Article 28 of the Convention.

Chapter IV
Jurisdiction

Article XXI   — Modification of jurisdiction provisions

For the purposes of Article 43 of the Convention and subject to Article 42 of the Convention, a court of a Contracting State also has jurisdiction where the object is a helicopter, or an airframe pertaining to an aircraft, for which that State is the State of registry.

Article XXII — Waivers of sovereign immunity

1.   Subject to paragraph 2, a waiver of sovereign immunity from jurisdiction of the courts specified in Article 42 or Article 43 of the Convention or relating to enforcement of rights and interests relating to an aircraft object under the Convention shall be binding and, if the other conditions to such jurisdiction or enforcement have been satisfied, shall be effective to confer jurisdiction and permit enforcement, as the case may be.

2.   A waiver under the preceding paragraph must be in writing and contain a description of the aircraft object.

Chapter V
Relationship with Other Conventions

Article XXIII — Relationship with the *Convention on the International Recognition of Rights in Aircraft*

The Convention shall, for a Contracting State that is a party to the *Convention on the International Recognition of Rights in Aircraft*, signed at Geneva on 19 June 1948, supersede that Convention as it relates to aircraft, as defined in this Protocol, and to aircraft objects. However, with respect to rights or interests not covered or affected by the present Convention, the Geneva Convention shall not be superseded.

Article XXIV — Relationship with the *Convention for the Unification of Certain Rules Relating to the Precautionary Attachment of Aircraft*

1.   The Convention shall, for a Contracting State that is a Party to the *Convention for the Unification of Certain Rules Relating to the Precautionary Attachment of Aircraft*, signed at Rome on 29 May 1933, supersede that Convention as it relates to aircraft, as defined in this Protocol.

2.   A Contracting State Party to the above Convention may declare, at the time of ratification, acceptance, approval of, or accession to this Protocol, that it will not apply this Article.

Article XXV — Relationship with the *UNIDROIT Convention on International Financial Leasing*

The Convention shall supersede the *UNIDROIT Convention on International Financial Leasing*, signed at Ottawa on 28 May 1988, as it relates to aircraft objects.

Chapter VI
Final Provisions

Article XXVI — Signature, ratification, acceptance, approval or accession

1. This Protocol shall be open for signature in Cape Town on 16 November 2001 by States participating in the Diplomatic Conference to Adopt a Mobile Equipment Convention and an Aircraft Protocol held at Cape Town from 29 October to 16 November 2001. After 16 November 2001, this Protocol shall be open to all States for signature at the Headquarters of the International Institute for the Unification of Private Law (UNIDROIT) in Rome until it enters into force in accordance with Article XXVIII.

2. This Protocol shall be subject to ratification, acceptance or approval by States which have signed it.

3. Any State which does not sign this Protocol may accede to it at any time.

4. Ratification, acceptance, approval or accession is effected by the deposit of a formal instrument to that effect with the Depositary.

5. A State may not become a Party to this Protocol unless it is or becomes also a Party to the Convention.

Article XXVII — Regional Economic Integration Organisation

1. A Regional Economic Integration Organisation which is constituted by sovereign States and has competence over certain matters governed by this Protocol may similarly sign, accept, approve or accede to this Protocol. The Regional Economic Integration Organisation shall in that case have the rights and obligations of a Contracting State, to the extent that that Organisation has competence over matters governed by this Protocol. Where the number of Contracting States is relevant in this Protocol, the Regional Economic Integration Organisation shall not count as a Contracting State in addition to its Member States which are Contracting States.

2. The Regional Economic Integration Organisation shall, at the time of signature, acceptance, approval or accession, make a declaration to the Depositary specifying the matters governed by this Protocol in respect of which competence has been transferred to that Organisation by its Member States. The Regional Economic Integration Organisation shall promptly notify the Depositary of any changes to the distribution of competence, including new transfers of competence, specified in the declaration under this paragraph.

3. Any reference to a "Contracting State" or "Contracting States" or "State Party" or "States Parties" in this Protocol applies equally to a Regional Economic Integration Organisation where the context so requires.

Article XXVIII   — Entry into force

1. This Protocol enters into force on the first day of the month following the expiration of three months after the date of the deposit of the eighth instrument of ratification, acceptance, approval or accession, between the States which have deposited such instruments.

2. For other States this Protocol enters into force on the first day of the month following the expiration of three months after the date of the deposit of its instrument of ratification, acceptance, approval or accession.

Article XXIX   — Territorial units

1. If a Contracting State has territorial units in which different systems of law are applicable in relation to the matters dealt with in this Protocol, it may, at the time of ratification, acceptance, approval or accession, declare that this Protocol is to extend to all its territorial units or only to one or more of them and may modify its declaration by submitting another declaration at any time.

2. Any such declaration shall state expressly the territorial units to which this Protocol applies.

3. If a Contracting State has not made any declaration under paragraph 1, this Protocol shall apply to all territorial units of that State.

4. Where a Contracting State extends this Protocol to one or more of its territorial units, declarations permitted under this Protocol may be made in respect of each such territorial unit, and the declarations made in respect of one territorial unit may be different from those made in respect of another territorial unit.

5. If by virtue of a declaration under paragraph 1, this Protocol extends to one or more territorial units of a Contracting State:

    a. the debtor is considered to be situated in a Contracting State only if it is incorporated or formed under a law in force in a territorial unit to which the Convention and this Protocol apply or if it has its registered office or statutory seat, centre of administration, place of business or habitual residence in a territorial unit to which the Convention and this Protocol apply;

    b. any reference to the location of the object in a Contracting State refers to the location of the object in a territorial unit to which the Convention and this Protocol apply; and

    c. any reference to the administrative authorities in that Contracting State shall be construed as referring to the administrative authorities having jurisdiction in a territorial unit to which the Convention and this Protocol apply and any reference to the national register or to the registry authority in that Contracting State shall be construed as referring to the aircraft register in force or to the registry authority having jurisdiction in the territorial unit or units to which the

Convention and this Protocol apply.

Article XXX   — Declarations relating to certain provisions

1.   A Contracting State may, at the time of ratification, acceptance, approval of, or accession to this Protocol, declare that it will apply any one or more of Articles VIII, XII and XIII of this Protocol.

2.   A Contracting State may, at the time of ratification, acceptance, approval of, or accession to this Protocol, declare that it will apply Article X of this Protocol, wholly or in part. If it so declares with respect to Article X(2), it shall specify the time-period required thereby.

3.   A Contracting State may, at the time of ratification, acceptance, approval of, or accession to this Protocol, declare that it will apply the entirety of Alternative A, or the entirety of Alternative B of Article XI and, if so, shall specify the types of insolvency proceeding, if any, to which it will apply Alternative A and the types of insolvency proceeding, if any, to which it will apply Alternative B. A Contracting State making a declaration pursuant to this paragraph shall specify the time-period required by Article XI.

4.   The courts of Contracting States shall apply Article XI in conformity with the declaration made by the Contracting State which is the primary insolvency jurisdiction.

5.   A Contracting State may, at the time of ratification, acceptance, approval of, or accession to this Protocol, declare that it will not apply the provisions of Article XXI, wholly or in part. The declaration shall specify under which conditions the relevant Article will be applied, in case it will be applied partly, or otherwise which other forms of interim relief will be applied.

Article XXXI   — Declarations under the Convention

Declarations made under the Convention, including those made under Articles 39, 40, 50, 53, 54, 55, 57, 58 and 60 of the Convention, shall be deemed to have also been made under this Protocol unless stated otherwise.

Article XXXII   — Reservations and declarations

1.   No reservations may be made to this Protocol but declarations authorised by Articles XXIV, XXIX, XXX, XXXI, XXXIII and XXXIV may be made in accordance with these provisions.

2.   Any declaration or subsequent declaration or any withdrawal of a declaration made under this Protocol shall be notified in writing to the Depositary.

Article XXXIII   — Subsequent declarations

1.   A State Party may make a subsequent declaration, other than a declaration made in accordance with Article XXXI under Article 60 of the Convention, at any time after the date on which this Protocol has entered into force for it, by notifying the Depositary to that effect.

2. Any such subsequent declaration shall take effect on the first day of the month following the expiration of six months after the date of receipt of the notification by the Depositary. Where a longer period for that declaration to take effect is specified in the notification, it shall take effect upon the expiration of such longer period after receipt of the notification by the Depositary.

3. Notwithstanding the previous paragraphs, this Protocol shall continue to apply, as if no such subsequent declarations had been made, in respect of all rights and interests arising prior to the effective date of any such subsequent declaration.

Article XXXIV — Withdrawal of declarations

1. Any State Party having made a declaration under this Protocol, other than a declaration made in accordance with Article XXXI under Article 60 of the Convention, may withdraw it at any time by notifying the Depositary. Such withdrawal is to take effect on the first day of the month following the expiration of six months after the date of receipt of the notification by the Depositary.

2. Notwithstanding the previous paragraph, this Protocol shall continue to apply, as if no such withdrawal of declaration had been made, in respect of all rights and interests arising prior to the effective date of any such withdrawal.

Article XXXV — Denunciations

1. Any State Party may denounce this Protocol by notification in writing to the Depositary.

2. Any such denunciation shall take effect on the first day of the month following the expiration of twelve months after the date of receipt of the notification by the Depositary.

3. Notwithstanding the previous paragraphs, this Protocol shall continue to apply, as if no such denunciation had been made, in respect of all rights and interests arising prior to the effective date of any such denunciation.

Article XXXVI — Review conferences, amendments and related matters

1. The Depositary, in consultation with the Supervisory Authority, shall prepare reports yearly, or at such other time as the circumstances may require, for the States Parties as to the manner in which the international regime established in the Convention as amended by this Protocol has operated in practice. In preparing such reports, the Depositary shall take into account the reports of the Supervisory Authority concerning the functioning of the international registration system.

2. At the request of not less than twenty-five per cent of the States Parties, Review Conferences of the States Parties shall be convened from time to

time by the Depositary, in consultation with the Supervisory Authority, to consider:

a.   the practical operation of the Convention as amended by this Protocol and its effectiveness in facilitating the asset-based financing and leasing of the objects covered by its terms;

b.   the judicial interpretation given to, and the application made of the terms of this Protocol and the regulations;

c.   the functioning of the international registration system, the performance of the Registrar and its oversight by the Supervisory Authority, taking into account the reports of the Supervisory Authority; and

d.   whether any modifications to this Protocol or the arrangements relating to the International Registry are desirable.

3.   Any amendment to this Protocol shall be approved by at least a two-thirds majority of States Parties participating in the Conference referred to in the preceding paragraph and shall then enter into force in respect of States which have ratified, accepted or approved such amendment when it has been ratified, accepted or approved by eight States in accordance with the provisions of Article XXVIII relating to its entry into force.

Article XXXVII — Depositary and its functions

1.   Instruments of ratification, acceptance, approval or accession shall be deposited with the International Institute for the Unification of Private Law (UNIDROIT), which is hereby designated the Depositary.

2.   The Depositary shall:

a.   inform all Contracting States of:

   i.   each new signature or deposit of an instrument of ratification, acceptance, approval or accession, together with the date thereof;

   ii.   the date of entry into force of this Protocol;

   iii.   each declaration made in accordance with this Protocol, together with the date thereof;

   iv.   the withdrawal or amendment of any declaration, together with the date thereof; and

   v.   the notification of any denunciation of this Protocol together with the date thereof and the date on which it takes effect;

b.   transmit certified true copies of this Protocol to all Contracting States;

c.   provide the Supervisory Authority and the Registrar with a copy of each instrument of ratification, acceptance, approval or accession, together with the date of deposit thereof, of each declaration or withdrawal or amendment of a declaration and of each notification of denunciation, together with the date of notification thereof, so that the information contained therein is easily and fully available; and

d.   perform such other functions customary for depositaries.

IN WITNESS WHEREOF the undersigned Plenipotentiaries, having been duly authorised, have signed this Protocol.

DONE at Cape Town, this sixteenth day of November, two thousand and one, in a single original in the English, Arabic, Chinese, French, Russian and Spanish languages, all texts being equally authentic, such authenticity to take effect upon verification by the Joint Secretariat of the Conference under the authority of the President of the Conference within ninety days hereof as to the conformity of the texts with one another.

ANNEX

FORM OF IRREVOCABLE DE-REGISTRATION AND EXPORT REQUEST AUTHORISATION

Annex referred to in Article XIII

[Insert Date]

To: [Insert Name of Registry Authority]

Re: Irrevocable De-Registration and Export Request Authorisation

The undersigned is the registered [operator] [owner] of the [insert the airframe/ helicopter manufacturer name and model number] bearing manufacturers serial number [insert manufacturer's serial number] and registration [number] [mark] [insert registration number/mark] (together with all installed, incorporated or attached accessories, parts and equipment, the "aircraft").

This instrument is an irrevocable de-registration and export request authorisation issued by the undersigned in favour of [insert name of creditor] ("the authorised party") under the authority of Article XIII of the Protocol to the Convention on International Interests in Mobile Equipment on Matters specific to Aircraft Equipment. In accordance with that Article, the undersigned hereby requests:

(i) recognition that the authorised party or the person it certifies as its designee is the sole person entitled to:

(a) procure the de-registration of the aircraft from the [insert name of aircraft register] maintained by the [insert name of registry authority] for the purposes of Chapter III of the *Convention on International Civil Aviation*, signed at Chicago, on 7 December 1944, and

(b) procure the export and physical transfer of the aircraft from [insert name of country]; and

(ii) confirmation that the authorised party or the person it certifies as its designee may take the action specified in clause (i) above on written demand without the consent of the undersigned and that, upon such demand, the authorities in [insert name of country] shall co-operate with the authorised party with a view to the speedy completion of such action.

The rights in favour of the authorised party established by this instrument may not be revoked by the undersigned without the written consent of the authorised party.

Please acknowledge your agreement to this request and its terms by appropriate notation in the space provided below and lodging this instrument in [insert name of registry authority].

                                                        _____

                                                         [insert name of operator/owner]

Agreed to and lodged this [insert date]   By: _____

                                                         [insert name of signatory]

                                            Its: _____

                                                         [insert title of signatory]

_____
[insert relevant notational details]

TABLE OF CASES

[References are to pages.]

[References are to pages.]

[References are to pages.]

[References are to pages.]

TABLE OF STATUTES

[References are to pages.]

[References are to pages.]

UNIFORM MODEL CODES

Uniform Commercial Code

[References are to pages.]

[References are to pages.]

[References are to pages.]

INDEX

[References are to chapters and sections.]

[References are to chapters and sections.]

[References are to chapters and sections.]

M

MODEL SECURITY AGREEMENT
Sample text . . . App B

P

PERFECTION
Generally . . . 4[A]
Accessions . . . 4[G][2]
Attachment distinguished . . . 4[C]
Automatic perfection . . . 4[B][3]
Commingled goods . . . 4[G][3]
Continuing perfected status in proceeds
    . . . 4[F][1][d]
Control of collateral, by . . . 4[B][4]; 4[E][1][b][v]
Exceptions . . . 4[C]
Filings
     Generally . . . 4[C]
     Method of perfection, as . . . 4[B][1]
     What to file (See WHAT TO FILE)
     Where to file (See WHERE TO FILE)
Fixtures, of security interest in . . . 4[G][1][c]
Methods of
     Generally . . . 4[B]; 4[G][1][d][iii]
     Automatic perfection . . . 4[B][3]
     Control of collateral, perfection by
       . . . 4[B][4]; 4[E][1][b][v]
     Filing, perfection by (See subhead: Filings)
     Possession of collateral, perfection by
       . . . 4[B][2]
Possession of collateral, by . . . 4[B][2]
Priorities (See PRIORITIES)

PERSONAL PROPERTY COLLATERAL, TYPES OF
Generally . . . 2[D][1]; 2[D][3]
Accounts . . . 2[D][3][d]
Commercial tort claims . . . 2[D][2][a]
Deposit accounts . . . 2[D][2][b]
Electronic chattel paper . . . 2[D][3][a]
Electronic documents of title . . . 2[D][3][h]
General intangibles . . . 2[D][3][e]
Health-care-insurance receivables . . . 2[D][3][b]
Instruments . . . 2[D][3][f]
Intellectual property rights . . . 2[D][4]
Investment properties . . . 2[D][3][g]
Leases on personal property . . . 2[G][7]
Letter-of-credit right . . . 2[D][3][c]
Software, security interests in . . . 2[D][4]

PRIORITIES
Generally . . . 4[D][1]; 4[D][2]
Accessions . . . 4[G][2]
Buyers of collateral, as to
     Generally . . . 4[D][2][g]
     Buyers out of inventory with knowledge vs.
       perfected interests in inventory
       . . . 4[D][2][g][i]
     Consumer buyers from consumer sellers vs.
       automatically perfected purchase money se-
       curity interest . . . 4[D][2][g][ii]
Chattel paper collateral, in . . . 4[D][2][h]

PRIORITIES—Cont.
CIIME, under . . . 6[C]
Commingled goods . . . 4[G][3]
First-to-file rule . . . 4[D][2][e]
Fixtures, as to (See FIXTURES, subhead: Priority
    issues)
Judgment creditors vs. debtors . . . 4[D][2][b]
Lien creditors vs. unperfected security interests
    . . . 4[D][2][c]
Liens arising by operation of law, creditors with
    . . . 4[D][2][f]
Perfect rule . . . 4[D][2][e]
Purchase money security interests
     Generally . . . 4[D][2][i]
     Consumer buyers from consumer sellers vs.
       automatically perfected purchase money se-
       curity interests . . . 4[D][2][g][ii]
Unsecured creditors v. debtors . . . 4[D][2][a]

R

REPOSSESSION
Generally . . . 3[B]
Disposition rights upon
     "Absolute bar" as factor . . . 3[C][3]
     Commercial reasonableness of disposition
       . . . 3[C][2]
     Compulsory disposition and redemption of col-
       lateral . . . 3[C][1]
     Deficiency or surplus as issues in litigation
       . . . 3[C][3]
     Rebuttable presumption, effect of . . . 3[C][3]
     Timeliness of notification . . . 3[C][2]

T

TRANSACTIONS SUBJECT TO ARTICLE 9
Attached and enforceable security interests (See AT-
    TACHED AND ENFORCEABLE SECURITY
    INTERESTS)
Drafting exercise for security agreement (See
    DRAFTING EXERCISE-SECURITY AGREE-
    MENT)
Establishing secured loan transactions
     Generally . . . 2[A]
     Demand promissory notes . . . 2[A][2]
     Documentation for . . . 2[A][1]
Exclusion standard . . . 2[B][2]
Inclusion standard . . . 2[B][1]
Personal property collateral, types of (See PER-
    SONAL PROPERTY COLLATERAL, TYPES
    OF)
Rights in collateral, note on . . . 2[C]
Scope of applicability
     Exclusion standard . . . 2[B][2]
     Inclusion standard . . . 2[B][1]
Separate security agreement, need for
     Generally . . . 2[E][1]
     Composite document compliance as sufficient
       . . . 2[E][2]

[References are to chapters and sections.]